D0911589

JEWISH FAMILIES IN EUROPE, 1939– PRESENT

The HBI Series on Jewish Women, created by the Hadassah-Brandeis Institute, publishes a wide range of books by and about Jewish women in diverse contexts and time periods. Of interest to scholars and the educated public, the HBI Series on Jewish Women fills major gaps in Jewish Studies and in Women and Gender Studies as well as their intersection.

The HBI Series on Jewish Women is supported by a generous gift from Dr. Laura S. Schor.

For the complete list of books that are available in this series, please see www.upne.com

HBI SERIES ON
JEWISH WOMEN

SHULAMIT REINHARZ,
GENERAL EDITOR

SYLVIA BARACK FISHMAN,
ASSOCIATE EDITOR

JEWISH FAMILIES IN EUROPE, 1939–PRESENT

HISTORY, REPRESENTATION, AND MEMORY

EDITED BY
JOANNA BEATA MICHLIC

BRANDEIS UNIVERSITY PRESS
WALTHAM, MASSACHUSETTS

Brandeis University Press

An imprint of University Press of New England

www.upne.com

© 2017 Brandeis University

This work is licensed under a Creative Commons
Attribution-NonCommercial-NoDerivatives 4.0
International License.

[cc] BY-NC-ND

Manufactured in the United States of America

Designed by Eric M. Brooks

Typeset in Skolar and Meran by
Passumpsic Publishing

For permission to reproduce any of the material in this book,
contact Permissions, University Press of New England, One Court
Street, Suite 250, Lebanon NH 03766; or visit www.upne.com

*This book was published through the generosity of the Laura S. Schor fund,
the Taube Foundation for Jewish Life and Culture, and Mr. Sigmund Rolat.*

Library of Congress Cataloging-in-Publication Data

NAMES: Michlic, Joanna B., editor.

TITLE: Jewish families in Europe, 1939–present: history, representation,
     and memory / edited by Joanna Beata Michlic.

DESCRIPTION: Waltham, Massachusetts : Brandeis University
     Press, [2017] | Series: HBI series on Jewish women | Includes
     bibliographical references and index.

IDENTIFIERS: LCCN 2016029651 (print) | LCCN 2016030060 (ebook) |
     ISBN 9781512600094 (cloth: alk. paper) | ISBN 9781512600100
     (pbk.: alk. paper) | ISBN 9781512600117 (epub, mobi & pdf)

SUBJECTS: LCSH: Jewish families—Europe,—History—20th century. |
     Jewish families—Europe,—History—21st century. | Jewish
     children in the Holocaust. | Holocaust survivors.

CLASSIFICATION: LCC HQ525.J4 J394 2017 (print) |
     LCC HQ525.J4 (ebook) | DDC 306.85/089924–dc23

LC record available at https://lccn.loc.gov/2016029651

5 4 3 2 1

CONTENTS

FOREWORD
SYLVIA BARACK FISHMAN

This groundbreaking volume, edited and introduced by Joanna Beata Michlic, illuminates the persistent impact of childhood Holocaust experiences from World War II until the present day. Twelve chapters written by Holocaust scholars from a broad range of countries and disciplines discuss the Holocaust not only as a cataclysm that brutally ripped apart families and murdered family members, but also as the generator of pathological environments in which social norms and expectations were inverted and social lacunae festered: husbands and wives, fathers and sons, mothers and daughters, brothers and sisters were deprived of each other, and they were also deprived of critical familial roles that the other played. *Jewish Families in Europe, 1939–Present* powerfully reveals the ongoing implications of these familial disruptions.

Historical Jewish societies considered families to be foundational social institutions, de rigueur for productive adult existence. Jewish law and culture created clear generational and gendered familial norms, norms that were expected to bolster the physical and spiritual Jewish well-being of adult generations as well as protect and nurture Jewish generations to come. Despite historical and geographical disruptions, and changes over time, Jewish families were expected to promote what today would be called Jewish religious "continuity," and to serve numerous educational, sociopsychological, and sexual functions. Not least, traditionally defined roles within Jewish families often helped to cushion family members in times of difficulty, compensating for personal and societal existential uncertainties.

In contrast, the Holocaust violently distorted normative family relationships. Several of the essays in this collection emphasize the ways in which new, ad hoc, family-like structures were created: both adults and young people tried to fill in the gaps by playing roles for each other that enhanced the possibilities for day-to-day survival. In this environment, children were robbed not only of loving family members but also of necessary developmental episodes. For the youngest children, those who could not remember an environment prior to the Holocaust, their daily living situations may have seemed "normal," some testimonies reveal. Nevertheless, other testimonies show that child Holocaust victims were not necessarily passive in the grip of moral distortions. On the contrary: isolated and without adults capable of playing protective adult roles, some children responded by consciously resisting and by playing quasi-adult roles and protecting each other. Ironically, many victimized children were much *less* passive than children with normal childhoods — they learned to depend on their own agency. During the Holocaust, these adultlike children understood that they must repress aspects of their childhood selves in order to function and survive. Later, in their postwar lives, such adult child survivors realized that their very childhoods had been stripped from them. Even those who succeeded economically and socially during adulthood were often haunted by such bereavements throughout their lives.

The testimonies of child survivors of the Holocaust are especially prominent sources in this volume. Many general readers will not have previously encountered testimonies of child-survivor experiences and losses, even though such testimonies were recorded and stored in various oral history and archival collections. For decades, the memories of people who had been "children" during the war were not considered reliable evidence for historians. Today, scholarly appreciation for the importance of child survivors' testimonies is growing — partially because of the pioneering work of scholars such as Michlic and her colleagues.

These compelling essays reveal that the often ignored, mistrusted, or sentimentalized testimonies of child survivors of the Holocaust differ in important respects from the recorded memories of adults — and from each other. They illuminate a range of childhood and familial experiences foundational to understanding how and why the Holocaust continues to play a profound role in Jewish lives and societies. In reclaiming the voices of these child survivors of the Holocaust, and in showing how an analysis of gendered and family-like relationships is foundational to understanding the ongoing impact of the Holocaust, Joanna Michlic's *Jewish Families in Europe* performs a scholarly task that is humanitarian, feminist, and very much in keeping with the mission of the Hadassah–Brandeis Institute: "promoting fresh ways of thinking about Jews and gender worldwide."

PREFACE

JOANNA BEATA MICHLIC

"Child survivors cannot recollect the Holocaust the way adult survivors do. Their contribution is bound to their experience. But their limited experience is a profound one."[1] This statement uttered by Aharon Appelfeld (1932–), an acclaimed Israeli writer and a child Holocaust survivor from Bukovina, can be viewed as one of the underpinning ideas for this collective volume. The book delineates key aspects of postwar histories and (self)-representations of mainly central east European Jewry through the lenses of Jewish parents, children, and youths, and to a lesser degree, through charismatic Jewish activists and educators and Jewish organizations and institutions. It does not claim to provide the final word on the subject, but instead, presents a rich sample of the most recent avenues of research into child survivors' postwar memories and into the coping mechanisms of Jewish families and youths during the Holocaust; the possibilities, limitations, and dynamics of the reconstruction of the post-Holocaust Jewish family; and the impossibility of the recovery of childhood in the aftermath of the genocide. It hopes to invite scholars from a variety of fields to engage in further stimulating intellectual conversations, debates, and research on the subject. It alerts the reader's attention to aspects of social history of the Holocaust and its aftermath of which our understanding is still patchy.

The volume records the experiences of Jewish families and children in central east Europe during and in the aftermath of the Holocaust. Some of these experiences are similar to the experiences of Jewish families and children from Nazi-occupied Western Europe.[2] However, some other aspects, such as the mistreatment of Jewish fugitives by those who could be defined as rescuers-abusers, are more specifically embedded in the historical experience of the Holocaust in Nazi-occupied Poland and other east European countries. The editor of this volume recognizes the need for a comparative study aimed at writing a comprehensive history of the rescue of Jewish children in Western and Eastern Europe and the history of European Jewish family reconstitution after the war. Comparative synchronic historical studies of specific issues such as the attitudes and behavior of rescuers toward Jewish children during the Holocaust and the attitudes and behavior of Turkish rescuers toward Armenian children, who had to convert to Islam during the Armenian genocide of 1915–1917,[3] might also be useful for a deeper understanding of the treatment of religious and ethnic minorities' children who are victims of genocide, though such studies may prove difficult to conduct because of sparse sources in the Armenian case. Another potential comparative synchronic study worth exploring, in order to deepen our understanding of young survivors' lives in the aftermath of genocide, is to compare the memories and self-perceptions of Jewish youths as they had emerged from the Holocaust with those of young victims of other twentieth-century genocides, such as the young Tutsi victims of the Rwandan genocide of 1994:[4] how both groups felt about and reflected on their own survival.

At the same time, I believe that present-day scholarly examination of the experiences of children in World War II and in the aftermath should reflect historical distinctions between various groups of child victims, and not be "colorblind" to the differences between Jewish children's experiences and those of children from other ethnic and national groups. It is crucial not only to discuss similarities of experiences, but to pay attention to historical differences and the different historical contexts of the varied child victims. By denying specific features of child victims' experiences in Nazi-occupied Europe, we are in danger of providing a rather a shallow and inaccurate picture of the impact of war and genocide on families and children, and societies as a whole. Of course, such a scholarly analysis should be free of any ideological goals and of attempts at ascertaining a hierarchy of child victims.

I would like to express my appreciation to a number of institutions and individuals who enabled me to work on this project. I am particularly grateful to Shulamit Reinharz, director of the Hadassah–Brandeis Institute, Brandeis University, for her continuous support and her great enthusiasm for this project. I would also like to thank Sylvia Barack Fishman and other members of the HBI staff for their support; Laura S. Schor of Hunter College and Jonathan Sarna of Brandeis University for their encouragement; Antony Polonsky for his beneficial comments and advice; Ariel Kochavi of the Weiss-Livnat International MA Program, School of History, Haifa University, where I spent a fruitful academic spring 2014 as a U.S. Senior Fulbright Scholar; and my graduate students at Haifa University for intellectually stimulating discussions. I would also like to thank Nahum Bogner, a pioneering scholar of Jewish childhood in Poland during the Holocaust and himself a child Holocaust survivor from Poland, for his constant enthusiasm for and support of my work, and many other child Holocaust survivors in Israel, Poland, France, the United Kingdom, and the United States, whom I was privileged to meet and interview over the last decade. I am also deeply indebted to Sigmund Rolat and Shanna Penn of the Taube Foundation for Jewish Life and Culture for their generosity, and to Ruth Abrams for her careful reading of the original chapters. I would like to thank all the contributors—and especially Henryk Grynberg for his poignant and masterly afterword.

Finally, I would like to thank my editors and copy editor at Brandeis University Press/University Press of New England for their care and continuous interest in this project, and for walking me through the steps necessary to turn this into a book, and the anonymous readers for the press, who offered an invaluable critique. Last but not least, I would like to thank my family and friends for their patience, enthusiasm, interest, and support. I dedicate this book to the child Holocaust survivors and their multigenerational families.

NOTES

1. Aharon Appelfeld, "A Different Testimony," in *Erinnerte Shoah: Die Literatur der Überlebenden*, ed. Walter Schmitz (Dresden: Thelem, 2003), 7.

2. On Jewish child survivors in the Netherlands, see the important works by Diane L. Wolf, *Beyond Anne Frank: Hidden Children and Postwar Families in Holland* (Berkeley: University of California Press, 2007), and Wolf, "Child Withholding as Child Transfer: Hidden Jewish Children and the State in Postwar Netherlands," *Journal of Human Rights* 12, no. 3 (2013): 296–308; on child survivors in Belgium and their rescuers, see the pioneering study of Suzanne Vromen, *Hidden Children of the Holocaust: Belgian Nuns and Their Daring Rescue of Young Jews from the Nazis* (Oxford: Oxford University Press, 2008).

3. On rescue and conversion to Islam during the Armenian genocide, see, for example, Ugur Ümir Üngör, "Conversion and Rescue: Survival Strategies in the Armenian Genocide," in *Resisting Genocide: The Multiple Forms of Rescue*, ed. Jacques Semelin, Claire Andrieu, and Sarah Gensburger (New York: Columbia University Press, 2011), 201–18.

4. For a collection of powerful accounts of survivors of Rwandan genocide, see Jean Hatzfeld, *Life Laid Bare: The Survivors in Rwanda Speak* (New York: Other Press, 2007). Originally published in French, *Dans le nu de la vie* (Paris: Seuil, 2000).

JOANNA BEATA
MICHLIC

JEWISH FAMILIES IN EUROPE, 1939– PRESENT

HISTORY, REPRESENTATION, AND MEMORY— AN INTRODUCTION

May 8 [1945]

It is over. Our liberation has come, but she wears a prosaic face. No one has died of joy. No one has gone mad with excitement. When we used to dream of freedom, we bathed her with our tears. We crowned her with the garlands of our smiles and dreams. Now that she is here, she looks like a beggar, and we have nothing to give her. With what desperation did we call for her in those dark days. With what power did her far-off shimmer flesh out our thin bodies? Now she is here and she beckons to us from every corner. She is right before our eyes, yet we cannot see her. She begs us: "Touch me . . . enjoy me . . ." But we are tired. Our past, like a hawk, circles overhead, fluttering its black wings, devouring our days with horrible memories. It poisons our nights with terror. Poor, sad Freedom! Will she ever have the strength to free us from those dark shadowy wings?[1]

For years my own feelings lay dormant like a fossil inside an amber bead. Now, fifty years after the war ended, I want to uncover my past and learn who I was. . . . For years I did not speak about the war. People were killed. Parents watched their children slain. I survived. What was there to tell? Only the dead can tell. But when my older son, Daniel, went to school, his teacher asked me to meet with the students to tell them about my life.[2]

The first passage is from the *Diary* of Chava Rosenfarb, today an acclaimed Yiddish writer, dated May 8, 1945, when she was twenty-two years old. The second is an excerpt from the memoir of Miriam Winter, a theater professor in the United States and a child survivor, who was, like Rosenfarb, born in the great prewar multicultural city of Lodz in 1933. Their writing encapsulates some central aspects of the Holocaust experience for young Jewish individuals. Both excerpts show common themes in the self-representations of young survivors and in the postwar social history of European Jewish youth.

That history is filled with multifactored silences. The war forced young Jews to suppress critical aspects of their own identity in order to survive. When that pressure abated, many pursued a sudden, compelling search for their prewar and wartime selves, while experiencing an overwhelming sense of the irreparable loss of their families. Memoirs and testimonies from young survivors are imbued with the realization that wartime experiences have a profound impact on one's adult life, even for people who achieved what is socially regarded as a successful familial and professional life.[3] They constitute a body of evidence that draws us as close as we can get to the young survivors' apprehensions regarding their identities, their mourning of their murdered families, and their explorations and interrogations of their own memories.

Since the late nineteenth century, European culture has regarded childhood as a temporary and impermanent phase of the life cycle and has always defined it as a loss in adult life. For Jewish children during the Holocaust, and for that matter, for other children under the conditions of genocide in the twentieth and twenty-first centuries, there was a total, violent loss of childhood experiences during the chronological phase of childhood. Their childhood was denied and destroyed.[4] Examining the history of these experiences has prompted an ongoing methodological discussion of how and what young survivors, especially children, remember from their wartime childhood. Historians are also concerned with when the memory comes, whether and by whom it is transmitted, and how the children of survivors, generation two, and the grandchildren of survivors, generation three, engage with the wartime memories of their parents and grandparents.

This collective volume, *Jewish Families in Europe, 1939–Present: History, Representation, and Memory*, is the outcome of an interdisciplinary, in-depth research project on "Families, Children, and the Holocaust," conducted at Hadassah-Brandeis Institute, and the vigorous academic discussions it prompted involving historians, sociologists, psychologists, literary scholars, and child survivors themselves, such as the acclaimed Polish Jewish American writer, Henryk Grynberg.

AIMS OF THE BOOK

The main goal of this work is to broaden our understanding of wartime and postwar histories and (self)-representations of mainly central east European Jewry through the lenses of Jewish parents, children, and youth, and to a lesser degree, through Jewish organizations and institutions. This work does not claim to provide the final word on the subject, but instead presents a rich sample of the most recent avenues of research into child survivors' postwar memories and into the coping mechanisms of Jewish families and youth during the Holocaust; the possibilities, limitations, and dynamics of the reconstruction of the post-Holocaust Jewish family; and the impossibility of the recovery of childhood in the aftermath of the genocide. The mortality rate for Jewish children and also for elderly Jews was especially high during the Holocaust. According to reliable estimates, only 6 to 11 percent of Europe's prewar Jewish population of children numbering approximately between 1.1 and 1.5 million survived, as compared with 33 percent of the adults, so the history of Jewish child survivors also represents a history of a small youth minority.[5]

The book demonstrates how the fields of the Holocaust and postwar social Jewish history have been changing and expanding as a result of scholarly engagement with new archival collections and oral histories in a variety of audio and visual forms. The access to new archival collections in post-communist Europe and the recently opened Red Cross International Tracing Services (ITS) records at Bad Arolsen, Germany, which is now also available in digitized form at the United States Holocaust Memorial Museum in Washington, D.C., have led scholars to ask previously neglected questions. It enables historians to conduct richly detailed microstudies of everyday life in concentration and death camps and on different aspects of life in hiding on "the Aryan side" in Nazi-occupied Eastern Europe, which was forbidden to Jews by the German laws and regulations. It also enables historians to conduct microhistories of children's lives and rehabilitation programs in Displaced Persons (DP) camps in occupied Germany in the early postwar period.[6] Thanks to the engagement with these recovered or newly discovered sources, scholars are now involved in in-depth historical examinations of the dynamics of relationships in prisoner society; in ghetto society; between Jewish men and Jewish women, and Jewish children and Jewish adults; and between Jews and non-Jews on "the Aryan side," including the still underresearched and in postcommunist Europe, greatly politicized, subject of the rescue of Jews, particularly children.[7]

Greater openness toward and critical engagement of historians with oral histories have enabled new interdisciplinary scholarly discussions on the memory and the postwar self-representations of young survivors. Nowhere is this as visible as in the growing scholarly interest in child Holocaust testimonies from different postwar periods, starting with the early postwar wave of 1945–1949[8] and ending with the latest and possibly the final postwar "boom" beginning in the 1990s, which is still continuing. After decades of denying agency to Jewish youths and children, historians began to acknowledge the agency of young survivors in ensuring their own survival and in helping others, especially siblings who were younger than they were.[9]

Conventional history has been suspicious of individual witnesses and lacked a vocabulary and methodology for dealing with ordinary people and their experiences and memories. Women and children have been ignored over a long period in conventional history. This historical school has viewed child survivors' testimonies with particularly great mistrust, though such testimonies were eagerly collected for psychological and educational purposes already at the end of the war. However, even the professional and amateur historians of the Jewish Historical Commissions in Hungary, Poland, and Germany,[10] established immediately in the aftermath of the Holocaust to document the physical and cultural destruction of Jews, did not know what to do with the child survivors' testimonies. These first collectors (*zamlers*) of child survivors' testimonies saw child survivors' accounts as being of little value to historians. In their eyes, child survivors' testimonies could not be treated as historical evidence because children at this stage of cognitive development lack the capacity to transmit their lived experiences and general information accurately. This was, for instance, the view of Genia Silkes (Sylkes) (1914–1984), herself a survivor and an active member of the Central Jewish Historical Commission (*Tsentrale yiddishe historische komisye*), a body first established in Poland in August 1944 and transformed into the *Żydowski Instytut Historyczny* (Jewish Historical Institute, ZIH) in October 1947. Among 7,300 personal testimonies collected by the members of the Central Jewish Historical Commission in Poland between 1944 and 1948, 419 child survivors authored 429 testimonies, as some wrote or dictated more than one testimony. More than three-quarters of these testimonies are in Polish, the second language of the testimonies is Yiddish, and a small minority of testimonies are in German and Russian. In 1945, Silkes compiled the instructions for interviewing child survivors that became the guidelines for the newly established Jewish Historical Commissions in Poland. In the guide, published in both Polish and Yiddish in Lodz, a major thriving center of Jewish life in post-1945 Poland, children's testimonies were considered valuable material for psychological and educational purposes rather than important documents for historians.[11] "When carrying out precise studies of children, we assume beforehand that they are less valuable than other evidentiary material; however, they have a psychological value that cannot be calculated, which adults are not in the position to give us."[12] Somewhat contradictorily, Silkes, and other like-minded activists of the Jewish Historical Commissions, viewed the children's testimonies as powerful emotional indices of resistance and heroism, demonstrating the young survivors' courage (*mut*), practical survival skills (*lebns hokhme*), and the vigor of their resistance (*vidershtands-kraft*). But she was unable to acknowledge the agency of child survivors, in spite of the fact that 199 child-survivor testimonies—ninety-nine of those by girls and one hundred by boys—named their own actions and wits as essential in the process of their own survival.

THE UNDERRESEARCHED HISTORY OF
JEWISH SURVIVOR YOUTHS AND FAMILY

The literary scholar Lawrence Langer has argued that by dividing the history of the Holocaust into two histories, perpetrators and victims, conventional historians have failed the victims and privileged the perpetrators, merely because the Nazi regime created official archival documents.[13] These historians created narratives concerned mainly with the perpetrators, ignoring or marginalizing the victims. They failed the youngest victims and survivors most by denying them not only agency, but also a legitimate place as a subject of historical inquiry.

Beginning in the late 1970s and through the 1980s and 1990s, new trends in scholarship in the form of the oral history, the history of everyday life, women's history, gender studies, and the history of childhood have facilitated the rise and expansion of the social history of the Holocaust and post-1945 Jewish history by the inclusion of the previously hidden subjects, women[14] and children. These developments have forced historians to look for analytical tools outside their discipline and to recognize that the study of history should be concerned not only with the past, but also with how collectives and individuals remember the past. Contemporary historians realize that the exploration of human subjectivity allows us to understand the emotional impact and the human meaning of events, and that therefore the subjectivity of children constitutes an appropriate topic for historical inquiry.[15]

This collective volume is part of this exciting shift and follows in the footsteps of such works as the pioneering study of Jewish children in Nazi-occupied Europe by Debórah Dwork, *Children with the Jewish Star: Jewish Youth in Nazi-Occupied Europe*,[16] published in 1991, which gives an overview of the different fates of Jewish children; and Nicholas Stargardt's *Witnesses of War: Children's Lives under the Nazis*,[17] which demonstrates the merits of a history of children, written from a child's point of view, and which places children's experiences within the broader social and cultural contexts of the Second World War. Two contributors to this volume, Dalia Ofer and Leonore Weitzman, are pioneering scholars of the history of women[18] and the Jewish family during the Holocaust, and their respective chapters represent the latest development of their approach to the modes of parenthood and survival strategies of Jewish families in the major ghettos in Nazi-occupied eastern Europe.

In addition to demonstrating the recent shifts in historical writing on the Holocaust and on post-Holocaust social Jewish history, *Jewish Families in Europe, 1939–Present* offers a vision for how these fields might develop in the future. It contributes to the deeper understanding of young individuals and families during and in the aftermath of the Holocaust. It provides insights into the role of children and youths in the post-Shoah reconstruction of Jewish family and society, and the complexities, paradoxes, and contradictions of that process. It alerts our attention to the areas of the social history of the Holocaust of which our understanding is still fragmentary.

This book focuses primarily on Jewish communities in central east Europe and does not include comparative analysis with other child-victims of the Second World War, a field that has generated increasing academic interest in the last decade.[19] This specific geographical focus demonstrates that there are still many underresearched historical and methodological topics and a wealth of understudied material that begs for a proper scholarly investigation. Even so, the need for more comparative studies is clear, for example, concerning the postwar modes of reconstruction of childhood experiences in biographical memory between Jewish children and non-Jewish children—victims of Nazi policies of violence, discrimination, and persecution. In agreement with Nicholas Stargardt's position,[20] I argue these studies should examine not only similarities but also the major differences between the different national and ethnic groups of children. It is crucial to pay attention to historical differences and the different historical contexts of the varied child-victims under discussion.

Jewish Families in Europe, 1939–Present does not attempt to make any comparisons with the experiences and memories of Jewish youths and families during and in the aftermath of the Holocaust in Western Europe. But it acknowledges the need for future comparative studies, involving Western and Eastern Europe, for example, of certain topics such as the rescue of Jewish children, the postwar reconstitution of Jewish families, the recovery of hidden Jewish children, and the wartime and early postwar experiences of antisemitism and its impact on young Jewish survivors. Certain parallels and similarities, between early postwar Poland and early postwar Holland, concerning the painful reconstitution of the Jewish family, the lack of reunion with Jewish parents, and the psychological problems of regaining a Jewish identity by hidden children have struck me while reading Diane L. Wolf's *Beyond Anne Frank: Hidden Children and Postwar Families in Holland*,[21] a sociological study based on interviews with former hidden Dutch Jewish children. Of course, in studying the nature of these similarities, one has to take into account major historical differences such as state-level family policy. In contrast to post-1945 Poland, in which family law at least theoretically guaranteed the right of surviving Jewish parents to be reunited with their offspring who were sheltered by individual Polish rescuers during the Holocaust, in the Netherlands, in August 1945, a special regulation was enacted that became a law concerning hidden Jewish children which made it almost impossible to reunite these children with their biological parents returning from concentration and death camps.

Jewish Families in Europe, 1939–Present demonstrates that the post-Holocaust history of central east European Jewish youths and family encompasses many transnational aspects, such as the reconstitution of Jewish families, adoption, and a variety of life trajectories of young survivors, including first loves, future marriages, lifelong friendships, and family-like relationships among youths who met in children's homes and kibbutzim established in central east Europe and in the West in the aftermath of genocide. It is a history that must be approached through a transnational lens. One of the underresearched issues regarding the transnational history of young Holocaust survivors is, for example, the treatment of youths from Poland, Czechoslovakia, and Hungary in early postwar British society. In her doctoral thesis,[22] Mary Fraser Kirsh explores the ways the Anglo-Jewish relief organizations and press, including the leading weekly *Jewish Chronicle*, portrayed child survivors from the war-torn continent in the early postwar era. She offers a rather disturbing picture of the utilization of child survivors in the Anglo-Jewry's propaganda and fund-raising campaigns in which the child survivor was reduced to a mere symbol of redemption and assimilation in middle-class British society. Adolescent survivors were always portrayed as serious, studious, and neatly dressed, and eager to learn a new trade, an antithesis of the delinquent youths so prominent in postwar British imagination. Despite the destruction written on children's bodies, the social workers and the journalists typically emphasized the attractive appearance and health of young survivors from Bergen-Belsen and Terezin camps. There is a need for systematic investigation of how the Anglo-Jewish tradition of invisibility and acculturation, rooted in collective anxiety over the spread and influence of anti-Jewish stereotypes in postwar British society, has affected the lives of young survivors from central east Europe in postwar Britain. A subtle version of British antisemitism and its influence on the second and third generations of British Holocaust survivors also requires a thorough scholarly analysis.

To understand the short-term and long-term impact of the Shoah on young survivors and the post-1945 multigenerational Jewish family, it is essential to study that history in both the wartime and postwar historical contexts rather than treat these two periods separately. Many Czech, Slovak, Polish, or Hungarian Jewish children found themselves in the Displaced Persons camps in the early postwar American, British, and French zones in divided Germany, and made their new postwar homes in the West: in the United States, Canada, and Australia, and to a lesser degree in the United Kingdom and France. Many child survivors, the full orphans, were shattered by the painful realization that no one would "come for them," because their immediate and extended families had been totally destroyed. As a result, they were attracted, not only in an ideological, but also in a primarily practical and existential sense, to

Zionism as the only attractive, meaningful alternative to build a future life.[23] The children's homes and kibbutzim that mushroomed in the early postwar period were the formative centers for young survivors in which the yearning for the "dreamed" safe Jewish homeland crystallized. These children emigrated mostly illegally to the Yishuv in Palestine/Israel between 1945 and 1950, but the sense of orphanhood did not disappear easily in their new homeland, as the simple poem by an unnamed child survivor written in Kibbutz Mishmar Ha'emek in 1946 exclaims:

> I have so much of everything
> But I have no parents
> At the same time
> I hear the wind whisper
> Child, don't listen to that voice
> There are many children like you
> Who have no mothers
> So don't cry
> You must sing, study, and dance
> And build our land.[24]

Other orphan children were adopted by unknown Jewish relatives or strangers in the United States through a variety of Jewish charities, such as the European Jewish Children's Aid, which became part of the United Services for New Americans (USNA).[25] The "lucky ones," who were reunited with at least one surviving biological parent or another close relative, emigrated to the West after their newly reconstituted families met all the bureaucratic emigration criteria and passed the difficult task of proving that they were "blood relations," often without possessing crucial documents such as birth and death certificates.

THE HIDDEN CHILDREN

Chapters on the postwar period in this volume throw new insights on the history of hidden children, whose wartime and postwar experiences and memories were barely known to historians in the early 1990s. Yet today, in 2016, hidden children have fully established active social networks, foundations, and associations not only in the United States, Canada, Australia, and Western Europe, but also in postcommunist Europe. With the help of Abraham H. Foxman, a former national director of the Anti-Defamation League and a child survivor from Poland, whose wartime rescue experiences, along with those of his parents, are also discussed in this volume, sixteen hundred former hidden children from twenty-eight countries met for the first time in late May 1991 in New York City at the First International Gathering of Children Hidden during World War II.[26] Thanks to this international gathering, which included a variety of social, cultural, academic, and psychotherapeutic events, hidden children for the first time publicly voiced their neglected wartime experience and thereby triggered and facilitated a scholarly interest in this group. Hidden children, the youngest born in 1939 or during the first three years of World War II, are the last living Holocaust survivors.

Hidden children are today part of the remarkable global social movement of memory among survivors, committed to the reconstruction of their prewar and wartime childhood and their postwar youth, which is characterized by a twisted sense of split identity and a complicated family history. Like other child survivors, many hidden child survivors are the driving force behind specific commemoration ceremonies in their *heimats* (places of their birth and childhood) and prewar homes of their ancestors. Some take on the role of survivor-educators, or "professional survivors,"[27] by teaching about their experiences and the Holocaust in schools, colleges, and universities, and in public engagements, promoting tolerance and multicultural understanding. Many have deposited their interviews and memoirs in major archives such as Yad Vashem in Jerusalem, the United States Holocaust Memorial Museum in Washington, D.C., the Imperial War Museum in London, or smaller local archives and museums. Between 1981 and 1995, the Fortunoff Video Archive for Holocaust Testimonies at Yale University collected 34,000 testimonies, while between 1994 and 2002 Steven Spielberg's Shoah Visual History Foundation collected 52,000. Many of these are those of child survivors.[28] At the same time, we have to remember that there are child survivors who still avoid giving public interviews and testimonies and may never be ready to do so. There are many reasons for their silence, including familial concerns, psychological reservations, personal life trajectories, and/or drastically violent memories of wartime and early postwar experiences, such as emotional and sexual assault by those who were supposed to be their guardians.

Studies of child survivors' testimonies unsettle a number of assumptions and popular conceptions about the Holocaust. First, they shatter the commonly accepted notion that the Holocaust ended in 1945. This sense that the Shoah is an ongoing trauma is poignantly expressed by Thomas Buergenthal, an internationally acclaimed American human rights lawyer and judge, and child survivor whose father was a Polish Jew from Galicia and whose mother was a German Jew: "That story, after all, continues to have a lasting impact on the person I have become."[29]

Second, an examination of child survivors' accounts questions heroic and martyrological traditions that tend to sentimentalize Jewish children and Jewish families and fail to recognize the complexity of the dilemmas they faced during the Holocaust and in its aftermath. For example, in the early postwar period, some hidden children struggled to function in the newly reconstructed family units in which their surviving parent represented a forgotten and emotionally distant figure because of the long years of separation during the Holocaust or because the parent had remarried a new spouse immediately after the war.[30] As a result, these children sometimes yearned for a reunion with their loving wartime rescuer. Of course, this latter pattern was common among certain groups of hidden children from all over Nazi-occupied Europe, as it is revealed in the powerful documentary film *Secret Lives: Hidden Children and Their Rescuers During WWII* (2002), by the documentary filmmaker Aviva Slesin,[31] herself a hidden child from Lithuania.

Third, child survivors' testimonies reveal how extremely vulnerable young fugitives were in the world of adults under the conditions of war and genocide in Poland and other eastern European countries. Even among those who were supposed to shelter and protect them, there were rescuer-abusers who tormented them mentally and physically and treated them as a source of free labor, although there were also those who treated their young Jewish charges with love, compassion, and total dedication, as if they were their own children.

The postgenocide era did not bring an end to the confusion and vulnerability of youth in the world of adults. The key features of their early postwar experience were shattered dreams and a deeply felt sense of orphanhood buried beneath the surface of their joy at having survived. Other features include different, and often contradictory, expectations of behavior and educational and career choices among the young survivors and their newly appointed guardians, and a lack of understanding and sympathy on the part of some adoptive parents in the West and institutionalized authorities. Despite obvious differences between then and now, perhaps these unsettling findings about Jewish youths during and in the aftermath of the Holocaust constitute important lessons on how young victims of current and future genocides and wars should be treated.

CONTENT OF THE BOOK

Jewish Families in Europe, 1939–Present consists of an introduction, twelve chapters divided into two chronological sections, and an afterword by Henryk Grynberg.

The first section includes essays on parenthood, childhood, and the relationships between Jewish youths and adults during the Nazi era. It opens with a chapter by Dalia Ofer that discusses a variety of modes of parenthood, with special attention being paid to fatherhood in the major ghettos of Eastern Europe, such as Warsaw and Lodz.[32] Ofer shows that the contemporaneous sources, such as personal diaries and letters, postwar memoirs, and oral histories, offer us only a fragmentary portrayal of the Jewish family, one that is filled with contradictions and complexities.

The sociologist Leonore Weitzman's chapter is in direct conversation with Ofer's essay. It offers us an interpretation of self-help within a family unit under ghetto conditions. Weitzman presents a dynamic interpretation of role reversal between husbands and wives and between children and parents, suggesting greater fluidity, modifications, and "on and off switching roles" than the rather static understanding of role reversal. Her interpretation is particularly helpful in demonstrating how "role sharing" was realized in a variety of small and large families through different stages of ghettoization.

Joanna Sliwa's essay investigates the survival strategies of children in the Kraków ghetto from the moment of its inception on March 3, 1941, until its final liquidation on March 13-14, 1943. On the eve of the Second World War, the Jewish community of Kraków numbered 56,000 inhabitants,[33] one-third of the entire population of this medieval Polish capital, which became the capital of the Nazi-established administrative entity *General Government*, headed by the infamous Hans Frank. Sliwa provides an in-depth analysis of the variety of children's survival strategies in the ghetto, through which the children emerge as historical actors exercising agency, albeit to varying degrees and with all restrictions imposed on that agency. Sliwa argues that smuggling goods and individuals in and out of the ghetto and food into the ghetto were two intertwined domains of Jewish youths. The acclaimed Polish French filmmaker Roman Polanski was one of such children of the Kraków ghetto.[34]

Kinga Frojimovics's chapter takes us into the discussion of a still largely neglected topic, the wartime and postwar experiences of disabled Jewish children.[35] Frojimovics's essay focuses on the survival of fifteen to twenty deaf and blind children in the Budapest ghetto, thanks to the efforts of a remarkable man, Dr Dezső Kanizsai, a children's speech therapist and director of the National Institute for the Israelite Deaf-Mute, and the Blind in Budapest between 1926 and its closure at the end of 1940s. She offers a novel way of looking at the institutionalized rescue patterns and their policies and practices toward the most unfortunate children during genocide, and invites scholars to conduct further comparative research on the subject.

Kenneth Waltzer's chapter examines patterns of social behavior among a group of 304 East European Jewish prisoners, sixteen years old and under, who were evacuated from Auschwitz-Buna (Monowitz) camp and Birkenau and taken on a death march to the west on January 19, 1945. Among them was the young Lazar (Eliezer) Wiesel (1928-2016), who documented his ordeal in the most well-known Holocaust memoir, *Night*, written first in Yiddish under the title *Un di Velt Hot Geshvign*.[36]

Waltzer offers a passionate critique of a Hobbesian interpretation of concentration camp prisoner society as devoid of solidarity, human connection, and compassion. Instead, he contends that prisoner society must also be understood as a world of small-scale solidarities and connections between adult men and boys that enabled the latter to survive under extreme genocidal conditions. His work invites historians to conduct research on the small clusters of young survivors after the liberation, a study that would allow us to understand the short-term and long-term impact of social bonding among young survivors in the aftermath of genocide.

Jennifer Marlow's chapter provides a historical reconstruction of the rescue of Jews through the lenses of former child survivors and also their parents. According to Marlow, the Nazi occupation and the Holocaust changed relationships between female Polish Catholic domestic workers and their former young Jewish charges whom they protected and sheltered, and the Jewish parents, the former employers of these domestic workers. The rescue dynamic unleashed, on the one hand, love, loyalty, and total dedication, and on the other, a darker mixture of emotions: possessive love, anger, cruelty, and jealousy.

The second part of *Jewish Families in Europe, 1939–Present* focuses on the complexities of the situation of Jewish children and youths during the early postwar period and examines the methodological and historical issues raised by survivor youths' accounts of their wartime experiences. It also addresses the transmission of Holocaust memories in postwar Jewish families.

Avinoam Patt, a historian of Zionism in Jewish Displaced Persons (DP) camps in postwar Germany,[37] discusses the early postwar life trajectories of 110 young survivors from two kibbutzim in the Polish Silesian towns of Bytom and Sosnowiec. This group spent fourteen months in the DP camps in the American zone of occupied Germany, where they named their united kibbutz after the Warsaw ghetto heroine Tosia Altman (1918-1943). Patt shows that for the young orphan survivors, the kibbutz came to serve as a substitute for the large Jewish families that the youths lost in the Shoah. Patt's analysis also examines the manner in which young survivors internalized, utilized, and also sometimes rejected the Zionist ideology. Further studies comparing growing up, on the one hand, in collective orphan survivors' centers and kibbutzim in DP camps in postwar Germany and in Israel, and on the other, in adoptive Jewish families of unknown relatives and strangers in the West would be a valuable tool in determining the role of peer groups in helping young survivors successfully adjust to a new life.

Joanna Beata Michlic and Rita Horváth discuss the importance of early postwar children's testimonies in the reconstruction of the complexities of wartime experiences and the immediate effect of the Holocaust on the children. Horváth's and Michlic's chapters derive from and contribute to the growing school of historical writing about children that recognizes the individual agency of children and views children as important historical co-creators of everyday life.[38] While arguing for critical examination and broader contextualization of youth accounts, both scholars insist that early postwar child survivors' testimonies show how the "granddaddy issue"[39] in childhood history — that there is no access to children's voices — can be overcome.

In their chapter, Boaz Cohen and Gabriel Finder reveal that the issue of the authenticity of children's testimonies caused heated discussions in the early postwar period. One such discussion took place between the collector and editor, Benjamin Tenenbaum (1914–1999), and David Hanegbi, the publisher, of one of the first immediate postwar collections of the early postwar children's testimonies, *ehad me-'ir u-shenayim mi-mishpahah* (*One from a City and Two from a Family*), which appeared in Hebrew in 1947.[40] Cohen and Finder discuss the history of this Hebrew language anthology, its origins, structure, and goals, and compare it to the other immediate postwar anthology of children's testimonies, *Dzieci oskarżają* (*The Children Accuse*), originally published in Polish in 1946 by the Central Jewish Historical Commission.

Uta Larkey's chapter looks at how the memories of Holocaust survivors are communicated and transmitted in family settings by members of the second generation (2G), any individual born in 1945 and after, and the third generation (3G), the grandchildren of Holocaust survivors. The passing of the first decade of the twenty-first century, with the growing awareness of the inevitable encroachment of the "postsurvivor" era, makes the issue of how to interpret the Holocaust memories of survivors by 2G and 3G a compelling and timely research subject. Not only does the subject engage historians, psychologists, sociologists, and literary scholars, but also neuroscientists, who have recently claimed to identify the mode of transmission of Holocaust survivors' stress to their offspring through their genes — "the epigenetic inheritance."[41]

Since 1977, there has been a growing global outpouring of fictional, life writings, and visual artistic works by the second generation, known as "the Heirs of the Holocaust,"[42] a term coined by Helen Epstein, the pioneering voice of 2G who made "an unidentifiable group identifiable."[43] As regards the transmission of the Holocaust memories by 3G, we have also recently witnessed an outpouring of fictional works, such as Safran Foer's *Everything Is Illuminated* (2002), Andrew Wiener's *The Marriage Artist* (2010), and Nathan Englander's *What We Talk about When We Talk about Anne Frank* (2012), and the emergence of new Holocaust memorialization projects. The latter includes tattooing oneself with a survivor's number by grandchildren of the Holocaust survivors as a way of remembering and raising the awareness of the Holocaust.[44] According to the Holocaust historian Michael Berenbaum, transmitting memories of the Holocaust with one's own body is a manifestation of a broader transition from "life" to "historical memories": "We're at that transition, and this is sort of a brazen, in-your-face way of bridging it."[45]

In her work, Larkey builds on research on familial transfer of memory, such as "postmemory," the most significant concept in the discussion of the 2G memory, introduced by Marianna Hirsch,[46] and the concepts of seeking a *tikkun* (mending repair) of self (*atzmi*), the world (*olam*), and (*am*) (healing of the Jewish people). Larkey offers a new conceptualization, "transmemory," to define the engagement with the Holocaust by the generation of grandchildren. She also calls for a further investigation of a gendered transfer of a family's memory in the 3G in a transnational context.

The second part ends with a chapter by psychologist and clinician Eva Fogelman, who is also a member of 2G. Fogelman argues that, for decades, the almost sole focus on and fascination with Anne Frank (1929-1945)[47] — the famous young Jewish victim-figure — contributed to the neglect of the child survivors by scholars, the general public, and reparation authorities. Nonetheless, Fogelman contends that the last three decades have seen the recognition of child survivors' suffering; and this development, in turn, has made a profound difference in the child survivors' waning years. Fogelman's essay offers a warning and important lesson for social workers, psychologists, and other professionals who deal with today's young victims of genocide and war. It clearly shows how crucial it is to acknowledge and listen to the voices of young victims immediately in the aftermath of genocide.

Jewish Families in Europe, 1939-Present ends with the afterword by Henryk Grynberg, a prolific writer and poet, who dedicated his entire oeuvre to the writings about child survivors, based on his autobiographical experiences.[48] In his essay, Grynberg, a child survivor born in 1936, was asked to comment on many academic essays included in this volume — a "reversal task," since it is usually the scholars who critically analyze child survivors' testimonies and statements. Grynberg offers intellectually sharp and poignant reflections about a variety of issues discussed in the volume. He makes us aware that children not only experience situations differently from adults, but they often face other horizons of experience: in contrast to adults, who had a normal past before the Holocaust, for many children the Holocaust was normality.

Grynberg also shares with the readers the ways in which he employed children's testimonies in his book *Children of Zion*,[49] based on the testimonies of 861 Polish Jewish children, mainly orphans, who in the fall of 1939 left Nazi-occupied Poland and found themselves under the Soviet occupation. In the summer of 1942, these children began their journey to Iran. They were a part of a group of 24,000 Polish civilians, who along with the recruits to the Polish Anders' Army, were allowed to leave the Soviet Union for Iran. Known as the

"Tehran children," they constitute one of the least-researched Jewish children's cohorts during the Second World War.[50]

Jewish Families in Europe, 1939-Present reveals that there are still many questions about the wartime experiences of the Jewish family and certain groups of Jewish children in east-central Europe, and about how the Holocaust affected child survivors and the post-Holocaust multigenerational Jewish family. These questions require unraveling by the employment of various interdisciplinary scholarly approaches and different analytical tools. It is my hope that the research we present here will serve as a useful and inspirational guide for scholars of the social history of the Holocaust, Jewish childhood, and the post-1945 Jewish family, and for scholars of memory, human rights, childhood, and young people and families during and in the aftermath of war and genocide.

NOTES

1. Chava Rosenfarb, *Diary*, written in the Displaced Persons camp in Bergen-Belsen after the liberation of the camp on April 15, 1945. The excerpts from the *Diary* were first published in Yiddish in 1948 as an addendum to Rosenfarb's first collection of poems, *Di balade fun nekhtikn vald* (The Ballad of Yesterday's Forest). Goldie Morgentaler, Rosenfarb's daughter and a professor of English at the University of Lethbridge, translated her mother's *Diary* and published its excerpts in *Tablet Magazine* (January 27, 2014); see Chava Rosenfarb, accessed on August 10, 2015, http://www.tabletmag.com/jewish-arts-and-culture /books/160640/rosenfarb-bergen-belsen-diary.

2. Miriam Winter, *Trains: A Memoir of a Hidden Childhood during and after World War II* (Jackson, MI: Kelton Press, 1997).

3. There is a lack of studies concerning the cultural, social, and economic achievements of young East European Jewish survivors in the West. For an interesting sociological analysis of socioeconomic achievements in the United States among young Jewish refugees from German-speaking Central Europe, see Gerhard Sonnert and Gerald Holton, *What Happened to the Children Who Fled Nazi Persecution* (New York: Palgrave Macmillan, 2006).

4. On the plasticity of the terms *children* and *childhood* in European society from the late eighteenth century and on the late nineteenth-century legacy of children becoming the emblem of the adult human condition, see, for example, Carolyn Steedman, *Strange Dislocations: Childhood and the Idea of Human Interiority, 1780-1930* (Cambridge: Harvard University Press, 1995).

5. For a short overview of the history of Jewish children during the Holocaust, see, for example, Keren Nili, "Children," in *The Holocaust Encyclopedia*, edited by Walter Laqueur, 115-19 (New Haven, CT: Yale University Press, 2001). For a rich collection of published primary sources on children during the Holocaust, see Patricia Heberer, *Children during the Holocaust* (Lanham, MD: AltaMira Press, 2011).

6. For an essay based on previously understudied records of UNRRA's child-tracing service held in the Archives of the International Tracing Service (ITS), see Verena Buser, "Displaced Children 1945 and the Child Tracing Division of the United Nations Relief and

Rehabilitation Administration," in *The Holocaust in History and Memory*, vol. 7: *Seventy Years after the Liberation of the Camps*, ed. Rainer Schulze, 109-23 (Colchester, UK: University of Essex, 2014). On the general history of Jewish life in Displaced Persons camps in occupied Germany, see Atina Grossmann, *Jews, Germans, and Allies: Close Encounters in Occupied Germany* (Princeton: Princeton University Press, 2007); Hagit Lavsky, *New Beginnings: Holocaust Survivors in Bergen-Belsen and the British Zone in Germany, 1945-1950* (Detroit: Wayne State University Press, 2002); and Zeev W. Mankowitz, *Life between Memory and Hope: The Survivors of the Holocaust in Occupied Germany* (New York: Cambridge University Press, 2002).

7. On the politics of memory of the Holocaust and its dark aspects, including the uses and abuses of the narratives of rescuers in the entire postcommunist Europe, see John-Paul Himka and Joanna B. Michlic, *Bringing the Dark Past to Light: The Memory of the Holocaust in Postcommunist Europe* (Lincoln: University of Nebraska Press, 2013).

8. On the first postwar wave of survivors' testimonies, see, for example, Henry Greenspan, *The Awakening of Memory: Survivor Testimonies in the First Years after the Holocaust and Today* (Washington, DC: United States Holocaust Memorial Museum, Monna and Otto Weinmann Annual Lecture Series, 2000), and Boaz Cohen, "The Children's Voice: Postwar Collection of Testimonies from Child Survivors of the Holocaust," *Holocaust and Genocide Studies* 21, no. 1 (2007): 73-95.

9. For an analysis of self-help and self-rescue among Jewish youths during the Holocaust, see, for example, Joanna Beata Michlic, "The Untold Story of Rescue Operations: Jewish Children in Nazi-Occupied Poland Helping Each Other," in *Jewish Resistance against the Nazis*, ed. Patrick Henry, 300-318 (Washington, DC: Catholic University of America Press, 2014),.

10. For discussion of the makeup of the Jewish Historical Commissions, see Laura Jockusch, *Collect and Record! Jewish Holocaust Documentation in Early Postwar Europe* (New York: Oxford University Press, 2012), and Jockusch, "*Khurbn Forshung*—Jewish Historical Commissions in Europe, 1943-1949," *Simon Dubnow Institute Yearbook* 6 (2007): 441-73.

11. *Instrukcje dla badania przeżyć dzieci żydowskich w okresie okupacji niemieckiej*, series 2, vol. 3: *Prace Metodologiczne* (Lodz: Centralny Komitet Żydów Polskich, Komisja Historyczna, 1945), 1-16, and *Metodologische onveyzungen tsum dem khurbn fun poylishn yidntum*, no. 5, Lodz, 31-47. For an analysis of the *Instrukcje*, see Joanna B. Michlic, "The Children Accuse, 1946: Between Exclusion from and Inclusion into the Holocaust Canon," in *Zwischen Zwangsarbeit, Holocaust und Vertreibung: Polnische, jüdische und deutsche Kindheiten im besetzten Polen*, ed. Krzysztof Ruchniewicz and Jürgen Zinnecker (München, 2007); and in *Newsletter of the Society for the History of Children and Youth*, no. 9 (February 2007), accessed on November 6, 2009, http://www.history.vt.edu/Jones/SHCY/Newsletter9/michlic.html.

12. *Metodologische onveyzungen tsum dem khurbn fun poylishn yidntum*, no. 5, 35.

13. See the seminal work by Lawrence L. Langer, *Holocaust Testimonies: The Ruins of Memory* (New Haven: Yale University Press, 1991).

14. On the challenges of the inclusion of Jewish women in modern Jewish history and the Holocaust, see, for example, Shulamit Reinharz, "The Individual in Jewish History: A Feminist Perspective," in *The Individual in History: Essays in Honor of Jehuda Reinharz*, ed. ChaeRan Y. Freeze, Sylvia Fuks Fried, and Eugene R. Sheppard, 285-300 (Waltham, MA:

Brandeis University Press, 2015); Paula Hyman, "Feminist Studies and Modern Jewish history," in *Feminist Perspectives on Jewish Studies*, ed. Lynn Davidman and Shelly Tennebaum, 120–39 (New Haven, CT: Yale University Press, 1991).

15. On the importance of studying the subjectivity of children by historians, see, for example, Nicholas Stargardt, "German Childhoods: The Making of a Historiography," *German History* 16, no. 1 (1998): 1–15.

16. *Debórah Dwork, Children with the Jewish Star: Jewish Youth in Nazi-Occupied Europe* (New Haven, CT: Yale University Press, 1991).

17. *Nicholas Stargardt, Witnesses of War: Children's Lives under the Nazis* (London: Jonathan Cape, 2005). Hereafter, Stargardt, *Witnesses of War*.

18. Dalia Ofer and Leonore Weitzman, eds., *Women in the Holocaust* (New Haven, CT: Yale University Press, 1998).

19. See, for example, the special issue of *European Review of History — Revue européenne d'histoire* 22, no. 2 (2015), with the introduction by its editors Machteld Venken and Maren Roger, "Growing up in the Shadow of the Second World War: European Perspectives," 199–220. For an important comparative study of state and humanitarian organizations' policies on children in the aftermath of the Second World War, see Tara Zahra, *The Lost Children: Reconstructing Europe's Families after World War II* (Cambridge: Harvard University Press, 2011).

20. Stargardt, *Witnesses of War*, 17.

21. See Diane L. Wolf, *Beyond Anne Frank: Hidden Children and Postwar Families in Holland* (Berkeley: University of California Press, 2007); hereafter, Wolf, *Beyond Anne Frank*, and see also Wolf, "Child Withholding as Child Transfer: Hidden Jewish Children and the State in Postwar Netherlands," *Journal of Human Rights* 12, no. 3 (2013): 296–308.

22. Mary Fraser Kirsh, "The Lost Children of Europe: Narrating the Rehabilitation of Child Holocaust Survivors in Great Britain and Israel" (PhD diss., University of Wisconsin-Madison, 2012).

23. See Avinoam J. Patt, *Finding Home and Homeland: Jewish Youth and Zionism in the Aftermath of the Holocaust* (Detroit: Wayne State University Press, 2009).

24. The poem called "Because My Life Is before Me," originally in Hebrew, composed in 1946, Kibbutz Mishmar Ha'emek Archive, from the collection of "Shahar Class," trans. and cited by Micha Balf, in "Holocaust Survivors on Kibbutzim: Resettling Unsettled Memories," in *Holocaust Survivors: Resettlement, Memories, Identities*, ed. Dalia Ofer, Françoise S. Ouzan, and Judy Tydor Baumel-Schwartz, 165–83 (New York: Berghahn Books, 2011); and in the same collective volume about different trajectories of child survivors, see also Joanna B. Michlic, "Rebuilding Shattered Lives: Some Vignettes of Jewish Children's Lives in Early Postwar Poland," *Holocaust Survivors*, 46–87.

25. On the history of Jewish child survivors in the United States, see Beth B. Cohen, *Case Closed: Holocaust Survivors in Postwar America* (New Brunswick, NJ: Rutgers University Press, 2007).

26. The history of the Hidden Children's annual gatherings is available online on the Anti-Defamation League website. The organization also publishes *The Hidden Child* magazine, http://www.adl.org/?_ga=1.266830667.432226445.1463022406?referrer=http://archive.adl.org/hidden/history.html.

27. Anna Sheftel and Stacey Zembrzycki, "Professionalizing Survival: The Politics of

Public Memory among Holocaust Survivor-Educators in Montreal," *Journal of Modern Jewish Studies* 12, no. 2 (2013): 1–22; July 1, 2013, accessed on August 10, 2015, http://dx.doi .org/10.1080/14725886.2013.796157.

28. For the discussion of the revival of interest in the testimony of the Holocaust survivors, see Geoffrey Hartman, *The Longest Shadow: In the Aftermath of the Holocaust* (Bloomington: Indiana University Press, 1996); see also Annette Wieviorka, *The Era of Witness*, trans. Jarek Stark (Ithaca, NY: Cornell University Press, 2006), 107–18.

29. Thomas Buergenthal, *A Lucky Child: A Memoir of Surviving Auschwitz as a Young Boy* (New York: Little, Brown, 2009).

30. On the difficulties of the reconstitution of Jewish family in postwar Holland, see Wolf, *Beyond Anne Frank*, especially chap. 6, 203–28.

31. For an interesting review of *Secret Lives* by Aviva Slesin, see Dave Kehr, "Film in Review: 'Secret Lives': Hidden Children and Their Rescuers during World War II," *New York Times*, May 16, 2003, accessed on August 20, 2015, http://www.nytimes.com/movie /review?res=9F00E3DB173EF935A25756C0A9659C8B63.

32. For the history of the infamous Lodz ghetto in English, see Gordon Horwitz, *Ghettostadt: Lodz and the Making of a Nazi City* (Cambridge: Belknap Press of Harvard University Press, 2008); and Isaiah Trunk, *Lodz Ghetto: A History* (Bloomington: Indiana University Press, 2006).

33. Sean Martin, *Jewish Life in Cracow, 1918–1939* (London: Vallentine Mitchell, 2004).

34. On Roman Polanski's wartime childhood, see, for example, the documentary film *Roman Polanski: A Film Memoir*, directed by Laurent Bouzereau and produced by Andrew Braunsberg, 2011.

35. On the treatment of mentally and physically disabled people in Nazi Germany, see, for example, Michael Burleigh, *Death and Deliverance: Euthanasia in Germany, 1900–1945* (Cambridge: Cambridge University Press, 1995); and Götz Aly, Peter Chroust, and Christian Pross, *Cleansing the Fatherland: Nazi Medicine and Racial Hygiene* (Baltimore: Johns Hopkins University Press, 1994).

36. *On the discussion surrounding different versions of Night* in Yiddish, French, and English, see, for example, Naomi Seidman, "Elie Wiesel and the Scandal of Jewish Rage," *Jewish Social Studies*, n.s. 3, no. 1 (autumn 1996): 1–19.

37. Avinoam J. Patt, *Finding Home and Homeland: Jewish Youth and Zionism in the Aftermath of the Holocaust* (Detroit: Wayne State University Press, 2009).

38. See, for example, Benita Blessing, *The Antifascist Classroom: Denazification in Soviet-Occupied Germany, 1945–1949* (New York: Palgrave Macmillan, 2006); Stargardt, *Witnesses of War*, 1–17; Hans-Heino Ewers, Jana Mikota, Jürgen Reulecke, and Jürgen Zinnecker, eds., *Erinnerungen an Kriegskindheiten: Erfahrungsräume, Erinnerungskultur und Geschichtspolitik unter sozial- und kulturwissenschaftlicher Perspektive* (Weinheim, DE: Beltz Juventa, 2006); and Joanna Beata Michlic, "The Aftermath and After: Memories of Child Survivors of the Holocaust," in *Lessons and Legacies X: Back to the Sources*, ed. Sarah Horowitz, 141–89 (Evanston, IL: Northwestern University Press, 2012).

39. Peter N. Stearns, "Challenges in the History of Childhood," *Journal of the History of Childhood and Youth* 1, no. 1 (2008): 35.

40. Benjamin Tenenbaum, ed., *'ehad me-'ir u-shenayim mi-mishpahah* [One from a city and two from a family] (Sifriat Poalim: Merhavia, 1947).

41. On the controversial issue of "the epigenetic inheritance," see, for example, David Samuels, "Do Jews Carry Trauma in Our Genes? A Conversation with Rachel Yehuda," *Tablet Magazine*, December 11, 2014, accessed on August 20, 2015, http://www.tabletmag.com/tag/rachel-yehuda; Helen Thomson, "Study of Holocaust Survivors Finds Trauma Passed on to Children's Genes?" *Guardian*, August 21, 2015, accessed on August 21, 2015, http://www.theguardian.com/science/2015/aug/21/study-of-holocaust-survivors-finds-trauma-passed-on-to-childrens-genes?CMP=share_btn_fb); and Michael Shapiro, "Intergenerational Transmission of Trauma: How the Holocaust Transmits and Affects Child Development," Working Papers series, HBI Project on "Families, Children, and the Holocaust," Brandeis University, accessed on August 20, 2015, http://www.brandeis.edu/hirjw/children holocaust/workingpapers/sapiroWP.pdf.

42. Helen Epstein, "Heirs of the Holocaust," *New York Times*, June 19, 1977, accessed on August 20, 2015, http://www.helenepstein.com/resources/NYT-Heirs-of-the-Holocaust-1977.pdf.

43. Deborah Lipstadt, "Children of Jewish Survivors of the Holocaust: The Evolution of a New-Found Consciousness," in *Encyclopedia Judaica Year Book 1988/89* (Jerusalem: Keter, 1989), 139–50.

44. For a critical assessment of Holocaust tattoos, see Yael Miller, "Holocaust Tattoos: Isn't There a Better Way to Educate?" *Haaretz*, October 22, 2012, accessed on August 20, 2015, http://www.haaretz.com/jewish-world/the-jewish-thinker/holocaust-tattoos-isn-t-there-a-better-way-to-educate.premium-1.471468.

45. Michael Berenbaum, cited in Jodi Rudoren, "Proudly Bearing Elders' Scars, Their Skin Says 'Never Forget,'" *New York Times*, October 1, 2012, accessed on August 20, 2015, http://www.nytimes.com/2012/10/01/world/middleeast/with-tattoos-young-israelis-bear-holocaust-scars-of-relatives.html?pagewanted=all. See also the audio recording "Tattoo to Remember," accessed on August 20, 2015, http://www.nytimes.com/interactive/2012/10/01/world/middleeast/01tattoo-slideshowwithaudio.html?ref=middleeast&_r=0.

46. See, for example, Marianne Hirsch, "Past Lives: Postmemories in Exile," *Poetics Today* 17, no. 4 (1966): 659–86; and Hirsch, "The Generation of Postmemory," *Poetics Today* 29, no. 1 (2008): 103–28. For a critical engagement with Hirsch's "postmemory," see Uta Larkey's chapter in this volume, and Jonathan J. Long, "Monika Maron's Pawels Briefe: Photography, Narrative, and the Claims of Postmemory," in *Memory Contests: The Quest for Identity in Literature, Film and Discourse since 1990*, ed. Anne Fuchs, Mary Cosgrove, and George Grote, 147–65 (Rochester, NY: Random House, 2006).

47. There is a huge literature written about Anne Frank, her legacy, and her *Diary*. For an informative short summary of Frank's biography and her legacy, see Dina Porat, "Biography of Anne Frank," *Jewish Women Encyclopedia*, accessed on August 20, 2015, http://jwa.org/encyclopedia/article/frank-anne.

48. See, for example, Henryk Grynberg's acclaimed *The Jewish War* and *The Victory*, published in English in one volume (Evanston, IL: Northwestern University Press, 1993). *The Jewish War* was Grynberg's first full-size prose volume, written and published in Polish in 1965. *The Victory*, its sequel, was written in California after Grynberg decided to leave Poland in exile because of the antisemitic purge of 1968 and the official communist ban on his books.

49. *Henryk Grynberg, Children of Zion* (Evanston, IL: Northwestern University Press, 1997).

50. For basic information on the Tehran Children, see the article on the website of the United States Holocaust Memorial Museum, accessed on August 20, 2015, http://www.ushmm.org/wlc/en/article.php?ModuleId=10007498.

PARENTHOOD AND CHILDHOOD UNDER SIEGE, 1939–1945

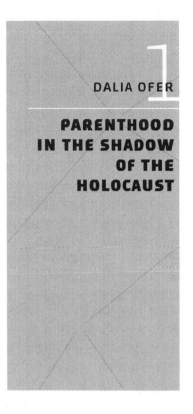

DALIA OFER

PARENTHOOD IN THE SHADOW OF THE HOLOCAUST

During World War II, Jewish parents under Nazi occupation experienced unimaginable difficulties as they tried to function according to what they believed was their parental responsibility. In the Eastern European ghettos the situation was extremely complex. When hunger, forced labor, and death became the daily experience, living conditions were next to impossible, and parents faced unbearable dilemmas in their efforts to maintain the family and their parental responsibility. Nevertheless, the family remained central to life in the ghetto, serving as both a support and a burden. Parents lived in constant tension trying to care for both their own lives and the lives of their children.

When we read the primary documents of the time — diaries, letters, memoirs, and other sources — as well as the oral testimonies that were recorded later in the postwar period, we confront a paradox. On the one hand, we see parents who are totally devoted to their children and ready to sacrifice their own lives to save a child. On the other hand, these same sources describe parents who neglect and desert their children. Because the contemporary documentation is fragmented, in both official and personal sources, it is difficult if not completely impossible to follow individual families from the years that preceded the war through their entire ghetto experience. Thus scholars should be careful with making sweeping generalizations in biographies of individual Jewish families during the Holocaust.

My recent work has examined two dimensions of family experiences in the ghetto. In "Cohesion and Rupture: The Jewish Family in the East European Ghettos during the Holocaust," I explored tensions within the family unit, and in "Motherhood under Siege," I looked at the pressures on mothers. In this chapter, in addition to these two aspects, I also explore a third dimension, the role of men as fathers and husbands in understanding the family and parenthood during the Holocaust.[1]

Parenthood has a life cycle that is based on the age of children and parents, and on the size of the family. Understanding parenthood is dependent on the relationship between couples and the structure of the family. Beyond the individual case of each couple and the particular relationships among family members, which will display a different reality in each case, parenthood is a cultural concept and contains a gendered code of conduct and responsibility of both father and mother.[2] The definition of responsibilities and norms reflects both the partnership and the particularity of each of the partners in organizing the family and caring for its members, in the context of society's cultural conventions, class, and gender relations.

I explore how parents endeavored to maintain their basic obligations and responsibilities toward their children, as they understood them, and how this affected their identity as parents and their self-image. What were the results of the traumatic events following the war and of confinement in the ghetto on their behavior as parents? Were parents aware of the ever-growing crisis in their ability to sustain and live according to norms and conventions that guided life prior to the ghetto enclosure, and how did they react to it?

One should bear in mind that the generations of parents of the 1930s and 1940s had experienced the hardships of the First World War and the economic and political crisis of its aftermath. The 1930s were difficult years for a majority of the Jewish population in Eastern Europe because of the new widespread economic crisis and the rise of antisemitism. It became more difficult to provide for the family, and thus a growing number of Eastern European Jewish women were compelled to work. Over 30 percent were employed in industry and commerce, but many more were working traditionally in small family businesses, and not included in that statistic.[3]

At the same time, parents were being educated differently. On one hand, many young Jews took advantage of public education, which became obligatory in the 1920s, and a considerable group participated in supplementary Jewish education of different forms. However, there were also many youngsters who continued to attend traditional religious institutions—the heder and the yeshiva. How different were the younger parents, who were raised in modern Polish-Jewish culture, from their parents and grandparents in their feelings and expressions of love and affection between spouses and between parents and their children?

The Israeli American historian Shaul Stampfer's research on the interwar period showed the increased importance of love, affection, and a romantic relationship between young Jewish men and women entering marriage. This was more prevalent among the lower and lower-middle classes, where economic considerations in marriage were less important than in the middle and upper-middle classes.[4] Can we follow this growing centrality of love and affection into the ghetto and see how it is manifested in strong mutual bonds between spouses and between parents and children in both the nuclear and the extended family, including the parents of married couples?

What were the major tasks of parents in the prewar years, and how did they change in the ghetto? Parents viewed their main responsibility in the family as an economic one—to care for the basic physical needs of both children and adults by providing them with food, clothing, and housing. The gendered roles of parents placed on the husband the provision of the financial foundation, while the wife managed the household, taking care of food preparation, clothing, and cleanliness. This gendered division of labor was normative even in middle- and lower-class families, where women worked.

In addition to its vital economic role, in all societies the family has been responsible for transmitting culture and social placement to ensure that children grow up to become productive members of society and conform to its values and conventions. Assumptions about gendered roles led to a distinction between the upbringing of boys and girls, in particular in the sphere of education. In addition to the formal schooling that boys and girls received, fathers were responsible for the religious education of their boys and so enrolled them in a religious institution, while mothers had to ensure that their daughters, through their home experience, would be able to manage a Jewish household. These functions were central to the achievement of the social goals of the family. In this respect the parents provided continuity and the transmission of tradition.

In this context one must also consider the impact of emancipation and revolutionary movements such as communism, Bundism, and Zionism on the ability of parents to be efficient agents of tradition. A growing number of Jewish youths experienced a mental and educational divide between their views and those of their parents, and this led to many conflicts. (Calel Perechodnik, whom we will discuss further, is one example of a son who felt estranged from his parents.) However, some scholars claim that these generational differences and conflicts, in perspective, enabled Jewish adolescents and young adults to become independent and follow their own way of realizing their life vision.[5] What happened to this sense of independence and freedom when the youths were confined to the ghetto? Did the conditions of living in the ghetto affect the solidarity between adolescent youths and their parents?

Another important responsibility of parents was to provide their children with psychological support and give them a sense of self-assurance. But we must remember that most parents during the 1920s and 1930s did not share a sense of the centrality of psychological self-confidence in rearing their children, as parents understand it today. In fact, we learn from the YIVO Institute for Jewish Research collection of more than six hundred autobiographies of youths, based on essays written in Poland and Lithuania in the 1930s, that many young children were critical of their parents as their emotional supporters. They complained that their parents did not understand their needs and ignored their emotional stress. Moreover, they often emphasized that parents considered provision of the basic economic needs as fulfillment of their obligations and were hoping that the children would soon grow up and participate in providing for the family's economic well-being. The authors of the autobiographies often criticized the relationship between themselves and their parents and testified to the lack of love and care. In the lower classes, both mother and father were absent from home for long hours, and often an older sister took care of the younger siblings. Boys spent long days in the heder, which made up for the absence of a parent from home. However, descriptions of neglect are apparent in a number of the autobiographies and in other sources as well.[6]

In middle-class families, the involvement of parents in their children's development was probably more evident. Calel Perechodnik, a young man from Otwock who left a diary in which he recorded his ghetto experience, provides us with a detailed portrayal of growing up in Poland, including a discussion of his home that focuses on his relationship with his parents. As he introduces himself, we learn

> I was born in Warsaw, on September 9, 1916, into a family of average Jews, a relatively well-to-do, so-called middle-class family. They were honest people, with a strong family instinct, characterized on the part of the children by affection and attachment to their parents and on the part of the parents by a sacrificial devotion to the material well being of the children. I emphasize "material" because there were no spiritual bonds that tied me or my siblings to our parents. They did not try, or perhaps were not able, to understand us. To put it briefly, each of us was raised on his own; influenced by schooling, friends, books we read; conscious of our won material independence; and living in an atmosphere of free expression and thought in the years 1925–1935.[7]

This citation is a good illustration of the fundamental understanding of responsibilities among Jewish parents toward their children, but also reveals the criticism of the younger generation, who were more educated and knowledgeable in psychology and lived by a set of different life expectations. Perechodnik wrote that his own marriage was a love marriage, and his strong emotional bonds to his wife and daughter are evident from his despair when they were deported from the ghetto to their death. I will later draw on Perechodnik's self-image as a husband and father and his attitude to his own father as examples of the complexity of parenthood under siege.

Historical research on the family and parenthood during the Holocaust confronts a number of major methodological questions that emerge from the difficulty of finding the adequate documentation to enter into the life experience of its members. The documentation on the family, as in many other topics of daily life during the Holocaust, is fragmented. Reflections on the situation of the family and parenthood are recorded in two types of documents. First, there are the formal documentations of the ghetto, such as Judenrat meetings, police reports, or the chronicles such as the one of the Lodz ghetto (Litzmannstadt ghetto). Alongside these sources are personal writings that typically discuss these issues in more detail, and more emotionally. The historical analysis endeavors to integrate all available sources and to contextualize them with the particular reality of each ghetto. Here I divide my discussion between nonpersonal records found in ghetto archives, such as official chronicles, and contemporary private diaries, of which some were also found in ghetto archives. I discuss each genre separately and integrate them in the final discussion.

NONPERSONAL GHETTO ARCHIVES DOCUMENTATION

The following entry is from the *Lodz Chronicle*, which was compiled under the auspices of the Judenrat. On January 12, 1941, the *Chronicle* reports under the title "The Little Denouncer": "An eight-year-old boy complained to the police that his parents had deprived him of his bread ration; he asked the police to punish them. Interpretations are redundant."[8]

Shortages of food and hunger were inherent in the daily life of the Litzmannstadt ghetto. However, the report of a child, who was deprived of the meager portion that was available, demonstrates at first glance a violation of the fundamental responsibility of the parents toward their children. It shows us that the ghetto authorities could intervene in the private sphere, and that ghetto institutions enabled a child to file a formal complain about his parents. Does it hint at recurring violations of this kind? From the comment of the author of this episode describing it along the lines of "interpretations are redundant," can we conclude that this was a common phenomenon?

The interpretation of this episode remains open. What information is available to the reader about this particular family? We know only that the child dared to complain. But we do not know why the parents were depriving him of his portion of food. Were there other children in the family that, for some reason, the parents thought should get a larger portion of the bread? Or perhaps there was a sick child or a sick parent in the family, and therefore the parents had to sell the bread ration to buy medicine. Or was this an act of parental punishment? Was it a regular behavior of negligence and inability to confront the hardship? The title that the writer of the *Chronicle* gave this episode is derogatory; does it hint at anything? We are unable to answer any of the questions and are left perplexed.

The issue becomes more complex when we read another section in the *Chronicle*, under the title "A Story That Repeats Itself," of a family in the ghetto that tried to save one of the children, who had contracted tuberculosis. The doctor recommended sending the boy to the hospital and then keeping him at home with good nutrition. The parents gave up part of their food allotment, and the mother became so weak that she could not go to work. The older sister, too, contributed some of her food for her brother and also asked to work night shifts, so that she could get a larger food allotment and give it to her brother. However, the condition of the boy did not improve. The family began selling the last household items, their shoes, and their clothing to buy better food. After some time the older sister also fell ill, her condition quickly deteriorated, and the doctor said that she would no longer be admitted to the hospital. Oskar Rosenfeld, who wrote this section in the *Chronicle*, concluded: "They tried the impossible to save the one that was going to die, and by doing this the other members of the family were joining the last road. [. . .] These [stories] reoccur every day, one family after the other is destroyed, the son, father, mother, sister — it is always the same story, but in a different order."⁹

This report and commentary in the *Chronicle*, which were written in 1944, the last year of the ghetto's existence, reveal the "high, high price" of love and devotion. The mutual responsibility of the parents, brothers, and sisters created a chain of death, which was typical of the unmanageable situation. Was the value of family cohesion stronger than the will to live of an individual family member? Was the life of one member of the family more important than the life of another? We are again left with unanswered questions.

The *Lodz Chronicle* also records one "typical document of life" — the request by a wife to divorce her husband:

> I ask to divorce my husband, because he is not ready to support his family. We are a family of five. A short time ago we were six — my thirteen-year-old daughter died of starvation. I beg for mercy for my other three children, since we are unable to live like this. My husband is working in the carpenters' *restore* [the term used in Litzmannstadt ghetto for the small ghetto workshops] and we get no allowances. For the last two years there is no peace at home — fights and battering occur every day. I cannot bear it any longer. I plead for help; I have no other way to save my life.¹⁰

One should ask: What was the meaning of divorce in the ghetto? Was the husband forced to leave the apartment or the one room that the family shared? With poor housing conditions, this could present a difficult problem for the man. Documents testify that men who held higher positions in the ghetto often had a lover or left their wives and took a younger woman as a wife or partner.¹¹

Returning to the specific case recorded in the *Chronicle*, here we may gain some information about relationships within the family in the years that preceded the ghetto period. The complaints about two years of a bad relationship go back to the beginning of the war and the confinement in the ghetto. However, the date may assist us in shedding some light on the time when the complaints were lodged. From December 1941, when the deportations from the ghetto to Chełmno extermination camp (Kulmhof) began, the tension among ghetto inmates mounted.[12]

During the fall of 1941, Jews from the Reich were deported to the Litzmannstadt ghetto, and the prices of food skyrocketed. Hunger and starvation increased, and working conditions in the ghetto deteriorated. The husband in this case, who was employed in the carpenters' *restore*, undoubtedly experienced the consequences of this new ghetto stage. Carpentry was an important industry in the ghetto, one in which the number of workers doubled in the course of two years: in 1943, there were 450 workshops in operation.

The carpenters' *restore*, however, went through a traumatic period in early 1941. Its seven hundred workers felt exploited and, in order to improve their working conditions, initiated a strike following the denial of their earlier requests by the head of the Lodz ghetto Judenrat, Chaim M. Rumkowski. They demanded a raise of ten to twenty pfenning per hour for the four categories of workers; that half the salary be paid in food products; that they be provided with an additional soup, not charged against the ration card; and that the supplement of five hundred grams of bread be reinstated. (Rumkowski had just set a bread ration of four hundred grams both for those working and for nonworkers.) The strike lasted some ten days (Jan. 23 to Feb. 2, 1941) and provoked a few other *restores* to join in, but in the end it failed. The workers went back to work after a number of them were arrested, food rations and payments were taken away from them and their families, and a few were injured by the Jewish police, who used violence against them. Following these events the workers' spirits were very low, and their sense of camaraderie was strongly undermined.[13]

What conclusions can we reach from these events — our general knowledge about the deteriorating work conditions in the carpenters' *restore* — in relation to the sore behavior of this particular husband toward his wife and children? What conclusions can we reach about this couple's parenting?

Could this help us to understand the timing of the divorce request? In just a few weeks massive deportations started, and single mothers were more vulnerable to be selected for deportation; thus, many single women tried to partner with available men in the hope that it would prevent their deportation.[14] In some ghettos, such as Vilna and Kovno, it was the policy of the Jewish Council to register single women and orphaned children with a man as the head of the family to avoid their selection or to secure them with a work permit. Under these harsh conditions, a request for divorce by a woman with three children seems very unusual. Could she count on the divorce and the allowance to improve her economic situation, and that she would be able to care for her three children?

We are unable to "push" the sources that far and apply our historical imagination to create a comprehensive narrative with the meager information at hand. However, when we juxtapose this episode with the information that 102 divorce requests were filed in the Lodz ghetto between September 1942—when a divorce board was established in the ghetto (abolishing the religious divorce ceremony)—and November 1943, we may question whether under the ghetto conditions divorce was more common then we had suspected. The bare number of divorce cases does not allow us to learn about motivations and the physical, mental, and emotional conditions of those spouses who filed for divorce.

The story of Bajli, a fifteen-year-old girl from Warsaw, as found in the Ringelblum archives, tells us a different story of a family that was on the brink of starvation.[15] The father was a furrier who had lost his business. The mother, daughters, and extended family, which consisted of an aunt and her children, are the protagonists of the narrative. The father decided to produce coats from old pieces of fur and sell them illegally on the Aryan side. This was definitely illegal, as all furs were confiscated, and selling anything outside the ghetto confines was a crime under Nazi regulations. Fifteen-year-old Bajli was to smuggle the coats out of the ghetto, contact merchants (whom the father probably knew from his previously established business contacts), carry out the transaction, and receive the money. The mother was extremely worried about the safety of her daughter, and she used to watch from a certain corner in the ghetto to see that Bajli crossed the walls safely. For almost a year the "business" ran smoothly. One day Bajli was caught and put in jail to await sentencing. The parents were extremely anxious because in November 1941, the Germans announced the death penalty for Jews found on the Aryan side. The parents tried to get her released from jail, but they failed. During the months in jail, they tried to help Bajli withstand the hardships she endured.

When a typhus epidemic broke out in the prison, Bajli pretended to be ill. She was moved to the hospital, where her parents were able to visit her. They brought her food, and her father tried to smuggle her out of the hospital and free her. He failed and Bajli was sent back to prison. She was released after many long months in a kind of amnesty for Jewish prisoners. At that point she was severely ill with tuberculosis. We do not know the final fate of Bajli and her family.

This case attests to the great pain of Bajli's parents, who struggled to sustain the family while being aware of the danger their daughter was facing. It seemed that they were unable to find an alternative to Bajli's contribution to the family income, when smuggling was the only way to sell the coats and the danger of starvation was imminent. Bajli herself felt satisfaction at being able to assist her family and her aunt's family. We learn that in this case it was the extended family that had to function as a whole economic unit. The story of this family displayed cooperation and a sense of solidarity and dependability among its members, with both parents acting together. The official ghetto documentation reported diverse examples of constructive and depressing cases of parents who worked out their responsibilities in extreme situations.

DIARIES

In the discussion of personal testimonies, I use the diaries of one man and a few women from different ghettos and of different social classes. I examine parenthood from the perspective of young parents, and the approach of young adults to their parents.

Unlike the previous sources, diaries provide a fuller narrative of different stages in individual life and present a continuous account of an individual life. Calel Perechodnik's diary is a good illustration of such a source. It was written from May 7 to October 19, 1943, while Perechodnik was in hiding. A large part of the narrative told the story of what had happened before he moved to his hiding place. The months in hiding are also a mixture of details and his recollections and insights about the past that do not leave him, in particular his strong feelings of guilt concerning his conduct as a husband and father in the deportation of his beloved wife and two-year-old daughter. The diary allows the reader to follow the Perechodnik family from the time that Calel and his wife, Anna Nusfeld, were lovers before they were married to their time as a couple before they became parents. We learn how they perceived parenthood and the nature of the impact of the war and occupation on their lives. The narrative also guides the reader into the relationship between Calel and his own parents, the older Perechodniks, with his father as a focal point, and examines the attitude of the elder Perechodnik toward his son Calel and his family, and vice versa.

Calel Perechodnik, born in 1916 to an Orthodox Jewish family, belonged to an educated, secular, and professional Polish Jewish elite. Because of the *Numerus Clausus* (admission limits on Jewish students) introduced in Polish universities in the second half of the 1930s, he was not accepted to the University of Warsaw and went to study engineering and agronomy at the University of Toulouse instead. He returned to his hometown, Otwock, in central Poland in 1938 to marry his beloved girlfriend, Anna Nusfeld. The couple worked hard in their own businesses and established a fine household with a desire to raise children.

The outbreak of war in 1939 confronted them with hardships and losses: Anna's two brothers were killed. Both of their businesses, the movie house Anna shared and ran with her brothers and Calel's storehouse in Otwock, were closed down and taken over by the German authorities. However, they did not lose their optimism: the war, they believed, would end soon, and they would be able to return to a normal routine and recover their lives. Moreover, Calel mentioned in his diary that despite the sadness over the death of his brother-in-law, he envied him for having left a living child, so his memory would not fade away. Under such difficult conditions, Calel and Anna decided to have their first child. In August 1940, almost one year after the Nazi occupation, Athalie (Annuska, Alinka) was born. The couple was as happy as could be and planned carefully how to raise their daughter in order to guarantee her a great future.

Calel and Anna were happy parents and were not counted among the poor. Calel Perechodnik was a good planner as the head of the family. Prior to the move to the Otwock ghetto in the late autumn of 1940, he stocked his room with food and wood for the winter. He gave his original apartment, which he had to leave with all its furnishings, to a Polish acquaintance he trusted. Therefore, he was able to sell household items that were kept with his friend and exchange them for food. Though Calel was aware of the hardship and suffering around them, and the disparity between the haves and have-nots in the ghetto, for him and Anna everything centered around their own shelter; they were cautious and enjoyed their parenthood.

> Thus I passed summer and winter 1941 in comparative peace, taking care of and raising my little Alinka. Although my wife and I denied ourselves many things, there was nothing too dear for my daughter's diet. She was treated royally, we never left her alone in the house and she therefore blossomed for us, developed and augured for us the best hope for the future.[16]

The next year, 1942, was a year with no peace or quiet. News of the deportations from Lublin followed other fateful tidings. Otwock was relatively calm until August 1942. When in 1943 Perechodnik was describing these calm months, he had already gained knowledge and insights that he had lacked during the first eight months of 1942. He thought he was safe since he served on the Jewish police force. He and his family were not hungry, nor were they candidates for forced labor. His thoughts centered on his work and the family, though it is clear from his writing that he was apprehensive about what would happen in the future, particularly to his daughter. While uncertainty caused alarm, his defense mechanisms and the options, even if limited, for his family to leave the ghetto helped discount the urgency despite his knowledge of the deportations from Warsaw. Wealthy Otwock Jews, Perechodnik wrote in his diary, who earlier had fled to Warsaw, believing that the big city was safer, returned to Otwock. Others left the ghetto, secretly crossing over to the Aryan side.

All these were events that one could have interpreted as alarming and as warnings. But Perechodnik, who considered a number of alternatives to ensure his family's safety, was unable to come to a clear decision. In his head, he heard two conflicting voices that were upsetting him: one that urged, "There is a danger in delay,"[17] and the other voice that reassured him, "Regardless of what was going on in the world, every individual ought to and needs to live normally, work, and earn a livelihood."[18]

However, at that time tension mounted between Calel and Anna. For Anna Perechodnik, news of the mass killings revived the memory of the murder of her brothers during the first months of the war. She wanted to obtain a false identity card that would allow her to pass as a (Christian) Pole, and in fact she planned to escape to the Aryan side, where she had the option of either passing as a Polish woman or hiding completely. Her non-Jewish appearance would have enabled her to pass as an Aryan, so she begged Calel to obtain the false identity papers for her and for the baby girl. Calel knew that he himself had no chance of passing as a Christian Pole, since he looked like a typical Jewish intellectual.[19] One might think that this asymmetry which suddenly emerged between the couple was affecting Perechodnik's decision making. He wrote with great bitterness and sincerity:

> I silently shrugged off her words, didn't even want to hear them, because they irritated me. It is possible that if I had had some ready hard currency, I could have arranged it—just to be left in peace. But first of all it was necessary to sell a suit, my English coat—that upset me. Besides, believing in all "assurances" I did not have a foreboding of danger.[20]

Calel did, however, inquire about a hiding place for his daughter, assuming that the child had a good chance to survive with a Christian Polish family. He thought that if only she would survive she would be the legitimate and sole heir to the family's considerable real estate. He initiated a deal with a decent Polish friend by which, for a large sum of money paid in advance for one full year, the child would be sheltered by a specific Polish family in the city of Lublin in eastern Poland. Alas, the deal did not come to fruition, and Perechodnik made no other efforts to seek shelter on the Aryan side for his beloved daughter. The spring and summer of 1942 were marked by unbelievable reports of massive deportations to unknown destinations from large Jewish communities in the General Government.

On August 17, 1942, just two days before the deportations began, the atmosphere in Otwock took a turn for the worse. Perechodnik noted in his diary a painful memory of a bitter quarrel with his wife. He came home very upset, and so was his wife. A small incident with the baby girl developed into a big argument, and Anna charged him with being indifferent to her plight and anxiety and preferring to save their fortune instead of saving her life: "She knows that when she is deported, she will leave it [her property] all behind, finally, that I did not procure for her *Kennkarte* (identity card) and that I generally did not protect her."[21] Her words pained him, and Calel left the house in a fury.

This incident stands out in the diary's narrative because the presentation of their personal relationship usually displayed love, solidarity, and great respect for each other. Reading the description of their personal behavior toward each other the two previous days, August 15 and 16, in which tension was already great, adds to the surprise of the reader at the angry outburst described previously. On Saturday, August 15, Perechodnik met Mr. Władysław Błażewski, a lawyer (magister) whom he had befriended since 1940. He trusted him as an honest man and thought offhand to give him a suitcase with some belongings to keep for them. He consulted with Anna, who approved of the idea, and they planned to have Błażewski come to their home two days later. Sunday, August 16 was a quiet laundry day at home, and Calel took care of the baby.

Thus it would seem that the row of Monday, August 17, was a result of tension that had accumulated for long months and was kept undercurrent by both Anna and Calel. However, one sad result of this fight was the one-day delay in the visit of Mr. Władysław Błażewski, the magister.

During the next day, Perechodnik was already certain that the deportation from the Otwock ghetto was around the corner. Following information obtained from the police, he and his wife acted rationally and phoned the magister, who came to their home. They shared the information with him and begged him to find a home for the baby. He took the suitcase and promised to return the next day with a plan for the little girl.[22]

Calel and Anna continued to act coolly and continued with their calculated steps; they prepared their rucksacks, went to the baker and baked bread with the flour they had, and Anna went secretly to a photographer to have a photo taken for a Polish *kennkarte* that would be ready the next day. However, the next day was too late. Calel was left without his family. On August 19, 1942, Anna and little Athalie were deported to Treblinka death camp.

Let us now analyze the roles of Calel and Anna as parents. They were a loving couple. Ten years before they married they became lovers, and their relationship endured the long separation when Calel was studying in Toulouse. Anna was not as educated as Calel. She was orphaned at an early age, and her two older brothers took care of her, but her economic position was sound. When she lost both brothers in the first months of the war, Calel felt that he served the role of a father, brother, and husband for her. They were true partners; he consulted Anna about his business and work, respected her partnership with her brothers, and later took care of her inheritance. Parenthood seemed to reinforce their sense of partnership and cooperation. After the birth of Athalie, Anna, like many middle-class women, devoted her time to the home and the child. Calel, too, spent time with his little daughter and took care of her when Anna was too busy with household chores.

As mentioned previously, though Athalie was born during the first year of occupation, her parents had planned the pregnancy. They wanted to have a child, and they thought that the war would not last more than one year. Having a child was a promise, Calel wrote, that "I shall not wholly die" ("Non omnis moriar").[23] This may hint that they were not blind to the dangers threatening them; but like many other Jews and non-Jews under the Nazi occupation in Poland at that time, they were still optimistic about their own destiny and the duration of the war. They sounded like a reasonable couple, calculating opportunities and risks.

Perechodnik continued to act rationally. As mentioned before, when in December 1940 Jews had to move to the Otwock ghetto, he gave his apartment with all that it contained to a Polish friend whom he authorized to sell items from his household, enabling Perechodnik to acquire food and other necessary items despite the increasing shortage in the ghetto. In February 1941, one month after the Otwock ghetto was sealed off with a fence, Perechodnik realized that there was increased danger of being conscripted for forced labor, so he joined the Jewish police, known as the Ghetto Police of Otwock. This promised some stability. His task was to supervise the bakers and make sure that they made proper use of the supply of flour. Thus, he wrote in his diary, he did not clash with people or have to use force; and in the ghetto situation, his specific responsibility as a policeman also promised some benefits.

Perechodnik was aware of the social gaps in the Otwock ghetto and the difficult situation of the poor, and he noticed how people's conduct changed. He followed political and military developments and conversed with the magister and other Polish friends on the political future, sharing with them the information about the fate of Jews. He did not hesitate to ask their advice and assistance in his efforts to shelter his daughter, but as noted earlier, only to a limited extent.

All these things demonstrated the thoughtfulness of Perechodnik and his ability to think clearly and make decisions. As noted, initially the tension in the ghetto increased when Germany turned against the Soviet Union in June 1941 and news began to be received about the mass killings on the Eastern Front. At first this seemed far away, but as reports and rumors about massive killing in the General Government reached Otwock, rational thinking was shattered and replaced by deep fear. Perplexity reigned over reason, and sound rules of action did not promise the expected results.

These circumstances destroyed the "safe nest" and the total trust between Anna and Calel. Though not at all confident, Calel pretended that he knew how to handle the situation. Anna was under more stress and may have had greater intuition; she realized what she and the child should do, but was unable to convince Calel and could not proceed on her own. In this respect, she followed the traditional gender roles, in which activities and responsibilities in the public sphere belonged to the man in the family. Just one day before the deportation, she went secretly, without informing Calel, to have her photo taken for a forged Polish identity card. The tension that transpired in the couple's relationship did not dissipate and developed into a real conflict, as Calel painfully recorded.

In view of the ensuing deportation, Calel, who failed to act in time to create conditions that would protect his daughter and wife, was crushed. The Nazi tactics of deceit led him to write, "I have brought my wife and daughter to their deaths."[24]

Perechodnik's diary is an honest testimony of a husband and father plagued with unbearable feelings of guilt and a deep sense of having betrayed his family. Calel did not write the diary until he reached a hiding place. In the last weeks of the ghetto and during his long months in a forced labor camp, he was unable to record such a painful account. He had to protect himself from the memory of both his action and inaction.

Writing and reflecting left him feeling exposed, almost unguarded, and his Self completely helpless. He was quite sure that he would not survive. The diary, he wrote, became his and Anna's second child—a child of love and revenge, a child from which he had to part so it would survive, and a child that testified to the great love of a husband and a father.[25]

THE ELDER PERECHODNIKS CALEL'S PARENTS

Perechodnik writes extensively about his own parents and describes how they acted during the war years. However, we should bear in mind that we do not have access to the parents' voices, but rather only to Calel's interpretation of their personalities, behavior, and parenthood. What stands out when reading Calel's descriptions of both his mother and father is a complex relationship between parents and son. In the first pages of his diary Perechodnik provided some background information about his youth, his family, and his parents. As noted previously, Calel discussed the lack of warmth and love in the relationship between the parents and the children. He did stress, however, that his parents were devoted and dedicated to the provision for the material needs of their children, and one may assume that they supported his education in Poland and in France. We may also assume that they favored his marriage to Anna, because he mentions in the diary that his parents loved Anna more than they loved him and that she reciprocated their love.

Calel stressed his respect for his parents, and he appreciated their hard work and honesty. He resented the materialistic approach of his father, who had gained his sound economic status through hard work as a self-made man, but he appreciated his father's practicality. Calel was critical, however, of what he understood to be his father's lack of spirituality.

The elder Perechodnik emerges from his son's diary as one who acts as the head of the family, a sort of patriarch. During the night before the deportation, however, he and Calel's mother secretly escaped from the ghetto without informing the children. The next morning, however, he came back to learn what had happened to his daughter and son and their families. Both Calel and his brother-in-law were serving with the Jewish police, and the father assumed that they were relatively secure. Indeed, his daughter hid in the cellar and, unlike Anna, did not report for deportation.

When Calel told his father what had happened with Anna and little Athalie, his father was furious; he could not understand how foolish Calel had been to believe the Germans and that he took his wife to the assembly place believing that they would be safe. "How could you have brought your wife to the square?" he yelled. "You know from the past that the Germans cannot be trusted."[26] This conversation rubbed salt into Calel's wounds.

Yet the elder Perechodnik did not let sorrow detract his attention from the steps he had to take to save his life and that of his wife. He conferred with Calel and called for concentration and alertness to carefully calculate their steps in order to save their lives. He was sure that he and his son's material situation was a crucial factor, so that they would be able to pay well for every service obtained from Poles. He asked Calel to take care of the remainder of the families' belongings that had not yet been pillaged by the Poles. These, he thought, should be safeguarded to meet the needs of the family.

In Calel's state of mind when this conversation took place, the message was unbearable, and he confided the following to his diary:

> I opened my eyes wide: He had just learned of the death of his daughter, sister-in-law, grandchildren, and he talks to me about pillows. Is this an animal or a human being? I am supposed to watch his bedding, as if the entire ghetto isn't piled high with pillows. What's the point? Who thinks of life in the future? I didn't say anything to him, gave him a few shirts, and led him to the boundary of the ghetto. This first visit did not leave me with feelings of happiness. It's true my parents were safe, but distaste stifled a son's feelings. There remains only a sense of obligation towards them.[27]

Despite these emotions, Calel cooperated fully with his father. He organized the suitcase, filling it with items to sell, and gave him his money. In many respects he admired his father's energy and determination to live. After one of their meetings, when Calel was in the forced labor camp to which the remnant of the Otwock ghetto were deported, he met his father to give him money to get his mother out of a forced labor camp. He described in the diary how he perceived his father during this meeting:

> There I see an older man with big gray whiskers, dressed in a black jacket. I open my eyes wide. . . . Yes it is my father. He has changed unrecognizably during this time, is considerably thinner, but thanks to that has a first-rate Aryan appearance. [. . .] my father had changed so much that he moves about fearlessly on the streets of Otwock.[28]

Calel understood from their conversation that his father was passing as an Aryan, because he claimed that if he remained among Jews only the bullet awaited him; but Calel was not ready to admit that his father was right. Was the alternative any better, Calel wondered, not sure that he himself desired to live with the fear and challenge of living in disguise; however, his father was ready to take up the challenge.

I will not go into the detailed story of the elder Perechodnik and how the relationship between father and son evolved. What stands out from the diary is that ambivalent feelings on the part of Calel were dominant, from which a love-hate relationship with his parents ensued. Calel suffered from what he interpreted as distrust of his father. Nevertheless, the father, who passed as an Aryan, was Calel and his mother's contact with the outside world during the long months in which they were in hiding in an apartment in Warsaw. For a long time, the father refused to let Calel know where he resided or his whereabouts. Was it distrust or an additional precaution hoping to save Calel from pressure should he fall prey to denunciation and be interrogated by the Germans about other Jews in hiding? Calel was sure that his father did not trust him and was offended. He was always faithful to his parents (though admitting that he did not love them) and spared nothing of the capital he entrusted to his Polish friends to support them. But it was the father who took all the meaningful steps for their survival. He displayed not only resourcefulness, but utmost devotion to his family.

READING DIARIES, READING PARENTHOOD

I elaborated on Calel Perechodnik's diary because his narrative centers on the crisis of his personal life and that of a spouse and a father. Similar problems feature in many other diaries. In what follows I discuss a number of the key issues as they appear in other diaries.

The care of parents for their children and the care of parents by their children is a theme that appears in the diary of Fela Szeps, a young woman from a well-to-do family. She was a student at the University of Warsaw when the war broke out and ruined her future.[29] The Szeps family of five lived in Dąbrowa Górnicza in Zagłębie. The diary was written in the Greenberg forced labor camp (Zielona Góra in present-day Poland), and it recorded reminiscences about the family and its cohesiveness, as well as the great partnership between the parents and between them and the children. The memory of her family and the hope of a reunion provided Fela with the motivation and energy to endure the cruelty of the camp. Fela recalled how her mother begged them not to obey the registration call. She did not trust the Germans' innocent-looking announcement for the young people to register. Following this call and the willingness of Fela and her sister Bath Sheva to register, an argument arose between the children and the parents. The sisters thought that since they were employed in an established workshop they were safe from forced labor. The father, anxious for his daughters, went with them to register, but waited in vain for their return. Fela and Bath Sheva were seized and sent to the forced labor camp.[30] In the first months in the camp, the caring parents sent them parcels of food and clothing. These were extremely helpful for both their physical and emotional endurance. As letters and parcels arrived more and more infrequently until they stopped altogether, the girls' urge to know what had happened to their parents and their hope to meet them again became an important source of energy for them to endure and survive.

Another diary, from the area of Zagłębie, refers to the relationship between young adults and their parents. Hajka Klinger, a zealous leader of a Zionist youth movement, *Hashomer Hatzair*, described a rift between her and her Orthodox parents. In the years preceding the war, she was critical of the Orthodox lifestyle of her parents and their inability to understand the reality around them.

During the years of Nazi occupation, despite different approaches to the necessary responses to the Germans in daily life, the devotion and assistance to each other of both the Klinger parents and their daughter Hajka was unquestionable. The parents were prepared to endanger themselves to protect their daughter, who was active in the underground and hiding from the police, while Hajka was ready to do the utmost to assist her ill father and support her mother and her sister, who was married and had a small child.[31]

An additional testimony of trust between parents and a grown-up married daughter transpires in the diary of Noemi Szac Wajnkranc.[32] In contrast to both Klinger and Perechodnik, for Noemi her professional, culturally assimilated parents served as a life model. She had wonderful memories from her childhood and travels abroad with them, and she admired the optimism and creativity of her father. She identified strongly with the difficulties they experienced when they had to move into the Warsaw Ghetto, leaving behind their belongings and social environment, but appreciated her father's positive approach. Noemi referred in her diaries to the extended family, an uncle and aunt and also her parents-in-law. She shared her income with her parents and her other relatives in need, and got extra food coupons for them. She visited her parents regularly and missed them when walking in the streets became too dangerous.[33]

Her parents were anxious about Noemi's safety and did not want to burden her with their needs and anxieties. Her father demonstrated great ingenuity in devising a hiding place. Thus they managed to escape the large deportations of the summer of 1942.

Noemi had married her husband Jerzy (diminutive Jurek) shortly before the outbreak of the war. They loved each other dearly and promised always to be completely honest and candid with each other and to share their troubles and doubts as well as their joy and happiness. The tension of ghetto life, however, created some rifts between them. Issues that may seem banal were the cause of conflict, with their promise to discuss all that troubled them and to never keep secrets from each other.

Caring for their parents resulted in an unexpected difficulty: how to divide the care between the two sets of parents. Jurek suspected that Noemi was ready to give everything they had to her parents, while she considered his parents as being overdemanding. She did not inform Jurek about the extra food coupons she brought to her parents and her brother, who were extremely poor. She expressed sadness about the first secret that stood between them.[34] Despite these sad feelings, Naomi expressed great love and devotion to Jurek and trusted their relationship as a couple.

Unlike in the preceding diaries, Irena Hauser, a forty-year-old Viennese woman deported to Litzmannstadt ghetto with her husband and six-year-old child, focuses on the lack of partnership with her husband and the absence of his sense of parental responsibility toward their child. She wrote with great anger and bitterness. Only fragments of her diary were found, and they testify to the horrible situation of a poor refugee family in the Litzmannstadt ghetto. The diaries referred to earlier were written by middle-class people who were confined to the ghetto in their own town. In contrast, Irena Hauser was part of the most destitute segment of the ghetto population: the poor refugees.

Irena Hauser's writings confront the reader with the bare facts of a cruel situation of despair and pain. It also shows Irena's endless efforts to endure in the swamp of poverty and wants of the Lodz ghetto. It is among the most difficult texts to study, and the reader senses that he or she is touching the utterly naked essence of pain and suffering.

Irena described her husband as a selfish, unreliable man, who was unable to provide for his family under the difficult conditions of the ghetto. From the early days of their arrival in Lodz, he lost any sense of direction and was preoccupied with immediate anxieties and personal necessities such as cigarettes. Thus he foolishly sold most of their belongings, and in a very short time they were left with next to nothing to sell for food or medicine. He was working in a *restore*, but did not share the food he received with his family. He held on to the food coupons, his only concern being for his food and cigarettes. Irena's description presents a dysfunctional family in which the father and husband lost all sense of partnership and responsibility. At a certain point she filed for a divorce, as he often became violent toward her and their child. His very presence became unbearable to her.

Though I cannot fully elaborate here on the difficult account of Irena Hauser, it is important to stress that she also wrote that her husband was hungry and very weak, and that he too was hardly able to climb the stairs to their apartment. She was not blind to his personal suffering, but was filled with anger at his desertion of his responsibilities as a father and a spouse.

She often wrote that she would rather have died than endured the hunger, pain, helplessness, and loneliness of that situation, yet her responsibility to her child prevented her from committing suicide. In September 1942, when the deportation of the children and the elderly took place, she played with the idea of joining the carloads of deported children and getting the loaf of bread that was distributed to the deportees, but her son, Erich Bobi, refused. The following sentence from her diary summarizes her despair: "The child cries [from] hunger, the father [smokes] cigarettes, the mother wants to die, family life in the ghetto."[35]

CONCLUSIONS

The preceding examples and other sources allow a modest discussion of the modes of parenthood and of the questions posed at the beginning of this essay.

It is clear that there are many methodological difficulties in dealing with the subject matter. The fragmented sources provided by the *Chronicle of the Lodz Ghetto*, and the scattered letters and diaries from the Ringelblum archive and other sources, confront the scholar with the inability to weave an integrated and comprehensive fabric of family life and parenthood. The sources demonstrate that it was impossible to carry out basic parental responsibilities — providing food for the children and protecting them physically — even before the deportations. We also learn that the norms and expectations of parents were deeply implanted in the minds of the ghetto inmates, who were tormented by the collapse of what they believed were their unquestionable responsibilities. From the chronicle of the Litzmannstadt ghetto, we learn that couples who lived separately hurried to the rabbi for a divorce when one spouse was deported. This suggests that couples were still thinking in terms of conventional behavior, even though they were already living outside of marriage with another spouse.[36] We may also learn from these fragmentary sources that the family was a source of strength that often preserved the wish and perhaps the ability to survive. The despair of parents who lost their children in deportations resulted in an inability to endure, and often the parents died soon after.[37] Despite their fragmentary nature, these sources are powerful and evoke a sense strong of empathy for and even an affinity with the tragic protagonists and their efforts to establish a semblance of normality in that chaotic and unprecedented reality.

One might assume that diaries or a more extensive body of correspondence would enable us to observe a continuous relationship between couples and their performance as parents and provide a fuller description of the reality that confronted parents trying to carry out their responsibilities. However, these descriptions are very limited, despite the relatively large body of diaries that were published and those that remained unpublished and hosted in the various archives in Europe, Israel, and the United States. Diaries capture the tragic events and often become a lamentation, or a text of memorialization and testimony. The window that the diaries open for scholars may be misleading and give an illusion of full realization and understanding of the multifaceted, complex, and painful reality.

The diaries' narrative is also a selection of details and events that may have been chosen to respond to the writer's needs and goals at the time that they were written, as in the case of Perechodnik, discussed previously. While the strength of the narrative lies in its authenticity and directness, it may lead the reader to come to general conclusions and grant it more authority than it deserves. The sources do not allow for a meaningful quantitative analysis; only a qualitative methodology is available. But even the qualitative methodology should be approached with caution.

In addition, because we often read diaries today that were written in a language other than the one we are studying them in, the style of the description may be "colored" by the translation process.

Nevertheless, some generalizations are in order and necessary. Parents lived in a state of continuous tension that served as a seismograph reflecting the events around them and the information they received from other ghettos. It is clear from all the diaries that people did not expect the war to last so long or that the fate of the Jews would develop so crudely. Therefore, as Calel Perechodnik wrote, they decided to have a child despite the shadows of war. Similarly, Arie Klonicki-Klonymus from Pinsk called his son, born in 1942,

Adam, in the hope that the universal vision of mankind would destroy the bestiality of Nazism.[38]

Middle-class Jews and professionals were able to activate contacts on the Aryan side and send their children to pass as Aryans or go into hiding. Miscalculations ended in tragedies, such as in the case of Perechodnik, or betrayal by gentile friends or acquaintances. Parents who survived the war carried this tragedy with them for the rest of their lives, and many reflected on this in their postwar writings.[39]

A description that narrates the events in some continuity, from the outbreak of the war, becomes more meaningful for understanding the protagonists and their environment in the course of the war. This is apparent in fathoming the relationship between Calel Perechodnik and Anna, and between Calel and his parents. The same holds true for the diaries of Fela Szeps and Noemi Szac Wajnkrac. Hajka Klinger, in her ghetto diary that related her life before the war, was able to demonstrate how a relationship evolved because of the duress experienced during the Nazi occupation and in what respects her perspective toward her parents changed. Nevertheless, the relationships between children and parents or of couples were crucial when facing the crisis of ghetto life and the threat of death.

The shock of deportation was an experience that the protagonists were unable to contain, and many lost their partners, children, or parents in this crisis. We also have to take into account that circumstances were very different in the various ghettos. The isolation of Litzmannstadt ghetto and the relatively easy movement in and out of Otwock ghetto were crucial to the ability to devise hiding strategies and contact Poles on the Aryan side. In places where pressure was somewhat less extreme, or among social groups that had connections or means, Jews were able to manipulate the efforts to sustain a semblance of normalcy that could continue almost until the last moments before deportation. This was the case with the Perechodniks and the Szeps.

I would like to end with a quotation that demonstrates the quest for preserving the family in situations that did not allow such preservation. I quote from a letter that Malvina, the wife of Arie Klonicki-Klonymus, wrote about their son, Adam, to her relatives in the United States (the letter was never sent but was enclosed with her husband's diary). Adam was in hiding with a Christian family, while his parents, Arie and Malvina, were in great danger wandering from one village to another. "I want so much to bring up my adored son, to get pleasure from him, is it possible? It is even difficult to dream about it."[40]

NOTES

First published in August H. Leugers-Scherzberg/Lucia Scherzberg (Hg.): Genderaspekte in der Aufarbeitung der Vergangenheit, Saarbrücken 2014 (theologie.geschichte, Beiheft 8).

1. Dalia Ofer, "Cohesion and Rupture: The Jewish Family in East European Ghettos during the Holocaust," *Studies in Contemporary Jewry* 14 (1998): 143-65; Ofer, "Motherhood under Siege," in *Life, Death and Sacrifice: Women and Family in the Holocaust*, ed. Esther Hertzog (Jerusalem: Gefen, 2008), 41-67.

2. There is a vast literature on the topic, but I rely mainly on the classic work of William J. Goode, *The Family* (Englewood Cliffs, NJ: Prentice Hall, 1982), because of the strong connection he draws between culture and family structure.

3. Bina Garnazarska-Kadary, "Changes in the Material Situation of the Jewish Workers in Poland, 1930-1931" [in Hebrew], *Gal'ed* 9 (1986): 169, table 8.

4. Shaul Stampfer, "How Jewish Society Adapted to Change in Male/Female Relationships in 19th/Early 20th-Century Eastern Europe," in *Gender Relationships in Marriage and Out*, ed. Rivkah Blau (New York: Michael Scharf Publication Trust of Yeshiva University Press, 2007), 65-83.

5. Matat Adar-Bunis, "Childhood in Middle-Class Jewish Families in Poland-Lithuania in the 19th Century: The Rise of Youth Movements" [in Hebrew], *Sociologia Yisraelit* 7, no. 2 (2005): 351-80. The divide between parents and children is apparent in the biographies and memoirs of Holocaust survivors; see Avihu Ronen, *Condemned to Life: The Diaries and Life of Chajka Klinger* [in Hebrew] (Haifa: University of Haifa, Yidiot Haharonot, Hemed Books, 2011); Bella Gutterman, *Zyvia the One* [in Hebrew] (Tel Aviv: Hkibbutz Hameuhad, Yad Vashem, 2011).

6. Jeffrey Shandler, ed., *Awakening Lives: Autobiographies of Jewish Youth in Poland before the Holocaust* (New Haven: Yale University Press, 2002), especially the autobiographies of Khane: 20-50; Esther: 321-43, and Yudl: 391-403. For an extensive description of the family and the internal relationship within the family based on the YIVO collection of autobiograpies, see Ido Basok, "Aspects of Education of Jewish Youth in Poland between the World Wars in Light of Autobiographies by Jewish Youth from the YIVO Collection" [in Hebrew] (PhD dissertation, Hebrew University of Jerusalem, 2009), 56-118.

7. Calel Perechodnik, *Am I a Murderer: Testament of a Jewish Ghetto Policeman* (Boulder, CO: Westview Press, 1996), xxii. Hereafter, Perechodnik, *Am I a Murderer*.

8. *Chronikah shel geto Lodz*, trans. and annotated by Arie Ben-Menachem and Joseph Rab, 4 vols. (Jerusalem: Yad Vashem, 1986-89), 1:5. A selection from the *Chronicle* was translated into English as *The Chronicle of the Lodz Ghetto 1941-1944*, ed. Lucjan Dobroszycki (New Haven: Yale University Press, 1984). Whenever a citation appears in the English version, I cite it; in all other cases, the citation is my own translation from the Hebrew version.

9. *Chronikah shel geto Lodz*, 4:389, May 29, 1944.

10. Ibid., 1:307, Dec. 21, 1941.

11. Leib Garfunkel, *The Destruction of Jewish Kovno* (Jerusalem: Yad Vashem, 1959), 255; Rachel Auerbach, *Warsaw's Testaments* [in Hebrew] (Tel Aviv: Sifriyat Hapoalim, 1985), 109-12.

12. During this period, 70,672 people were deported from the ghetto, and the 92,054 who remained lived through lesser crises until the final liquidation of the ghetto during

July–August 1944. Michal Unger, *Lodz: The Last Ghetto in Poland* [in Hebrew] (Jerusalem: Yad Vashem, 2005), 311.

13. Joseph Zelkowicz, *In Those Terrible Days: Notes from the Lodz Ghetto* [in Hebrew] (Jerusalem: Yad Vashem, 1994), 201-28; Isaiah Trunk, *Lodz Ghetto: A History* (Bloomington: Indiana University Press, 2006), 324-28, 372-78; the latter pages are a translation from the Yiddish of Zelkowicz's notes. The paragraph describing the workers' demands uses the translation of Trunk, p. 372.

14. Unger, *Lodz*, 331-34.

15. "The Story of Bajli" [in Polish], related in the document titled *Przed uwięzieniem* [Before imprisonment], Archives of Ringelblum 1/470 (ARI 1/470), Yad Vashem Archive (YVA), Jerusalem.

16. Perechodnik, *Am I a Murderer*, 9.

17. Ibid., 23.

18. Ibid., 22.

19. Ibid., 23.

20. Ibid., 24.

21. Ibid., 26.

22. Ibid., 29.

23. Ibid., 7.

24. Ibid., 17.

25. Ibid., 191-92.

26. Ibid., 85.

27. Ibid.

28. Ibid., 118.

29. Fela Szeps, *A Blaze from Within: The Diary of Fela Szeps, the Greenberg Forced-Labor Camp* [in Hebrew], ed. Bella Guterman (Jerusalem: Yad Vashem, 2002), 7-19.

30. Ibid., 35, 43-45.

31. Ronen, *Condemned to Life*.

32. Noemi Szac Wajnkranc, *Gone with the Fire: Notes on the Warsaw Ghetto Written in Hiding* [in Hebrew], ed. Bella Guterman (Jerusalem: Yad Vashem, 2003).

33. Ibid., 21, 41.

34. Ibid., 46-47.

35. Quoted from Alexandra Garbarini, *Numbered Days: Diaries and the Holocaust* (New Haven: Yale University Press, 2006), 123; Unger, *Lodz*, 279-80, 276-77.

36. *Chronikah shel geto Lodz*, 1:352.

37. Ibid., 1:531.

38. Arie Klonicki-Klonymus, *The Diary of Adam's Father* [in Hebrew] (Tel Aviv: Hakibbutz Hameuhad, 1969), 17.

39. For examples, see Baruch Milch, *Can the Heavens Be Void?* [in Hebrew] (Jerusalem: Yad Vashem, 2003); Klonicki-Klonymus, *Diary of Adam's Father*.

40. Klonicki-Klonymus, *Diary of Adam's Father*, 46.

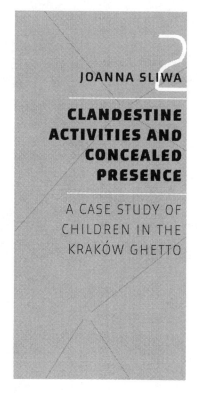

JOANNA SLIWA

CLANDESTINE ACTIVITIES AND CONCEALED PRESENCE

A CASE STUDY OF CHILDREN IN THE KRAKÓW GHETTO

Janka Warshavska began smuggling in the Kraków ghetto when she was eleven years old. Submitting her testimony at age fourteen, she explained, "Did I have a choice? We didn't have what to live off in the ghetto so I had to become a provider." The Germans deemed bringing in food from the Aryan side a criminal activity and, as Janka pointed out, "It was very difficult to get back into the ghetto with merchandise. We had to be very careful and watch that a policeman didn't grab us and take any merchandise. It would take weeks to recoup that which was lost." She admitted to being embarrassed by the way she earned a living. "At first I was very ashamed to go around from house to house with our merchandise, or to stand in the doorways and bargain. Later, however, we got used to it."[1] With the impending actions in the ghetto, Janka's tasks extended to smuggling out children to the Aryan side. She recalled the first time she took out a boy: "I didn't know what to do with him. Aside from that, I myself was still a child and didn't know what to do to get him to listen to me. When we got close to the fences I was so frightened that I pleaded with him not to cry. To this day I still feel the fear."[2]

Janka's testimony provides a glimpse into the smuggling operations of both goods and people, and the dangers associated with them. Her activities were not limited to obtaining food products for her family and those that she sold or bartered in the ghetto. In fact, Janka actively participated in transferring children from the ghetto for temporary "safety" during raids, and for permanent placement with gentile families. Janka's story is but a small piece of the larger history of children in the Kraków ghetto and the way that illegal—and thus clandestine—activities led to the children's (often temporary) survival. From the German point of view, Jewish life became illegal. For the Jews, this meant that their lives had to assume a circumspect and concealed form. In effect, Jewish survival depended on camouflaged presence and inconspicuous activities. German authorities held activities such as hiding, lying about age, and sneaking out and smuggling in and out of the ghetto illegal. Yet they were essential to the well-being and survival of children and their families. Here I examine the ways, reasons, risks, and consequences of such actions, and how these activities contributed to young people's prolonged survival in the ghetto. Jewish children and their caretakers realized that deception, evasion, and disobedience comprised tactics necessary for, but not guaranteeing, children's existence. Therefore, youths were routinely encouraged and supported in undertaking covert endeavors by their own families, and they often received assistance from gentiles. At other times, however, young people took their own initiative, unbeknownst to their families.

In analyzing the life circumstances of Jewish children[3] trapped in the Kraków ghetto from the moment of its inception (March 3, 1941) until its final liquidation (March 13–14, 1943), the Jewish child emerges as a historical actor exercising (extremely stringent) agency. *Agency* refers to the child's capacity to respond to his or her position as a participant in the events as they were occurring. Nazi anti-Jewish policy and German actions against Jews shaped children's experiences. The lives of the youngest members of the persecuted group were also influenced by the responses of their gentile neighbors, Jewish institutions, and family dynamics. In their own actions, children were constrained by factors including racial categorization, religion, ethnicity, gender, and their membership in a child subculture of society. Yet children appeared not only as curious observers of the reality that was happening around them, or as invisible appendages to their parents, but also as avid agents influencing their own fates. They acted both independently and with the assistance of adults.

SOURCE MATERIAL

Jewish and some gentile individuals and organizations viewed Jewish children as the most vulnerable segment of the victimized people and one that symbolized the future. Yet historical studies have largely neglected children's experiences. And scholars have overlooked the child's voice for all too long. With the exception of several significant studies that grasp the fates of Jewish children in wartime Europe,[4] the scholarship on Jewish children's experiences during the Holocaust, particularly in Poland, is slim.[5] Yet children under the age of fourteen numbered nearly one million out of Poland's prewar Jewish population of more than three million.[6]

Reconstructing the experiences of such young people during the Holocaust poses several constraints. In her groundbreaking book *Children with a Star: Jewish Youth in Nazi Europe* (1991), the American historian Debórah Dwork noted the fragmentary documentation on Jewish child life in Nazi Europe and discussed the reasons for this. Dwork has argued that it is justifiable to use the survivors' accounts to speak for others, as their lives were parallel to the lives of those who perished until the moment of death. Allowing children's voices to be heard, oral histories provide a valuable source of information.[7]

While they must be used with discretion, postwar accounts are invaluable. The memories, feelings, thoughts, behavior, and actions of those who were children during that time can, in the final analysis, be recalled by only those who lived through it. In her article "The Aftermath and After: Memories of Child Survivors of the Holocaust," British historian Joanna Michlic observed that "child survivors' wartime biographies remain durable and almost intact in the child survivors' memories despite the passage of time."[8] Michlic claimed that child survivors have retained memories of a set of emotionally charged and personally momentous experiences that defined their wartime lives. Children's accounts shed light on aspects of young people's lives during the Holocaust that cannot be gleaned from official German documents, or those produced by adult witnesses. Therefore, as Michlic argued, "Child survivors' testimonies are a necessary and irreplaceable source in historical investigations concerning the lived experiences of the young survivors. Though they cannot be viewed as the sole or self-sufficient evidence, they are nevertheless essential for the writings of *Alltagsgeschichte* (everyday history) of Jewish children both during and after the war."[9]

On the one hand, perpetrator documents, such as German decrees against Jews, defined the terms and boundaries of Jews' existence. On the other hand, records maintained by the Jewish community that operated inside the ghetto provide information about the situation of children and include official statistics of the Jewish population, offering estimates on the number of children. This study relies on children's (and in some instances, on their caretakers') testimonies, which are, in turn, divided into several categories. The Central Committee of Jews in Poland collected a large number of written accounts from both adults and children in the immediate postwar years.[10] They provide an invaluable source of information about events witnessed by children whose memory was not yet influenced by the subsequent acquisition of historical knowledge.[11] Later postwar compilations of survivor accounts contain rather short descriptions of children's lives, which are nevertheless crucial for research on Jewish childhood during the Holocaust.[12] Then too, memoirs expound on important issues while presenting survivors' interpretations of events. In addition, the oral histories collected by the Shoah Foundation Institute act as a lens on multiple aspects of a child's life, otherwise inaccessible.[13]

WHY KRAKÓW?

The topic of children's illicit activities aimed against and in response to Nazi anti-Jewish policies, but that nevertheless served to prolong children's lives, offers insight into Jewish life under German occupation in Poland, particularly in Kraków (Cracow), the capital of the General Government and seat of the Kraków District (both German-created administrative entities). The German army invaded the city on September 6, 1939, and immediately began to introduce and enforce laws restricting Jewish presence and mobility in public life. Forced isolation (legal and physical) severed Jewish Krakovians from the Polish nation, to which they believed they belonged and to which they had to a large extent integrated. The prewar historical and cultural role of Kraków[14] and the self-identification of its Jewish minority as Polish Jews frame the impact of German occupation on its inhabitants and on their responses to persecution. Yet, surprisingly little has been written about Jews in wartime Kraków.[15] The German occupation of the city affected the lives of all of the more than 250,000 Krakovians. However, the war and the ensuing genocide influenced the fates of some sixty thousand Jewish residents of the city differently from those of their gentile Polish neighbors.[16]

German plans for Kraków stipulated the disappearance of Jews from the urban landscape. Following the expulsions from the city between May and August 1940, only some twenty thousand Jews were permitted to remain. In tandem with the policy of dispersion, the Germans instituted a strategy of concentrating the remnant of Kraków's Jews. On March 3, 1941, the governor of the Kraków District, Dr. Otto Wächter, announced the establishment of the *Jüdischer Wohnbezirk* (Jewish living quarter), giving health and safety reasons for the creation of the ghetto.[17] The territory destined for Jews was actually an enclosed and guarded area where Jews were forcibly concentrated and persecuted. Located in the Podgórze district of the city, where few Jews had lived before the war, the ghetto was separated from the former Jewish district and the city proper by the Vistula River and two bridges. It was surrounded by barbed wire, and later a wall was built with four entrances (including one for the brisk passage of trams catering only to Aryan customers). Othmar Rodler became the commissar of the ghetto, which fell under the jurisdiction of Gestapo and ss Oberführer Julian Scherner in April 1941. Increasingly harsh regulations ensued. Jews who attempted to leave the ghetto without special permits faced the death penalty as of October 15, 1941. The decree specified that the same punishment applied to gentiles providing aid to Jews. Beginning the same day, Jews were responsible for acquiring their own food supply. And reversing their earlier directive, the German authorities forced all Jews from Kraków and the vicinity to report to the ghetto.

POPULATION POLICY

Based on the estimates of May 1, 1941, there were 10,873 Jews in the Kraków ghetto, consisting of 5,034 men (including 870 boys up to the age of twelve) and 5,839 women (including 912 up to the age of twelve).[18] The ghetto's population swelled when the German authorities forced all Jews from Kraków and its surrounding areas to enter the city's Jewish quarter in October 1941. In total, some 25,000 Jews lived in the Kraków ghetto throughout the two years of its existence. Sources vary on the number of children. According to official reports of Jewish organizations that operated inside the ghetto, about 2,500 children lived there at its peak in December 1941.[19] The census takers of Jewish organizations who worked in the ghetto may not have included all children on the official forms, being mindful of the fact that children's clandestine presence might offer future protection. Moreover, a number of children remained in the ghetto illegally by sneaking in and failing to register with the authorities. Then too, some children deceived the authorities about their age. Finally, the reports are only fragmentary and were drafted by various organizations.

In order to control the ghetto's population and fulfill the objectives of the program of genocide, the German authorities staged three major actions in the Kraków ghetto. Between May 28 and June 8, 1942, approximately seven thousand Jews were deported to the death camp in Bełżec. This raid was overseen by Wilhelm Kunde and led by ss Obersturmführer Otto von Mallotke. According to Heinrich Himmler's order of July 19, 1942, all ghettos in the General Government had to be eliminated by December 31, 1942. Hence, the Germans unleashed the second big dragnet operation on October 28, 1942, under the direction of ss Sturmbannführer Willi Haase. About six hundred Jews were murdered on the spot (including approximately three hundred children) and more than forty-five hundred others were shipped to Bełżec. Hans Frank, the governor of the General Government, declared the zone *Judenrein* (free of Jews) on November 14, 1942, except for five closed ghettos in Kraków, Radom, Warsaw, Lwów, and Częstochowa. At this time, approximately five thousand Jews remained in the Kraków ghetto. The German authorities divided it on December 26, 1942, into "Ghetto A," for Jews who were assigned work, and "Ghetto B," for those without work and as a dumping ground for Jews from the Kraków area. Both sections were dissolved in the final liquidation on March 13–14, 1943, under the direction of Amon Goeth, the commandant of the Płaszów camp.[20] The Jewish inmates of Ghetto A were marched to Płaszów, while those from Ghetto B were killed.

DECEPTION

The German authorities required all Jews over the age of fourteen to perform forced labor.[21] They were detailed in various ways. Youths were rounded up or obliged to report to a specific place, from which they were taken to work sites. The *Arbeitsamt* (labor office) in the ghetto also assigned children to workplaces where they went on a regular basis. Realizing that working might protect them against deportation, Jews in the ghetto used their networks of family and friends to look for jobs. Youths sent by the Germans to work outside the ghetto received special permits. They usually worked alongside adults, including their parents.

Children often lied about their real age in order to be spared deportation and be considered useful through work. At times, it was sufficient to deceive German officials by telling them that the child was older.[22] In other instances, youths had their birth certificates falsified. Jane Schein's falsified document, purchased by her mother from the Kraków *Judenrat* (Jewish Council), recorded that she was sixteen years old, when in fact she was only eleven. She spoke about that experience many years after the events. "I was eleven, looked like I was going on five, and was passing for a sixteen-year-old."[23] Mieczysław Staner also had his birthday "formally" adjusted in order to assure his survival. He recalled half a century later: "Somehow, my parents arranged a change of my birth date to show that I was 16, otherwise I would have been classified as a useless child and therefore be disposed of. I grew up rapidly and my struggle for survival had just begun."[24]

Some children were made to look older. Changing hairstyle, applying makeup, and wearing more adult clothing helped deceive the authorities. One trick involved braiding long hair around a girl's head so that she appeared more mature. Other girls donned long dresses or wore long coats or hoods to cover up their bodies and appear fuller. Still other girls were disguised as full-fledged women wearing high heels, lipstick, and stuffed bras.[25] Presumably boys, too, participated in activities meant to fool the authorities about the boys' young ages.

Misleading through age distortion and physique camouflage allowed some children to lead clandestine lives in the ghetto. Classified as useful Jews, they could avoid instant death during an action or being sent to a death camp. At the same time, because of their status as laborers, these youths received food rations. In this way, children helped contribute to their family's well-being. They exercised their agency by agreeing to work, thereby understanding the implications of employment for Jews in the ghetto. Youths were actors in their own right since they chose to follow the demands related to multifaceted deception. Irrespective of the type, forced labor was dangerous for young people. Apart from their young age, exhaustion, stress, and fear, coupled with being terrorized, made them prone to injuries in the workplace. The benefits associated with their work capability category, however, often outweighed the disadvantages and risks.

HIDING

Masquerading as an adult served as one of the ways in which youths engaged in covert activities. Physical concealment constituted another tactic.

Hiding inside the ghetto emerged as an important way for children to avoid violence, deportation, and death during raids. Hiding was a constant in the lives of a number of children in the ghetto, and finding hiding places was an endeavor in its own right.[26] Some youths were trained by their parents to conceal their presence or, fearing any type of commotion, hid instinctively. Jane Schein was precocious for her age. Her parents felt relatively secure leaving her alone at home while they went to work. Whenever she heard any kind of noise, Jane knew to hide so that she would not be caught.[27] Other children hid in various places: in the sewers, under a heap of potatoes, behind a cupboard, in cellars and attics.[28] All that Jerzy Cyns remembered was being camouflaged. Half a century later he recalled: "Until March 1943, during the deportations, I was hidden in various places." His memory is limited to images of things and people that "accompanied" him during that time. "Little remains in my memory other than stacks of dirty laundry, under which my older brother, Henryk, a girl cousin, and I sat for many hours when they were conducting 'selections.'" During one such action, the laundry basket caught the attention of a German officer, who poked the clothes with a rifle butt. However, the children, who were well trained and subconsciously understood that their lives depended on silence, did not utter a sound.[29]

Some youths concealed their presence during actions in previously arranged places that their parents or caretakers considered relatively safe, and which would serve as a meeting point for the family after the deathly assault against the ghetto population had ended. The course of events, however, sometimes required the young person to think and act quickly, not always strictly according to the plan. During one of the raids, Jane Schein ran near the assembly place, Plac Zgody. She saw what was happening and decided to go to the "safe house" — the Jewish police building. Instead, she hid in a garbage can that stood in the courtyard of the Jewish police headquarters. She was petrified and afraid to move. After several hours, Jane eventually reached the "safe house" and was reunited with her parents.[30]

As opposed to hiding outside the ghetto, it was fairly common for an entire family, or at least all the children, to hide together inside the ghetto for the duration of an action. Hiding in a group was often necessary since there were limited concealment opportunities in the ghetto. And families wanted to remain together. Also, the ghetto was, paradoxically, perceived to be the safest place because the Polish gentile informants and blackmailers operated on the Aryan side. Jews were conscious of the constant risk of discovery by the Germans and the fact that they and their families would eventually have to emerge from their hiding places and continue their clandestine lives.

If some families remained together, others chose to separate when hiding in the ghetto. This was motivated by safety reasons or simply by the lack of one hiding spot that would accommodate the entire family. Sometimes, families identified multiple hiding places within their building. In a case such as this, children frequently evoked ingenuity, courage, maturity, and responsibility. Jerzy Aleksandrowicz's eight-member family had been assigned various hiding places in case there was a raid. When he overheard a German officer conducting a search of the house, Jerzy took the initiative. He grabbed the keys from his mother and dropped them out the window to the building's caretaker, who then opened the cellar door and took out Jerzy's aunt and grandmother, who were hiding there, into the street and into safety.[31] This undertaking required quick decisions and swift action. In a sense, Jerzy became responsible for his family's survival. His situation also shows that Jews selected hiding arrangements being mindful of protecting each member of the household. They did so in anticipation of roundups, and not just in response to a raid already in progress.

At times, parents placed their children with other Jews hiding in the ghetto mainly because they had not managed to smuggle out their offspring in time, or there was not enough space for the child to join his or her parents in another hiding place. This allowed parents with other means to escape a raid to do so with the knowledge that their children were taken care of. Before the liquidation of the ghetto, Janka Warshavska's father placed her two sisters, Gusta, age fourteen, and Reina, age sixteen, in hiding with one Mrs. Drenger. The well-camouflaged space provided a hiding place for twelve people. Janka described the inconspicuous bunker: "The entrance was through the lavatory, which was almost impossible to enter because of the revolting stench. There was a well-concealed door, which opened on a dimly lit corridor, where there was a dirty old cupboard. By going through a cupboard, a small room was reached, which could not be detected from the outside."[32] Emerging too early from the hiding place resulted in immediate death at the hands of the Germans, the tragic fate met by Mrs. Drenger and her children.

Boys in particular took up the role of caretakers of those in hiding. Janka Warshavska recalled how Victor Tenenbaum took care of her sisters' group, being the only one to exit the hiding place to obtain food and water. He sought to resist the oppressors in any way possible. "He prepared bars of iron and announced that the Germans would not take him alive."[33]

While in hiding, children were overwhelmed by the fear of ensuing danger, brutality of the persecutors, and possible discovery. Their reactions varied. Some youths experienced adverse physical responses induced by stress.[34] Older and more religiously observant children in particular, thinking of an impending end, prayed or said the Kaddish (prayer for the dead).[35] Many years after the event, Roma Ligocka, a very small child during the war, recalled a specific incident, or rather the feelings associated with it, which dug deeply into her memory. During one raid when the Germans entered their apartment, her grandmother hid Roma under the table. The girl was numb with fear. She covered her ears so as not to hear her grandmother's screams as she was brutally taken away. Several hours later, Roma's father found her under the table. She knew that something terrible had taken place, but she did not ask questions. She stayed under the table that night.[36] While the chronology was not recorded in the small girl's mind, the memory of the emotions experienced at that specific moment never escaped her. Roma's reactions to the event signify the immense trauma she suffered when her loved one was violently pulled away. She herself might have met the same fate had she disobeyed her grandmother's request to hide silently under the table.

Hiding in a group with younger children posed a certain risk of discovery. Especially in a group of strangers, adults were skeptical and often outright denied children the right to shelter in communal hiding places. They (understandably) feared that the noises made by young children would expose everyone.[37] The ideal of solidarity sometimes crumbled in face of such danger. Yet, the perseverance of parents and the voices of other people in the room often quelled those on the offensive, and children were allowed to stay. Many children bore witness to tragic scenes while hiding with others. During the October 1942 action, Aneta Weinreich was hidden in an apartment together with approximately thirty people, including two babies. When the babies started crying, the mothers put cushions over their mouths; one baby suffocated. Aneta believed that this incident probably saved her life.[38] Before the ghetto's liquidation, Janina Pietrasiak's father and other men created a hiding place to accommodate several people. "Dantesque scenes took place there," she recalled. Janina witnessed the accidental death of a child. "One of the little children began to cry, so his mother covered his head with a pillow to silence him. The child suffocated."[39] The older children surely understood that infanticide, however horrible it was to witness, had nevertheless saved their own lives and the lives of other people.

Life in hiding forced many children to endure horrifying experiences. They saw adults fall apart or some of the older people lose their minds. They saw individuals commit suicide.[40] During the liquidation of the ghetto, four-year-old Roma Ligocka and her mother were hidden with several others in a hole under a paint store. In the darkness, Roma came upon an unidentified figure, which she thought was a corpse, and screamed. Others, scared of the possibility of being discovered, tried to calm the girl by holding her and pressing their hands over her mouth to the point of near-suffocation. They reasoned that sacrificing one girl for the sake of the others' safety was plausible; however, Roma's mother persuaded the people to leave her daughter alone.[41] In essence, children were expected to stop behaving like children and control themselves and adjust their reactions the way adults do.

SNEAKING INTO THE GHETTO

Throughout the existence of the Kraków ghetto, children practiced still other forms of deception, evasion, and disobedience. Many youths were either smuggled into the ghetto or they sneaked in themselves. Some had been hidden on the Aryan side and entered the ghetto to join their parents or relatives. Others were smuggled into the ghetto when their caretakers on the Aryan side wanted to get rid of the burden of harboring them, or when the danger to their lives became imminent. Finally, some children sneaked in from neighboring ghettos to wait until the raids passed and the situation calmed down. Their presence was rarely, if ever, recorded. Hence, their entire life and presence within the ghetto was clandestine; they were off the books, as it were.

Mendel Feichtal's case exemplifies how some children entered the Kraków ghetto only temporarily because it appeared a safer alternative to the smaller ghettos in the vicinity. Mendel testified in the immediate postwar years that on hearing rumors of an action in the Brzesko ghetto (about fifty-three kilometers away), his mother sent him with a Polish woman to the Jewish quarter in Kraków. Once he reached the ghetto's gate, Mendel bribed a Jewish policeman with approximately 3,000 złoty and entered the ghetto with Jewish workers. He stayed there with his aunt for about two weeks, until it was rumored that the raids had stopped in Brzesko. To exit the ghetto, Mendel once again bribed a Jewish policeman and also a Polish policeman with money and a gold watch. The policemen pretended to take him to the precinct, when in fact they escorted him to the railway station.[42]

Mendel's history demonstrates the Jews' desperate search for safe havens, including visiting ghettos. As a medium-size ghetto, Kraków offered opportunities to meld in with the crowd, something difficult to accomplish in the Brzesko ghetto, because of the ghetto's small population and area size. Mendel's furtive entrance into the Kraków ghetto illustrates, too, that Jews' mobility was possible despite the German's efforts to curb it. Certainly difficult and dangerous, and even life threatening, Jewish secret—and thus illegal—entry into the ghetto was often facilitated by bribery, but also depended on the timing. Mendel entered the ghetto before the October 1942 action. Following this particular action, the German guardianship of the ghetto intensified, relieving Polish and Jewish policemen from certain duties and abolishing outside labor groups, limiting opportunities for sneaking in and out. The Germans and their henchmen dissolved most ghettos in the area by the end of 1942, concentrating the remnant of Jews from the smaller ghettos, and those previously not subject to ghettoization, in the larger ghettos of the General Government, including Kraków.[43]

German restrictions failed to impede Jews' efforts to survive, and children assumed a vital role in those endeavors. Sneaking out of the ghetto, purchasing foodstuffs on the Aryan side, and smuggling the score back into the ghetto were closely intertwined domains in which young people predominated. Adult Jews who were sent to work on the Aryan side, or obtained permission to exit the ghetto, also brought in the contraband. But after the October 1942 action in the ghetto, those avenues of smuggling were cut off. An important reason that young people filled the niche was that children under the age of twelve were not yet subject to the laws requiring Jews to wear a visible marking on their clothes. The order had already gone into effect on December 1, 1939, and applied throughout the ghetto years. Severe punishments awaited those who disobeyed the law.[44] The wording of the regulation, however, opened a legal loophole that offered a solid reason for sending the youngest members of the family on smuggling missions. When exiting the ghetto, child smugglers were formally breaking only one law — the prohibition against existence outside of the ghetto.

The ability to interpret the law for one's own purposes facilitated a parent's decision to send off their child on smuggling missions, or instilled confidence in a child to serve as a potential smuggler. Yet, more factors contributed to the reasons that children undertook illicit activities. They were small enough to pass undetected, yet old enough to understand the risks, follow their parents' instructions, and make fast decisions. As children, they aroused less suspicion and evoked more sympathy. Inconspicuous, they blended in among gentiles. Inside and outside of the ghetto children displayed flexibility and adaptability to situations that could change instantly. At the same time, they exhibited courage, even if they were afraid of their actions and terrified of the consequences, and showed responsibility for themselves and their families. Youths had to use cunning strategies when leaving and reentering the ghetto and finding places whence they could obtain food, as well as ingenuity once they returned to the ghetto and parceled out their products. The situation required them to become manipulative, resourceful, and independent, although they were still young people, who needed to be cared for and catered to. These children matured quickly and understood that their actions influenced their own and their families' fates. For many families, whose adults could not leave the ghetto, the children's illicit smuggling activities contributed to their families' well-being.

Young people slipped out of the ghetto illegally with or without the help of German guards, or Jewish and/or Polish policemen. Sometimes children took advantage of the guards' silent consent, sensed a moment of inattention, or offered a bribe. Once on the Aryan side, Jewish children relied primarily on their "Aryan looks,"[45] proficiency in the Polish language, knowledge of Catholic rituals, and if they could obtain them, falsified papers that declared them non-Jews. All of these acts were prohibited by the German authorities, who rendered severe punishments on individuals caught in the act.

Methods of evasion and deception proved useful for child smugglers once they crossed to the Aryan side. Jewish girls with the so-called "Aryan look"[46] had an easier time fooling the watchful eyes of informers outside the ghetto. For Jewish boys who had been circumcised, sneaking out of the ghetto posed an additional and substantially greater danger of disclosure than it did for females. When recognized by a prewar neighbor or schoolmate, pointed out by a stranger, stopped randomly by a Polish policeman, or suspected by a German, the young man was often forced to pull down his pants to show his physical marking as a Jew. Nevertheless, some took the risk. In order to deal with fear, danger, and risk of discovery, many child survivors recalled that they employed a strategy of not drawing attention to themselves.

Deemed illegal by the German authorities, smuggling acquired a positive connotation among ghetto inhabitants, for whom it became a crucial means of support. Children also recalled mixed feelings about their smuggling assignments. While some recognized the importance of their activity for their family's well-being, others felt uncomfortable with their tasks. Initial embarrassment, however, disappeared in the face of food scarcity. Even though many child survivors referred to their wartime smuggling missions as "stupid,"[47] they acted out of necessity, pushed by their parents to fulfill a role they themselves could not.

ESCAPING THE GHETTO

Escaping the ghetto and hiding on the Aryan side for the duration of an action was another way for Jewish children to survive. Such covert activity carried its own set of risks, of course. With the imposition of Hans Frank's "Third Decree about Limiting Jews' Presence in the General Government" of October 15, 1941, providing any form of assistance to Jews became legally prohibited.[48] From then on, Jews who left the ghetto without a permit risked the death penalty; and gentiles who aided them and offered shelter faced the same punishment, although certain cases (as determined by special German courts) qualified for arrest or imprisonment. This law was instituted early in the existence of the ghetto evidently because instances of gentiles' helping Jews had occurred, which the Germans had noticed. This law terrorized the Polish gentile population and served to deter it from engaging in activities that would ameliorate the Jews' situation.

Yet despite the strict law, parents searched for ways to whisk their children out during danger and sought out prewar friends, acquaintances, coworkers, maids, nannies, teachers, neighbors, building supervisors, or even strangers, asking them to keep the child in a secure place on the Aryan side until the situation in the ghetto had calmed down. Some parents made arrangements before moving into the ghetto, and the child either was spirited away by an adult or a child smuggler,[49] or left the ghetto on his or her own accord and went to a prearranged place. Some individual Jews undertook organized actions to bring children to the Aryan side for safekeeping.[50] In some cases, Jewish women, who lived on the Aryan side or left the ghetto for the purpose of finding potential rescuers, solicited gentiles willing to care for a Jewish child until the raid was over and prepared smuggling routes.[51] Such endeavors provided hope for the children's clandestine survival, if only temporarily.

Once a gentile caretaker had been secured, the parents needed to devise an avenue of escape. People used their ingenuity to invent ways to smuggle out children. At times, Jews staged a fight to divert the guards' and policemen's attention.[52] Often, however, children were physically camouflaged and removed from the ghetto, carried out in knapsacks or baskets.[53] At other times they were injected with a sleeping medication to avoid disclosure.[54] Roma Ligocka's parents, for example, realized that children were being targeted, and they also knew that some of the youngest members of their extended family, such as their cousin Roman Polanski, were hiding on the Aryan side. They gave Roma some liquid to drink and put her into a suitcase. Her screams, however, were too much too bear.[55] Roma's history demonstrates the intricate ideas adults came up with in order to remove the child until the immediate danger had passed. It also shows the issues that parents wrestled with when faced with exposing their children to the unknown.

The approach to children's temporary survival soon changed diametrically. Sensing an impending major action, which turned out to be the liquidation of the Kraków ghetto in March 1943, parents made the desperate decision to permanently relinquish their children in the hope that their lives might be spared. On the Aryan side, some youths were placed with gentile families, while others were left to face the uncertain situation on their own. In some cases, parents made arrangements with individual Poles; in other instances, an informal underground network composed of Jews with contacts on the Aryan side, or the Kraków branch of ŻEGOTA (Council for Aid to Jews), an underground organization run jointly by Jewish and ethnic Polish socialist and Catholic activists, took upon itself to find safe havens for children. The latter began its activities in the Kraków ghetto only in March 1943 as the ghetto was being liquidated.

A common escape route led through the barbed wire or a hole in the wall. Frequently, a child's "illegal" exit from the ghetto depended on the assistance of other children and teenagers. A number of children managed to sneak out through the sewers. Janina Fischler and her brother Joseph escaped through a manhole into the sewers. Janka Warshavska's sister, thirteen-year-old Helena, and her fifteen-year-old brother Ignatz escaped in the same manner. According to Janka, when Helena descended into the sewer, many children surrounded her and begged her to take them with her. Helena was mindful of the fact that bigger children had a better chance of successfully making it to the other side, while smaller children were in greater danger of drowning.[56] If some children escaped through the tunnels by themselves or in groups, others left together with adults, often with their parents.[57]

Some children left the ghetto by a combination of their own devices and outside assistance. Ten-year-old Roman Polanski recalled the events of his escape. "On the day the Kraków Ghetto was finally liquidated, March 13, 1943, my father woke me before dawn. Taking me to Plac Zgody, to a blind spot just behind the ss guardhouse, he coolly snipped the barbed wire with a pair of pliers. He gave me a quick hug, and I slipped through the fence for the last time."[58] Finding the door locked to the apartment of the Polish gentile Wilk family, with whom he was acquainted, Roman decided to go back to the ghetto. He saw a marching column of Jewish men, among them his father. When Roman finally got his father to notice him, his father hissed, "Shove off!" Roman explained the reason for his survival: "Those two brusque words stopped me in my track. I watched the column recede, then turned away. I didn't look back."[59]

During the liquidation of the ghetto, all children under the age of fourteen were to stay behind. Amon Goeth, the commandant of the Płaszów labor camp, promised the parents that all children would eventually arrive at the camp. But some parents, unwilling to be separated from their children, attempted to smuggle them into the camp.[60] Henryk Zvi Zimmerman, a witness to the events, recounted the stories of parents smuggling their children in backpacks, so that they could stay together in Płaszów. They did so at great risk. "Groups of ss-men walked between the suitcases and bags and kicking with their hobnailed boots, and poking with guns, they checked whether there were any children hidden in the baggage. Blood was dripping from the luggage." One particular incident stood out in his memory. "In front of me and the Waldmans stood the wife of Harry Zweig with 12-year-old daughter Sylwia, dressed to look older than she really was." In addition to her daughter, who was posing as an adult, "Zweigowa carried a big backpack. Seeing her terrible despair, we understood, that their three-year-old son Jerzyk was hidden in that backpack." The quick action of a fellow ghetto inmate saved the child. "Cunning old Waldman, standing behind Zweigowa, whispered to her 'Drop the backpack!' Zweigowa, hypnotized, did what he said. I also understood Waldman's intentions. The bag was now lying on the ground in front of us. With full force we kicked it towards the baggage that had already passed control. We made it, because the policemen were paying attention to some tumult in front of us."[61]

A number of children were smuggled out of the ghetto in carts among furniture or medical equipment.[62] Other children tried to leave the ghetto with the columns of prisoners marching to the camp. Janek Weber's father understood that children had bleak chances for survival. Janek's father put the eight-year-old boy into a suitcase and smuggled him on a cart going to Płaszów. Janek recounted the incident half a century later: "I felt, surprisingly enough, that it was an adventure, and I don't recall being frightened. My luck, there is luck in such circumstances, is that I was sufficiently adult and grown up, mature enough to cope with the situation but unable to grasp the tragedy of it all."[63]

Only a small number of children survived the liquidation. Some did so by hiding in the ghetto. They were either subsequently smuggled out or they sneaked out to the Aryan side. The remaining children were killed. During the liquidation, Janina Pietrasiak, her sister Ewa, and their mother had hidden in a wooden outhouse; her mother and Ewa held the latch, while Janina squatted. After two days in the outhouse, the mother looked through a crack and saw a German soldier standing at ease. She gave him the little remaining jewelry that she had, and they escaped to the Aryan side.[64] On March 14, 1943, Roma Ligocka came out of the hiding place in the cellar. Her mother just managed to whisper to Roma that her last name was Ligocka, not the original Liebling. Both were among the last to be smuggled out of the now defunct ghetto in a cart transporting suitcases and other possessions.[65] On the day of the ghetto's liquidation, Janka Warshavska had just returned from smuggling out a child. Horrified at what she witnessed in the ghetto, Janka took advantage of the commotion and ran away to the Aryan side.

CONCLUSIONS

An analysis of children's concealed existence and illicit activities in the Kraków ghetto demonstrates that young people led multilayered covert lives in order to survive. Securing a hiding spot inside a medium-size ghetto such as Kraków was not an easy task. It required ingenuity, courage, and often the help of others.

In tracing children's covert existence and activities, young people emerge as active participants in the events, exercising agency, albeit in a limited way, along every step of the deception process. Several factors played a part in that. Age influenced children's perception of reality. Older children understood that cooperating with their family members in lying about age, assuming a mature look, hiding, and sneaking out and smuggling into the ghetto were necessary to stay alive. Younger children, in comparison, were often not fully aware of the gravity of events and the ensuing dangers, but knew they needed to make themselves invisible the moment a commotion began. They also knew to remain silent while in hiding. Gender was an important aspect in hiding and smuggling operations. When hiding in a group with mostly women and girls, boys appeared to assume the role of caretakers. This was either because of the traditional gender roles assigned to males or a spontaneous decision made by the boys. A child's background also played a role in the success of clandestine activities. Young people who spoke fluent Polish, were familiar with local customs, and even knew Catholic prayers were better positioned to avoid the watchful eyes of Germans and Polish informants.

The case study of the Kraków ghetto illuminates the centrality of children for the Jewish community in their efforts to sustain their lives and for the German authorities in their systems to destroy them. Children participated in various degrees in assuming a covert existence in the ghetto, and methods considered illicit by the perpetrators were necessary to assure Jewish continuity.

NOTES

Note: This article is part of the author's doctoral dissertation: "Concealed Presence: Jewish Children in German-Occupied Kraków" (PhD diss., 2016, Strassler Center for Holocaust and Genocide Studies, Clark University, Worcester, Massachusetts).

1. "Janka Warshavska's Story," 12. I thank Shelly Tenenbaum, Clark University, for bringing her aunt's (postwar name: Janette Warshavska Geizhals) written testimony to my attention and for providing a copy of it. Janka's account is deposited at the Archives of the Auschwitz-Birkenau State Museum in Oświęcim (Wspomnienia t. 192/1046, inw. 173940). Azriel Eisenberg recalls the story of Janka, but refers to her as "Manya," in *The Lost Generation: Children in the Holocaust* (New York: Pilgrim Press, 1982), 120.

2. "Janka Warshavska's Story," 15.

3. According to Nazi laws, "Jewish children" denote individuals up to the age of fourteen racially defined as Jews. Jewish organizations, which continuously stressed the importance of child care as it concerned the entire ghetto population, applied the same age limit. "Ogólny bilans wydatków na opiekę za pierwszy semester 1942 roku," YIVO [YIVO Institute for Jewish Research], 335.1, folder no. 91.

4. For studies on Jewish child life during World War II, see Debórah Dwork, *Children with a Star: Jewish Youth in Nazi Europe* (New Haven, CT: Yale University Press, 1991); Lynn Nicholas, *Cruel World: The Children of Europe in the Nazi Web* (New York: Knopf, 2005); Nicholas Stargardt, *Witnesses of War: Children's Lives under the Nazis* (New York: Knopf, 2006); Diane L. Wolf, *Beyond Anne Frank: Hidden Children and Postwar Families in Holland* (Berkeley: University of California Press, 2007); Suzanne Vromen, *Hidden Children of the Holocaust: Belgian Nuns and Their Daring Rescue of Young Jews from the Nazis* (Oxford: Oxford University Press, 2008); Patricia Heberer, *Children during the Holocaust* (Lanham, MD: AltaMira Press, 2011).

5. Feliks Tych, Alfons Kenkmann, Elisabeth Kohlhaas, and Andreas Eberhardt, eds., *Kinder über den Holocaust: Frühe Zeugnisse 1944-1948* (Berlin: Metropol Verlag, 2008);

Joanna B. Michlic, "Jewish Children in Nazi-Occupied Poland: Early Postwar Recollections of Survival and Polish-Jewish Relations during the Holocaust," in *Yad Vashem's Search and Research Lectures and Papers* (Jerusalem: Yad Vashem, 2008); Justyna Kowalska-Leder, *Doświadczenie Zagłady z Perspektywy Dziecka w Polskiej Literaturze Dokumentu Osobistego* (Wrocław: Wydawnictwo and Uniwersytetu Wrocławskiego, 2009); Joanna B. Michlic, "The Raw Memory of War: The Reading of Early Postwar Testimonies of Children in Dom Dziecka in Otwock," in *Yad Vashem Studies* (Jerusalem: Yad Vashem, 2009); Emunah Nachmany Gafny, *Dividing Hearts: The Removal of Jewish Children from Gentile Families in Poland in the Immediate Post Holocaust Years* (Jerusalem: Yad Vashem, 2009); Nahum Bogner, *At the Mercy of Strangers: The Rescue of Jewish Children with Assumed Identities in Poland* (Jerusalem: Yad Vashem, 2009).

6. Jacob Lestschinsky, *Crisis, Catastrophe and Survival* (New York: Institute of Jewish Affairs of the World Jewish Congress, 1948), 60.

7. Dwork, *Children with a Star*, xvii–xlii.

8. Joanna B. Michlic, "The Aftermath and After: Memories of Child Survivors of the Holocaust," in *Lessons and Legacies X: Back to the Sources: Reexamining Perpetrators, Victims, and Bystanders*, ed. Sara R. Horowitz, 141–89 (142) (Evanston, IL: Northwestern University Press, 2012). I would like to thank Joanna Michlic for providing me with a copy of her text.

9. Michlic, "The Aftermath and After," 148.

10. For more information about the committee, see Laura Jockusch, *Collect and Record! Jewish Holocaust Documentation in Early Postwar Europe* (New York: Oxford University Press, 2012).

11. On the topic of immediate postwar testimonies, see Joanna B. Michlic, "The Raw Memory of War: Early Postwar Testimonies of Children in Dom Dziecka in Otwock," *Yad Vashem Studies* 37, no. 1 (2009): 11–52; Alan Rosen, *The Wonder of Their Voices: The 1946 Holocaust Interviews of David Boder* (New York: Oxford University Press, 2010).

12. Some examples include: Maria Hochberg-Marianska and Noe Grüss, eds., *The Children Accuse* (Portland, OR: Vallentine Mitchell, 1996); Lena Kichler-Silberman, *One Hundred Children* (Garden City, NY: Doubleday, 1961); Wiktoria Śliwowska, Jakub Gutenbaum, Agnieszka Latała, Julian Bussgang, and Fay Bussgang, eds., *The Last Eyewitnesses: Children of the Holocaust Speak*, 2 vols. (Evanston, IL: Northwestern University Press, 2005); Azriel Eisenberg, *The Lost Generation: Children of the Holocaust* (New York: Pilgrim Press, 1982); Kerry Bluglass, *Hidden from the Holocaust: Stories of Resilient Children Who Survived and Thrived* (Westport, CT: Praeger, 2003).

13. For studies on the use of oral testimonies see, for example, Lawrence Langer, *Holocaust Testimonies: The Ruins of Memory* (New Haven, CT: Yale University Press, 1991); Shoshana Felman and Dori Laub, *Testimony: Crises of Witnessing in Literature, Psychoanalysis, and History* (New York: Routledge, 1991); Suzanne Kaplan, *Children in the Holocaust: Dealing with Affects and Memory Images in Trauma and Generational Linking* (Uppsala: Uppsala Programme for Holocaust and Genocide Studies, Uppsala University, 2002); Daniel Baranowski, *Ich bin die Stimme der sechs Millionen: Das Videoarchiv im Ort der Information* (Berlin: Stiftung Denkmal für die Ermordeten Juden Europas, 2009); Henry Greenspan, *On Listening to Holocaust Survivors: Beyond Testimony* (St. Paul, MN: Paragon House, 2010).

14. The city served as an important historical and cultural hub for Poles, and as a center of rabbinic study and expertise in *Halakhah* (Jewish religious law). For many Krakov-

ian Jews, who viewed Kraków as the Jerusalem of Galicia, the city stood at the crossroads of eastern and western Jewry.

15. Aleksander Biberstein, *Zagłada Żydów w Krakowie* (Kraków: Wydawnictwo Literackie, 1985); Yael Peled, *Krakow ha-yehudit 1939-1943: Amidah, mahteret, ma'avaq* [Hebrew] (Tel Aviv: Hakibbutz Hameuchdad, 1992); Katarzyna Zimmerer, *Zamordowany świat: Losy Żydów w Krakowie 1939-1945* (Kraków: Wydawnictwo Literackie, 2004); Monika Bednarek, Edyta Gawron, Jerzy Jeżowski, Barbara Zbroja, and Katarzyna Zimmerer, eds., *Kraków: Czas okupacji 1939-1945* (Kraków: MHMK, 2010); Andrea Löw and Markus Roth, *Juden in Krakau unter deutscher Besatzung 1939-1945* (Göttingen, DE: Wallstein, 2011); Andrzej Chwalba, *Okupacyjny Kraków w latach 1939-1945* (Kraków: Wydawnictwo Literackie, 2011).

16. The city's prewar population statistics can be found, for example, in Sean Martin, *Jewish Life in Cracow, 1918-1939* (London: Vallentine Mitchell, 2004), 16.

17. "Zarządzenie o utworzeniu dzielnicy mieszkaniowej dla żydów w Krakowie. 3.III.1941. Wachter," March 3, 1941, ANK (Archiwum Narodowe oddział w Krakowie) [Polish State Archive with a branch in Kraków], J13922, p. 33.

18. Gmina Żydowska and Biuro Ewidencji Ludnosci, "Ludność żydowskiej dzielnicy w Krakowie na podstawie płci i wieku. Stan z 1 maj 1941," ANK, J13871, p. 1.

19. Żydowska Samopomoc Społeczna, "Protokół spotkania Żydowskiego Komitetu Opiekuńczego Miasta Krakowa z 17.XII.1941," December 17, 1941, USHMM [United States Holocaust Memorial Museum, Washington, DC], 1997, A.0124, reel 31.

20. At first a labor camp, Płaszów became a concentration camp in January 1944.

21. At the beginning of the German occupation, the order to perform forced labor applied to Jews over twelve years of age (decrees of October 26, 1939 and December 12, 1939), ANK, J13907, p. 287. In February 1941, the Germans specified another age limit for Jews performing labor—over fourteen years old. ANK, J13910, p. 167.

22. Celina Biniaz, interview 11133, Visual History Archive (online), University of Southern California (USC) Shoah Foundation, Los Angeles, 2013; Louise Gruner Gans, interview 40851, Visual History Archive (online), USC Shoah Foundation, Los Angeles, 2013.

23. Eisenberg, *The Lost Generation*, 216; Isaiah Trunk, *Jewish Responses to Nazi Rule* (New York: Stein and Day, 1978), 117-22; Jane Schein, interview, 415, Visual History Archive (online), USC Shoah Foundation, Los Angeles, 2013.

24. Mieczysław Staner, *The Eyewitness* (Kraków: Hagada, 1999), 12.

25. Frances Gelbart, interview 12003, Visual History Archive (online), USC Shoah Foundation, Los Angeles, 2013; Aneta Weinreich, interview 14405, Visual History Archive (online), USC Shoah Foundation, Los Angeles, 2013; Miriam Bruck, interview 21495, Visual History Archive (online), USC Shoah Foundation, Los Angeles, 2013.

26. For an in-depth analysis of hiding places, see Marta Cobel-Tokarska, *Bezludna wyspa, nora, grób. Wojenne kryjówki Żydów w okupowanej Polsce* (Warsaw: IPN, 2012).

27. Jane Schein, interview 415, Visual History Archive (online), USC Shoah Foundation, Los Angeles, 2013.

28. Frances Gelbart, interview 12003, Visual History Archive (online), USC Shoah Foundation, Los Angeles, 2013; Paul Faynwachs, interview 14951, Visual History Archive (online), USC Shoah Foundation, Los Angeles, 2013; Renee Stern, interview 22644, Visual History Archive (online), USC Shoah Foundation, Los Angeles, 2013; Louise Gruner Gans, interview 40851, Visual History Archive (online), USC Shoah Foundation, Los Angeles, 2013.

29. Jerzy Cyns, interview 635, Visual History Archive (online), USC Shoah Foundation, Los Angeles, 2013; "Testimony of Jerzy Cyns" in Śliwowska, *The Last Eyewitnesses*, 269–70.

30. Jane Schein, interview 415, Visual History Archive (online), USC Shoah Foundation, Los Angeles, 2013; Eisenberg, *The Lost Generation*, 215.

31. "Testimony of Jerzy Aleksandrowicz," in Śliwowska, *The Last Eyewitneses*, 5–10.

32. Kichler-Silberman, "Janka Warshavska's Story," in *One Hundred Children*, 28–29; Eisenberg, *The Lost Generation*, 120. Eisenberg refers to Janka Warshavska as "Manya."

33. Ibid.

34. Miriam Bruck, interview 21495, Visual History Archive (online), USC Shoah Foundation, Los Angeles, 2013.

35. Louise Gruner Gans, interview 40851, Visual History Archive (online), USC Shoah Foundation, Los Angeles, 2013.

36. Roma Ligocka, *The Girl in the Red Coat* (New York: St. Martin's Press, 2002), 15–16, 19.

37. Anita Lobel, *No Pretty Pictures: A Child of War* (New York: Greenwillow Books, 1998), 46–50; Tadeusz Pankiewicz, *The Cracow Ghetto Pharmacy* (Washington, DC: USHMM, 2000), 120.

38. Aneta Weinreich, interview 14405, Visual History Archive (online), USC Shoah Foundation, Los Angeles, 2013.

39. "Testimony of Janina Pietrasiak," in Gutenbaum and Latała, *The Last Eyewitnesses*, 197–207; Janina Pietrasiak, interview 22050, Visual History Archive (online), USC Shoah Foundation, Los Angeles, 2013.

40. Esther Stuhl, interview 1243, Visual History Archive (online), USC Shoah Foundation, Los Angeles, 2013.

41. Ligocka, *The Girl in the Red Coat*, 25.

42. Testimony of Mendel Feichtal, 301/609, AŻIH (Archiwum Żydowski Instytut Historyczny) [Jewish Historical Institute Archive], Warsaw.

43. For more information about the development, history, and timeline of ghettos in the Kraków district and the General Government, see Guy Miron and Shlomit Shulhani, eds., *The Yad Vashem Encyclopedia of the Ghettos during the Holocaust* (Jerusalem: Yad Vashem, 2010); Martin Dean and Mel Hecker, eds., *The United States Holocaust Memorial Museum Encyclopedia of Camps and Ghettos 1939–1945*, vol. 2: *Ghettos in German-Occupied Eastern Europe* (Bloomington: Indiana University Press in association with the US Holocaust Memorial Museum, 2012).

44. "Des Distriktchef von Krakau Wächter; Rozporządzenie o znamionowaniu żydów w okręgu Krakowa. 18.XI.1939," November 18, 1939, ANK J13922.

45. For a discussion of factors necessary to survive on the Aryan side, see Natan Gross, "Days and Nights in the Aryan Quarters, the Daily Worries of a Jew Carrying 'Aryan Papers,'" in *Yad Vashem Bulletin*, no. 5 (Jerusalem: Yad Vashem, 1959); Małgorzata Melchior, *Zagłada a tożsamość: Polscy Żydzi ocaleni na "aryjskich papierach": Analiza doświadczenia biograficznego* (Warsaw: IFiS Academy of Sciences, 2004); Joanna Nalewajko-Kulikov, *Strategie przetrwania: Żydzi po aryjskiej stronie Warszawy* (Warsaw: Neriton, 2004); Lenore J. Weitzman, "Living on the Aryan Side in Poland: Gender, Passing, and the Nature of Resistance," in *Women and the Holocaust*, ed. Dalia Ofer and Lenore J. Weitzman, 187–222 (New Haven, CT: Yale University Press, 1998).

46. During the Holocaust, an "Aryan appearance" meant possessing certain physical characteristics: fair skin, preferably light and straight hair, eyes that did not "evoke sad-

ness," facial features that did not invoke associations with the Semitic stereotype, as well as emotional features that included an overall composure and confidence, and a particular way of carrying oneself.

47. Louise Gruner Gans, interview 40851, Visual History Archive (online), USC Shoah Foundation, Los Angeles, 2013; Max Pelton, interview 38075, Visual History Archive (online), USC Shoah Foundation, Los Angeles, 2013.

48. "Trzecie rozporządzenie o ograniczeniach pobytu w Generalnym Gubernatorstwie," *Verordnungsblatt für das Generalgovernement*, no. 99 (October 25, 1941).

49. Knowing particular escape routes, confidently treading on the Aryan side, familiar with the map of the city, and possessing connections in the city, Jewish child smugglers became sought out as suitable smugglers of not just goods, but also of other children.

50. Jack Geizhals, interview 7863, Visual History Archive (online), USC Shoah Foundation, Los Angeles, 2013.

51. Pearl Benisch, *To Vanquish the Dragon* (Jerusalem: Feldheim, 1991), 171.

52. Max Pelton, interview 38075, Visual History Archive (online), USC Shoah Foundation, Los Angeles, 2013.

53. Amy Hauer, interview 9628, Visual History Archive (online), USC Shoah Foundation, Los Angeles, 2013; Esther Stuhl, interview 1243, Visual History Archive (online), USC Shoah Foundation, Los Angeles, 2013.

54. Mordecai Paldiel, *Sheltering the Jews: Stories of Holocaust Rescue* (Minneapolis: Fortress Press, 1996), 115.

55. Ligocka, *The Girl in the Red Coat*, 19.

56. George Eisen, *Children and Play in the Holocaust: Games among the Shadows* (Amherst: University of Massachusetts Press, 1988), 119.

57. "Testimony of Jerzy Aleksandrowicz," in Śliwowska, *The Last Eyewitnesses*, 6–7; Julian Aleksandrowicz, *Kartki z dziennika doktora Twardego* [Pages from the diary of Dr. Tough] (Kraków: Wydawnictwo Literackie, 1983).

58. Roman Polanski, *Roman* (New York: Morrow, 1984), 34.

59. Ibid., 34–35.

60. Testimony of Leah Bladberg-Muskatenblut, YVA [Yad Vashem, Jerusalem], 0-33/1801, quoted in Felicja Karay, *The Women of the Ghetto Kraków* (Tel Aviv, 2011).

61. Henryk Zvi Zimmerman, *Przeżyłem — Pamiętam — Świadczę* (Kraków: Baran i Suszczyński, 1997), 157.

62. Celina Rose, interview 42011, Visual History Archive (online), USC Shoah Foundation, Los Angeles, 2013; Tosia Gringer, interview 28313, Visual History Archive (online), USC Shoah Foundation, Los Angeles, 2013; Klapper-Karpiński, "My Nanny" in Gutenbaum and Latała, *Children of the Holocaust Speak*, 107–109.

63. "Testimony of Janek Weber," in Bluglass, *Hidden from the Holocaust*, 71.

64. Janina Pietrasiak, interview 22050, Visual History Archive (online), USC Shoah Foundation, Los Angeles, 2013; Janina Pietrasiak, "I Am One of the Lucky Ones," in Gutenbaum and Latała, *The Last Eyewitnesses*, 197–207.

65. Ligocka, *The Girl in the Red Coat*, 27.

LENORE J. WEITZMAN

RESISTANCE IN EVERYDAY LIFE

FAMILY STRATEGIES,
ROLE REVERSALS,
AND ROLE SHARING
IN THE HOLOCAUST

What happens to family roles and functions in conditions of extreme stress, such as the Holocaust? In theory, the family is one of the most effective social structures for withstanding external assaults because it has a built-in system for taking care of its members, especially those who are younger and weaker. Ideally it provides for the physical, economic, social, and emotional well-being of its members: a place to live, financial security, normative guidance, social status, and unconditional acceptance and love.

In his classic book *The Family*,[1] sociologist William J. Goode theorized that these basic functions of the family are incorporated into the concrete actions of individuals through social roles. Those who occupy a specific status within the family — as a mother, father, son, or daughter — learn to adopt the social roles for their status.[2] Thus, for example, in the typical Jewish family in Eastern Europe in the interwar period, it was assumed that a husband would be the "head" of the household, the family's moral authority, and that he would be responsible for financial support of the family. His wife, in contrast, would focus on homemaking and child care (although she might also help out in the family business — or even run it if her husband was devoted to Jewish scholarship).

How did Jewish families try to maintain these basic family functions during the Holocaust and, more specifically, in the ghettos? After reading hundreds of diaries, memoirs, and testimonies, I concluded that most families adopted a collective strategy of pooling their skills and resources to protect each and every member of the family, especially those who were most vulnerable and who could not have survived on their own.

What surprised me was that instead of trying to maintain their prewar roles and responsibilities, the most effective mechanisms for families to implement this collective strategy appeared to be for them to engage in two forms of role reversals: reversing the prewar roles of husbands and wives, and reversing the prewar roles of parents and children. In fact, it appeared that families who were the most flexible in erasing the traditional dichotomy between the roles of husband and wife, and between the roles of parents and children, were those who were the most successful in coping with the constraints in the ghettos and who were most able to adapt and respond to trying conditions and challenges. We therefore begin examining family strategies by looking at these two types of role reversals: those between husbands and wives, and those between parents and children.

However, I soon found that role reversals explain only part of what was happening in many families. When we look at their experiences in more detail, which we do by focusing on one family in the third section of this chapter, we find much more fluidity and creativity in the type and rapidity of role changes that occur. For example, there is often more "role sharing" than a complete abandonment of old roles or a complete assumption of new roles. In addition, changes in roles are often nonlinear so that one member of the family might assume another's role, then share it, and then abandon it—before assuming it again. Finally, this case study shows that different components of a single role can vary independently, such as when a father is no longer the breadwinner but is still the moral authority and recognized head of the family. While there is always some fluidity in roles in normal situations, the shifts described in the case study that follows are, as we shall see, more extensive and more of a departure from a normal role set.

In the last section of this chapter, I discuss the larger impact of these family coping strategies and how they explain previously misunderstood aspects of the Holocaust.

HUSBAND-WIFE ROLE REVERSALS

When one considers the systematic targeting of Jewish men in the early days of the German occupation of Poland, and the very real threats men faced when they ventured outside of their homes—harassment, humiliation, physical assault, arrest, and even murder—it is easy to understand why men would want to avoid being outdoors during daylight, and why their wives would take on many of their husbands' prewar roles, such as providing for the family and representing the family outside the home. In fact, it became common for women to leave home during the day to stand in line for bread, trade personal belongings for food, petition the *Judenrat* (the Jewish Council) for permission to retrieve personal belongings from their confiscated homes, and organize the repair of damaged businesses.

As Emmanuel Ringelblum (1900-1944), the noted historian of the Oneg Shabbat underground archive in the Warsaw ghetto, wrote in his diary:

Men don't go out. . . . She stands on the long line. . . . When there is need to go to Aleja Szucha [the Gestapo] the daughter or wife goes. . . . The women are everywhere . . . [Women] who never thought of working [out of their homes] are now performing the most difficult physical work.[3]

Adam Czerniakow (1880–1942), chairman of the Warsaw *Judenrat*, also wrote about the increasingly assertive role that Jewish women were assuming in public space.[4] His diary describes how these fearless women would argue with the Germans who came to confiscate family belongings or to take their husbands to forced labor. Czerniakow even recounts the different techniques that women used to convince the Germans. He was impressed by their tenacity and observed their fearlessness in exposing themselves to danger.

One of the most important roles that women assumed was their husband's prewar responsibility for financial support of the family. We are indebted to the Israeli historian Dalia Ofer for introducing us to the invaluable source for following women's efforts to assume this role, the work of Cecilia Slepak, the journalist and translator whom Emmanuel Ringelblum commissioned to undertake research on the experiences of women in the Warsaw ghetto.[5] Ofer reports that in early 1942 Slepak interviewed sixteen women representing a diversity of prewar statuses.[6] She found that each one showed a remarkable determination to support her family. Because the survival of their families often depended on their ability to become the provider, they not only sought out "conventional" jobs, such as engaging in a trade or working in a ghetto "shop," but when these were not available, the women were willing to pursue less conventional paths and invent ad hoc ways to support their families. Some, for example, took up the dangerous "occupation" of smuggling and had to escape from the ghetto to trade on the "Aryan side." Relying on their ingenuity, they renewed past contacts and exchanged clothing, jewelry, and linens for food and other scarce resources.[7]

PARENT-CHILD ROLE REVERSALS

The second type of role reversal common in ghetto families was when children assumed their parents' prewar responsibilities for providing food, leadership, and emotional support when their parents were barred from or unable to perform these roles. Consider two examples from interviews I conducted with children who became family breadwinners.

Hasia Bornstein (Bielicka), a young woman who gradually assumed her father's prewar role of provider, lived in Grodno, a city near Białystok that was part of Poland between the First and Second World Wars (and is now in Belarus and known as Hrodno).[8] Her father owned a small soda factory, and they were comfortably middle class. When the Nazis marched into Grodno on June

22, 1941, Hasia, who was born in 1921, had just finished a sewing course sponsored by ORT (Russian Obshchestvo Rasprostraneniya Truda Sredi Yevreyev, the Organization for Rehabilitation through Training), a Jewish organization devoted to providing Jews with the skills and vocational training they need to secure practical jobs. Five months later in November 1941, when Grodno's Jews were forced into the two split ghettos, Ghetto One in the Old Town suburb and Ghetto Two in the Słobódka suburb, and had to leave behind anything they could not carry, Hasia carried her sewing machine and a few items of clothing.[9]

It proved to be a wise choice. Because her father was cut off from his factory and his means of earning a living, and because her family lost their savings, their home, and all their possessions when they were forced into the ghetto, only Hasia had the means to earn money to help her family survive. Like many young people in the Grodno ghetto, Hasia was conscripted into forced labor for the Germans and was sent to work in a German-owned brick factory. There were also some non-Jewish Polish workers at the factory who found out that Hasia could sew, and they asked her to do some mending for them in exchange for food. The only time Hasia could work for them was late at night, after a full day's work at the factory. But it was worth it; they paid her with bread and cabbage, which she could then smuggle into the ghetto for her family. Since there were great food shortages in the ghetto, and since only young people like Hasia who worked received any food during the day, the rest of Hasia's family was always hungry. They urgently needed the food from Hasia's sewing.[10]

The second example of a young person who took on his father's prewar role of family provider and breadwinner is David Efrati, who was a teenager in the Warsaw ghetto established in November 1940.[11] In the early days of the Warsaw ghetto, before being caught outside the ghetto became a capital offense for Jews, David's mother suggested that he sneak out to buy some food. His father had no work, and the family had nothing to eat. She thought David would not be identified as a Jew because he spoke "good Polish" (that is, fluent Polish that was grammatically correct and without a Jewish accent) and had the manners of a street-smart kid. That was because David had insisted on going to a Polish public school before the war, instead of the traditional Jewish *heder* his parents had wanted him to attend. Unlike his parents and sister, who spoke only Yiddish at home, David therefore spoke colloquial Polish without a Jewish accent thanks to his prewar schooling.[12] David thought of his mother's suggestion as a challenge and a lark, and he soon became a successful smuggler:

> I got some clothes that I could hide food in and it just looked like I was fat. I didn't always succeed and sometimes the police caught me. They would

take all my food and throw it away and beat me until I was bloody and throw me into the ghetto . . . But for me it was an adventure, and I became very successful.[13]

By the time he was sixteen, David had established a network of suppliers and smugglers and was supporting his family in a grand style. He was doing so well that his family could afford to buy chocolate in the ghetto, a rare luxury when people were starving to death, and his mother was able to distribute food to other relatives.[14]

A final example of a parent-child role reversal is provided by the well-known memoir (and feature film) *The Pianist*, by the Jewish Polish musician and composer Władysław Szpilman (1911–2000).[15] While his father retreated from the world by "playing his violin for hours on end," Władysław assumed many of his father's former roles by trying to watch over and take care of other members of the family.[16]

WHAT IS MISSING? FLUIDITY, CREATIVITY, RAPID CHANGES, AND ROLE SHARING

While these examples illustrate the effectiveness of these two types of role reversals, a closer examination of individual families suggests that the concept of role reversals is too simplistic to describe the rapidly changing, fluid, and complicated role shifts that occurred.

For example, roles were often *shared*, rather than being truly reversed. Because restrictions and opportunities were constantly changing, it was more common for a man to share the provider role with his wife or children, rather than to relinquish it completely.

In addition, the pattern of role changes was not always linear—that is, it was not always from a husband to his wife, or from a parent to a child. Instead it was often cyclical or reversible or inconsistent and might move in one direction and then in another.

It is also evident that the definition of various family roles was often reformulated to include or to emphasize different responsibilities. Thus, it is too simplistic to refer to "the role of *the* mother," or *the* father, because various components of that role varied independently. For example, a father who was unable to support his family might still retain his role as the family's strategist, moral authority, and "decider."

In addition to noting these rapidly changing, fluid, and nonlinear shifts in roles, and in addition to the possibilities of role sharing and parsing out different components of a single role, the following analysis is complicated by the possibility of a discrepancy between a person's behavior and the social label that was attached to it. In fact, because people were so attached to the normative expectation that they fulfill their role obligations, it was evident that individuals were likely to label their behavior as consistent with their idealized view of their role, even though an observer might see the very same behavior as a major change.

For example, when Dalia Ofer examined the accounts of the women in the Warsaw ghetto who were interviewed by Cecilia Slepak, Ofer described the women as setting aside conventions and assuming new roles to support their families. According to Ofer, these women were embarking on uncharted territory. However, as Ofer noted, the women themselves viewed and explained their behavior as a continuation of their traditional roles as wives, mothers, and daughters, emphasizing their duty to sustain their husbands, children, and parents.[17] For example, a woman might talk about her involvement in smuggling as if it were a "normal way" to provide food for her children. By labeling her activities as part of conventional "mothering," she did not have to explain her willingness to engage in unconventional and dangerous activities.

A final complication arises from the fact that resources and contributions to the family were typically pooled. Therefore, the social definition of what one contributed might be the result of one's status or position in the family, rather than the true measure of one's contribution.[18]

In addition to these complications in analyzing behavior in a "stable" family, the composition of the family itself was often changing in the ghetto as individual family members became sick, died, were captured for forced labor, or were deported.[19]

Before examining these fluid role adjustments in a single family, one brief note on methods is in order. When I began this study of family coping strategies, I started out by making a long list of families I knew about from reading diaries, memoirs, and testimonies and by conducting my own interviews. I decided to focus on Eastern European ghettos (thus eliminating Western Europe, where there were no ghettos) and to eliminate places where the ghetto period was less than several months. I then applied a "thought test" to the families on my list. At first, the instances of role reversals were most prominent. However, as noted above, when I examined individual families more carefully, more complex patterns in role adjustments emerged. It therefore seemed heuristically useful to scrutinize role changes in a single family and to use a published text that would allow the reader to examine and analyze this material with me.

ROLE SHARING AND ROLE SHIFTS
SARA SELVER-URBACH'S LODZ GHETTO MEMOIR

Through the Window of My Home: Recollections from the Lodz Ghetto, by Sara Selver-Urbach, is a chronicle that underscores the overwhelming forces arrayed against the survival of any single family in the ghetto.[20] But it is also a chronicle of a family that consistently adopted a collective strategy to care for and save those who were or became weak, sick, or disabled.

While it is impossible to know if this family was "typical," I chose it primarily because it provides what the anthropologist Clifford Gertz referred to as "thick description" — that is, a full and detailed narrative of the individuals and their collective experiences — which enables us to track the dynamics of role adaptations in a single ghetto family.[21]

Sara's memoir begins with her prewar family life: her father was a bookkeeper and proficient in English, German, Russian, Polish, and Yiddish. But more important than his occupation, and above everything else, was his passion for studying *Torah*. Though he was forced to earn a living, he dedicated every free moment to his studies.[22] As she wrote:

> The rhythm of his life was determined by his Judaism which was the very essence of his existence. . . . We children especially enjoyed father's *zmirot* — special songs chanted on the Sabbath. His singing and soulful melodies surrounded us by day, lulled us to sleep at night, and enveloped us anew when we woke up in the morning.[23]

Sara describes their standard of living as "not plentiful, but they never lacked essentials." There was a clear division of labor between her mother and father, with her father solely responsible for the family's economic support. As she wrote:

> Father alone carried the heavy burden of breadwinner, mother's help being limited to encouraging his endeavors. Father was thus compelled to work very hard, but we children never noticed it, because the mood at home was cheerful and happy. The father we saw was always ready to either joke with us or hold "serious conversations" which infused us with pride and a sense of "maturity" and increased importance. As children and like all children, we did not probe beneath appearances, including the few shadows that we noticed, yet misinterpreted or misunderstood. We listened to father's comforting singing when sick, delighted in his fascinating "tales" about Josef and his brothers, Hannah and her seven sons, etc.[24]

"We children" refers to Sara and her older brother, Fulek, her three younger brothers, David, Leizer, and Yankush, and her younger sister, Branulka. Sara's mother is described as a "beautiful and totally feminine woman, . . . but also a modern woman with a college education who loved reading and going to the movies."[25] Her love for her husband was "truly boundless" and he returned her love fully.

Sara's idyllic portrait of life before the German occupation is completed by her enthusiasm for school. She was always an excellent pupil and attended a

Bais Yaakov school, a network of primary and secondary schools established to provide Orthodox Jewish girls with a first-rate education.

As soon as the German army took over Lodz in early September 1939, family roles begin to change with what looks like a classic parent-child role reversal.

The family's first problem was getting food. When their supplies ran out, Sara's older brother, Fulek, "whose blond hair and fair eyes lent him an 'Aryan appearance,'" set out for Kalisz, in western Poland, where her mother's family owned a grocery store. He returned with supplies and further assumed the role of family provider by standing in lines for bread (from which Jews were barred), protected by his non-Jewish looks.[26]

The family lived "in perpetual fear" of the terror that surrounded them — the constant kidnapping of Jews for forced labor, with those who returned from the labor coming home battered and bleeding; targeting Orthodox Jewish men on the streets for humiliation, beatings, and ripping off their beards; and assaulting Jews at home, with soldiers marching into private apartments to terrorize the occupants and confiscate whatever they fancied. But Sara's parents believed they did not have the money or resources to escape, and they resigned themselves to staying in Lodz.[27]

When the winter of 1940 arrived "with its snows and piercing cold," they could not afford to heat their three-room apartment and had to move into a single room. Sara described the days as "bleak and filled with anxiety." Sara's father was attacked on the streets and had his beard cut off. But he tried to make fun of the whole incident and to retain his otherwise positive demeanor.[28] Adopting his perspective, Sara noted that he was "lucky," because they had not ripped out his beard as they had done with other Jews, who had also been forced to sing and dance while the German soldiers assaulted them.[29]

But Sara's mother showed signs of the physical strain: she lost weight and frequently had to lie down because of severe headaches.[30] In a double example of role reversals, Sara started assuming her mother's tasks in the home, and her father became her helper. She wrote: "I kept the house as best I could. On heavy wash days, father would don an apron during curfew hours and lend a hand."[31]

During this period, Sara's father was constantly trying to find work that would enable him to provide for the family. His first venture was to set up a home-based workshop for crocheting caps. He managed to find some wool, and they "knitted caps from morning to night."[32] Sara's brothers also learned to knit and helped out. While her father organized the production, they all shared the work.

By March 1940, Sara's family and all the Jews of Lodz were forced to move into the Lodz ghetto, the second largest ghetto in all of German-occupied Europe, after the Warsaw ghetto. Unable to find an apartment in the slum area designated for the ghetto, they squeezed into her grandfather's one-room apartment, shared with another aunt and her children.[33] They slept on the floor and "huddled together for warmth" because they were unable to get fuel. But despite these dismal conditions, Sara remembers her parents playing their traditional roles in leading the family celebration of the Jewish festival of Purim, with her father and grandfather singing and cursing Haman (the villain) and enjoying all the double meanings of the curses (applied to Hitler), and her mother, grandmother, and aunt somehow finding the ingredients to prepare cookies and sweets.[34]

But these memories of Purim were bittersweet, because it was to be her father's last Jewish holiday with the family.

After Purim, her father resumed his role as the family leader-provider by finding them a one-room apartment of their own and starting a new business as an illegal smuggler. As Sara wrote:

He began sneaking out of the ghetto, at high risk, to trade with Poles.

At that time, the Ghetto was not totally cut off. Some contacts still continued with the outside world, as well as some vestiges of trade with the Poles. Father . . . managed to sneak out at dusk with a bundle hidden under his clothes . . . and sell all sorts of embroidery silks.

He was almost caught once (and) his face grew more and more haggard from day to day. Mother helped him as much as she could. In those matters, she was bolder than father . . . ingenious and resourceful, and could improvise schemes and escapes from predicaments on the spur of the moment.

Father (continued to poke) fun at things . . . and made us laugh at the absurdities in our new circumstances. But his bright, intensely blue eyes reflected his anxiety . . . and dread for the future.[35]

Two weeks later, Sara's father came down with influenza, which developed into pneumonia. Despite her mother's efforts to nurse him, he died. The entire family was terrified and devastated.[36] As Sara wrote:

Mother was crouching over him, sobbing her heart out, dazed with grief and almost unrecognizable. "Oh, how I am shamed! How I am shamed!" This lament that my mother kept repeating was meaningless to me at the time. It was only much later that I understood how vulnerable and exposed to disgrace and mortification a woman can become when bereft of her husband.

Though reality was staring at us terrifyingly from the floor, we were unable to grasp that this appalling thing had really happened to us, that our father would no longer talk to us, be with us, care for us, protect us, sing to us, encourage us.[37]

Sara described a family so numbed by grief that they were "incapable of exerting the energy and vigilance required by the growing hardships."[38] Sara felt as if her "mother also died," even though her body was still there, and she continued to feed her children.[39]

But Sara believed that her mother never felt any hunger herself:

> Throughout the long years of starvation, mother was never hungry. Literally. . . . as though nothing could affect her physically. Since father's death, she was plunged in a state of dazed torpor which made her insensible to all physical needs and requirements. She undertook any number of activities in the hope of increasing a little our scanty diet, and would not be deterred from her purpose no matter the efforts or inescapable humiliation. And yet, it was evident that her thoughts and feelings were focused on one single person—father. Her life was over; it ended with father's. Since his death, she merely existed, and this solely for us.[40]

The next shift in family roles occurred in the summer of 1940 after the death of the father, when a dysentery epidemic spread through the ghetto, and everyone in Sara's family became ill. At first, when her older brother Fulek got sick, Sara's mother nursed him day and night. But when her mother and the youngest sister, five-year-old Branulke, fell ill, the other children assumed that role. A visiting doctor saw that their efforts were inadequate and insisted that their mother be sent to the hospital. The children were left alone at home to nurse Branulke, who was soon diagnosed with pneumonia. For several days she struggled between life and death: as Sara held her in her arms and tried to infuse her with her warmth and vitality, her brothers recited psalms to pray for her recovery. But she died in the arms of her fourteen-year-old brother David and left her brothers and sisters in a state of utter despair, "numb with pain."[41]

The children were not allowed to visit their mother in the hospital because she suffered from a contagious disease, and they were terrified that she too would die. At the same time they were also terrified of telling her about Branulke. How could they tell her she had died in their care?

There was no joy when their mother did return from the hospital, just fear and the dread of telling her: when she realized what had happened, they all broke down into uncontrollable sobbing and fell into each other's arms.

Despite their tragic failure in assuming their mother's role as the family's caretaker, the children were forced to continue in that role and nurse their mother, who was still ill, when she returned from the hospital. In addition, because she could not assume the provider role of her former husband, the children became responsible for obtaining food as well. But they were not very good at it, and the family was soon on the verge of starvation. As Sara wrote:

Mother's recovery lasted a long time . . . We were in dire circumstances . . . (because) we did not know how to force our way, a very necessary skill in those days. Somehow we always found ourselves at the tail end of the queue, and when the supply was limited, we were among those who came away empty-handed. Mother was quicker and smarter than we, and knew how to get around, not with brute force but thanks to her keen astute mind. But she was still bedridden and would get up for one hour a day to test her strength.[42]

Fortunately, Sara's older brother, Fulek, who was then working at the ghetto post office, received a large portion of soup at work, along with some grits and potatoes. He filled the void by bringing some of it home to share with the others.

At this point, there were family arguments about the roles and responsibilities of the children. Sara's mother wanted the seventeen-year-old Fulek to assume his father's role—especially his role as the family's spiritual leader on Shabbat. But Fulek, who was involved in a nonreligious youth movement in the ghetto, disagreed and showed his reluctance to observe the Shabbat and other Jewish holidays. As Sara wrote: "In his youthful enthusiasm, he—like all young people—considered his ideas superior to everything else, and our home played only a secondary role in his eyes."[43]

Sara also yearned for a "normal" life of her own. She had become involved in a group of Orthodox girls, B'nos Agudas Yisroel, guided by an inspiring teacher and mentor. She also had a new best friend, who shared her enthusiasm and hunger for learning.[44] Some of the clashes between Fulek and his mother became daily fights and developed into ugly arguments and quarrels. She chastised him for neglecting his younger brothers and sister by spending all of his after-work time on his youth movement activities. Although she asserted her authority as their parent, Sara's mother was disabled by her sickness, and her effectiveness was visibly diminished. It was with considerable shame, in hindsight, that Sara wrote about how her children "ganged up" on her:

> Mother was so defenseless against our rude tongues. Full of youthful arrogance, we dared teach her how children ought to be raised, dared analyze to her the psychological causes for her behavior, had the audacity to claim and prove that she was in the wrong. And mother would often face us helplessly, cut to the quick, a childlike despair in her imploring eyes, with no father to stand up for her, to thunder at us and silence us. There was no longer a father whose mere presence would have prevented us from "lecturing" our mother on such topics. And so we threw off every rein, and mother could not restrain us.[45]

But not long after this phase of what appeared to be a complete breakdown in family solidarity, Sara's mother regained her strength; and sometimes in the summer of 1940, she opened a small vegetable store in their apartment, selling the meager produce from a large ground-floor window. While her children were not particularly enthusiastic and hampered their mother "by acting like stupid snobs because it never occurred to us that mother was sacrificing her own dignity in an effort to improve her ungrateful children's material circumstances,"[46] nevertheless, some people stopped to buy something and once again, the family had some food to eat.

The most significant improvement in the family's material circumstances occurred two months later, after the family's shop failed, when a wealthy neighbor, who was handicapped, hired Sara's mother to shop and cook for her—and paid her generously. In addition, there was leftover food that she could take home so that everyone in the family had something to eat. Their mother was once again the primary breadwinner. While their newfound good fortune was tinged with some "shame at eating leftovers," their mother's practicality won out, and she once again assumed the authority and leadership of the family.

From here on we see a family with an effective and forceful parent-leader: they coped collectively and met each ensuing crisis successfully. For example, they always had problems keeping themselves and their clothing clean because they did not have any hot water for washing, nor any fuel to boil water. Nor could they afford to pay for electricity. In the winter their room was so cold and damp that icicles hung in the corners.[47] Their inability to wash themselves and their clothing reached what they defined as an embarrassing crisis when they started to itch and found lice in their clothes. David, who always had a technical knack, came up with a solution by rigging up illegal electricity and "fabricating an electrical gadget that could warm and even boil water."[48] Then they were able to carry out a big cleaning operation and keep themselves, their clothing, and the apartment clean.

Sara wrote that the spring of 1941 was the happiest time of her life, "no matter how incomprehensible that might sound."[49] With her family back on a relatively firm footing, Sara was freer to enjoy being eighteen, spending Sabbath mornings with her friends, often accompanied by her beloved teacher, under a solitary tree studying and taking in the spring air. Sara and her new best friend, Haya Gutterman, a kindred soul who shared her love of learning, talked about their innermost feelings about life and love, and their profound and sincere faith.[50]

Some of the pressure on the family was reduced because the children were working and were fed lunch at work. Sara had a very good job in the storeroom of Glazer Clothes, where David worked in electrical appliances, and Leizer and Yankush worked in the carpet department. Fulek worked at a youth farm in Marysin, the section of the ghetto where all the youth movements were based.[51] Only their mother could not find a job and was in a precarious position as a target for deportation because everyone in the Lodz ghetto was required to work.

But her children somehow managed to get her a work permit and averted another potential crisis. It was Fulek who secured the valuable card that meant the difference between life and death: the card verified her employment, even though she did not actually have to go to work. As Sara explained: "One needed pull for such an arrangement, and this was one very rare occurrence where our family profited from Fulek's connections."[52] It was not only a major feat for Fulek, but also reflected the fact that he was once again fully attached and dedicated to his family.

In addition to family cohesion, it is evident that their mother's power, authority, and leadership were, once again, firmly established. For example, at one point she decided to use the money she earned to pay for Sara to have lessons in Latin, German, and world history.[53]

While this must have been a strain on family resources, it signaled her ability to determine how family resources would be spent. In addition, it probably reflected her new awareness of the importance of Sara's lessons and her sons' involvement in underground political activities in combating the apathy that overcame many in the ghetto.

At another point, when her son David contracted pleurisy, she made the previously unimaginable decision to bring nonkosher horse meat into the house—just for David. Sara wrote about how difficult that was for observant Jews:

> We never brought meat into our house (before then) because the miserly amount that we were allotted was non-kosher; either pork or horse meat. But when David fell ill, mother determined that we had reached a crucial stage and should start using non-kosher meat. At first, only David ate this meat, and we kept two separate kitchens, one kosher and one not kosher. At the end of a year, however, we found it very difficult to observe punctiliously every rule of *Kashrut*, and as the two other boys started showing symptoms of ill-health, we gave in and ate the non-kosher meat.[54]

This level of family cooperation and coordination was also palpable in the winter of 1942, when a typhoid epidemic swept through the ghetto. Each of them "fell ill, one after another, suffering fits of violent shivering."[55] Although it was primarily their mother who "was beside herself with worry and overwork, nursing us night and day," each of them nursed each other in turn.[56] Later on, when their mother became seriously ill, they mobilized to help her and secretly traded their own rations for food they thought would help her. As Sara wrote:

> Mother was ill and had become so emaciated that it frightened me. The two of us slept together in the same bed and I was aware of [her] thin and protruding bones. . . . Mother always gave us part of her rations, and when we refused to eat her food, she would say that she did not need all of it since she had stopped growing long ago. The reasons she invented were amusing . . . (and she persuaded us). Now that mother lay ill, we knew we had to give mother some of our food. Mother fought us on this issue, but we managed to save up a loaf of bread, secretly, and I traded it for a small amount of butter [which they believed would help her recover].[57]

In retrospect, however, Sara berated herself for this "futile achievement," and bemoaned her inability to be more effective in helping her mother because she was not like others who managed to unearth extra ration cards and get help from "protectionists" in the ghetto. But even if Sara was correct, and even if others "could" have done more, that does not undermine our analysis about the depth and strength of her concern and commitment to her mother. If anything, the depth of her guilt underscores the analytic point.[58]

The most dramatic example of the family's coordinated effectiveness in a crisis occurred in the *Gehsperre* (*Sperre*), a massive, terrifying *Aktion* and roundup of over fifteen thousand Jews, mostly children under the age of ten, the elderly, and the infirm, for deportation between September 5 and 12, 1942. At that time the Germans demanded a comprehensive and strictly organized series of inspections to separate the strong and healthy workers from those deemed "unproductive"—children, elderly, and sick, who would be deported to the Chełmno death camp. At first lists were compiled, but then the Germans took over and went from door to door taking anyone who looked unfit.[59] Sara and Fulek were terrified that their mother, David, and Yankush looked too weak to pass the inspection, so they decided to hide them from the Germans:

> (First) Fulek came running home to warn us that a group of ss troopers was approaching. We hurried mother out of the house because she was skinny and looked unhealthy. She hid with a relative who lived on a street which, so it was assumed, the Germans would not inspect on that day. Our two sick boys, David and Yankush, were taken by wonderful Mrs. Goldman, whose kindness I shall never forget. She hid them in a secret recess in her attic and locked them in. . . . and dragged a cupboard so that it screened the whole wall, including the locked door.
>
> And then, Fulek, Eliezer and I went home and waited. They came. "*Alle*

raus! Everybody out!" their roar rent the air. We went out into the court-yard, trembling . . .⁶⁰

[After they each passed inspection and the Germans left, they stumbled upstairs and opened the locked door with trembling hands.]

The boys were . . . ashen faced, petrified with fear, but alive! It is truly a wonder how they managed to stifle their sneezes and coughs during those fateful moments . . . We all burst out crying, and Mrs. Goldman gave us some water because we were on the verge of fainting.

[Their mother returned later, having to slip furtively through the sur-rounded streets . . . and] we burst into renewed tears [that we] remained together . . . (and were) saved from the Germans' clutches.⁶¹

After these events, Sara realized that they had experienced a fundamental change in their relationship with their mother. They once again appreciated everything she had done for them and "her tremendous spiritual courage." They bonded with her in "a close, precious relationship which enabled us to discuss everything with her as freely as we wished."⁶² They saw that she, in turn, "understood and empathized" with them, and "shared so fully in our frustration at the waste and loss of our youth, she now allowed and forgave our every whim, letting [each of us] look for our own individual solace and support."

They also gained a new appreciation for her strength and bravery in the final days of the ghetto. As Sara wrote, "Mother withstood everything. . . . When the regular distribution of rations was cut off entirely, mother would get us a loaf of bread by standing on a number of queues simultaneously and rushing from one to the other, regardless of the constant, deadly dangerous 'Aktions' that the Germans were conducting."⁶³ Even Fulek started spending more time at home because "home had suddenly become the most treasured place on earth for us."⁶⁴

Months before their momentous decision to leave the ghetto, Sara observed that "It was as though we sensed that our end was growing near and were cherishing the final moments we were given to spend with her. . . . [I]t was so wonderful to feel that we could get close to her, that we could cling to her love and understanding."⁶⁵

In the end, in the summer of 1944 when the final liquidation of the Lodz ghetto began on June 23, they made their final collective decision as a fam-ily. By then, Sara wrote, life in the ghetto had descended into total chaos: no rations were distributed, all public services had stopped, people were forced to loot the stores for provisions, and it seemed as if only the strong managed to get any food. They were scared by the rapidly deteriorating health of their mother and the younger boys, and they knew that the ghetto was "about to be liquidated": "We shivered with fright, fearing the horror that was about to befall us in the coming liquidation."[66]

When Fulek suggested that their only hope was to hide in a bunker with his friends, they "recalled the still vivid horror of the *Sperre*" and were terrified. Because they were sure that nothing could be worse than what they were facing in the ghetto, they decided, unanimously, as a family, that they would leave the ghetto on the next transport—to be "resettled." They had no idea of what awaited them on the trains, and no idea that only Sara would survive Auschwitz.

CONCLUSIONS

I conclude with two observations.

First, with respect to the theory, examining the coping activities in Jewish families during the Holocaust has allowed us to broaden the sociological model of maintaining family functions through "role reversals" in four respects.

First, we observed considerable role sharing when parents did not relinquish their role as the family authority but nevertheless shared their responsibilities with other members of the family. When Sara's mother became ill, the older children took on many of her parental roles, such as getting food, cleaning the home, taking care of younger children, and planning a family strategy, but their mother still retained considerable power and authority as the head of the family.

Second, we observed many examples of role shifts that were nonlinear, in which different family members were breadwinners and nurturers at different points in time. For example, early on the role of family breadwinner passed from the father to the eldest son, Fulek, when he was the only one who could stand in line for bread. But then their father resumed his role by organizing the family to crochet caps and by sneaking out of the ghetto to trade with Poles. After the father's death in the early summer of 1940, Fulek again assumed the provider role by sharing his daily soup, but then their mother became the main provider first with her vegetable stand and next with her work for their rich handicapped neighbor.

Along the same lines, we saw their mother's prewar role as nurturer and caretaker shift—first to Sara, the oldest daughter, and then to everyone else, as each nursed and cared for the others who became sick. The caregiver role shifted back to their mother when she recovered, and then once again back to the children when she became ill again. Thus, roles shifted from one person to another, depending on who was able to provide food and care, and who was incapacitated. The shifts were not all in one direction: there were many back-and-forth shifts over time.

Third, we noted that each role, such as that of parent, had several components, and each of these could vary independently. Some remained fixed, others were shared, and still others were lost. For example, if we think of the initial role of Sara's father, the three most important components of his role were providing religious leadership, economic support, and emotional sustenance. As long as he was alive, he continued to be the family's religious leader and the father who sustained them emotionally with his optimism and upbeat interpretation of events. For example, when his beard was cut off, he defined himself as "lucky" that it had been cut off—and not ripped off—by the Germans. However, he shared the breadwinning component of his role: at times it shifted to Fulek, and at other times everyone in the family contributed their labor to the family "business," even though he was usually the one who organized and directed their work. Finally, we saw many roles, such as those of provider and caretaker, that were taken on collectively and did not remain the responsibility of a single individual. The best example of this family's collective action was during the *Sperre*, the terrifying mass roundup for deportation in September 1942, when everyone played a role in their collective planning and activity.

My second conclusion is more controversial: Many observers have commentated on the importance of the Jewish family during the Holocaust. This chapter illustrates how and why it was important: the family protected and sustained the weaker members of the family—and gave them a chance to survive.

Obviously, the measure of the success of the family cannot be that everyone survived. We know that survival as a family was virtually impossible. So the measure of family success must be the extent to which family members were willing to forgo the exclusive pursuit of their own self-interest in order to support or care for or sustain other members of their family. My reading of the literature is that most family members were engaged in collective caring and sharing, even if they did not ultimately survive.

These activities of Jewish families during the Holocaust allow us to explain a previously enigmatic fact about Jewish survival in the ghettos prior to their liquidation: the fact that there was such a large discrepancy between the anticipated death rate and the actual death rate of Jews in the ghettos. How did so many Jews manage to survive the draconian conditions in the ghettos when it was assumed that many more of them would die? I believe that the reason why so many Jews were able to stay alive can be traced directly to their strong family bonds, collective strategies, and to the "rescue operations" undertaken by hundreds of Jewish families.[67] Consider, for example, how many members of Sara's family would have starved to death, or died from disease, if they had not been rescued by the other members of their family?

In fact, there was a time when every person in Sara's family would have starved to death if someone in the family had not shared his or her food with that person. In addition, there was a time when every person in Sara's family would have died of dysentery or typhoid or pleurisy if someone in the family had not nursed him or her back to health. It was only because the family took collective responsibility for rescuing and sustaining each person that six members of this family—Sara, her mother, and her four brothers, Fulek, David, Leizer, and Yankush—all survived more than four years in the ghetto instead of succumbing to starvation and disease. This collective response of the family—and their flexibility in assuming and changing family roles—not only illustrates the theory of family roles, but takes it one step further by showing the dynamic aspects of role shifts as successful coping mechanisms to rescue family members in extreme circumstances, such as during war and genocide.

NOTES

1. William J. Goode, *The Family*, 2nd ed. (Englewood Cliffs, NJ: Prentice Hall, 1982), 5. Goode showed that while the pattern of family relationships may vary—with tribal societies giving priority to extended kinship networks, in contrast to modern industrial societies emphasizing the nuclear family unit—the family serves the same basic functions in all societies. As the social unit for reproduction, the family provides for the physical maintenance of family members. It socializes and educates children, and provides social status for family members in the larger society. The family is an agent of social control that establishes and enforces norms for social behavior by defining what is socially appropriate in each society. In many, but not all societies, the family also provides unconditional love and affection for all family members, or at least it is supposed to do so.

Although Goode wrote about the worldwide diversity of family patterns, he noted that these basic functions are rarely separated from the family. Even though it would be theoretically possible to assign some of these family functions to other societal institutions, all attempts to do that—from the Republic that Plato envisioned, to the (real-life) experiments in Oneida and the Israeli kibbutz—either have not succeeded or not been implemented, or have gradually returned to more traditional family roles.

2. In all societies there is a division of labor in these role assignments, and in all societies role assignments are based on both gender and age (Goode 1982, 7).

3. This entry, written in 1940, is a quote from the 1992 Hebrew edition published as Emanuel Ringelblum, *Ketavim aharonim*, vol. 1 (Jerusalem: Yad Vashem, 1992), 51–52. An abridged version of Ringelblum's notes were published in English as *Notes from the Warsaw Ghetto*, ed. and trans. Jacob Sloan (New York: McGraw-Hill, 1958).

4. Raul Hilberg, R., Stanislaw Staron, and Joseph Kermish, eds., *The Warsaw Diary of Adam Czerniakow: Prelude to Doom* (New York: Stein and Day, 1979), 88, 92–93, 102–3, 122, 162–63, 184–86, 202, 204–5, 214.

5. Dalia Ofer, "Gender Issues in Diaries and Testimonies of the Ghetto: The Case of Warsaw," in *Women in the Holocaust*, ed. Dalia Ofer and Lenore J. Weitzman, 152–62 (New Haven, CT: Yale University Press, 1998); and Dalia Ofer, "Her View through My Lens: Cecilia Slepak Studies Women in the Warsaw Ghetto," in *Gender, Place and Memory in Modern*

Jewish Experience: Replacing Ourselves, ed. J. T. Baumel and Tova Cohen, 29–50 (London: Vallentine Mitchell, 2003).

6. Cecilia Slepak's research is preserved in the Ringelblum archive, ARI/49, Yad Vashem (YVA), Jerusalem, Israel.

7. Ofer, "Gender Issues in Diaries and Testimonies of the Ghetto"; and Ofer, "Her View through My Lens."

8. Hasia Bornstein, interviewed by Lenore J. Weitzman, June 14, 1994, Kibbutz Lahavot Ha Bashan, Israel.

9. Ibid.

10. Ibid.

11. David Efrati, interviewed by Lenore J. Weitzman, June 6, 1994, Jerusalem, Israel.

12. For further discussion of the importance of speaking Polish without an accent, see Lenore J. Weitzman, "Living on the Aryan Side in Poland: Gender, Passing, and the Nature of Resistance," in *Women in the Holocaust*, ed. Dalia Ofer and Lenore J. Weitzman, 187–222 (New Haven, CT: Yale University Press, 1998).

13. David Efrati, interviewed by Lenore J. Weitzman, June 6, 1994, Jerusalem, Israel.

14. Ibid.

15. Władysław Szpilman, *The Pianist* (New York: St. Martin's Press, 1999).

16. Ibid., 17–18, 43, and 91. Among the many examples that reflect his assumed responsibility for the whole family are his discussion of the impossibility of getting the vaccine for everyone (17–18) and the impossibility of getting six certificates for the entire family (91). This is not limited to Władysław; see, for example, the text on p. 71 about his brother Henryk.

17. Ofer, "Gender Issues in Diaries and Testimonies of the Ghetto"; and Ofer, "Her View through My Lens."

18. Ironically, the reverse was also apparent when some families saw and labeled something as a significant change, when an outsider, or at least this outsider, would not have labeled it in the same way. For example, many families attributed their survival to a specific contribution of food, such as when children augmented the family's resources by picking berries or mushrooms, or when a son or daughter sent a food parcel. This food was defined as "what saved the family" and "kept the family alive." See, for example, Henryk Grynberg, *Children of Zion* (Evanston, IL: Northwestern University Press, 1994), 93, 100. But an outsider might view that as attributing more credit to the mushrooms or food parcel than its actual value. I believe this discrepancy can be explained by the extra "marginal utility" of the food when it was received.

19. These upheavals also led to a pattern in which other social groups, such as the youth movements, assumed many of the functions of the family and became surrogate families. This is similar to women who adopted each other as "camp sisters" and formed surrogate families in the camps. In both instances, these surrogate families fulfilled some of the traditional family functions and sought to protect and sustain each other—even though the odds were stacked against them.

20. Sara Selver-Urbach, *Through the Window of My Home: Recollections from the Lodz Ghetto*, trans. Siona Bodansky (Jerusalem: Yad Vashem, 1986). It was originally published in Hebrew in 1964 as *Mi-be'ad le-halon beiti: Zikhronot me geto Lodz* (Jerusalem: Yad Vashem, 1964).

21. Other important portraits of life in the Lodz ghetto include: Michal Unger, *The*

Internal Life in the Lodz Ghetto, 1940–1944 [in Hebrew] (PhD diss., Hebrew University of Jerusalem, 1997); Michal Unger, ed., *The Last Ghetto: Life in the Lodz Ghetto, 1940–1944* (Jerusalem: Yad Vashem, 1995); Dawid Sierakowiak, *The Diary of Dawid Sierakowiak: Five Notebooks from the Lodz Ghetto*, ed. Alan Adelson and trans. Kamil Turowski (New York: Oxford University Press, 1996); and Sierakowiak, *Lodz Ghetto: Inside a Community Under Siege*, ed. Alan Adelson and Robert Lapides (New York: Viking, 1989), 320–21, 336–47; and Lucjan Dobroszycki, ed., *The Chronicle of the Lodz Ghetto 1941–1944* (New Haven, CT: Yale University Press, 1984).

22. Selver-Urbach, *Through the Window of My Home*, 16.

23. Ibid., 15.

24. Ibid., 18.

25. Ibid., 20.

26. Ibid., 32.

27. Ibid., 32.

28. Ibid., 33–34.

29. Ibid., 33–34.

30. For a more sequential understanding of Sara's mother, Malka Selver, see Lenore J. Weitzman and Dalia Ofer, "A Conceptual Framework for Explaining the Presence and the Disappearance of Traditional Gendered Behavior during the Holocaust," keynote talk presented at the International Conference on Gender in the Holocaust, Warsaw, Poland, November 2011; and Lenore J. Weitzman and Dalia Ofer, "The Sequential Development of Jewish Women's Coping Strategies (in the Ghettos) during the Holocaust: A New Theoretical Framework," in *Women and the Holocaust: New Perspectives and Challenges*, ed. Andrea Peto, Louise Hecht, and Karolina Krasuska (Warsaw: Wydawnictwo Instytut Badań Literackich PAN [Literary Institute of the Polish Academy of Sciences], 2015).

31. Selver-Urbach, *Through the Window of My Home*, 34.

32. Ibid., 35.

33. Ibid., 37.

34. Ibid., 40.

35. Ibid., 41.

36. Ibid., 42–43.

37. Ibid., 43.

38. Ibid., 44.

39. For a more extensive discussion of the difficulties of being a single mother in the ghetto and of motherhood more generally in the ghetto, see Dalia Ofer, "Motherhood under Siege" and "Cohesion and Rupture: The Jewish Family in East European Ghettos during the Holocaust," *Studies in Contemporary Jewry* 14 (1998): 143–65.

40. Selver-Urbach, *Through the Window of My Home*, 45.

41. Ibid., 49.

42. Ibid., 52.

43. Ibid., 54.

44. Ibid., 59. This hunger for learning was true in all the youth movements (64). The other children in the family were also finding their own way: David was a loner immersed in the study of Torah; Leizer joined the religious Zionist *Mizrachi* party.

45. Selver-Urbach, *Through the Window of My Home*, 55.

46. Ibid., 65.

47. Ibid., 67.

48. Ibid., 67.

49. Ibid., 73.

50. Ibid., 73. Her friendship with Haya Gutterman continued to sustain her through the hard times as well. For example, at the end of 1943, she wrote that "in those bleak days she (Haya) was my source of strength. . . . We studied the Bible together and tried to find in it the strength and the solace that would enable us to carry on" (ibid., 115–16).

51. Ibid., 69–70.

52. Ibid., 70.

53. Ibid., 68.

54. Ibid., 85, n. 9. In addition to the meat, the whole family cooperated in giving David richer, more highly nourishing food until he was feeling better (ibid., 86). A year later, when Fulek came down with pneumonia, they again pooled their resources to get him more nourishing food until he also recovered (ibid., 109).

55. Ibid., 86.

56. Ibid., 86.

57. Ibid., 109.

58. Even though Sara was too timid to offer the doctor "gift money" to induce her to visit her sick mother at home, and even though Sara felt "anger and shame at my impotence," the doctor came to see her mother anyway, and she prescribed some injections that helped (ibid., 110).

59. For other descriptions of the mass inspections and deportations of September 1942 in the Lodz ghetto, see the heartbreaking entry in the diary of Dawid Sierakowiak about his mother's deportation (*The Diary of Dawid Sierakowiak: Five Notebooks from the Lodz Ghetto*, ed. Alan Adelson and trans. Kamil Turowski (Oxford: Oxford University Press, 1996), 214–26. See also Lucjan Dobroszycki, ed., *The Chronicle of the Lodz Ghetto 1941–1944* (New Haven, CT: Yale University Press, 1984), 248–55.

60. Selver-Urbach, *Through the Window of My Home*, 95.

61. Ibid., 95–96.

62. Ibid., 119.

63. Ibid., 120.

64. Ibid., 120.

65. Ibid., 119–20.

66. Ibid., 121.

67. I am not arguing that the protection of the weak is confined to the Jewish family. As stated above, this is one of the universal functions of the family.

THE NATIONAL INSTITUTE FOR THE ISRAELITE DEAF-MUTE IN BUDAPEST, 1938–1948

A CASE STUDY FOR THE RESCUE STRATEGY OF CONTINUOUSLY OPERATING JEWISH COMMUNAL INSTITUTIONS

On January 18, 1945, on the day when the Red Army liberated the large ghetto of Budapest, about fifteen to twenty half-frozen, deaf-mute and blind children led by the director, Dr. Dezső Kanizsai, returned from the ghetto to the building of the National Institute for the Israelite Deaf-Mute.[1] One of these children was the then not yet eleven-year-old Izráel Deutsch. In his memoirs—which were set down in writing in English by his daughter, Eleanor C. Dunai (a specialist in deaf-mute education)—he described their liberation, that is, the moments when he realized that the Hungarian fascist Arrow-Cross men had disappeared from the ghetto:

> I went outside to join hundreds of other souls to sit and die. Everybody was quiet. We had come to terms and had accepted our fate.
>
> Out of nowhere, Russian soldiers began appearing in the ghetto. Each had a red star on his uniform. They were holding their guns pointed out in front of their bodies. The Jewish people, including myself, were on the ground in the middle of Klauzál Square [the main square of the ghetto].
>
> [. . .]
>
> Dr. Kanizsai gathered all of us and said we were returning to the institute. I wanted to run as fast as I could to get out of the zone, but I could barely walk. All around me, people were scrambling to leave, though some were too weak to move and stayed right where they were. The journey back felt like an eternity. My feet were frostbitten, and my head was spinning.[2]

How did these handicapped Jewish children survive the Holocaust in Budapest? Being both Jewish and handicapped, they belonged to not one but two categories of people that Nazi Germany aimed to completely eliminate. How were they able to survive the German occupation and the homemade fascist Arrow-Cross reign of terror?

Researchers of the history of Nazi Germany all agree that one of the first groups that the new Nazi regime wanted to eliminate was the one constituted by physically and mentally disabled people. On July 14, 1933, just a few months after Hitler rose to power, the Law for the Prevention of Offspring with Hereditary Diseases (*Gesetz zur Verhütung erbkranken Nachwuches*) was passed. This law, which came into force in January 1934, led to the sterilization of from 375,000 to 400,000 persons, who suffered from a hereditary illness or were mentally handicapped.[3] This number does not include those individuals who had been sterilized in the concentration camps.

In late 1939, Operation T-4, the so-called euthanasia program, began, which signified the systematic killing of mentally challenged people and sufferers from hereditary illnesses. The euthanasia program commenced with the murder of about five thousand physically and mentally handicapped children in 1939. They were either starved to death or given a lethal injection. In January 1940, adults were also subjected to the program. The large-scale murder went on in six killing centers equipped with gas chambers and crematoria. Even though Hitler officially discontinued Operation T-4 in August 1941 as a response to the public opinion in the Nazi Reich,[4] in reality, it was continued clandestinely during the entire existence of Nazi Germany. As a result, about 200,000 to 250,000 mainly institutionalized handicapped persons were murdered.[5]

In Germany, handicapped Germans were sent to the killing centers as a consequence of the report of their own physicians, teachers, and other caretakers. The majority of the people who were sent to the killing centers had been living in various state and church institutions, hospitals, or boarding schools. Horst Biesold was the first to research systematically the participation of the teachers of institutions for the deaf-mute in Germany in the sterilization of their students, and then, in their murder within the framework of the euthanasia program. Biesold's research demonstrates that heads of the institutions for the deaf (and mute) almost without exception served the Nazi regime by turning over the individuals, who had been entrusted to their care, to Nazi racial eugenics experts for sterilization and euthanasia.[6]

Interestingly, the Nazi regime persecuted handicapped Jews receiving care in German Jewish institutions chiefly for being Jewish and not for being physically and/or mentally challenged. The fate of the students of the Israelite Deaf (and Mute) Institute in Berlin (*Israelitischen Taubstummenanstalt*) clearly illustrates this point. Felix Reich—the son of the institute's founder, Markus Reich, a Bohemian Jew, who established it in 1873—was the director of the institute in the Nazi era. About fifty to sixty deaf-mute children studied there in the 1930s. Reich was able to leave Nazi Germany for London with the eight youngest pupils of the institute in August 1939. Then, as a result of the outbreak of the war on September 1, 1939, Reich was unable to get anyone else out from among his former students. The students of the institute were deported together with the Jews of Berlin in 1941 and 1942. Very few of them survived.[7]

THE NATIONAL INSTITUTE FOR THE ISRAELITE DEAF-MUTE IN BUDAPEST DURING THE HOLOCAUST

Antal Fochs, who died in 1874 and left a large part of his fortune for the establishment of the National Institute for the Israelite Deaf-Mute in his will, made it possible for the foundation school to be built in 1876. The institute accepted deaf and mute children from Hungary regardless of their religious affiliations. The institute functioned as a military hospital from the beginning of World War I until 1916. In 1926 the Neolog Jewish Community of Pest, which was responsible for maintaining the institute, united it with the Wechselmann Educational Institute for the Blind, founded by the knight Ignác Wechselmann and his wife, Zsófia Neuschloss. As a consequence of this fusion, in the autumn of 1928, the Institute for the Israelite Deaf-Mute moved to Mexikói Avenue, no. 60, where the Educational Institute for the Blind operated from the beginning of the twentieth century.[8]

In the interwar period, about forty to forty-five deaf and mute and five to ten blind children studied at the institute. The overwhelming majority of them were Jewish, but a few Christian children also received their education in the institute, which was maintained by the Neolog Jewish Community of Pest.[9] Dr. Dezső Kanizsai was the director from 1926 onward. He was born in 1886 and began to work at the Institute for the Deaf-Mute in 1907, after obtaining his diploma in special education for handicapped children. Kanizsai, together with his family, resided at the institute. Kanizsai's major field as a researcher was speech therapy, and he worked on special education methods for deaf children and children who are hard of hearing. In 1951, he became a professor at the Teachers Training College for Special Education in Budapest, where he headed the Speech Therapy Department until 1962. Kanizsai's work was internationally acclaimed, and his studies on the prevention and improvement of childhood speech impediments are still used by speech therapists.[10]

The overwhelming majority of the boarders of the Institute for the Deaf-Mute came from poor Jewish families with many children from the Hungarian provinces. The children typically did not receive any kind of education prior to arriving at the institution. Since they usually communicated with merely a few rudimentary, commonsensical signs with their families, when they became six years old and had to go to school, they were very far behind and knew only a few elementary things about their environment. Izráel Deutsch, whose memoirs I have already quoted, was born in 1934 as the ninth child of an Orthodox family in a small village in the sub-Carpathian region (*Kárpátalja*) called *Magyarkomját*. He lost his hearing in an accident when he was one year old. Accompanied by his mother, Izráel arrived at the Institute for the Deaf-Mute in Budapest in September 1940 for the second time. In September 1939, he could not start his studies because he was found completely unready even for the school's preparatory class. In his memoirs, Deutsch relates the trauma of being left at the institution in 1940:

> I was excited that I could visit Budapest again. However, I was still unaware of the real purpose of our trip. The communication between my family and me was still limited to body language. My voice conveyed only grunts, groans, moans, screeches, and laughter. My knowledge was acquired strictly from observations. I was able neither to express my full thoughts nor to ask any detailed questions. . . .
>
> [When they arrived, Kanizsai guided them through the school and then] they told me to sit out in the hallway while they spoke in private. . . . My mother came out of the office. She rubbed her stomach, which meant she needed to go to the bathroom. She told me to wait. What I didn't know was that Dr. Kanizsai had suggested she leave me in the corridor and then wait in his office.
>
> As soon as she walked away, one of the counselors motioned for me to come into his classroom, which was filled with children. I refused, indicating that I was waiting for my mother. The counselor again motioned for me to follow him. Again, I refused. He came toward me and gently grabbed a hold of my wrist, pulling me into the room with the other children. I had no voice to say no or to speak up for myself. I fought with the counselor, and he failed to get me into the classroom. Finally, a couple of counselors grabbed me and pulled me into a dorm room. I was screaming with a lion's voice. I could not scream words because I didn't know any. For more than an hour, I screamed like a lion. The principal was one floor below me. Apparently, he couldn't stand hearing my outcries. He came up to the dorm and grabbed me. He shook me, placing me firmly on the ground and telling me, "Shush! Shush!" He never smacked me, but as I continued to scream, he kept me until I finally calmed down. Then, the nurse came and gave me some pajamas. I was very upset and cried myself to sleep.[11]

This description is remarkable, as it shows both the well-meaning standard pedagogical methods at that time—such as making the mother leave without saying goodbye and promising to be back—and their thoroughly traumatizing effects on the children. The narrator's point of view concerning time is very complex, because he attempts to articulate from the present his experience of being left alone, which is, as all traumas are, timeless, and which occurred at a time when he had not yet acquired the capability to be articulate. An additional reason for me to quote this incident at length is that this utterly bewildering and unanticipated, and therefore traumatic experience of loss serves as a model for all the subsequent traumatic losses and insecurities that Deutsch experienced during and in the aftermath of the Holocaust. The memory of being abandoned at the institute and Kanizsai's role in it also explains Deutsch's ambivalent feelings toward Kanizsai, which otherwise would be utterly mystifying, since this ambivalence informs a Holocaust memoir that relates the story of how the director of the institute kept the children entrusted to his care together and made every effort to help all of them survive.

Deutsch's memoir recounts how quickly—similarly to the majority of the children who studied in the Institution for the Deaf-Mute—the special education provided by the school, which took into account both the needs and strengths of every individual pupil, produced dramatic results. At the end of the first school year, little Izráel, stepping down from the train, was able to greet his family members, and he learned many new words and expressions from them throughout the summer vacation.

At the end of the 1930s and the beginning of the 1940s, it became increasingly difficult for more and more Jewish parents to educate their children in specialized institutions. For parents who had lost their livelihood, having lost their professional licenses, jobs, or small businesses as a consequence of the (anti-)Jewish laws, paying for the fare to travel home and back was way too expensive. Little Izráel, for example, had to travel home alone by train—he had to change trains!—in the summer of 1941. The grocery shop that provided for his family was taken away by the Hungarian state, so they could not afford to pay for an additional train ticket.

After the first (anti-)Jewish law came into force, it became more and more common that children from the provinces could not travel home for every vacation. They usually traveled home only for the summer vacation. This burdened the school, as it had to take care of the children not only during the teaching periods, but also during the Hanukkah and Pesach vacations. The boarding school also had to entertain and teach the children by providing them with special programs during the vacations. Moreover, it was increasingly difficult for the Jewish Community of Pest to collect the tuition from parents who had lost their livelihoods. Among the documents of the Jewish Community of Pest, we find a great many sad and humiliating letters concerning tuition between the recently impoverished parents, the Institute for the Deaf-Mute, and the Jewish Community of Pest, which wanted to collect the money that the parents owed by legal action.[12]

Despite the difficulties, mostly financial ones, the institute functioned more or less unhindered until March 1944, when the German Army occupied Hungary. The realities of the war and the official policy of antisemitism had, of course, permeated the daily life of the school until then as well: some of the teachers, Director Kanizsai among them, were called up for forced labor service in the Hungarian army for various lengths of time. In the school year of 1942–43, antiaircraft battery no. 203 was stationed in the school. From December 18 to 23, 1942, during the winter vacation, forced labor company no. 110/26 was put up on the second floor of the institute.[13]

On March 19, 1944, the Wehrmacht occupied Hungary. In the yearbook of the institute concerning the month of March, we read the following enigmatically laconic "chronicle":

> On the 15th, on our national holiday, there was no teaching;
> On the 20th, we held a ceremony to commemorate the fiftieth anniversary of the death of Lajos Kossuth;[14]
> On the 31st, we concluded the school year as it had been decreed by the Hungarian Royal Minister of Religion and Education.[15]

Kanizsai did not mention at all in the yearbook that the German army occupied Hungary on March 19, 1944. The entry about celebrating one of the greatest Hungarian freedom heroes ever, of course, amounts to a statement against the Nazi occupation as well as to a passionate confession of a belief in Hungary and freedom. Kossuth also stood up for the Jews of Hungary on several important occasions; therefore, by honoring his life, Kanizsai also declared his deep-seated belief in the fruitfulness of the Hungarian Jewish coexistence, and therefore, in the value of a Hungarian-Jewish identity. Overtly the yearbook only says that the 1943–44 school year had ended on March 31, 1944, as a result of the decree of the minister of Education. The immediate consequences of the German occupation of Hungary for the Jews and their institutions had been, of course, much graver than that. It was not only the school year that ended in all of the Jewish schools in Hungary in March 1944. All of these institutions were closed, and the Jewish communities were dissolved. The German occupying forces, in close collaboration with the enthusiastic and efficient Hungarian authorities, started the preparations for the ghettoization and subsequent deportation of the Jewish population of Hungary.

In April 1944, the institute building became the police quarters and home for the paramilitary and premilitary youth organization "Levente."[16] Some of the students, those who were still able to board trains, went home. Since the overwhelming majority of them were from the provinces, they were deported with their families from May through July 1944. Those who could not leave for home, about thirty children, ended up in the nearby Orphanage for Boys of the (Neolog) Jewish Community of Pest (*A Pesti Izraelita Hitközség Alapítványi Fiúárvaháza*) at no. 25, Vilma királynő Avenue, in the Seventh District of Budapest.[17]

The children from the institution were put up in the orphanage, but they were given food only Monday through Friday. Therefore, it was imperative for the teachers to find accommodation for the pupils during the weekends. It was not an easy task, because the Hungarian government had issued a great number of anti-Jewish decrees from the end of March 1944, severely restricting every aspect of the lives of the Jewish community.

The first measure taken in order to physically separate the Jews from the rest of the society was a decree concerning discriminative marking (decree no. 1240/1944), issued by Prime Minister Döme Sztójay on March 31, 1944. According to this decree, from April 5, when not at home, every Jew over the age of six had to wear a canary yellow, six-pointed fabric star, ten by ten centimeters in diameter, sewn onto the left side of the upper part of his or her outer garment.[18] In addition to children under the age of six, there were other Jews who were exempt from wearing the yellow star, mainly those who had received medals in World War I.[19] On April 7, 1944, prime ministerial decree no. 1270/1944, restricting the movement of Jews, was published and immediately took effect.[20] The decree forbade Jews who had to wear the yellow star to travel or ship anything by car. Furthermore, Jews were allowed to travel by public transportation only with special travel permits issued by the police or the gendarmerie. According to the decree, the Jews of Budapest could travel by public transportation within the territory of the capital; but Jews were routinely stopped and ordered to show their identity documents, and they were interned if the smallest irregularity was discovered.

In spite of the difficulties, the teachers of the Institute for the Deaf-Mute, and the Blind tried to take care of their pupils. Ignác Kardos, for example, visited Jewish families one after the other in the Seventh District of Budapest, which was densely populated by Jews, in order to find accommodation and dinner invitations for the deaf, mute, and blind children living in the orphanage during the week. He succeeded: each child had a place to go for the weekends.[21]

In May 1944, however, the orphanage was directly hit during an air raid. The children survived in the shelter, but the building became uninhabitable. Deutsch described the event:

Hundreds of planes crowded the sky. We all evacuated the building, heading directly to the bomb shelter. . . . I watched as the counselors instructed the hearing children to place their hands over their ears and hold them there while keeping their mouths open. We deaf children followed exactly what the hearing children were doing.

The building began shaking like we were having an earthquake. Then, the big bomb came with a direct hit to our building. Each floor came collapsing down, floor by floor, to the ground level. The lights flickered.

Pushing and shoving, we panicked, trying to exit the building. I made it to the staircase, crawling up toward the door. The cloud of dust made it impossible to see. I felt my way up to the building's main floor and continued to crawl upward until I made it out to the yard.[22]

A new location had to be found for the children. In the chaos following the bombing, a few children wandered alone in the streets and individually sought a place for themselves. Deutsch was among them. A Jewish family with one child took him in. He spent two weeks with this family, when his favorite teacher, Aunt Sári (Mrs. Dr. J. Pogány, born Sarolta Balkányi), came for him and took him to the Balkányi family villa in Buda. Aunt Sári's father, an economist, and brother, a banker, were prominent Jewish plutocrats. As such, they were so-called "exempted" Jews, whom Regent Miklós Horthy, taking into account their pivotal role in the Hungarian economy, exempted from falling within the anti-Jewish laws. Deutsch lived with the Balkányis until August 1944. Then, however, the family decided that it was too dangerous for them to hide the Jewish child any longer, since from the middle of June 1944, Jews, apart from the exempted Jews and forced labor servicemen, had to live exclusively in the so-called "yellow-star houses" (houses marked with the yellow star of David).[23] Therefore, Aunt Sári escorted the child back to Pest, to the institute,[24] where Deutsch met again the majority of his schoolmates. The teachers had led the children back to the institute after the bombing of the orphanage. In addition to the children initially in Kanizsai's care, the Jewish children who had been ousted from the National Association to Assist the Blind (Vakokat Gyámolító Országos Egyesület) and the National Home for Handicapped Children (Nyomorék Gyermekek Országos Otthona) were also taken to the institute.

Soon after the return of the bombed-out children, in June 1944, the institute became part of an internment camp that was established by the Gestapo. More than 3,600 Jews were interned in the camp. Dr. Kanizsai became responsible for all the handicapped children there.[25]

The beginning of the story of how the former Institute for the Israelite Deaf-Mute, and the Blind became an internment camp dates back to 1943. It is an integral part of the famous and controversial rescue operation called the Kasztner train, which until the present day elicits extremely strong emotions.

In Hungary, a number of Zionist groups formed the Rescue Committee of Budapest (Budapesti Mentőbizottság, the Vaadah) in January 1943. Ottó Komoly, the president of the Hungarian Zionist Alliance, became the president of this new organization, and Rezső (Yisrael) Kasztner, a Zionist leader (lawyer and journalist) who moved to Budapest from Transylvania in September 1940, became his deputy. The Vaadah set three goals for itself: to save Jewish lives by smuggling Jews through the borders of Hungary, to assist Jewish refugees in

Hungary, and to prepare for Jewish self-defense. After the occupying German forces arrived in Hungary, the main objective of the *Vaadah* became simply to save the Jews of Hungary. In order to attain this goal, the leaders of the *Vaadah* immediately began negotiations with ss officer Dieter von Wisliceny, and from May onward, with Adolf Eichmann. The Kasztner train rescue operation was the result of these negotiations. In May 1944, Kasztner offered five million Swiss francs' worth of jewelry and cash in exchange for the lives of a hundred thousand Jews. As part of the negotiations, certain Jews from various ghettos were taken to Budapest as future passengers of the train. First, 388 Jews from the ghetto of Kolozsvár (today Cluj-Napoca, Romania; Kasztner's birthplace) were taken to Budapest on June 10, 1944. They were placed in wooden barracks built at the courtyard of no. 46, Columbus Street, previously the Institute for the Deaf-Mute. The institute became part of the internment camp, which was guarded by ss soldiers.[26]

The passengers of the train were Jews selected by the *Vaadah* and the Central Council of the Hungarian Jews in Budapest (*Magyar Zsidók Központi Tanácsa*), but the final list was altered by von Wisliceny, who supervised the deportations. The Kasztner train finally left Budapest on June 30, 1944, with 1,684 passengers; the train arrived in Bergen-Belsen on July 8, 1944. Among them were many prominent Jewish personalities: political and community leaders, scientists, artists, Zionists, as well as Jewish refugees from Poland and Slovakia. The train traveled through Vienna and Linz, arriving in Bergen-Belsen on July 8, 1944. The passengers of the Kasztner train were placed in a new camp: the so-called *Ungarnlager* (Hungarian camp).[27]

The situation of the Jews of Budapest suddenly changed for the worse when in October 1944, Regent Miklós Horthy (1868–1957) had tried to pull out from the war. The German answer was to help the coup of the extremist right-wing Hungarist Arrow-Cross party, under the leadership of Ferenc Szálasi (1897–1946). The unrestricted terror of the Arrow-Cross broke loose. Almost immediately following the Szálasi takeover on October 15, 1944, men between the ages of sixteen and sixty and women from sixteen to forty were assembled from the yellow-star houses in order to be taken to forced labor. Until October 26, about 25,000 Jews were gathered. At first, the majority of them were taken to work on fortifications around the capital and in various military factories. On November 6, 1944, the ill-famed death marches commenced; many Jews who had already been taken to forced labor or who had just arrived were marched on foot from Budapest to Nazi Germany. Those who survived the march and the work on fortifications at the borders were then taken to various concentration camps inside the Third Reich. The two ghettos—the so-called "little" or international ghetto[28] and the large ghetto: the ghetto of Pest[29]—were soon established in Budapest following the Szálasi coup. Armed Arrow-Cross bands frequently broke into the yellow-star houses and later into the so-called "protected" houses, as well as into the large ghetto and the Jewish hospitals. They rounded up the Jews and dragged them away. They also routinely rounded up Jews on the streets. Many thousands of Jews were murdered during the few months of the homemade Arrow-Cross terror. The majority of them were shot into the Danube by Arrow-Cross men.

The camp at no. 46 Columbus Street was not liquidated after the passengers of the Kasztner train had left. On December 3, 1944, Arrow-Cross men broke into the Columbus Street camp, which by then was under the authority of the International Red Cross. They dragged away about 3,200 Jews. The students of the institute who were fifteen years old or older were among them. Some of these people eventually arrived in the large ghetto of Pest, but many of them were taken on the death marches and perished. During the raid on the camp, the Arrow-Cross men murdered about seventy people on the spot. Leó Wachtenheim, a fourteen-year-old deaf student of the institute, was among them. Horror-stricken Izráel Deutsch described his death: Leó started to hurriedly make his way out of the institute to the street together with the others, in response to the orders of the Arrow-Cross men. He was doing what people around him were doing. When he was running down the stairs, an Arrow-Cross man shouted at him from behind to stop. The deaf youngster did not hear the order and continued to run. Seeing his "insolent disobedience," the Arrow-Cross man shot six times into the child's body.[30]

Concerning the December 3 Arrow-Cross raid on the Columbus Street camp, we have two contemporaneous testimonies that were taken down in the so-called "Glass House" (Üvegház) on the same day. The official name of the "Glass House" was the Swiss Embassy's Office for the Protection of Foreign Interests, Emigration Division (Svájci Követség Idegen Érdekek Képviselete Kivándorlási Osztály), after July 24, 1944.[31] It was protected by Switzerland, and various Zionist organizations worked there from the summer of 1944 onward.

The history of the rescue operation that was connected to the Glass House started when Regent Miklós Horthy forbade subsequent deportations of Jews from Hungary on July 7, 1944. Hitler, in response to that, decided on July 10 to allow the emigration of seventy-eight hundred Jews from Hungary, if the Hungarian government permitted the immediate continuation of the deportations. After Switzerland had offered to take in the emigrating Jews, the Hungarian government officially charged Swiss consul Carl Lutz and Miklós Krausz, who was the head of the Palestine office that was responsible for matters of emigration, to put together a list of seven thousand Jews. Lutz suggested the designation of a building near the Swiss embassy for the people on the list. No. 29 Vadász Street in the Fifth District of Budapest was chosen. Glass wholesaler Arthur Weiss had offered his own house for this purpose.

The building was given extraterritoriality as the Swiss embassy's Office for the Protection of Foreign Interests, Emigration Division.

The emigration office in the Glass House started to operate on July 24, 1944, and Krausz with Lutz began to put together the list; but they interpreted the seven thousand people as seven thousand heads of families. In the end, the group could not emigrate, but thanks to Lutz's initiative, thousands of Jews were able to survive the Holocaust in the Glass House and other buildings under Swiss protection. In addition, the Glass House became the center of the *Halutz* (Zionist youth) movements and rescue operations.[32]

The Glass House also functioned as a last resort for many Jews in the capital. Escaped forced laborers, Jews, who had fled from the ghettos or had been trying to pass as non-Jews but something went wrong, as well as survivors of the Arrow-Cross massacres, who were often wounded, made their way to the building. Many of them were taken in. From November 1944 onward, some of these escapees, especially survivors of massacres, dictated testimonial protocols concerning their experiences, which they just had survived. Therefore, the leaders in the Glass House had up-to-date reports from eyewitness survivors about all the aspects of the Arrow-Cross reign of terror: the massacres on the streets, Jews shot into the Danube, forced laborers, the death marches, Jews digging trenches in the vicinity of Budapest, the interned, and the ghettos. Among the collection of these testimonies, one can find two protocols that relate what happened in the Columbus Street camp on December 3, 1944. I am citing the more detailed one, which was dictated by two former inmates.[33] The other testimony given by one person[34] corroborates the information given by the testimonial protocol that I quote:

> Until today, we had been inhabitants of the Columbus Street camp under the protection of the International Red Cross. This morning at about 9 o'clock, a police officer, disregarding our protected status, came into the camp and went to the office. Then about 30 policemen entered the building and ordered the inhabitants of the camp . . . to take their most necessary belongings and line up in the yard within half an hour. When the policemen entered the building, one of them fired in the air.

The survivors continue their story:

> In the meantime, Arrow-Cross thugs surrounded the building and its vicinity. . . . The Arrow-Cross men took away the money and every article of value from everybody and then took everybody, except the handicapped, to the nearby κιsoκ-*pálya* (a sports stadium). Here, they separated the men from the women, and divided them into groups according to their age.
>
> Before dispatching [leaving for the κιsoκ-*pálya*], delegates of the Red

Cross appeared and handed a document to the police officer in charge. After a few minutes, the officer and the delegates of the R.C. [Red Cross] departed together by car. Seeing this, we started to have some hope, but our hope was soon extinguished, when the police officer came back and stated that everybody had to leave together with us, including those who were holding protective documents issued by neutral countries. They took away even the babies; the marching mothers were pushing baby strollers in the procession. Before we left, we heard a constant rattling of guns for about ten minutes. One of the policemen coming from the camp said in a loud voice, "These should be shot to death just like those had been." In all probability, they shot those to death who were hiding in the building or stayed behind. We left with the last group. Small children as well as sick and old people stayed behind (to march with this last group to the KISOK-pálya). They also had to march on foot all the way (to the KISOK-pálya). There was much crying, panic, and wailing in the group; children were searching for their parents who had been torn away from them and the elderly could not deal with the children. The people on the street (word by word translation: "the spectators of the streets") were indifferent; one could see by the look of the people that the sight of marching Jewish groups was a routine matter.

During our march, the skeleton staff (the guards) went to the back of the procession in order to keep an eye on those who were planning to escape, and they threatened everybody with being shot on the spot. One of us saw (the bodies of) two young men who had been shot dead at the gate of the KISOK-pálya. One of the policemen said: "That's what happens to anyone who attempts to escape." Many of us were harshly beaten with rifle butts.[35]

Some Jews, therefore, were able to escape and went from one place that seemed safe because it was under the protection of the International Red Cross to another place that seemed safe, the Glass House that was under Switzerland's protection. The fate of the handicapped children was different, as the previous testimonial protocol also mentions. After the break-in and the mass killing by the Arrow-Cross men, they remained in the almost entirely vacated camp for more than a week. Then, on December 12, the Arrow-Cross men took them, together with Kanizsai, to the large ghetto of Pest.[36] Izráel Deustch described their march from the camp to the ghetto:

Of course, none of us knew where we were headed. We were forced to walk six kilometers in the cold—not an easy undertaking with my one pair of rubber shoes. I had no socks or stockings, and I had to wrap my feet in towels and sheets. My feet were frostbitten, but I knew if I limped or took a short rest, I'd be shot. I continued on in the bitter cold.[37]

Kanizsai tried to keep the children together in the ghetto. They were starving, and because of the overcrowdedness and the lack of water and sanitary conditions in the ghetto, they all became infested with lice, and many of them became sick. All of them grew weak. The Red Army liberated them on January 18, 1945.[38]

THE INSTITUTE AFTER THE LIBERATION

After the liberation of the ghetto, the survivors returned to the institute, which they found in an awful state. It was completely plundered, badly damaged, and covered in dirt. The returnees had to try to make it livable. The International Red Cross and an American Jewish organization, JOINT, provided the children with food and clothing. The Neolog Jewish Community of Pest took on itself the partial reconstruction of the building and provided the institute with fuel. The Jewish self-relief organization, the National Jewish Relief Committee (Országos Zsidó Segítő Bizottság), replaced the necessary school equipment. Therefore, teaching could commence once again in the institute. At first, only Dezső Kanizsai and Sarolta Balkányi began to teach. Some of the other teachers retired, or went to work in another place. Two teachers did not survive the Holocaust: Ignác Kardos was murdered by Arrow-Cross men in Budapest, and Irén Strelisky perished in Bergen-Belsen.[39]

In the first school year after World War II, in 1945–46, four teachers taught in the institute, and only the director, Dr. Kanizsai, remained from among the former teaching staff. The majority of the students were boarders; and since the overwhelming majority of them had lost their deported parents, they lived in the institute during the summer as well. We do not have statistical data concerning the students in the first postwar school year, but in the next two years, twenty-three and twenty-seven deaf and mute pupils, respectively, studied in the institute.[40] Only two of them were not boarders. Thus, the institute operated after the war for a few years as an orphanage providing special education. This continued until the Communist regime, after coming into power, abolished many denominational institutions. The National Institute for the Israelite Deaf-Mute, and the Blind was among them. The year of 1947–48 was the last school year that the Jewish deaf and mute children could spend in the institute. Blind children were not studying there even then. After closing down the institution, various state institutions took in the children; and the older ones became independent, usually with the help of various deaf-mute clubs and other organizations.

CONCLUSIONS

Pre-Holocaust Jewish organizations and Jewish communal institutions which extended help — that is, the Foundation Institute for the Israelite Deaf-

Mute, and the Blind of the Neolog Jewish Community of Pest—and continued their activities during the Holocaust as well, when they attempted rescuing Jews, employed basically different rescue strategies from the ones employed by the Jewish self-help organizations that emerged during the Holocaust. The former organizations usually continued to care for and tried to rescue those people who had already been their charges before the Holocaust, unlike the newly formed organizations that had to define and redefine which groups or individuals they attempted to assist and/or rescue from among the great masses of Jews in response to the constantly changing circumstances. These extremely difficult and morally controversial decisions, which depended on various ideological convictions, genealogical characteristics, and cultural factors, were always the result of conscious deliberations. By contrast, the continuously operating institutions, such as hospitals, orphanages, and special schools, usually chose not to select a new group of people to help, but continued to assist those who had already been in their care. These institutions tried to devise rescue operations for their charges.

The Kasztner train clearly epitomizes the rescue operations established during the Holocaust. The list of the Jews to be rescued was put together and then several times altered by the *Vaadah* and the Central Council of the Hungarian Jews in Budapest. In the end, it was also altered by von Wisliceny, who supervised the deportations. Among the 1,684 Jews on the train, there were mainly Zionists and their family members, political and community leaders, as well as prominent representatives of the Jewish intelligentsia. There was one especially vulnerable group among the passengers: Jewish refugees from Poland and Slovakia. They were chosen because the members of the *Vaadah*, and the Zionists in general, thought that without knowing Hungarian and having no connections, they had no chance of survival. However, they constituted a small minority among the passengers, and many of them, in addition to being refugees, were also Zionists.

In contrast to the leaders of newly established self-help committees and organizations, the staff of Jewish help organizations that operated continuously before and during the Holocaust usually did not feel the burden of being called upon to select specific groups—that is, children, the intelligentsia, young people, people with special expertise—to rescue in order to ensure the survival of the Jewish people. Therefore, these institutions constitute a very special category within the history of Jewish self-help during the Holocaust: they rescued without selection those who had already been entrusted to their care before the Holocaust. In the case of the National Institute for the Israelite Deaf-Mute, and the Blind, the teachers of the institute with the leadership of Director Kanizsai aimed at rescuing deaf and mute and blind children, who probably would not have been selected as a group to rescue by any newly formed rescue organization.

NOTES

1. The full name of the institution was the National Institute for the Israelite Deaf-Mute and the Sir Ignác Wechselmann and his wife Zsófia Neuschloss Educational Institute for the Blind (*Az Izraelita Siketnémák Országos Intézete és a Lovag Wechselmann Ignác és neje Neuschloss Zsófia Vakok Tanintézete*).

2. Eleanor C. Dunai, *Surviving in Silence: A Deaf Boy in the Holocaust—The Harry J. Dunai Story* (Washington, DC: Gallaudet University Press, 2002), 63 (henceforth, Dunai, *Surviving in Silence*). After the war, Izráel Deutsch changed (Hungarianized) his name to Imre Dunai. Later, when he immigrated to the United States, he changed his given name to Harry. He communicated his memoir in English sign language to his daughter, and she took it down in English.

3. Sufferers of the following hereditary illnesses were to be sterilized: congenital feeblemindedness, schizophrenia, *la folie circulaire* (manic-depressive psychosis), hereditary epilepsy, hereditary St. Vitus's dance (Huntington's chorea), hereditary blindness, hereditary deafness, severe hereditary physical deformity, and severe alcoholism on a discretionary basis. See, for example, Henry Friedlander, "Holocaust Studies and the Deaf Community," in *Deaf People in Hitler's Europe*, ed. Donna F. Ryan and John S. Schuchman (Washington, DC: Gallaudet University Press and United States Holocaust Memorial Museum, 2002), 20–21.

4. For resistance concerning Operation T-4, see the case of Protestant clergy leader Paul Braune in Walters LeRoy, "Paul Braune Confronts the National Socialists' 'Euthanasia' Program," *Holocaust and Genocide Studies* 21, no. 3 (2007): 454–87.

5. On the euthanasia program, see Götz Aly, "Medicine against the Useless," in Götz Aly, Peter Chroust, and Christian Pross, *Cleansing the Fatherland: Nazi Medicine and Racial Hygiene*, trans. Belinda Cooper, 22–98 (Baltimore: Johns Hopkins University Press, 1994); and Patricia Heberer, "Targeting the 'Unfit' and Radical Public Health Strategies in Nazi Germany," in *Deaf People in Hitler's Europe*, ed. Donna F. Ryan and John S. Schuchman (Washington, DC: Gallaudet University Press and United States Holocaust Memorial Museum, 2002), 49–70.

6. Horst Biesold, "Teacher-Collaborators," in *Crying Hands: Eugenics and Deaf People in Nazi Germany* (Washington, DC: Gallaudet University Press, 2002), 42–83. See a copy of a questionnaire filled in by the institutions that ensured being selected for the euthanasia program, viz. to be killed, in Biesold, 66–67. (The filled-in questionnaire is from the Schleswig Provincial Institution for the Deaf, Schleswig, Germany, from June 1943.)

7. See the history of the Israelite Deaf-Mute Institution in Berlin (*Israelitischen Taubstummenanstalt*) in Horst Biesold, "The Fate of the Israelite Asylum for the Deaf and Dumb in Berlin," in *Looking Back: A Reader on the History of the Deaf Communities and their Sign Languages*, ed. Renate Fischer Harlan Lane, 157–69 (Hamburg, DE: Signum, 1993).

8. On the history of the institute in its yearbooks, see Dezső Kanizsai, *Az Izraelita Siketnémák Országos Intézete és a Lovag Wechselmann Ignác és neje Neuschloss Zsófia Vakok Tanintézete Évkönyve* [The yearbook of the National Institute for the Israelite Deaf-Mute and the Sir Ignác Wechselmann and his wife Zsófia Neuschloss Institute for the Blind]

(Budapest, 1938–1948); Ferencz Zsuzsa, *A Herminamező regénye*, accessed on April 7, 2016, http://epa.oszk.hu/01400/01434/00007/23.htm; and Dezső Kanizsai, *Az Izraelita Siketnémák Országos Intézetének Évkönyve, 1947–1948* (Budapest: Izraelita Siketnémák Országos Intézete, 1948), 1–2.

9. In the 1940–1941 academic year, for instance, thirty-six Jewish and five Roman Catholic boarders studied in the institute. In the 1943–44 academic year, there were thirty-six Jewish, three Roman Catholic, and two Calvinist boarders. See the relevant yearbooks.

10. See Kanizsai's biography, accessed on March 21, 2010, http://www.beszed.hu /kanizsai_dezso. His major works are *A gyermekkori beszédhibák megelőzése* (Budapest, 1954); *A beszédhibák javítása* (Budapest, 1955, 1961, 1968); *Elméleti fonetika* (Budapest, 1959); *Logopédia* (Budapest, 1960).

11. Dunai, *Surviving in Silence*, 13–14.

12. See, for example, Yad Vashem Archives, M.61. JM/28586, 2044–2113. (The original registered documents of the Neolog Jewish Community of Pest are kept in the Hungarian Jewish Archives in Budapest, PIH iktatott iratai, 1938/01096.)

13. Dezső Kanizsai, *Az Izraelita Siketnémák Országos Intézetének Évkönyve az 1942–1943 iskolai évről* [The yearbook of the National Institute for the Israelite Deaf-Mute for the school year of 1942–1943] (Budapest, 1943), 4–6.

14. March 15 is the anniversary of the 1848–49 Revolution and Freedom Fight. It is an official state holiday in Hungary. Lajos Kossuth was one of the leaders of the revolution and the subsequent freedom fight.

15. Dezső Kanizsai, *Az Izraelita Siketnémák Országos Intézete és a Lovag Wechselmann Ignác és neje Neuschloss Zsófia Vakok Tanintézete Évkönyve az 1943–1944. iskolai évről* [The yearbook of the National Institute for the Israelite Deaf-Mute and the Sir Ignác Wechselmann and his wife Zsófia Neuschloss Institute for the Blind concerning the 1943–1944 school year] (Budapest, 1944), 3–4.

16. This organization was formed in Hungary between the two World Wars and continue to exist during World War II.

17. Dezső Kanizsai, *Az Izraelita Siketnémák Országos Intézete és a Lovag Wechselmann Ignác és neje Neuschloss Zsófia Vakok Tanintézete Évkönyve az 1944–1945. iskolai évről* [The yearbook of the National Institute for the Israelite Deaf-Mute and the Sir Ignác Wechselmann and his wife Zsófia Neuschloss Institute for the Blind concerning the 1944–1945 school year] (Budapest, 1945), 1.

18. *Budapesti Közlöny*, no. 73, March 31, 1944. See the decree in its entirety in the following collection of documents: Ilona Benoschofsky and Elek Karsai, eds., *Vádirat a nácizmus ellen*, vol. 1 (Budapest: MIOK, 1958), 53–54 (henceforth, Benoschofsky and Karsai, *Vádirat* 1).

19. Finally, a decree published on May 13, 1944, decree no. 1730/1944 ME, defined the categories of exempted Jews. *Budapesti Közlöny*, no. 108, May 13, 1944. See the decree in its entirety in the document collection Benoschofsky and Karsai, *Vádirat*, 1:250–53.

20. *Budapesti Közlöny*, no. 79, April 7, 1944. See the decree in its entirety in the document collection Benoschofsky and Karsai, *Vádirat*, 1:127–29.

21. Dunai, *Surviving in Silence*, 43.

22. Ibid., 44.

23. According to the plans of the Hungarian and German authorities, the ghettoization and deportation of the Jews of Budapest would have been carried out after turning

the Hungarian provinces "*Judenrein.*" As the first step in the concentration of the Jews of the capital, the mayor of Budapest issued several decrees in June 1944 in order to designate so-called "yellow-star houses." These houses were established in all the fourteen districts of the capital, and from June 24, 1944, the more than two hundred thousand Jews of Budapest were compelled to live in them exclusively. In the end, more than two thousand yellow-star houses were marked for the Jews to move in. Those buildings became yellow-star houses in which more than 50 percent of the inhabitants were already Jews. Kinga Frojimovics, Géza Komoróczy, Viktória Pusztai, Andrea Strbik, *Jewish Budapest: Monuments, Rites, History* (Budapest: Central European University Press, 1999), 382–83.

24. Dunai, *Surviving in Silence*, 45–47.

25. Kanizsai, *Az Izraelita Siketnémák*, 1–3.

26. In the next few weeks, two synagogues in Budapest also became internment camps for privileged Jews (possible future passengers of the Kasztner train): one on Aréna Boulevard and another on Bocskai Boulevard.

27. From the moment when the Kasztner train left Budapest, the fate of its passengers depended on the negotiations between the Nazis and the Allied Forces that commenced in the second half of August. In a gesture intended to demonstrate the supposed change in their policies toward the Jews, the Nazis let the passengers of the Kasztner train leave for Switzerland in two groups. The first group, consisting of 318 people, arrived in Switzerland on August 21, 1944. The second group, consisting of 1,368 people, arrived on December 7, 1944.

Concerning the 1944 activities of the Vaadah, see Kasztner's 1946 report: Rudolph (Rezső) Kasztner, *Der Bericht des jüdischen Rettungskomitees aus Budapest, 1942–1945* (Basel, 1946); Randolph L. Braham, *The Politics of Genocide: The Holocaust in Hungary* (New York: Columbia University Press, 1994), 1069–1104; and Yehuda Bauer, *Jews for Sale? Nazi-Jewish Negotiations, 1933–1945* (New Haven, CT: Yale University Press, 1994).

28. The first ghetto, the so-called little or international ghetto, was set up in Budapest in November 1944, for about 15,600 Jews having protective documents issued by embassies of neutral countries or holding passports of those countries. The "protected" Jews had to move into apartments in which, until then, only 3,969 people had lived.

29. On November 29, 1944, Gábor Vajna, the minister of interior, issued the decree (no. 8935/1944. BM.) that ordered the establishment of the ghetto of Pest, or the so-called "large ghetto," for the Jews of the capital in the Seventh District, which had already been densely populated by Jews in the vicinity of the three grand synagogues: the Dohány Street synagogue, the Rumbach Street synagogue, and the Kazinczy Street synagogue. The Jews had to move into it from the yellow-star houses until December 2. The large ghetto, which was surrounded by a plank fence, was closed down on December 10. The ghetto had four gates oriented like the four points of a compass, guarded by Arrow-Cross men and policemen. Gentiles were forbidden to live or work in the ghetto.

30. Dunai, *Surviving in Silence*, 55.

31. Frojimovics, Komoróczy, Pusztai, and Strbik, *Jewish Budapest*, 408–9.

32. Asher Cohen, "The Halutz Resistance as a Revolt against Assimilation," in *The Holocaust in Hungary: Fifty Years Later*, ed. Randolph L. Braham and Attila Pók, 425–40 (New York: Columbia University Press, 1997).

33. Yad Vashem Archives, O.15H/181/14.

34. Ibid., O.15H/181/15.

35. Ibid., O.15H/181/14.

36. Kanizsai, *Az Izraelita Siketnémák*, 1–3.

37. Dunai, *Surviving in Silence*, 56.

38. Concerning the period between the closing down of the institute for the deaf-mute and liberation, see also: John S. Schuchman, "Hungarian Deaf Jews and the Holocaust," in *Deaf People in Hitler's Europe*, ed. Donna F. Ryan and John S. Schuchman (Washington, DC: Gallaudet University Press and United States Holocaust Memorial Museum, 2002), 169–201, and John S. Schuchman and Donna F. Ryan, "Deaf Survivors' Testimony: An Edited Transcript," in *Deaf People in Hitler's Europe*, 202–12.

39. Dezső Kanizsai, *Az Izraelita Siketnémák Országos Intézete és a Lovag Wechselmann Ignác és neje Neuschloss Zsófia Vakok Tanintézete Évkönyve az 1944–1945. iskolai évről* [The yearbook of the National Institute for the Israelite Deaf-Mute and the Sir Ignác Wechselmann and his wife Zsófia Neuschloss Institute for the Blind concerning the 1944–1945 school year] (Budapest, 1945), 1–3; and Dezső Kanizsai, *Az Izraelita Siketnémák Országos Intézetének Évkönyve az 1946–1947. iskolai évről* [The yearbook of the National Institute for the Israelite Deaf-Mute for the school year of 1946–1947] (Budapest, 1947), 1–3, 7.

40. See the data in the relevant yearbooks cited previously.

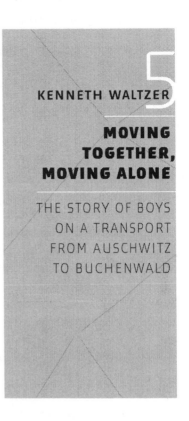

KENNETH WALTZER

MOVING TOGETHER, MOVING ALONE

THE STORY OF BOYS ON A TRANSPORT FROM AUSCHWITZ TO BUCHENWALD

On January 18, 1945, a large group of predominantly Jewish prisoners was evacuated from Auschwitz-Buna (Monowitz) and Birkenau and taken on a death march to the west. First, ten thousand prisoners were marched out in the frigid cold and snow for two days and nights toward Gleiwitz, a railhead and the site of several Nazi satellite camps. Prisoners too sick or exhausted to continue were summarily shot by ss guards along the roads. Then, at Gleiwitz, the Nazis loaded 3,935 surviving prisoners onto open coal cars and transported them to Buchenwald, a huge Nazi concentration camp near Weimar in Thuringia. The weather was so cold that some prisoners sat on frozen dead bodies as benches. According to Nazi records, the transport arrived January 26, 1945, with 3,784 prisoners. Of this number, 304 youths, sixteen years old or under, comprised about 8 percent of the human cargo.[1]

To better identify it, this transport brought Lazar (Eliezer) Wiesel from Auschwitz-Buna to Buchenwald. Wiesel, born in September 1928, from Sighet, in northern Transylvania, Romania, under Hungarian rule during World War II, was deported with his family to Auschwitz-Birkenau in late May 1944, and was selected for work with his father Abraham (Shlomo). He and his father slaved in Auschwitz-Monowitz (Buna) for seven months and now, with thousands of others, were being moved ahead of the advancing Red Army to Germany. Wiesel wrote about his ordeal later in a remarkable memoir, *Night*, which is known all over the world.

On arrival at Buchenwald, the prisoners were placed in large barracks down in the *kleines lager* (the little camp), a festering transit camp at the bottom of the Ettersburg hill on which the camp was built. Late in the war, Buchenwald functioned as a huge base camp and distribution center serving a far-flung expanding Nazi industrial slave empire. Prisoners were forced under harsh conditions of terror and privation to work digging tunnels, building shelters, making ammunition and antitank weapons, and helping in brown coal operations. Wiesel entered with his father, but Abraham soon died. The boy was then moved into a children's block in the little camp, block 66. "I was transferred to the children's block, where there were six hundred of us," he wrote in a single unelaborated line in his memoir.[2]

In total, some 223 prisoners from the transport (about 6 percent) were moved with Wiesel into the children's block. These included half the boys sixteen and under (150, or 49 percent), plus a few score slightly older "boys," eighteen or under. Among these were several older brothers permitted to stay with their younger brothers, such as Alex (Sandor) Moskovic and his older brother Zoltan from Sobrance, in the former Czechoslovakia, and Israel (Sruly) Stuhl and his older brother Vilmos from Akna Slatina, on the Slovakian-Romanian border. Many additional brother pairs, with individuals both above and below the age barrier, were in the *kinderbarrack*. Groups of unrelated boys functioning as surrogate brothers also were in the block.

The recent opening of the Red Cross International Tracing Services records long held behind closed doors at Bad Arolsen, Germany, now permits scholars to view the surviving records (transport lists, camp documents, etc.) and ask questions about and conduct microstudies of groups of prisoners, prisoner society, and everyday life in the camps. So too does the rich USC Shoah Foundation archive of survivor testimonies, with testimonies completed in the 1990s by many boys, now elderly men, from this and other transports. A major idea about prisoner society that appears prominently in classic memoirs about the camps, including by Primo Levi, which is restated in contemporary studies, including Wolfgang Sofsky's important *The Order of Terror*, is that prisoners were radically alone or became so in the camps. They comprised a coerced, seriated mass without solidarity or connection—they existed amid a deformed sociality.[3]

This large literature stresses that life in the Nazi camps approximated a war of all against all; prisoners were separate and apart, and social relations among prisoners were egoistic and pathogenic. The current essay is a preliminary working effort that seeks to explore this proposition for youths by closely studying the group of young prisoners who were on the same transport as Wiesel and, like him, were in block 66 or were housed elsewhere or sent from Buchenwald out to satellite camps. It is also an effort to fill out the larger social history behind Wiesel's narrowly focused tale in *Night*.

These were mostly Slovak, Hungarian, and Romanian Jewish boys, who had survived terrible family losses on entering Birkenau in late May 1944 and were in Buna under difficult conditions. Then, eight months later, they were in Buchenwald; and many were relocated to the *kinderbarrack*, while others were not. In this group of youths, there were surprisingly numerous social clusters—boys with their fathers like Elie Wiesel, boys with other boys, especially brothers or cousins, and boys with relatives or friends, often from the same towns. Many were acting out deep commitments, they say in their testimonies, to stay together and help one another under all pressures. Also, many were alone.

This microhistory asks in what ways these youths at Buna and Buchenwald were moving together and also moving alone during their tormented experiences. It shows how, focusing in a detailed way on a distinctive group within prisoner society, we can study the remarkable and diverse forms of solidarity that continued to coexist in prisoner society alongside separateness and aloneness among youths. In this case, we can also discover the fates of nearly all the boys on the transport—those like Wiesel who were in block 66, those who were not, and those who were sent outside of Buchenwald to the killing satellites.

DEPORTATION TO AUSCHWITZ-BIRKENAU AND TO BUNA

After Nazi Germany took control of Hungary in March 1944, Berlin detailed Adolf Eichmann to quickly organize the Final Solution of the Jewish Question commencing outside of Budapest. Under Eichmann's direction, hundreds of thousands of Slovakian, Hungarian, and Romanian Jews under Hungarian rule were quickly rounded up by Hungarian police and placed in makeshift ghettos, often in brick factories, located near rail lines. Then, a few weeks later, after they were robbed, beaten, and abused, the unknowing Jews were brought in family groups in closed cattle cars to Auschwitz-Birkenau, and most were quickly murdered by gassing. A remnant of this forced migration was selected under confusing conditions on the ramp, told to step right, shaved, disinfected, showered, and uniformed. Then, in a few days, most were tattooed and moved to Auschwitz III-Buna or other camps, where they were terrorized and exploited for months. Then, a remnant of this remnant was evacuated months later as the Red Army neared the Auschwitz complex.

Based on close study of the transport list, a large proportion of the boys under sixteen had entered Birkenau with their families from May 22 through May 31 and had undergone similar experiences mostly in Buna before the terror migration to Buchenwald. Most were from cities such as Ungvar, Munkacs, Nyirigyhaza, Huszt, and Akna Slatina and nearby towns and villages in Subcarpathian Ruthenia; or they were from Satmar and Sighet and nearby environs across the Tisa River in Maramures in Transylvania. A small minority (7 percent) were Polish from the Lodz ghetto and towns in the Radom district. A few (6 percent) were from Germany, France, and Holland, with one youth from Italy.

At Auschwitz-Birkenau, these boys suffered the shock of family losses on the ramp and, amid chaos and brutality, were inducted into a new modern slavery. Most got tattooed on their left forearms at Auschwitz I and then were brought by truck or marched to the I. G. Farben complex at Buna. KL Auschwitz III-Monowitz, built during 1941–42, became a Nazi *konzentrationslager* in November 1943; it was a huge camp and housed the headquarters of numerous additional camps. Thousands of prisoners worked here in synthetic rubber operations, making liquid fuels, and in construction, materials handling, and transportation activities. Boys sixteen and under, many of whom had been warned to lie upward about their ages by other prisoners at Birkenau, worked in labor *kommandos* hauling heavy concrete blocks to construct thirty-foot-high fire walls in the Buna warehouses. They worked digging ditches and repairing buildings and roads after frequent Allied bombings; carrying heavy cement sacks, stone, and wood; building air raid shelters; and loading and unloading equipment and materials. Some boys, like Elie Wiesel, were in barracks with adult men, such as fathers, uncles, or older brothers. Some boys were not with fathers or relatives, though, and several hundred boys were in barrack 44, a *jugendblock*.

Conditions were cruel and difficult at Monowitz (Buna), and the plight of the young prisoners was marked by beatings, terror, starvation, and exhaustion. There were dangers from work and starvation; there were also dangers from disease. Many boys recall periodic "hanging parades," where SS guards hanged young prisoners and required all prisoners to stand at attention and watch. Elie Wiesel described one such hanging in *Night* linked with his crisis of faith in the camps.[4] Other witnesses mention the same event; one volunteers that hangings took place nearly "every Sunday." Many boys also recall SS guards setting loose German shepherds to attack and tear the prisoners apart or SS guards cutting off young prisoners' ears if they failed to respond to commands in German. They also remembered periodic selections where, stripped to the waist, they paraded before SS doctors; and those less healthy or strong looking were selected to be returned to Birkenau and killed.

After a time in this universe, most boys knew well that they should keep themselves looking human and fit, walking erect, hiding any and all blemishes and sores, and that they must respond quickly to all orders, saluting and removing hats as required. The block elders and the *kapos* (overseers) in Buna were mostly German criminals with green badges and, like the SS guards, also treated the prisoners brutally. There was also a traffic involving children in the camp who were made "pets" of debased prisoner officials and shared their rooms at night. Wiesel remarked on this in his memoir.

A few examples will suffice to provide a sense of who these boys were, whom they were with, and what work they did. Alex (Yankele) Gross from Palanok, a village near Munkacs, was a fifteen-year-old prisoner with his brother Samu, who was older but looked younger; they were separated at

Buna but met again at Gleiwitz on the death march. Alex Gross recalled that he carried large industrial blocks and built cement fire walls in the warehouses; he subsequently dug ditches and hand loaded railroad cars and trucks. Alex and Sam were in separate blocks and saw each other infrequently, mostly at a distance. Years later, though, Alex recalled: "It was very important to me to know that someone else in my family was still alive."[5]

Chaim (Hersz) Grossman, from Huszt, was a boy who was alone. He initially worked building cooling towers and carrying heavy steel I beams, but later entered a *maurerschule* (a brick mason school), created by a German criminal *kapo* named Eddie, with many other boys. Ultimately, he worked carrying mortar and water in a brick mason *kommando* (work unit) constructing ss barracks outside the camp.[6] Alexander Berkowits (Avrum Srul Bercovics) was a fourteen-year-old from Sighet, Elie Wiesel's hometown. He was sent with other family members to a coal mine in Janinagrube, but was returned to Buna to the *jugendblock*, where he too learned bricklaying from Eddie and a German-Jewish assistant, Rudi. After that, Srulik worked as a brick mason, rebuilding bombed-out buildings and keeping small makeshift shelters against the weather warm for others in his detail.[7]

Zoltan Ellenbogen, a Hassid from Nyirbator, a border town in eastern Hungary, was also alone after losing his parents and siblings and was in *der jugendblock*. Ellenbogen linked up quickly with two older boys from his town, the Jakubowicz brothers, who had contiguous numbers with him, and all members of the trio looked out for each other. Ellenbogen counted nuts and bolts, and served as a *laufer* (messenger).[8] Samuel Jakubowicz (no relation), like Srulik Berkovics, was a seventeen-year-old from Sighet, was a friend of Elie Wiesel's, and also was in the boys' barrack. He recalls being marched to Buna, where he was taken "to a block of kids." He linked up there with a cousin.[9]

David Moskovic, a fourteen-year-old, also was in the youth block. Moskovic carried galvanized pipes and then trained as a bricklayer. Moskovic was part of a group of seven youths in the barrack, he recalled. "We were like a pack of wolves. We weren't scared of no man. We stuck together."[10] Simon Neumann from Vojnatina, Czechoslovakia, another fourteen-year-old, was also in the group. By sticking together, these youths helped themselves to more effectively organize resources and deal on the black market.[11]

Sam Cin (Samu Cin) was a fourteen-year-old from Huszt, from a large family with nine children. He wound up with his father and cousin in Birkenau, but he and his father were soon separated. He then linked up with his cousin Salomon Czen, a boy the same age from his town; both boys got contiguous numbers in Auschwitz I and were in the youth barrack in Buna. Cin and his cousin worked cleaning the barrack and then later building a factory. They got contiguous new numbers again when they arrived at Buchenwald as well; indeed, they were linked at the hip until the final two weeks before liberation.[12]

Israel (Sruly) Stuhl was a fifteen-year-old Vischnitzer Hassid from Slatinska Doly, in the former Czechoslovakia. He, his father, and two brothers were inducted into slavery together. All the Stuhl men and boys got contiguous numbers, but were spread out in Buna: Sruly's father was in one block; the older brother, Wolf (Vilmos) (seventeen), was in another; and Sruly and his younger brother, Ferencz (thirteen), were in the youth block. Sruly and Ferencz worked unloading paper from transports at Buna, and then Sruly was in a locksmith unit, where he became the "go-fer" for the group. Stuhl recalled frequent bombings at Buna, during which prisoners were barred from entering the air raid shelters they had built.[13]

Sigmund (Zsigismund) Weiser, a Hassid from Satmar, whose father was abroad in America, quickly lost his mother and siblings at Birkenau. Weiser recalled the remarkable fear and confusion he felt as they entered. "We were mostly women, children, and older men. The young men were in the Hungarian labor brigades. We were leaderless. . . . We didn't know."[14] Weiser saw prisoners shot; he saw naked women who appeared as utterly strange and foreign "creatures." He didn't know or understand any of what was happening initially. He wound up in Buna with several cousins, including Zisha, a boy his age. He worked digging ditches, filling up trolleys with dirt and emptying them. Later, like Chaim Grossman, he worked building houses for the s s outside Buna and lived in the youth barrack. When his cousin Zisha died in the hospital, Sigmund was left on his own.

Ted (Tibor) Gross, sixteen years old, also from Satmar, was initially with his father. He dug ditches for pipelines and then was in *Kommando* 90, a mechanical unit, one of the largest in Buna. Gross became the "pet" of a German criminal *kapo* named Karlin, an alcoholic. The extra rations Tibor got from work in the *kommando* and from Karlin he shared with his father.[15] Jakob Rozental, from Comlausa, in northern Transylvania, and sixteen years old, had been deported with his mother and five siblings from Sevlus, but he was alone in Birkenau. He recalled later with terrible shame that he had sent his younger brother Mordcha to his mother and hence to the gas chamber. In Buna, Rozental was also in *Kommando* 90 under Karlin, where he joined a boy from his town, Sam Izak.[16] The two youths were later paired on the march to Gleiwitz and the train to Buchenwald and remained together there in block 66.

Even Elie Wiesel, moving with his father, had links with other boys in his barrack and *kommando* at Buna. Wiesel wrote in *Night* of Tibi and Yossi, two boys from Czechoslovakia, who joined with Eliezer and his father in a work group in the electrical warehouse. These brothers "lived for each other body and soul," Wiesel observed, and "they quickly became my friends."[17] The young Zionist youths knew Hebrew songs, and the three boys spoke often about Palestine, vowing they would go there if they survived. Later, when Elie Wiesel was transferred to another barrack and was apart from his father, he was with Tibi and Yossi at a selection. Wiesel reported good news to his friends when he saw that the ss doctor failed to write down their numbers; the brothers then did the same for Wiesel.

Elie Wiesel was in a group of men and boys from Sighet when he was tattooed in Auschwitz I. Anton Meisner, another boy from Sighet, a year older than Elie, was in the same religious school class and had studied with the same rabbi. Anton recalled that he and his father, Maximilian, Elie Wiesel and his father Abraham (Shlomo), and others from Sighet were all together. But at Buna they were separated when they were placed in different barracks and given different work assignments. Anton Meisner and his father were in *Kommando 72*; they transported heavy machinery used to produce other machinery. Maximilian weakened under the harsh burden, and he died en route to Buchenwald on the transport.[18]

Alex (Sandor) Moskovic was a thirteen-year-old from Sobrance, near Ungvar, in Slovakia when he entered Birkenau. His father, Josef, and his older brother, Zoltan, were sent to Buna, but Sandor was kept behind with other boys in Birkenau. He was one of thousands of youths held in barracks 11 and 13 in camp BIId, possibly for medical experimentation, but after two months was tattooed and shifted to camp BIIa, where he was assigned to *Schiesse Kommando*. Alex worked with thirteen boys, all from the Carpathians, who determined they would stick together and look out for one another. They wore harnesses and pulled a large wagon into which others dumped garbage, moving regularly among Birkenau's multiple subcamps, accumulating goods in the women's camp and from several kitchens. Alex (Sandor) caught up with his father and brother only during the evacuation, at first failing to recognize them. At this point, Alex left his comrades—family loyalty trumped friendships—and rejoined his father and sibling. Like Wiesel's father, Alex's father, Josef, soon died at Buchenwald, and Alex and Zoltan transferred together into block 66.[19]

Three boys from Nagykarola at Birkenau were gradually separated from close family members and then determined to try to stay together as a group. Paul Kaszovitz, in America later called Paul Kassy, and Istvan Gutman and Imre Hirsch were schoolmates who took the same last name (Hirsch) in the camps. If they had the same name or numbers next to one another, they reasoned, they could stand together at roll calls. At Buna, Istvan Gutman was initially part of a *kommando* carrying cement bags for construction, then in a mechanical *kommando* indoors. Paul, Istvan, and Imre were first tied to others—Paul to an uncle, Imre to his father and brother. But then they were on the death march and the transport together, and they chose strategically to be together as fictive "brothers." Initially, they were in block 59 at Buchenwald, and then were moved to block 66. They shared the same barrack roost until the end and had contiguous numbers—no. 121480 (Imre), no. 121481 (Istvan), and no. 121482 (Paul)—in the Buchenwald numbering system.[20]

Finally, Lajos Weitzen and Gyulia Moskovics, neighbors in Ungvar who attended school together and who, after discriminatory laws shut down all education for Jews, were apprentice plumbers together, also linked up at Buna. Lajos Weitzen lost his parents at Birkenau and was in Buna, working in *Kommando* 26, carrying cement bags, and subsequently in *Kommando* 1, in an electrical warehouse. Gyulia Moskovics lost his mother and younger siblings, but was together with his father for a time; then they were separated and Gyulia was alone, cleaning pipes with a wire brush and carrying hoses. He and Lajos Wietzman got together after the loss of family members and as they came to Buchenwald, and then they were together in the new camp until after liberation.[21]

DEATH MARCH AND OPEN RAIL CARS TO BUCHENWALD

The death march from Buna that began on January 18, 1945, was an especially gruesome travail. The prisoners marched five abreast in the snow and ice in thin prisoner pajamas with wooden shoes. Alex Gross's barrack was the first to be led out. "The cruel wind howled and the snow blew in our faces, making it difficult to walk," he recalled.[22] Gross did not want to go, had no idea where the prisoners were being taken, and feared he would not make it; but he would not give up, hoping he would find his brother Sam, who was still alive and was marching too. Over time, Alex remembered, marching became increasingly difficult, as the ice built up on the prisoners' legs and marchers in front tamped down the snow, making it more and more slippery. Gross and others remembered the freezing cold and snow vividly. Sam Cin recalled, simply: "People froze." "They lay down on the ground, they collapsed; they were shot."[23] Gross remembered that the prisoners sometimes helped each other— Gross himself briefly carried another boy—but those who could not continue were shot by the Nazi guards and left where they fell. The bodies were thrown on military trucks and periodically buried in roadside ditches.

Many of the boys walked with someone they knew in Buna from before they entered Auschwitz. Sam Cin walked with his cousin Salomon Czen from Huszt. Jakob Rozental from Comlausa marched with his friend Sam Izak; Tibor and Wilhelm Berman, brothers from Munkacs, marched together. Tibor Grosz was with his father at this point; Lazar Wiesel, who was hobbled by a diseased foot, was still with his father. Anton Meisner walked with his father, but his father soon expired in the cars. Sruly Stuhl was with his father and his brothers Wolf and Ferenc. Alex Moskowicz reunited with his father and brother Zoltan. What seems most remarkable, a group of boys marched together with some older adults from Akna Slatina, all named Slomovics, eight prisoners total, all with contiguous numbers. The Slomovics stayed together at Buchenwald and were herded into barrack 59 with the three Hirsch boys from Nagykarola. Sol Culang (Szlama Zulang), a Polish Jewish boy from Warsaw who had been in Majdanek and Buna, marched with other boys with whom he'd schemed in the *jugendblock* to organize food.[24]

After Gleiwitz, conditions worsened. Prisoners were in open coal cars unsheltered from the elements on trains that—given Allied mastery of the skies—moved in fits and starts, hiding under overpasses, then moving with increased speed and purpose. The prisoners ate snow scooped from the sides of the cars: prisoners made snowballs and ate them like apples, Sam Cin said. Samuel Isakovich, another boy from Sighet, told David Boder, the American psychologist who interviewed survivors in France after the war: "Snow. . . . we ate the snow." "We didn't have anything else to eat."[25] The cars were full of the dead, and the living sat on the bodies. Sigmund Weiser recalled severe fighting among the prisoners on these "half trains," especially when passersby in Czechoslovakia threw bread and food down from the overpasses. Srulik Berkowicz also remembered the free-for-alls when food was thrown; he was small and knew it was best to lurk safely behind in the corners.[26]

Elie Wiesel recalled the march and transport in *Night*, telling of Rabbi Eliahu's son, who marched quickly ahead, abandoning his father, then of another son who stole food from his father. God seemed to be testing his chosen people, as God had tested Abraham and Isaac earlier. The journey was also a continuing test of the bonds that tied men together and kept them human. Wiesel wondered if he would pass the challenge.

> We received no food. We lived on snow; it took the place of bread. The days resembled the nights, and the nights left in our souls the dregs of their darkness. The train rolled slowly, often halted for a few hours, and then continued. It never stopped snowing. . . . Our eyes closed, we merely waited for the next stop, to unload our dead.[27]

Samuel Isakovich told Boder that the struggle for food on the train resulted in outright murder, confirming Wolfgang Sofksy's picture of a world of all against all. Isakovich told of one prisoner who used his wooden shoe to smash another "over the head," and the other prisoner simply "never used to get up anymore."[28] Wiesel too wrote about men hurling themselves viciously at one another, mauling each other, to possess crumbs of bread. "Beasts of prey, unleashed, animal hate in their eyes," he wrote.[29] But such radical Hobbesian behavior, as if the prisoners were in a precivilized state of nature, each against the other, was at the same time matched by continued strong small-scale solidarities — men and boys under extreme conditions sticking together as possible and doing what they could to help sustain a father, a brother, a cousin, or a friend.

On January 26, eight days after starting out, the prisoners arrived. Scores of dead bodies were left in the coal cars, and the surviving prisoners climbed down and entered KL Buchenwald. They assembled first on the *Appelplatz* (the location for the daily roll calls) inside the main gate to be counted, standing in fives. A veteran prisoner announced that they would be taken to the showers and issued clothing and then sent to the blocks. After a long time standing, during which Srulik Berkovics was beaten for stooping to gather snow, the prisoners were shaved, doused in disinfectant, and then — after a further long delay standing outside to complete camp questionnaires — they showered. After that, they received uniforms, were registered with new numbers and badges, and then were driven down into the *kleine lager*.

Startlingly, many of the prisoners who had been moving together in the concentration camp universe managed to obtain new Buchenwald numbers alongside one another — trace elements in the prisoners' personal documents of familial or friendship contiguity — and then to be placed in the same barracks together. Israel (Sruly) Stuhl and his brother Vilmos got contiguous numbers and were sent to block 51; Jakob Rozental and his friend Samuel Izak got numbers together and were also in block 51. Hersz (Chaim) Grossman was in block 51, so too was Samuel Iszakowics. Lazar Wiesel was temporarily separated from his father, who according to the transport list was placed in block 51; Lazar was with Samuel Jakobowicz from Sighet in block 57. Samu Cin and Salamon Czen got numbers together and were in block 58; Anton Meisner was there too. The three Hirsch brothers got three numbers in a row and were placed in block 59; so too were the Moskovic brothers, Alex (Sandor) and Zoltan, with their father.[30]

The initial assignments of the prisoners from Buna were all in blocks 51, 55, and 57–59, large barracks with multilevel bunks lacking straw or mattresses. The prisoners crowded in, fighting for space and knowingly coveting the higher-level roosts. Sigmund Weiser remarked about the sleeping arrangements in blocks 57–59: they were so tight that, "if somebody wanted to turn around, everybody had to turn around."[31] Included in the barracks were tough men from all over Nazi-occupied Europe, including large numbers of Ukrainians, Russians, and Poles, many of whom hated Jews; there were also Jews speaking many tongues who came from many different places. Little solidarity existed among the prisoners, and it was especially dangerous for youths in the large blocks, who were confronted repeatedly by bigger, older, rougher men. Daily the prisoners went to the line to the *kinohalle* (cinema building), where food was distributed, and then returned to the barracks. Most prisoners remained idle during quarantine, staying in their barracks or wandering in small confines, as the *kleine lager* was guarded and surrounded by barbed wire. Many older youths recall being put to work early in Kommando 53, the quarry. Later, some went to Weimar to clean up after bombings or were assigned to Kommando 20a, the wood yard.

The German communist-led international underground had created block 66 not long before the arrival of the transport from Buna. Antonin Kalina, a veteran Czech communist in Buchenwald since September 1939, was the block leader. Kalina's deputy block elder was Gustav Schiller, a Polish Jewish communist from Lvov, also in the camp since late 1939. Since mid-1944 Schiller had been working with Polish Jewish boys arriving from labor camps in Poland in a second Jewish block, block 23, in the main camp. Now Polish Jewish boys were moved down to one side of block 66, while Hungarian and Romanian Jewish boys were put on the other side. The large, cavernous barrack was staffed by veteran Czech, Hungarian, and Polish Jewish prisoners, and additional Polish Jewish and Czech Jewish men were recruited from new transports to serve as cadres, teachers, and mentors. From early February into mid-March, Kalina and Schiller went around to the barracks where the youths from the Buna transport were mixed with adult prisoners and offered them the voluntary opportunity to move to the *kinderblock*, where they would find improved conditions and be safer.

Sigmund Weiser from Satmar later recollected clearly the moment these veteran prisoners appeared. "We were becoming animals," he recalled in his USC Shoah history testimony. In the large wooden barracks where the boys were placed initially, dead cadavers were piled up outside the barracks daily until they were carted away to the crematorium. Death was a growing presence as the camp population increased, reaching nearly eighty thousand in early 1945, and the food supply diminished because of the bombings. There was also danger in everyday experience, as larger, older prisoners preyed on the young. A large Russian robbed Weiser of his food, and then a *kapo* struck the boy and opened a large gash on his head. Then on the day the veteran prisoners came, Weiser recalled, all the youths sixteen years old or so were told to line up and were offered the choice to go to a different barrack. "We [for Weiser was now paired up with another boy, Lipot Ciment, also from Satmar] were taken to a different barrack," Wieser said. "Here there were blankets, mattresses. . . . ! They showered us; they cleaned us up!" Weiser recalled especially the Czech communist block elder, Antonin Kalina, who was "a very nice man." "He guarded us like his children."[32] The Slovak, Hungarian, and Romanian Jewish youths were less effusive about Gustav Schiller, who yelled at and abused them, favored the Polish Jewish boys, and was violent. Polish

Jewish youths, who had arrived earlier from the Auschwitz farms, however, viewed Red Gustav clearly as their father figure.

Inside *kinderblock* 66, the youths occasionally got extra food, but generally everyone remained deeply hungry. Some boys say they had more and better food at Buna than at Buchenwald. The camp underground distributed a little extra food to the youths, using its network to gather Red Cross packages from veteran political prisoners and distribute their contents in the block, dividing all evenly. Sigmund Weiser recalled "relatively good" conditions in the block; Samuel Isakovich told interviewer David Boder that "we had a very good man for a *blakovy*," who worked to keep the youths alive.[33] Alex Moskovic said the block elders shared information about the war regularly; and there were occasional classes, and the boys put on special shows and performances, singing in different languages. Abraham Gottlieb (today Abraham Ahuvia) from Kozlov (Kozlow), near Miechów, in Galicia, who kept a Buchenwald diary and whose older brother Chaim Meir Gottlieb was a resident teacher in block 66, recorded several visits to see his brother and to watch the youth performances in the block. Gottlieb observed that the presence of the youth block in Buchenwald amid the deteriorating conditions in February and March was a remarkable phenomenon.[34]

Not all the boys who were sixteen years old or so, and not all the groups of brothers from Buna, went into block 66 when invited. In many cases, such choices depended on whether they could stay together with others important to them and with whom they were paired in Buna or on the march. Sons with fathers had to decide whether to take advantage of the opportunity if it meant abandoning a father, who would be sent to an outlying satellite camp. Fathers had to decide to let go of a son or in some cases let go of two or more sons, putting them in others' hands. Brothers who wished to remain together had to gauge whether this could be done better by staying in the base camp and moving to the children's block or, alternatively, taking one's chances and going out on transport to a satellite camp. In some cases, communist block elders in the blocks cajoled and persuaded younger boys to move, while in others boys who knew intuitively that Buchenwald was different from Buna influenced each other. But some youths were suspicious, for the idea of a children's block had multiple meanings, and some recalled bad experiences at Auschwitz or elsewhere. In other cases, like that of Alex and Zoltan Moskovic from Sobrance, the boys asked if the older brother could accompany the younger one and got permission. Sam Gross, who looked younger, was taken into block 66; Alex Gross, who looked older but was younger, was not accepted at first, but went there repeatedly and Kalina permitted his visits.[35]

As best as can be determined from the study of the transport list and other materials gathered from the Red Cross ITS documents, there were forty-five

boys born 1928 or later on the transport, who were moving together in forty social clusters with fathers, brothers, cousins, or in a few cases friends, totaling
ninety-eight persons. These included eighteen older men born 1893–1904, who
were mostly fathers, and twenty-five young men born 1923–1927, who were
older brothers and in a few cases cousins. None of these forty-five age-eligible
boys transferred into block 66. Several sets of brothers (or cousins) marked
by contiguous numbers at Buna and then again at Buchenwald stayed in the
dangerous adult barracks. Jeno Berger was with his older brother, Moritz, and
father, Josef, in block 57. Szmul Frydrich, a Polish Jewish boy from Ostrowiec,
was with his brother, Hemja, in block 58. The three Kaufman brothers, Bela,
Josef, and Matyas, from Akna Slatina, also stayed in block 58, as did cousins
Sam Cin and Salomon Czen. The Atlasz brothers from Kassau, the Fulop brothers from Tiszanagyfalu, and the Schleger brothers from Satmar all remained
in these initial blocks.

At the same time, several additional clusters of brothers and of fathers and
sons were broken up by the choice for the *kinderblock*. There were an additional forty-one boys born 1928 or later on the transport, who were moving together in another forty clusters involving ninety-three additional persons. Of
these forty-one boys, thirty-two were moved to block 66. In most cases, older
brothers did not follow or were not permitted to do so. Only Hersz Bandman
of four brothers from Kozienice went to block 66. Mendel Fischman, another
boy from Sighet, was in block 66, but his older brother, Herman, was not. Samuel Slomovics was in block 66, but his older brother, Salomon, and his father,
Elias, were not. Josef Herskovicz from Lipose left his father to enter 66; Franz
Steinberg from Munkacs was separated from his father, Moric; Wolf Kornblum from Lodz, Poland, via Starachowice, separated from his father, Natan,
and brother, Moniek, to enter block 66; and Emilio Todesco from Venice, the
sole Italian Jew, parted from his father, Eugenio, and his older brother, Mario,
to enter the *kinderblock*.

Finally, seventeen additional boys born 1928 or after from the transport,
who were in eleven social clusters totaling twenty-five additional persons,
were placed in block 66 with their brothers, including their older brothers.
Alexander Berkowicz and his brother, Elias, from Ungvar were in block 66
together; Jakob and Mendel Dawidowicz from Ajbriviso were together; and
Alex and Samu Gross from Varpolanka visited often together. The three al-
leged Hirsch brothers, Imre, Paul, and Istvan, were in block 66. Alex Moskovic
and his older brother, Zoltan; Israel (Sruly) and Vilmos Stuhl; Jakob Rosental
with Samuel Izsak; and Gyulia Moskovicz and Lajos Weitzen were in the *kinderblock*. Elie Wiesel bunked near Samuel Jakubowitz from Sighet; and later,
after liberation, they referred to each other in their military interviews as
someone who could vouch for the other. At the same time, there were scores

of individual boys apparently moving alone, some of whom also found ref-
uge in block 66. Of those mentioned earlier, they included Hersz (Chaim)
Grossman from Huszt and David Moskovic from Konus; another boy, Miklos
Grüner, from Nyiregyhaza, who had lost his father at Buna, was also included.
Additional boys in block 66 who were alone were Andor Katz from Munkacs,
Jakob Lender from Alsoviso, and Jerzy Zyskind, from Lodz, who memorably
tap-danced in the block to a famous Polish Jewish Julian Tuwim poem about a
locomotive ("*Lokomotywa*"). Years later, many boys remembered the boy who
tap-danced in the block.

REMAINING IN BUCHENWALD OR BEING SENT
ON TRANSPORT TO SATELLITE CAMPS

The boys from Buna came at a moment when Nazi satellite camps — created in mid- and late 1944 in the Harz Mountains and nearby to host projects
that involved digging massive subterranean production facilities for German
corporations manufacturing aircraft engines, parts, and ammunition — were
sharply expanding their demand for slave labor. The Allied bombing effort
over German territories necessitated the creation of new, protected underground spaces to continue producing for the war effort. Of the 304 boys sixteen and under who arrived January 26, and of the 154 boys not moved into
block 66, some fifty or so boys were sent out from several of the large barracks
at Buchenwald to these camps. Another twenty-four died in the barracks at
Buchenwald during February or March and presumably were too sick or weak
to be transported. Thus nearly half the boys sixteen and under who were not
in block 66, and roughly a quarter of all the youths from the transport, were
sent out from Buchenwald or died in the base camp within two months of
arriving.

Among the camps in the Harz Mountains was Langenstein-Zwieberge at
Halberstadt in the foothills of the Thekenbergen in Saxony-Anhalt. The Nazis
called this camp *Kommando* "BII," and also referred to it as "Malachite" or
"Malachyt." The camp opened in June-July 1944, and by February 1945, was
reaching five thousand prisoners. At BII-Malachyt, prisoners were sent to
work on an enormous tunnel excavation and road and railway construction
project for the Junkers Aircraft Company.[36] The central goal was to provide a
safe underground space for the Junkers Company to make jet engines and V-2
rocket parts. Workers slaved in the sandstone with primitive equipment in in-
humane working conditions creating enormous tunnels. Postwar testimonies
about terror labor here told of youths forced to carry cement sacks weighing
fifty kilograms, who routinely collapsed under the weight. Survivors describe
a high death rate, with prisoners working in the tunnels dying on average
within six weeks.[37]

Another camp in the Hils area in central Germany west of Halberstadt in Lower Saxony was Eschershausen near Holzen; the Nazis referred to this camp as *Kommando* "Hecht" or "Hecht/Stein." This camp was created in September 1944 and was similarly expanding in early 1945, although it was smaller than Malachyt, reaching only eleven hundred prisoners. Here, too, prisoners were driven to extraordinary lengths to drive a tunnel system into a mountain, beginning from five existing asphalt mines, with rocks broken and transported by hand from the tunnels. Hecht workers performed earth moving, construction, and digging for Organisation Todt, the German Asphalt Corporation, and for several armaments companies. The lead company was actually the Volkswagen Company at Wolfsburg, which sought to distribute its manufacturing sites and create several hundred thousand square meters of underground space to make Fi 103 (V-1) buzz bombs and engines and wings for a new Focke-Wulf high-altitude fighter.[38] Some Stein workers worked as metal workers or mechanics in armaments production.

Finally, yet another outlying satellite camp, this one southwest of Buchenwald, south of Gotha in Thuringia, was *Kommando* "SIII," or Ohrdruf, the largest of these satellites and today the most well-known. Created in November 1944, this camp grew through March 1945, reaching 11,700 prisoners. Here the prisoners were also set to work tunneling, but the focus was on building an immense communications center to serve as a redoubt for the German high command in case it had to retreat from Berlin, and perhaps also a secret site for advanced rocket development. Prisoners dug large caverns, picked up rocks, and did other related work without protective equipment under immense pressure from ss guards and prisoner *kapos* to work quickly and continuously. Other prisoners worked in the kitchens and other camp institutions, and some worked on cadaver *kommando*, pulling dead corpses from the work sites and transporting them for burial in mass graves.[39]

Fifty boys from the Buna transport who remained in blocks 51 and 57–59 were sent out to these three satellite camps beginning two weeks after arrival at Buchenwald. On February 9, the first group, numbering about a dozen, was transported as part of a group of one thousand prisoners (some seven hundred from the Buna transport) to BII: Langenstein-Zwieberge. The boys included Max Salamonovics and his older brother, Josef, from Ungvar, and the Schleger brothers, David and Iszak, from Satmar. Several boys with younger brothers in block 66 were also aboard, including Martin Taub from Akna Slatina, who was sixteen years old (his brother Bernat in block 66 was fifteen). Herman Stuhl, the father of Sruly, Vilmos, and Ferenc Stuhl, was also aboard this transport.[40]

Less than a week later, on February 14, the next group, also numbering a dozen boys, mostly from block 51, was sent out in a transport of one thousand prisoners to SIII Ohrdruf.[41] In this group were brothers Eugen and Tomas Atlasz from Kassau; also on the transport were the closely bonded cousins, Sam Cin and Salomon Czen. Wolf Kornblum's older brother, Moniek, was on this transport and would later die at Bergen-Belsen. At Ohrdruf, Salomon Czen weakened and got sick, and the ss shot him in the infirmary near the end; but Sam Cin worked building shelters for ammunition and carrying cement bags. Somehow he endured. Emil Weisz from Munkacs, another boy trained earlier as a brick mason when in Buna, was also in this group and worked in a stone mine at Ohrdruf.[42]

Finally, on February 17 and March 3, the largest group of youths sixteen and under numbering twenty-one was sent out to Hecht/Stein. This group also included several youths and slightly older young men tapped as mechanics and metal workers for Stein. Vilem and Salomon Slomovits from Akna Slatina were included with five others in their huge familial cluster. Jeno Berger from Munkacs, David Nutovits from Munkacs, Szmul Frydrich from Ostrowiec, now apart from his brother, Hemja, who was at Langenstein-Zweiberg, and Zoltan Weisz from Nyiregyhaza also went. Majer Klein and his older brother, Markusz Klein, from Potkonoyoc were mechanics chosen February 17 who arrived at Hecht on March 3.

One example of the youths who were taken to the satellites was Max Salamonovics, sixteen years old, from Ungvar, who was with his brother, Josef. "Both my brother and I were always together," Max emphasized in his usc Shoah testimony in 1995. "We made a pact, whatever happens we will stay together."[43] At Buchenwald, they were in barrack 51. But in their minds, the best chance to stay together was to go out on transport, and so they were soon on a closed train to Langenstein-Zwieberge. The second day, the train was attacked by Allied aircraft, and Max and Josef were each hit—Max in the hand, Josef in his leg. Even now, they hid their injuries so they could stay together and went on to Halberstadt, where they worked digging tunnels. This camp was the worst of all camps, where prisoners, as Max described, were "dying like flies." Others recalled that they worked inside tunnels never seeing daylight and endured numerous beatings, as well as frequent large explosions.[44]

Yet other boys were shifted around inside Buchenwald with surprisingly positive effects, avoiding transports until the end. Several boys stayed in or moved to block 58 and survived there under a communist block elder named Max. These included Anton Meisner, who was soon moved to the hospital; they also included the three Kaufman brothers, Matyas, Josef, and Bela—sixteen, fifteen, and thirteen years old, respectively—from Akna Slatina. Other boys were shifted into different blocks. One was moved to another children's block, block 8 in the *grosse lager* headed by German communist Wilhelm Hamann; eight were put in the two Jewish blocks, block 22 headed by German communist Emil Carlebach, and block 23 led by German communist Karl Siegmeyer; and more than a dozen were placed in block 49 headed by German communist Walter Sontag. A few additional boys were in blocks 62 and 63, convalescent barracks. Through March, traffic moved back and forth involving blocks 62, 63, and block 66. Some dozen or more boys moved into block 66 died in March, however, including the single Italian Jew, Emilio Todesco.

As time wore on into March and early April, those youths in Buchenwald in block 66 and elsewhere grew increasingly anxious about what would happen as the Allies drew near. Would the Nazis turn over the camp to the Allies intact, permitting all to survive; or would Buchenwald, like Auschwitz-Buna, be evacuated, with all the prisoners once again put onto the roads? Youths from Buna who had endured the death march and terrible transport did not wish to be taken out again. Then, in the afternoon April 4, 1945, the loudspeaker at Buchenwald blared out a command that all Jews were to report to the *Appelplatz*. Everyone knew the meaning: Buchenwald was being evacuated, and the Jews, including Jewish youths, were to be the first ones sent out. In block 66, where there were now over nine hundred boys from the Buna transport and other transports, Antonin Kalina and Gustav Schiller told their charges not to report and to stay in or near the *kinderblock*.

At this point, in a concerted action sanctioned by the communist-led underground at Buchenwald, Kalina arranged to change the identities on all the boys' uniforms. Red triangles with national markings identifying the boys as Polish, Hungarian, and Czech political prisoners were substituted for the yellow triangles they had worn below such triangles, which identified them as Jews. One boy recalled: "Instead we got other letters such as F P C U B R that masked our Jewish identity. Now we were just like all the other Christian prisoners in the camp." Srulik Berkovics from Sighet remarked that Kalina "made up signals [badges] for us with not any yellow in it."[45] A day or two later, when SS guards appeared down the hill outside block 66 to take the Jewish children, Kalina, with great personal courage and confidence, told the guards who confronted him that all such children were already gone and that only non-Jewish prisoners remained. The SS guards started to push past him into the block, but chaos in the camp above distracted them and they departed.

The Nazis led out several thousand Jews from other barracks during these first days, but were ultimately disappointed by the numbers. Now they began evacuating prisoners from all the barracks. They proceeded block by block, leaving children's blocks 8 and 66, and also the invalid blocks, until the end. Boys in the two Jewish blocks 22 and 23 were forced to hide outside these barracks, some coming down the hill and actually increasing the number in block 66. Then, on April 10, SS guards again descended on *kinderblock* 66 with guns and dogs, and boys were soon caught and led up the hill to the main gate. Until that moment, many boys had hidden in the attic between the ceiling and the roof of the barrack, underneath the barrack and in nearby barracks, and in empty water pipes in the ground; but all these were now rousted from their havens and pushed up the Ettersberg Hill as well. Some dropped out and fled to other barracks in the main camp; others hid in piles of the dead that lay all over the camp.

About mid-afternoon, most of the boys from the barrack were on the *Appelplatz* waiting for the gate to be opened—a couple hundred boys in an advance section of the group had already been taken out, including little Srulik Berkovics and Israel (Sruly) and Vilmos Stuhl—when Allied planes flew overhead, the air-raid sirens sounded, and the SS guards fled into the shelters. At this juncture, the youths were left standing, as Wiesel describes in *Night*,[46] and Kalina then told hundreds of the boys to return to the barrack. It was too late for the Nazis to round them up again that afternoon, so they were in the block the next day taking cover below the windows when American forces neared, the SS guards left the camp, and Buchenwald was liberated.

"On the 9th and 10th of April 1944, the Nazis attempted to assemble us for evacuation," Alex Gross recalled. "We were told the camp had to be emptied by nightfall, but the sound of air-raid sirens interrupted those plans. The guards and the SS men disappeared into the air-raid shelters and underground tunnels." Alex Gross and his brother Sam were saved. Alex Moskovic was too, although his brother Zoltan went or was taken out in the preceding days and was shot by the Nazis near Buchenwald. Louis (Lajos) Weitzen believed Kalina had arranged for the *kinderblock* to be led out last; his friend Julius (Gyulia) Moskowits emphasized: "All I can say about this man [Kalina] is thank you, thank you, thank you. He was trying to help us, and console us, and say hold on [because] better days are coming."[47] Anton Meisner, Simon Neumann, and Paul Hirsch, as well as Zoltan Ellenbogen, survived in the hospital, while Imre Hirsch and Istvan Hirsch hid near the end in nearby invalid block 67.

THE MEANINGS OF THIS MICROSTUDY

This microstudy of boys on a transport from Buna to Buchenwald, their social relations in the camps, and what happened in Birkenau, Buna, and Buchenwald, offers some insights about the social processes and prisoner social system among youths in the camps and also accounts for most of the boys' fates. In pioneering work forty-five years ago, amid early studies that highlighted some psychosocial processes of trauma and aloneness in the camps, the sociologist Elmer Luchterhand emphasized the importance of prisoner relations in small groups, especially in pairs. Luchterhand stressed the presence and salutary role of human groups in the struggle for survival, particularly the role of stable pairs and small groups. Many, perhaps most, survivors shared relationships of mutuality with one or more persons, he suggested.[48] While massive obstacles existed to sustaining such pairs and groups in the Nazi universe—for prisoners were killed, died, were moved in barrack or work assignments, or were put on transports—stable pairs, replacement pairs, and other social clusters nonetheless played important life-sustaining roles. In these clusters, prisoners shared and cooperated, helped each other in need, strategized and organized, looked out for one another, and above all, provided one another with reason and motivation to survive.

Regarding the boys at Buna and Buchenwald, we are helped to understand how such social clusters existed when we think back to their entrance into the camp system at Auschwitz-Birkenau and their experiences at Buna. They entered the concentration camp universe together with family members and fellow townspeople. Despite suffering horrific, traumatic losses on the ramp at the selections, many (but not all) were able to pair up with a father, a brother or brothers, or a cousin. Even in cases where this was impossible, it was still possible for some to find a colleague in a barrack or work group thereafter, especially a friend or friends from the same hometown or region and in the same age group. At Buna, too, it was possible for many fathers and sons, brothers, and others in family fragments or small clusters to live in the same barracks and work in the same *kommandos*. Even boys moving alone in the Nazi universe or finding themselves suddenly alone by the death of a father could find others with whom to connect, as they were concentrated in the *jugendblock* in Buna, where many trained as brick masons, or were in specialized work groups such as *Schiese Kommando* at Birkenau.

The existence of such social clusters, involving at least 102 of 304 youths for whom we have information on the Buna transport, helps us understand some of the complex social dynamics of life beyond extremity in the camps. They offer insights not only about the will to endure that many of these adolescent boys exhibited; they also may help explain choices made along the way, such as the decision in Buchenwald to go to the protective *kinderblock* or to avoid doing so. A barrack for youths located in a base distribution camp in most cases automatically meant separating from fathers or older brothers. However, there was nothing completely rigid about access to this barrack, and some brothers of different ages prevailed on veteran political prisoners to allow them to stay together. In other cases, presumably shaped by mistrust and suspicion, others thought that it would be best to stay together at all costs, even by going out on transports to satellite camps rather than going to a *kinderblock*. In still other cases, some boys accepted going into block 66 knowing at least initially that their older brothers were nearby.

The Israeli psychologist Shamai Davidson also wrote eloquently about human reciprocity in the camps, postulating that interpersonal bonding,

TABLE 5.1 BOYS ON BUNA TRANSPORT TO BUCHENWALD IN THIS MICROSTUDY

Name	Town of Origin, Country	USC Shoah Testimony	Interview
Srulic Berkovics (Alexander Berkowits)	Sighet, Romania	X	—
Szlama Zulang (Sol Culang)	Warsaw, Poland	X	—
Sam Cin	Huszt, Czechoslovakia	—	
Salomon Czen	Huszt, Czechoslovakia	—	—
Zoltan Ellenbogen	Nyirbator, Hungary	X	X
Berek Erlich	Warsaw, Poland	X	—
Harry Fischman	Sighet, Romania	X	
Samu Gross (Sam Gross)	Palonok, Czechoslovakia	X	
Szandor Gross (Alex Gross)	Palonok, Czechoslovakia	X	X
Tibor Gross (Ted Gross)	Satmar, Romania	X	—
Chaim Hersz Grossman (Henry Grossman)	Huszt, Czechoslovakia	X	
Istvan Hirsch (Stefan Guttman)	Nagykarola, Czechoslovakia	X	X
Paul Hirsch (Paul Kaszovitz, Paul Kassy)	Nagykarola, Czechoslovakia	X	X
Sam Isakowics	Sighet, Romania	—	Boder
Sam Izsak	Comlausa, Romania	—	—
Samuel Jakubowitz	Sighet, Romania	—	Josepher
Wolf Kornblum (William Kaye)	Lodz, Poland	—	X
Anton Meisner (Anton Mason)	Sighet, Romania	X	—
Sandor Moskovic (Alex Moskovic)	Sobrance, Czechoslovakia	X	X
David Mangarten	Starachowice, Poland	X	—
David Moskovic	Konusz, Czechoslovakia	—	—
Gyula Moskovics (Julius Moskowits)	Uzhorod, Czechoslovakia	—	—
Simon Neumann (Tommy Newman)	Vojnatina, Czechoslovakia	X	—
Jacob Rozental (Jack Rosenthal)	Comlausa, Romania	X	X
Israel (Sruly) Stuhl	Slatinska Doly, Czechoslovakia	X	—
Max Salamonowics (Max Sands)	Uzhorod, Czechoslovakia	X	—
Josef Salamonowics	Uzhorod, Czechoslovakia	X	—
Abby Weiner	Sighet, Romania	X	X
Sigmund Weiser	Satmar, Romania	X	—
Emil Weiss	Munkacs, Czechoslovakia	X	—

Name	Town of Origin, Country	USC Shoah Testimony	Interview
Lajos Weitzen (Louis Weitzen)	Uzhorod, Czechoslovakia	—	Tzugaris
Lazar Wiesel (Elie Wiesel)	Sighet, Romania	*Night*	X
Leopold Ziment	Satmar, Romania	—	—
Jerzy Zyskind	Lodz, Poland	—	Widow

NOTES: "Boder" refers to the interviews that were done by David Boder in 1946 after Liberation, which have been collected at the Illinois Institute of Technology in the Voices of the Holocaust Archive, which is online at https://voices.iit.edu/david_boder. The relevant citation is Samuel Isakovitch, July 30, 1946, http://voices.iit.edu/interview?doc=isakovitchS&display=isakovitchS_en.
"Josepher" refers to the interview with Samuel Jakubowitz by Brian Josepher (undated).
"Tzugaris" refers to the interview with Misty Tzugaris, daughter of Louis Weitzen, by Kenneth Waltzer (undated).
"Widow" refers to the interview with the widow of Jerzy Zyskind by Kenneth Waltzer (undated).
References to *Night* are to Elie Wiesel's memoir, *Night*.

reciprocity, and sharing were essential sources of strength for "adaptation" and survival. Such interpersonal support sustained the motivation to carry on the struggle to live and also assisted people in numerous ways, helping them organize and engage in the black market.[49] We see evidence of such active dyads, two-person clusters, in this case in the documents exhibited by contiguous numberings across two camp systems, in the tattoos at Auschwitz, and also in the badges at Buchenwald; we even sometimes see slightly larger groups together, coexisting as groups in the camp universe alongside clear evidence of anomie and alienation. We also see that some of these boys remember in testimonies many years later that they were sworn to stick together as brothers and as friends, and these mutual relationships were the primary commitments they made.

Alex Moskovic, the boy who left his work group comrades from Birkenau to rejoin family at Gleiwitz, today a survivor educator in Florida, explains it straightforwardly: "Trust was the main thing. You couldn't always stay or be together—it was just beyond your control. But having someone you could trust, where this was possible, was often a matter of life and death."[50]

As to the fates of all the many boys on the transport, the answer is about half—with Wiesel—were moved into block 66, where they found invaluable protection from members of a clandestine movement who were committed to saving them; about a quarter remained in the other large barracks with adult prisoners in Buchenwald, with some subsequently shifted about knowingly and strategically; and about a quarter were transported to horrific satellite camps, where they faced deadly labor assignments or they died soon after arriving at Buchenwald. Even Elie Wiesel was never completely alone in Buchenwald after his father died: although he wrote that he fell into a deep depression where "nothing mattered" anymore, he was also at the same time in a protected barrack with many other youths and with someone else from Sighet. Even after liberation, the rebuilding of many boys' lives and personalities and the beginning of new lives would also proceed based on pairs and small groups and on the forging and deepening of group bonds in transitional homes in France and elsewhere.[51]

NOTES

Acknowledgments: Special thanks to my undergraduate assistant Justine Brunet and researcher Bill Bilstadt, and also to Bob Houbeck, director of the University of Michigan–Flint, Frances Willson Thompson Library, for creating a feed from the USC Shoah Archives. Special thanks also to Alex Moskovic, who reviewed and commented on an earlier version.

1. Transport List of New Prisoners from KL Auschwitz to Buchenwald, January 26, 1945, doc. no. 5285826#1- 5285893#1 (1.1.5.1/0001–0182/0148A/0004 to 0071) (67 pp.), International Tracing Services (ITS Archives), Bad Arolsen, Germany.

2. Elie Wiesel, *Night* (New York: Hill and Wang, 2006), 113. See also Wiesel, *All Rivers Run to the Sea: Memoirs* (New York: Knopf, 1995), and *And the Sea Is Never Full: Memoirs* (New York: Knopf, 1999).

3. See Primo Levi, *Survival in Auschwitz* (New York: Touchstone, 1995); Wolfgang Sofsky, *The Order of Terror: The Concentration Camp*, trans. William Templer (Princeton, NJ: Princeton University Press, 1999). See also critical essays on Sofsky in Jane Caplan and Nikolaus Wachsmann, eds., *Concentration Camps in Nazi Germany: The New Histories* (New York: Routledge, 2010).

4. Wiesel, *Night*, 61–65.

5. Interview with Alex Gross, January 24, 1996, USC Shoah Foundation Testimony, no. 11272; Alex Gross, *Yankele: A Holocaust Survivor's Bittersweet Memoir* (Lanham, MD: University Press of America, 2002); author interview with Alex Gross, June 9, 2005, Boca Raton, Florida.

6. Interview with Henry Grossman (Hersz Grossman), USC Shoah Foundation Testimony, no. 14431. Also, Dori Laub interview with Henry Grossman, March 17, 2006, Fortunoff Archives, Yale University, New Haven, Connecticut.

7. Interview with Alex Berkowits (Szrul Bercovics), March 29, 1996, Winnipeg, Canada, USC Shoah Foundation Testimony, no. 13792.

8. Zoltan Ellenbogen, telephone interview with the author, December 11, 2006.

9. Samuel Jacubowitz, interview with Brian Josepher, shared in e-mail from Samuel Jacubowitz to the author, May 8, 2009.

10. Interview with David Moskovic, June 26, 1998, Ottawa, Canada, USC Shoah Foundation Testimony, no. 43392.

11. Interview with Thomas Newman, December 1, 1994, Toronto, Canada, USC Shoah Foundation Testimony, no. 316.

12. Interview with Sam Cin, July 14, 1996, Skokie, Illinois, USC Shoah Foundation Testimony, no. 17077.

13. Interview with Sruly Stuhl, July 13, 1998, Denver, Colorado, USC Shoah Foundation Testimony, no. 43116.

14. Interview with Sigmund Weiser, July 30, 1996, Staten Island, New York, USC Shoah Foundation, no. 17919.

15. Interview with Ted Gross (Tibor Gross), September 8, 1997, Kingston, Pennsylvania, USC Shoah Foundation, no. 32863.

16. Interview with Jack Rosenthal, February 7, 1995, Roslyn, New York, USC Shoah Visual History Foundation, no. 1072; Jack Rosenthal, interview with the author, January 11, 2007, New York City.

17. Wiesel, *Night*, 50–51, 71–72.

18. Interview with Anton Mason (Anton Meisner), September 16, 1998, USC Shoah Foundation Testimony, no. 45764. Another boy, Abby Weiner, was also in this group. Abby Weiner, interview with the author, November 14, 2012, New Haven, Connecticut.

19. Interview with Alex Moskovic, USC Shoah Foundation Testimony, no. 11302. Alex Moskovic, interview with the author, June 2, 2005, New York City. Alex Moskovic, interview with Steve Moskovicz for *Kinderblock 66*, April 2010, Hotel Elephant, Weimar, Germany.

20. Paul Kassy (Kaszovitz), telephone interview with the author, May 8, 2011; Ken Waltzer to Paul Kassy, May 11, 2011. See also Ken Waltzer to Stephan Guttman, June 1, 2011; Stephan Guttman, interview with the author, July 28, 2011, Basel, Switzerland.

21. Louis Weitzen's daughter, Misty Tzugaris, provided invaluable information and leads about Lajos Weitzen. Misty Tzugaris, e-mails to the author, March 6, May 3, May 5, 2012; Ken Waltzer to Misty Tzugaris, March 3–4 and May 5–6, 2012. Julius Moskowits, April 11, 1995, Toronto, Canada, USC Shoah Foundation Testimony, no. 4351.

22. Alex Gross, *Yankele*, p. 63.

23. Sam Cin, July 14, 1996, Skokie, Illinois, USC Shoah Foundation Testimony, no. 17077.

24. Interview with Sol Culang (Szlama Zulang), July 10, 1995, Los Angeles, California, USC Shoah Foundation Testimony, no. 3808.

25. Samuel Isakovitch, interview with David Boder, July 30, 1946, Paris, France, Voices of the Holocaust Archive, Illinois Institute of Technology, accessed on April 8, 2016, http://voices.iit.edu/interview?doc=isakovitchS&display=isakovitchS_en.

26. Alexander Berkowits (Srulik Bercovics), March 29, 1996, Winnipeg, Canada, USC Shoah Testimony, no. 13792

27. Wiesel, *Night*, 100.

28. Samuel Isakovitch, interview with David Boder, July 30, 1946, Paris, France, Voices of the Holocaust Archive, Illinois Institute of Technology, accessed on April 8, 2016, http://voices.iit.edu/interview?doc=isakovitchS&display=isakovitchS_en.

29. Wiesel, *Night*, 101.

30. Block assignments are identified on "List of 3935 Victims from Auschwitz in Buchenwald on January 26, 1945," record group: M.8.ITS, subsection: M.8.ITS.BD, file no: BU 17; original file no: GCC 2/181 I B / 9, ITS Archive, Bad Arolsen, Germany.

31. Sigmund Weiser, USC Shoah Foundation Testimony, no. 17919.

32. Sigmund Weiser, July 30, 1996, Staten Island, New York, USC Shoah Foundation Testimony, no. 17919.

33. Sigmund Weiser, USC Shoah Foundation Testimony, no. 17919; Samuel Isakovitch, interview with David Boder, July 30, 1946, Paris, France, Voices of the Holocaust Archive, accessed on April 8, 2016, http://voices.iit.edu/interview?doc=isakovitchS&display=isakovitchS_en.

34. Kenneth Waltzer, "Abraham Gottlieb's Buchenwald Diary" (paper presented at the Forty-Fourth Association of Jewish Studies Conference, December 18, 2012, Chicago, Illlinois). Gottlieb's unpublished diary, "A Human Being at Buchenwald," is an important eyewitness document on the final months in Buchenwald and on the *kinderblock* 66.

35. Alex Gross says he could not find a permanent place in the block, but went there repeatedly.

36. See U.S. Holocaust Memorial Museum, *Encyclopedia of Camps and Ghettos, 1933–1945*, vol. 1, ed. Geoffrey Megargee, 357–60 (Bloomington: Indiana University Press, 2009), s.v. "Halberstadt-Langenstein-Zwieberge ('Malachit,' 'BII')," by Christine Schmidt van der Zanden.

37. Ibid., 358.

38. See U.S. Holocaust Memorial Museum, *Encyclopedia of Camps and Ghettos, 1933–1945*, vol. 1, ed. Geoffrey Megargee, 339–41 (Bloomington: Indiana University Press, 2009), s.v. "Eschershausen ('Stein') and Holzen ('Hecht')," by Therkel Straede. See also the catalogue of the permanent exhibition, *Place of Remembrance of Forced Labor in the Volkswagen Factory*, which opened in 1999 on the site of the Wolfsburg plant.

39. See U.S. Holocaust Memorial Museum, *Encyclopedia of Camps and Ghettos, 1933–1945*, vol. 1, ed. Geoffrey Megargee, 402–4 (Bloomington: Indiana University Press, 2009), s.v. "Ohrdruf ('SIII')," by Christine Schmidt van der Zanden.

40. Transport List of Prisoners to Aussenkommando Halberstadt ("Malachyt"), February 9, 1945, doc. no. 5318265#1–5318269#1 (0183-0356/0300/00063@1.1.5.1 to 0183-0356/0300/00068@1.1.5.1), ITS Archives, Bad Arolsen, Germany.

41. Transport List of Prisoners to Aussenkommando Ohrdruf ("Slll"), February 14, 1945, doc no. 5320505#1 to 5320509#2 (/0183-0356/0312/0191@1.1.5.1 to 0183-0356/0312/0194@1.1.5.1, ITS Archives, Bad Arolsen, Germany.

42. Sam Cin, July 14, 1996, Skokie, Illinois, USC Shoah Foundation, no. 17077; Emil Weiss, September 19, 1998, Encino, California, USC Shoah Foundation, no. 46612.

43. Interview with Max Sands (Max Salamonovics), February 10, 1995, Westwood, California, Shoah Visual History Foundation, no. 849.

44. Interview with Max Sands, no. 849. David Fiszl described Langenstein-Zwieberge as "a death trap" and said, "We worked inside a tunnel, never seeing daylight." Paul Gottesman from Ungvar recalled moving equipment and carrying heavy materials. See interviews with David Fiszl, October 26, 1995, Des Moines, Iowa, USC Shoah Foundation, no. 8003; Paul Gottesman, July 18, 1998, North Hollywood, California, USC Shoah Foundation, no. 43171.

45. Victor (Zeev) Borger to Dr. Irena Steinfeld, Director, Department of the Righteous, Yad Vashem, May 26, 2011 (copy to the author). Interview with Alexander Berkowits (Srulik Bercovics), March 29, 1996, USC Shoah Foundation, no. 13792. Kalina was named a Righteous Among the Nations in June 2012.

46. Wiesel, *Night*, 114–15.

47. Interview with Julius Moskowitz (Gyula Moskovics), April 11, 1995, Toronto, Canada, USC Shoah Foundation, no. 4351.

48. Elmer Luchterhand, "Prisoner Behavior and Social System in the Nazi Camp," *International Journal of Psychiatry* 13 (1967): 245–64.

49. Shamai Davidson, "Human Reciprocity among the Jewish Prisoners in the Nazi Concentration Camps," in *The Nazi Concentration Camps: Proceedings of the Fourth Yad Vashem Historical Conference* (Jerusalem: Yad Vashem, 1984), 555–72; also Davidson, "Group Formation and Human Reciprocity in the Nazi Concentration Camps," in *Holding on to Humanity: The Message of Holocaust Survivors: The Shamai Davidson Papers*, ed. Israel Charney, 121–42 (New York: New York University Press, 1992).

50. Alex Moskovics, conversation with the author, October 2012. I must thank Alex Moskovic for reading and commenting on an earlier version of this essay.

51. See Wiesel, *Night*, 113; see Eva Fogelman, "The Role of Group Experiences in the Healing Process of Massive Childhood Holocaust Trauma," *Journal of Applied Psychoanalytic Studies* 4, no.1 (January 2002): 31–47. "We became like brothers," Sigmund Weiser recalled of his days at Ambloy and Taverny with the OSE in France. Weiser, July 30, 1996, Staten Island, New York, USC Shoah Foundation testimony, no. 17919.

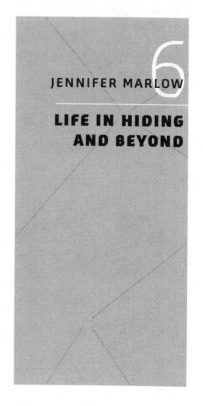

LIFE IN HIDING AND BEYOND

Elizabeth Grotch, born in 1938, referred to her nanny, Janina Zillow, as the mother "she knew" before the war.[1] Zillow was present in the home providing the daily, hands-on child-rearing tasks, making sure she was dressed, bathed, and carefully looked after. After Janina Zillow removed Grotch, along with her cousin Lillian Trilling, from the Warsaw ghetto, the trio went to the former nanny's sister's home; but they could stay only a few days because Zillow's sister, a laundress, was afraid to keep them any longer.[2] The nanny told people the girls were her nieces and that she was caring for them because her brother had been killed. The girls called her aunt in public, but sometimes mixed up details, adding to the serious danger. Zillow obtained papers for Grotch and Trilling, and the three of them traveled by train to Lviv (Lwów), where Zillow had been living.[3] To avoid scrutiny, Zillow kept the girls inside the apartment all day while she worked, but the landlord denounced them. During her encounter with the Germans, Zillow was thrown against the wall and feared that she would be sent to work in Germany, so she and the two girls had to leave the area. The three of them parted ways; Trilling was provided with papers to work in Warsaw, and Grotch and Zillow went to stay with the nanny's family in Lublin.

Life with Zillow's family, whom she described as "pro-Nazi," was difficult for both Grotch and her caregiver.[4] While the rest of Zillow's family treated her well, the mother was openly hostile toward her. Upon their arrival, the mother said to Zillow, "Well, when you were a child you used to bring stray cats, now you bring stray Jews."[5] Grotch lived in a formerly Jewish-owned apartment with Zillow and Zillow's mother, brother, and sister. The family was also running a formerly Jewish-owned business, and hiding a Jewish child in this home led to a great deal of conflict. Grotch was generally kept concealed because the family was afraid that people would see her and recognize her typically Jewish features. Zillow's family denounced people, looted their belongings, and directly benefited from the persecution of the Jewish population by receiving both an apartment and a business. Grotch described the mother as fiercely antisemitic. Yet this family was willing to risk its members' lives to hide a Jewish child in their home, which seems contradictory in the face of their other behavior.

Grotch suggested that Zillow's mother was desperate to have Zillow there, and the former maid wanted a child of her own.[6] Zillow had kept a Jewish baby in her Lwów apartment while she was hiding Trilling and Grotch; but when they were denounced, the baby had to be sent away. Grotch recalled Zillow frequently commenting that it was a shame about that other baby.[7] While Zillow's mother may have had ambivalent or negative feelings about Grotch, Zillow was "her daughter, her youngest child, so it was better to have her even if she had to put up with that (a Jewish child in their home)."[8] For Zillow, the desire to have a child and her feelings of attachment to her prewar charge were enough motivation to take an enormous risk and suffer her mother's displeasure.

Despite the animosity of the mother, Grotch was in many ways treated as part of this family. They celebrated the holidays together, and she was taken to church sometimes even though that was quite risky. Grotch believed she stayed with the family in Lublin at least one-and-a-half years, and she stayed with Zillow until she left Poland in 1946. This was a very uncomfortable and sometimes hostile environment for the child, and yet she was with the one person she felt safest with, Janina Zillow. Her maid was willing to deal with her mother's disapproval and risk not only her own life, but the lives of all of her immediate family to keep this child.

Zillow's age, the nanny's role as the child's primary caregiver before the war, and the time they spent together in hiding contributed to making their bond become even stronger during the Nazi occupation while staying briefly in Lwów and then in Lublin. When Grotch was approximately four or five years old, Zillow told her that her mother had been killed. Grotch replied, "Thank God it wasn't you," and her caregiver responded by yelling at her for saying such a thing and asking her if she was ashamed of herself.[9] Zillow had been quite attached to Grotch's mother, acting very nurturing and protective toward her employer before the war, and was likely upset at the news of her death. Though it was jarring for Zillow to hear the child express her lack of attachment to her mother, perhaps her reaction should not have been unexpected. Grotch was very young at the outbreak of the war and said that by the end of the war she thought Zillow was her mother. The memory of her own mother was so vague by then that she did not even want to think about her or about being Jewish.[10] Her age, the time spent with her caregiver, and the need to pretend and live as if she were Zillow's child certainly reinforced such forgetting.

Grotch survived the war with Zillow and was claimed by her extended family, whose members were living in the United States. Zillow traveled with the child to Sweden and Cuba for two years, until they were finally able to reach the family in the United States. This woman left her family and home in Poland rather than be separated from her charge. Many other female Polish Catholic domestic workers who protected Jewish children under Nazi occupation loved their charges even before the war, but the time spent together living in fear as part of a conspiracy formed a new and deeper bond. Some of these women risked everything to keep these children, not just discovery by the authorities that could result in death, but the loss of their families of origin, loved ones, acquaintances, and friends. The children themselves sometimes were old enough to be aware of the situation or sometimes were so young, as in the case of Grotch, that the identities they took while passing became their primary identities. They did not always realize how abnormal the situation was. The moving, the tension in the home, the adoption of an entirely new identity — for some children this was the only childhood they would remember. Thus, it was not until later that they would understand exactly what was happening. Even for older children, the lines were also not so clear. They may have had clear memories of their parents and missed them very much, but they also became increasingly attached to their caregivers and to their new identities. As we can see in the case of Elizabeth Grotch and her nanny, Janina Zillow, while caring for a prewar charge or being cared for by a prewar maid or nanny were in fact extensions of prewar life and provided a degree of normalcy, the situation also distorted and complicated every aspect of life for those involved in these conspiracies.

This chapter argues that the Nazi occupation and Holocaust changed relationships between Polish Catholic domestic workers and their former Jewish charges that they later protected, their former employers, and often their own acquaintances, family, and friends.[11] The rescue dynamic led to a greater intimacy between the caregiver and charge as they became partners in conspiracy, even while their clandestine activity greatly narrowed their universe and altered the prewar pattern of authority between the former employers and employees.

AN EVER SHRINKING UNIVERSE

Nazi policy was intended to sever ties between Polish Jews and gentiles, and in many cases this policy was overwhelmingly effective. However, in many cases where rescue by a former household servant occurred, Nazi policy had exactly the opposite effect. Rather than cutting ties and ignoring the fate of their Jewish employers, these women who engaged in clandestine rescue and aid activities bound their own fate to that of the Jews they were aiding.

In order to protect a Jewish child, it was necessary either to pass that child off as a gentile or to conceal his or her existence completely. As these women had ties to these children from before the war, even in urban areas they ran the risk that the child would be recognized as their prewar Jewish charge. As a result, when a former caregiver took a child from the ghetto, they either had to conceal the child completely from anyone who could recognize them, or to relocate to where the two of them would not be recognized.

In the case of Zillow and Grotch, Zillow could not stay in the city and needed to take the child someplace else, so she returned to her family of origin in Lublin. This created conflict in the family and also required a cover story for the appearance of this child. In a small town or village, people were familiar with one another, and the sudden appearance of someone who had been away with a child they had never heard about before and no husband roused suspicion and demanded a cover story. Some women passed their charges off as their own offspring. It was, of course, much easier to explain the presence of a child without a husband to strangers than to one's own family and friends. Former nanny Wictoria Rodziewiecz removed Sarah Wall from the Vilna ghetto and initially stayed in the city so the child could continue to have contact with her mother.[12] In June 1941, after a former neighbor recognized Wall and Rodziewiecz, the Gestapo took Rodziewiecz for questioning. They released her, but this incident made it apparent that she would have to leave the city. She fled alone, returning the child to her mother temporarily, and within weeks she removed the child from the ghetto permanently.[13] In preparation, Rodziewiecz went to her priest to ask for papers for her charge; but since she told the clergyman that the child was Jewish, he would not oblige her request and suggested she ask another priest she did not know. She took his advice, told another priest that Wall was her illegitimate child, and had her baptized as Irena to obtain legal documents. Rodziewiecz then returned to her family of origin in the village of Grauzyszki (Graużyszki), located today in Belarus, with a baby and unmarried. Initially, Wall says her caretaker did not know whom she could trust, so she did not tell her family this secret. Wall says, "You can well imagine this devout Catholic woman" who had to bear this shame.[14] Soon it was apparent that her family could be trusted; and even after the child's identity was revealed, the family continued to treat her well. Just to be safe, however, anytime people came around they would start admonishing the child, yelling at her, "You bastard!" for good measure.[15] This was a common means of concealing the identity of a Jewish child, even though it was certainly not without its problems and there was a stigma attached to this mode of deception for the caretaker.[16]

INCREASED INTIMACY

The conspiracy that Wall and Rodziewiecz participated in, just as in the previously mentioned case of Zillow and Grotch, firmly cemented the relationship between caregiver and charge as one of mother and child. Like Grotch, Wall was very young when she was placed in Rodziewiecz's care, and eventually this woman would be the only mother she remembered. Wall slept with Rodziewiecz every night. She remembers these wartime years as hard for everyone, but she recalls feeling fairly secure and being treated with love.[17] She always felt that she was the most important person in Rodziewiecz's life.[18] The nanny would bleach Wall's hair blond to ensure she looked Polish; Wall did not realize until later that this was not a normal activity. They celebrated all the Catholic holidays, and she describes herself as just like all the other (gentile) children, meaning antisemitic.[19] One night Rodziewiecz and Wall had to leave in the middle of the night because people seemed to be suspicious; and her caregiver made it into a game, "like everyone just leaves in the middle of the night."[20] These abnormal activities that were necessary to conceal the true identity of a child often did not seem particularly abnormal to the children at the time. Depending on their age or the situation, they did not know the difference or they became accustomed to this. Wall, for example, did not have any idea at the end of the war that this woman who had raised her was not her biological mother. After she was reunited with her own mother, who survived the war, she continued to miss her caregiver; but she did not ever share this sadness with her mother because she knew it would be hurtful to her to hear.[21]

Rodziewiecz and Wall developed this strong mother-daughter relationship that was strengthened by the absence of the child's mother and by the conspiracy in which they engaged. The family treated Wall as if she were a member and behaved as if Rodziewiecz were the child's mother. Wall did not know any of this was abnormal. She did not realize that having her hair bleached regularly was to conceal her Jewish identity; it was just something she did. The family closed ranks and all became responsible for this secret and all bore the risks. They pretended that the child was a "bastard," and it stands to reason that this would have been the cause of gossip and shame for the family as a whole, but especially for Rodziewiecz. So while Rodziewiecz was able to maintain her connections with her family of origin, she did have to leave her home and acquaintances in Vilna and bear the shame of having a child out of wedlock, thus restricting her social life and relationships. Rather than just her own universe shrinking, this conspiracy restricted the universe of the entire family unit.

Most caregivers were not fortunate enough to have the support of their families in their rescue activities; and even when they did have some assistance from their own family or friends, they still had to conceal their activities from everyone else. This included neighbors, landlords, coworkers, shopkeepers, and even priests. Nothing could appear out of the ordinary. Karolina Sapetowa was employed as a nanny for the Hochweiser children—Samus, Salusia, and Iziu—before the war; and after they were confined in the Kraków ghetto with their parents, she continued to have contact with the family, taking food and needed items to them. The youngest child came to stay with her at her home in Witanowice, and she would take the older children from the ghetto temporarily whenever the situation became especially unstable. She worried and missed the children when they were confined and thought of them as her own.[22] In March 1943 when the ghetto was liquidated, Sapetowa and her aunt went to the ghetto and caught sight of the older children, Iziu and Salusia, with their mother; and as soon as their mother caught sight of Sapetowa, she urged the children to "Go to Karolcia."[23] Salusia "slipped like a mouse between the heavy boots of the Ukrainians," who did not notice the child.[24] The little girl ran to Sapetowa with her "hands stretched out imploringly."[25] Iziu stayed with his mother, and they were both loaded aboard a transport and Sapetowa never saw them again.

Sapetowa took Salusia back home to Witanowice, where she was already keeping her little brother, Samus. At first, the children were able to play outdoors and her neighbors did not harass her much, but this did not last long. When relations grew difficult with the other villagers, she began keeping the children indoors; but the threats from her neighbors increased rapidly. Her neighbors implored and threatened her to turn the children in to the Gestapo before they all were punished for harboring Jewish children. She responded to their demands by "telling them off" or bribing them, until one day in 1944, shortly before the Soviets liberated Witanowice, the local farmers came to her and told her that they must "get rid of the children."[26] Their plan to do so involved taking the children to the barn and cutting their heads off while they slept.[27]

Sapetowa lived with her elderly father, and he was of course alarmed at this turn of events, and the children themselves were aware of what was happening. She remembers, "The poor children knew everything, and before they went to bed they would say to us, 'Karolcia, do not kill us just today!'"[28] These children knew that their caretaker, who loved them as her own, was being pressured not just to send them away but to take them into the barn and let the neighbors execute them. Sapetowa resolved that she would "not hand over the children at any price."[29] Instead, she put the children on a cart and paraded them around the village, telling everyone she was taking them outside of the village to drown them. She then took them out into the surrounding countryside and hid them, until she could smuggle them back into town that evening and hide them in a neighbor's attic. The children suffered there, concealed from the other neighbors in a hot, filthy attic, while Sapetowa worked to earn enough money to pay for food and to pay the neighbor for this hiding place. Eventually, she could not make the payments, and they were in turn evicted from this hiding place. Sapetowa, then, with no other choices available, brought the children back to her home and hid them in a shed with the cattle until the Red Army liberated them. The children remained with Sapetowa after the war; she became their sole guardian. She wrote, "I shall never part from them again, and even if they were to go to the ends of the earth, I would go with them. They are like my children; I love them more than anything in the world, and I would do anything for them."[30] Sapetowa never remarried (she was a widow), and she stayed with the children, leaving Poland with the children for Denmark. Later in life she cared for Salusia's children.[31]

While Sapetowa had the support of her father, she was surrounded by hostile neighbors, who believed she was putting all of them in danger. They threatened her regularly until she concealed the children completely to appease them. Neighbors she had likely known for years became openly hostile toward her, demanding that she murder or at least consent to the murder of the children she loved as her own. She also must have been cognizant of the danger into which she was placing her elderly father. In addition, the children's world shrank, as Sapetowa became the only one protecting them. "Normal" changed from confinement in the ghetto to staying for short periods with Sapetowa, with whom they "felt at home," to then staying full-time and being allowed to play outdoors. Soon, however, the children realized that every single person living in that town did not want them there, and some of those people wanted to harm them physically.[32] They went from playing outside to total concealment. Their father had been shot, their mother and older brother had disappeared, and they became fearful that the one person they loved and who cared for them might take them into the barn and cut off their heads. For these children and others living in hiding, the outside world not only became smaller, it became unimaginably hostile.

ALTERED CAREGIVER-CHARGE RELATIONSHIPS

While rescue brought increased intimacy to the relationship between caregiver and charge, further cementing familial bonds and emotional attachment, the situation also brought new anxieties and pressures to the relationship. As mentioned previously, Salusia and Samuś Hochwieser started to fear that their beloved caregiver, Karolina Sapetowa, would succumb to the pressure of her neighbors and murder them. Elizabeth Grotch also acknowledged the love that she felt for her caregiver and felt very much loved by Zillow in return, but recalled that there were also tense moments which made her fearful. At one point, Janina Zillow's mother threw her and the child out of her home. Zillow went to a convent seeking shelter for herself and the child, but they were refused. Zillow was upset and did not know where to turn, so she told Grotch they would go to the church and stand in front of the Holy Virgin and "if she nods her head that I should give you away I will have to. If she doesn't I'll stay with you."[33] Grotch remembers feeling terrified standing there, an unwilling player in a game of Christian roulette. Mary, of course, did not nod. It was not uncommon for caregivers, who were under extreme stress, to lash out at the children they cared for or exhibit abnormal behavior during these periods of extreme pressure.

Bernhard Kempler and his sister, Anita, spent the war passing as the daughters of their former caregiver, Franciszka Ziemiańska.[34] Bernhard had to act, convincingly, in order to pass as a little girl, Bernadette, since it was especially dangerous for male Jews because their circumcision could easily confirm their Jewish identities. Kempler was very young during the war, born in May 1936; but he recalls he had to make his voice sound like that of a girl, he remembers having his hair braided, and he recalls wearing a dress. He passed as a little girl for at least four years. He also became Catholic: learning all the prayers, attending Mass, and performing the rituals very naturally with his caregiver. His whole identity, gender as well as religion and ethnicity, had to be transformed to pass as his nanny's child.

Separated from his parents and living with a new identity as a Catholic girl was an extreme hardship for the young boy; and the relationship between Kempler, his sister, and his caregiver, whom he relied on for stability and protection, was also fraught with tension. Yet Kempler recalls kindness, and he felt that Ziemiańska loved the children. Kempler explained:

> Of course we had been with her before the war as well so it wasn't that big a change, but there were times when she was frightened, she had terrible headaches and sometimes if we didn't do something exactly the way she wanted she would be very upset. She would threaten to leave us, asking "What did she need this for?" It was dangerous for her to be taking care of us and hiding us like that. And I remember that it was frightening to me that she would leave us.[35]

In order to please his caregiver, who was a devout Catholic, Kempler acted "very religious as a Catholic" and would get her water and headache powders when she was not feeling well.[36] He explains that he felt close to her, but was also aware that she did not have to keep him and his sister; so he behaved in a manner as good, obedient, and helpful as possible.[37] Before the war, his nanny had looked after him, but this relationship became distorted under Nazi occupation policy. Now, under this new circumstance, he faced insecurity and fear that the woman who loved him might leave him at any moment. This compelled him to constantly attempt to please her as he concealed his true identity.

The relationship between Ziemiańska and Kempler's sister was also newly complicated by this precarious situation. His sister was "more of a problem" for their caregiver, so Kempler felt a need to compensate for her behavior by being especially obedient and doing everything precisely the way he thought Ziemiańska wanted him to.[38] According to Kempler, this created conflict between the three of them, placing them in a situation in which he always wanted his sister to behave better, but she would not. So he would behave better, as he was afraid they would be abandoned. This created what he describes as a sort of psychological triangle between and among them.[39] In her biography, Kempler's older sister, Anita Lobel, writes that when the nanny's mother became ill, Ziemiańska resented that she was unable to leave the children to go and be with her before she died, and sometimes she also had to miss Mass because of the children.[40] The constant threat of discovery altered the dynamic between caregiver and charges and between the siblings.

Unimaginable stress and resentment are often left out of the narrative of rescue because it does not fit the image of a heroic rescuer, who is usually portrayed as selfless and brave. This understanding of rescuers as more human and less heroic is in conversation with the current scholarship on Holocaust rescuers.[41] In reality, we know that caregivers were humans, with human emotions. They sometimes snapped at their charges, threatened to leave them, and at times resented the burden of their commitment to them.

Even with the continuity of a prewar caretaker, life for these children was forever altered, often more than the children even understood while it was happening. Relationships between caregivers and children were distorted and complicated under the pressure and circumstances of the Nazi occupation. Sarah Wall recalls that after the war, when she realized what had really happened, "nothing was the same."[42] Her whole life was, in her words, "fractured." Elizabeth Grotch became a part of her caretaker's family and was socialized in antisemitic attitudes, and she became accustomed to living with a woman who openly disliked her presence and believed that the Jews were "getting what they deserved."[43] Bernhard Kempler went from just being a little boy living in a middle-class home being cared for by his nanny to the keeper of the peace between his sister and their nanny as he also took on the identity of Catholic girl. For children who were not completely concealed and had to assume a new identity, this meant that one's life depended on convincingly taking on the role of Catholic, working-class child; and often this meant losing parts of their own prewar self in the process. Kempler hid with his nanny disguised as a little girl, but also went through the camp system as a girl to stay with his sister.[44] While a prewar caregiver provided a measure of comfort and continuity, there was only so much protection from the damage inflicted upon these children that she could give. The stress from the situation, changed relationships, and the acts of masking one's identity was extremely taxing even on the most resilient of children.

NEW PATTERNS OF AUTHORITY

In many of the testimonies given by child survivors of the Holocaust, it is apparent that household servants often had earned the trust or even affections of their employers before the war. The importance of their role was understood by household members, and they were sometimes treated as if they were a member of the family. Many child survivors recall the central role in their lives played by their maids and nannies and the mutual affection between themselves and their caregivers. However, at the end of the day, even when these women were trusted and treated in a familial manner, they were still employees and a power dynamic was associated with that employer/employee relationship. The primary purpose of their relationship was based ultimately on an economic arrangement, and this shaped the basic power dynamic.

Under the Nazi occupation, this power dynamic shifted. Gentile household employees found themselves higher on the social ladder than their former employers based on their status as non-Jews. While under the Nazi racial hierarchy Slavic peoples were considered inferior to Germans, they were above Jews. Not only did the power dynamic between lower-class Poles and middle-class or affluent Jews change in the public realm, it also changed dramatically in the intimate realm in cases where former domestic employees protected their former charges. Their role changed from servant to potential savior. Former employers entrusted these women with becoming the primary decision makers in a new role in which their decisions ultimately had life-or-death consequences. The former employers were completely at the mercy of their former employees. A domestic servant had the power to attempt to protect their child, to refuse, and to betray the family at any moment once she became a part of their conspiracy. Sometimes a former domestic servant was the natural choice for this role, based on the prewar relationship she had with her former employers, and sometimes she was just the only choice.

In the case of Abraham Foxman's protection by his former nanny, Bronisława Kurpi, this household employee did not begin working for the family until after the outbreak of the war.[45] When the Germans ordered that Jews move into the Vilna ghetto, the maid approached the couple and asked what they would do with the baby. His mother, Helen Foxman, replied that the baby, then thirteen months old, would go with them into the ghetto and what happened to them would happen to the child. Kurpi proposed that the family allow her to take little Abraham instead. Helen Foxman said that when Kurpi offered there was no time to think about it.[46] With no time for discussion, Mrs. Foxman looked to her husband, who replied, "Okay, take him," and she accepted this under the assumption that he knew better than she did and the decision was for the best.[47] The couple gave Kurpi all their possessions, with the exception of 180 rubles, so that she could sell them to support herself and the child; and Mr. Foxman promised he would continue to support them from the ghetto.[48] At Kurpi's request, the couple gave her a statement saying that they were giving her the child as her own; and Kurpi had the child baptized as Czesław Kurpi, registering him as her own offspring.[49] Both parents continued to earn money while confined in the ghetto and continued to pass funds along to Kurpi to care for their child. Once a week Helen Foxman would slip away from the ghetto to go check on the child in Kurpi's home in Vilna, and Kurpi would continually pressure Mr. Foxman for money. The child recognized Mrs. Foxman, but thought she was his aunt. The baby knew Kurpi as his mother, and Mrs. Foxman was not allowed to hold or kiss him when she visited.[50]

Kurpi, when she was employed by the Foxmans, had acted as the child's caregiver on their directives; but now in this new situation, she held all the power and dictated the terms of when the couple could see their child, how they were to behave around him, and how the child should understand who they were. When Kurpi requested that they sign the document stating that they gave her their child, they complied. The Foxmans were a religious family, and now under this new social situation and time of need, they felt they had to comply with Kurpi: allowing their child to be baptized and raised as a Catholic, and giving up control of their child's spiritual life, along with all other decisions about his upbringing and health.[51] This is a powerful example of how the power dynamic changed under this new situation. This maid, marginalized through her sex and class status, now dictated the new terms of this relationship with her former employers.

In her testimony, Mrs. Foxman stated that Kurpi threatened her husband, telling him that if he refused to pay she would go to the Gestapo and turn in the circumcised child.[52] Given her attachment to the child, this may have been merely an attempt to secure more money from the couple. The couple at one time also demanded that the child be returned, but Kurpi refused. Joseph Foxman testified that he realized then that the nanny who was raising their baby was, in fact, blackmailing them.[53] This former employee, rather than acting as a conduit of the parents' values, controlled their access to their own child. The parents had no say in his upbringing anymore, and the child's survival was left in the hands of this woman.

When the couple felt they had to leave the ghetto in order to survive, Mr. Foxman went to stay with a Polish family and Mrs. Foxman stayed with Kurpi.

She was initially "afraid to go to the *goya*," since Kurpi was already sheltering the child and Mrs. Foxman did not want to upset the situation there and was not even sure if Kurpi would agree to take her.[54] According to Mrs. Foxman, the two women got along fairly well while Mr. Foxman was away before the war; but once he returned, there was conflict in the household.[55] Kurpi agreed to shelter Mrs. Foxman and helped her obtain papers so she could work, and Mrs. Foxman in turn passed as a gentile working to pay for her upkeep. Kurpi found a place for the two women and the child to live on the outskirts of Vilna. Joseph Foxman wrote, "Even while Helen stayed with Bronia she suffered from her outbursts," and every so often Kurpi would force Mrs. Foxman to leave, occasionally along with the baby.[56] Mr. Foxman states that, "On the whole, Bronia treated the child well. She fed him and kept him clean, but if he made any sign of even leaning toward Helen, Bronia would spank him."[57] Despite this, the child was very close to his caregiver and displayed his affection toward her with hugs and kisses.

The relationships between the Foxmans and Kurpi were complicated. Both Helen and Joseph Foxman recognized that without her efforts their child would have not survived and likely neither would they, as her care for the child freed them initially to focus on their own survival. Kurpi also sheltered Helen Foxman when she left the ghetto herself, and this relationship was extremely tenuous. Helen Foxman stated that Kurpi did "plenty of harm" to her during the time she sheltered her.[58] She described Kurpi as "a sick, vicious woman."[59] Helen had to work at 6:00 a.m., and Kurpi would keep her awake at night, would not allow her to so much as touch her own child even though he slept in the bed with Kurpi right next to her own bed, and frequently threw her out of the house. Helen Foxman had to deal with being relegated to being her own child's "aunt" and lived in constant fear that their protector would betray them. We do not have access to Kurpi's version of events or her motivations for her actions. After the war, she did not want to surrender Abraham to Helen and Joseph Foxman. This is evident in her attempts to obtain legal custody of the child and her attempted kidnapping of the child when legal means failed her. Kurpi wanted to continue in her role as the boy's mother after the war, so it can be assumed that this conflict over her desire to be Abraham's mother complicated her feelings toward Helen Foxman. However, she also did extend aid to this woman, even while her behavior was sometimes erratic and cruel.[60]

This case is illustrative of the extreme shift in power that took place when a former household employee took on the role of rescuer, even when it was not as pronounced as it was in this particular case. In the interwar period, domestic employees were clearly subordinated to their employers; but in the new social order of the Nazi era and in this new role of rescuer, these women had an unprecedented level of power over their former employers. Sometimes the former employee had fond or even familial feelings toward the parents of the charges they took, but this was not always the case, as we see evidenced in the Foxman/Kurpi case. Even when relations between the parents and caregiver were strained, their collaboration was nevertheless often vital for the success of the rescue. Kurpi received financial support from the Foxmans, easing the financial burden of caring for a small child during extremely difficult economic times. This collaboration between Kurpi and the Foxmans was strained, but it nonetheless had them all laboring toward a common cause — to keep this young child alive and safe during a time when his very existence was outlawed by the ruling regime.

LIBERATION

The war had changed relations and relationships between caregivers and charges, former employers and employees, and Polish Catholics and Polish Jews. Abnormal became normal; safety was turned into insecurity. The end of the war did not bring an end to these changes or to the connections between these particular groups of Poles and Jews. Aid providers and recipients were forever changed by their experiences. Children and their caregivers became closer through their participation in their mutual conspiracies, although their relationships became far more complicated. Caregivers suffered consequences for their decision to shelter children and had to reaffirm their decision day after day as new difficulties arose. Children lost track of their prewar identities and aspects of those identities, and suffered emotional damage even when they were in the care of someone who loved them so much she was willing to risk her own life to try to keep them alive. When the Nazis were pushed out of Poland, the happy endings still did not come. Children were emotionally scarred, and their protectors were reluctant to have their wartime secrets exposed. Many of the children they had risked their lives to keep were reclaimed either by family members or Jewish organizations, leaving the caregivers grieving.[61]

The caregivers took great risks participating in rescue and aid activities. Entering the ghettos, passing goods into the ghettos, or ferrying children out of the ghettos; obtaining housing, legal documents, or employment for Jews living clandestinely outside the ghetto walls; or concealing or passing off a Jewish child as their own were tremendously risky endeavors. These activities required a great deal of knowledge, the ability to seek out and take advantage of resources, and the ability to exploit a situation when needed. Sometimes when these women were essentially caught, their brazenness and quick thinking were all they had to rely on. This could mean feigning outrage or becoming aggressive when confronted by someone suspicious of their activity, being able to stick to a story under extreme stress, or knowing whom to contact when they needed emergency aid. The women who engaged in this behavior had already become empowered to some degree as a result of leaving their families of origin and assuming responsibility in their employers' home, but this new situation pushed them even further.

The act of rescuing and protecting a Jewish charge built on this newfound independence, empowering former domestic servants even further. This would result in a new set of expectations for their postwar lives. Many of these maids would come to believe they had earned the right to raise the children they protected independently and that the extended families of these children should be grateful to them for their efforts, but often this did not happen. Former maids who had been working in other capacities may have also felt as if they had transcended the social barriers that kept them in the lower class before the war, but when they went abroad they were expected to become maids again.

Former domestic servants who had saved their charges were also disappointed when after the war they were often not allowed to keep the children they had protected. In the case of the Foxmans and their nanny, Bronisława Kurpi, both parents survived; so they had a natural claim to the child they had placed in her care, even though she felt justified in keeping him. In cases in which a child's immediate family was murdered during the Holocaust, many Jewish children were still removed from their wartime rescuer even though she was the only parent figure they had left. Sometimes they would be sent to extended family members, but other times they were removed from the care of their rescuers to be placed in an institution either in Europe, Palestine, or the United States. Prior to the Holocaust, there were roughly a million Jewish children under the age of fourteen in Poland.[62] According to a report of the Central Jewish Committee of Poland, only about 3 percent of those children survived. Polish Jews were among the hardest hit of all of the victims of Nazi persecution, with only about 10 percent of the once thriving community surviving.[63] Children were especially hard hit in the Nazi death tolls, and so the recovery of these children by the Jewish community was a top priority.

The women of this chapter and my larger study knew their charges from before the war and then expended a great deal of energy protecting them from harm during the Nazi occupation and Holocaust. They risked their own lives and sometimes the lives of their friends and family. They sometimes had to cut ties with people they cared about and lived with the stress of knowing they could be caught at any moment. Often, the bond between the caregivers and their charges grew even stronger as a result of their participation in this conspiracy. Many of these women felt like mothers to these children, and their separation was heartbreaking.

These women, who went to great lengths to thwart the Nazi authorities and hide their activities from potential denouncers, could not freely talk about their experiences after the war. Joanna Michlic argues that in the postwar period dedicated rescuers were unable to reveal their wartime activities because it would result in stigmatization for their efforts.[64] During the interwar period, ethnonationalistic press labeled ethnic Poles who defended the rights of the Jewish minority against antisemitic violence or persecution as "Jews," "Jewish uncles and aunts," or "Jewish protectors and Jewish saviors."[65] These people were, according to Michlic, perceived and treated like traitors to the Polish collective by ethnonationalists and were thought to have violated cultural codes.[66] She argues that during the war, aid to Jews was perceived in the same fashion.

After the war, there was still this stigmatization for dedicated rescuers for their attachments to Jews. Rescuer accounts of their activity served as a reminder that rescue was a minority activity among ethnic Poles and a reminder of Polish persecution of their Jewish population (and their Polish helpers) by many while under Nazi occupation.[67] Violent acts of antisemitism occurred regularly in Poland *after* the war, such as the Kielce pogrom that was perpetrated on July 4, 1946. As a result, rescuers likely would have perceived that it could be dangerous to talk openly about their activities during the war, which meant that they had to continue keeping secrets from people and masking their wartime lives and suffering. More practically, hiding a Jewish charge during the occupation put others at risk, including members of a household. Sometimes these household members were a part of the conspiracy, and sometimes they did not know they were actually hiding someone. Many Poles saw the idea that a Pole would knowingly put their own family at risk to save a Jew as questionable behavior. In short, though rescue and aid activities did serve to thwart the aims of the Nazi occupiers, the majority of Poles did not see rescue in the same way as other clandestine resistance because it was associated with the protection of Jews, not ethnic Poles.

Many rescuers were disappointed with their treatment after the war. They were disappointed either because they were expected to resume their lives as domestic servants as if nothing had changed, or because they were separated from their charges after the war, or because after the war they had to continue to carry the burden of their clandestine activities for years to come.

NOTES

1. Videotaped testimony of Elizabeth Grotch, file no. 26284, tape 1, USC Shoah Foundation Visual History Archive, 9:14, Los Angeles, California.

2. Grotch had just turned four when she was removed from the ghetto, so this was likely in 1942. Videotaped testimony of Elizabeth Grotch.

3. Lwów was invaded by the Soviets in 1939 under the terms of the Nazi-Soviet pact. The Germans would invade the Soviet Union and take Lwów in June 1941.

4. Videotaped testimony of Elizabeth Grotch, file no. 26284, tape 2, USC Shoah Foundation Visual History Archive, 25:12, Los Angeles, California.

5. Ibid.

6. Videotaped testimony of Elizabeth Grotch, file no. 26284, tape 3, USC Shoah Foundation Visual History Archive, 2:17, Los Angeles, California.

7. The testimony does not indicate where the baby was sent.

8. Ibid., 2:52.

9. Videotaped testimony of Elizabeth Grotch, file no. 26284, tape 2, USC Shoah Foundation Visual History Archive, 27:48, Los Angeles, California. The death of Grotch's mother was likely quite upsetting for Zillow, as she had assumed a mothering role toward her employer before the war.

10. Videotaped testimony of Elizabeth Grotch, file no. 26284, tape 3, USC Shoah Foundation Visual History Archives, 3:25, Los Angeles, California.

11. See also Maria Hochberg-Mariańska and Noe Grüss, eds., *The Children Accuse* (London: Vallentine Mitchell, 1996); Wiktoria Śliwowska, ed., *The Last Eyewitnesses: Children of the Holocaust Speak*, vol. 1 (Evanston, IL: Northwestern University Press, 1998); Jakub Gutenbaum and Agnieszka Latała, eds., *The Last Eyewitness: Children of the Holocaust Speak*, vol. 2 (Evanston, IL: Northwestern University Press, 2005); Elaine Saphier Fox, ed., *Out of Chaos: Hidden Children Remember the Holocaust* (Evanston, IL: Northwestern University Press, 2013); Kerry Bluglass, ed., *Hidden from the Holocaust: Stories of Resilient Children Who Survived and Thrived* (London: Praeger, 2003); Emunah Nachmany Gafny, *Dividing Hearts: The Removal of Jewish Children from Gentile Families in Poland in the Immediate Postwar Years* (Jerusalem: Yad Vashem, 2009); Nahum Bogner, *At the Mercy of Strangers: The Rescue of Jewish Children with Assumed Identities in Poland* (Jerusalem: Yad Vashem, 2009); Joanna Michlic, "Rebuilding Shattered Lives: Some Vignettes of Jewish Children's Lives in Early Postwar Poland," in *Holocaust Survivors: Resettlement, Memories, Identities*, ed. Dalia Ofer, Françoise S. Ouzan, and Judy Tydor Baumel-Schwartz (New York: Berghan Books, 2012); Joanna B. Michlic, "Who Am I? Jewish Children Search for Identity in Postwar Poland," in *Polin: Studies in Polish Jewry*, vol. 20: *Making Holocaust Memory*, ed. Gabriel Finder, Natalia Aleksiun, Antony Polonsky, and Jan Schwarz (Oxford: Littman Library of Jewish Civilization, 2008); and Joanna B. Michlic, *Jewish Children in Nazi-Occupied Poland: Survival and Polish-Jewish Relations during the Holocaust as Reflected in Early Postwar Recollections* (Jerusalem: Yad Vashem, 2008).

12. Videotaped interview of Sarah Wall, file no. 42189-1, tape 1, June 14, 1998, USC Shoah Foundation Visual History Archive, Los Angeles, California.

13. Ibid. Rodziewiecz offered to take the child's mother with her; but her mother believed that the more people Rodziewiecz had to hide the greater the danger, so she declined this offer.

14. Ibid., 18:30.

15. Videotaped interview of Sarah Wall, file no. 42189-1, tape 1, June 14, 1998, USC Shoah Foundation Visual History Archive, Los Angeles, California.

16. Genia Olczak also passed off her charge, Gabriel, as her illegitimate child, as did Franceszka Ziemiańska. See the interview of Genia Olczak, Warsaw, Poland, October 4, 2005, translated and transcribed by Bianka Kraszewski, who had interviewed Olczak and provided the author of this chapter with a copy of the interview. Introduction to interview, Bianka Kraszewski, February 1, 2006, provided by Paul Zakrzewski. Anita Lobel,

No Pretty Pictures: A Child of War (New York: Harper Collins, 1998). Videotaped testimony of Bernhard Kempler, file no. 33193, September 12, 1997, USC Shoah Foundation Visual History Archive, Los Angeles, California.

17. Ibid., 22:49.

18. Ibid., 27:40. She actually says, "Never was there a time when I felt like I wasn't treated like I was the most important person both in my nanny's life and my mother's life," when recollecting her childhood and the bonds she would feel all her life with both of these women.

19. Ibid., 27:58. She clarifies: she did not learn these ideas from the family or her caregiver, but rather from the neighborhood kids she played with.

20. Videotaped interview of Sarah Wall, file no. 42189-1, tape 2, 26:10, June 14, 1998, USC Shoah Foundation Visual History Archive, Los Angeles, California.

21. Ibid.

22. Maria Hochberg-Mariańska and Noe Grüss, eds., "Karolina Sapetowa," in *The Children Accuse* (London: Vallentine Mitchell, 1996), 277-79.

23. Ibid.

24. Ibid., 278.

25. Ibid.

26. Ibid., 278.

27. Ibid.

28. Ibid.

29. Ibid.

30. Ibid.

31. Michlic, *Jewish Children in Nazi Occupied Poland*, 89-91. Sepetowa was declared Righteous Among the Nations by Yad Vashem.

32. Hochberg-Mariańska and Grüss, "Karolina Sapetowa," in *The Children Accuse*, 277.

33. Videotaped testimony of Elizabeth Grotch, file no. 26284, tape 3, 7:14, USC Shoah Foundation Visual History Archives, Los Angeles, California.

34. Videotaped testimony of Bernhard Kempler, file no. 33193, tape 2, September 12, 1997, USC Shoah Foundation Visual History Archives, Los Angeles, California.

35. Videotaped testimony of Bernhard Kempler, file no. 33193, tape 2, 8:32-9:00, September 12, 1997, USC Shoah Foundation Visual History Archives, Los Angeles, California.

36. Ibid., 9:09. Kempler's caregiver was actually suffering from cancer at this time.

37. Ibid., 9:39.

38. Ibid., 9:55-10:00.

39. Ibid., 10:07-10:28.

40. Anita Lobel, *No Pretty Pictures: A Child of War* (New York: HarperCollins, 1998).

41. This work contributes to the existing scholarship on Holocaust rescuers not only by shedding light on motivations, but also by depicting these rescuers in a much more human and less heroic fashion. For further reading on rescuers, see also Martin Gilbert, *The Righteous: The Unsung Heroes of the Holocaust* (New York: Holt, 2003); Mordecai Paldiel, *The Path of the Righteous: Gentile Rescuers of Jews during the Holocaust* (New Jersey: KTAV Publishing, 1993); Carol Rittner and Sandra Myers, eds., *The Courage to Care: Rescuers of Jews during the Holocaust* (New York: New York University Press, 1986); Mark Klempner, *The Heart Has Reasons: Holocaust Rescuers and Their Stories of Courage* (Cleveland, OH: Pilgrim Press, 2006); Ellen Land-Weber, *To Save a Life: Stories of Holocaust*

Rescue (Chicago: University of Illinois Press, 2000); Nechama Tec, *When Light Pierced the Darkness: Christian Rescue of Jews in Nazi-Occupied Poland* (New York: Oxford University Press, 1986); Samuel P. Oliner and Pearl M. Oliner, *The Altruistic Personality: The Rescue of Jews in Nazi Europe* (New York: Macmillan, 1998); Patrick Henry, *We Only Know Men: The Rescue of Jews in France during the Holocaust* (Washington, DC: Catholic University of America Press, 2007); Eva Fogelman, *Conscience and Courage: Rescuers of Jews during the Holocaust* (New York: Doubleday, 1994); and Malka Drucker, *Rescuers: Portraits of Moral Courage in the Holocaust* (New York: Holmes and Meier, 1992).

42. Videotaped interview of Sarah Wall, file no. 42189-1, tape 2, June 14, 1998, USC Shoah Foundation Visual History Archives, Los Angeles, California.

43. Videotaped testimony of Elizabeth Grotch, file no. 26284, tape 3, 3:51, USC Shoah Foundation Visual History Archives, Los Angeles, California.

44. The children were first imprisoned in Montelupich and then sent to Płaszów, where they were protected by their aunt and uncle; later they were transported to Ravenbruck and then Auschwitz.

45. Second Generation of Long Island Collection, interview of Helen Foxman, tape 1, July 6, 1983, United States Holocaust Memorial Museum, RG 50.205*0028, Washington, DC.

46. Brana Gurewitsch, ed., "Helen Foxman," in *Mothers, Sisters, Resisters: Oral Histories of Women Who Survived the Holocaust* (Tuscaloosa: University of Alabama Press, 1998), 35.

47. Ibid.

48. Second Generation of Long Island Collection, interview of Helen Foxman, tape 1, July 6, 1983, United States Holocaust Memorial Museum, RG 50.205*0028, Washington, DC.

49. Joseph Foxman, *In the Shadow of Death* (New York: Yad Vashem and Holocaust Survivor's Project, 2011), 17.

50. Ibid., 18–19.

51. Many wartime protectors obtained baptismal certificates for their charges because it was necessary. This allowed the children to pass as Polish Catholics.

52. Translation of testimony of Helen and Joseph Foxman, RG 301/ file no. 3605, March 17, 1947, Jewish Historical Institute [Yiddish] in Foxman, *In the Shadow of Death*, 72.

53. Ibid.

54. Helen Foxman interview, tape 1, July 6, 1983, Second Generation of Long Island Collection, United States Holocaust Memorial Museum, RG 50.205*0028, Washington, DC.

55. The source of this conflict is not readily apparent in any of the sources, but in her testimony Mrs. Foxman attributes it to Kurpi being a lesbian.

56. Foxman, *In the Shadow of Death*, 20.

57. Ibid.

58. Gurewitsch, "Helen Foxman," in *Mothers, Sisters, Resisters*, 41.

59. Ibid.

60. There was very little housing available, so when Joseph found an apartment, the entire family lived there with Kurpi. Joseph wrote in his memoir, "After having saved the child, she was regarded as a part of the family" (21). See Foxman, *In the Shadow of Death*.

61. For the postwar plight of children, see Gafny, *Dividing Hearts*; Bogner, *At the Mercy of Strangers*; Michlic, "Rebuilding Shattered Lives"; and Michlic, "Who Am I?" For the postwar plight of rescuers, see Joanna Michlic, "The Stigmatization of Dedicated Polish

Women Rescuers during the Second World War and Its Aftermath," *East European Memory Studies*, no. 13 (2013), 1–6 (journal of the Memory at War project, Digital Humanities Network, Cambridge University, UK).

62. Bogner, *At the Mercy of Strangers*, 15.

63. Ibid.

64. Joanna B. Michlic, "Daily Life of Polish Women, Dedicated Rescuers of Jews during and after the Second World War," in *Ethics, Art, and Representations of the Holocaust: Festschrift in Honor of Berel Lang*, ed. Caroline S. Gould, Simone Gigliotti, and Jacob Golomb (Lanham, MD: Lexington Books, 2014), 215–23.

65. Ibid., 215–20.

66. Ibid.

67. In Jan T. Gross, *Fear: Antisemitism in Poland after Auschwitz: An Essay in Historical Interpretation* (New York: Random House, 2007). Gross argues that the guilt and shame of Polish behavior toward their Jewish cocitizens was manifested by acts of violence toward the Jews who survived the Holocaust and remained in Poland immediately after the war. He credits these feelings of guilt and shame as the real root cause of the Kielce pogrom on July 4, 1946.

II

AFTER THE WAR

REBUILDING
SHATTERED LIVES,
RECOLLECTING
WARTIME
EXPERIENCES

AVINOAM PATT

A ZIONIST HOME

JEWISH YOUTHS
AND THE
KIBBUTZ FAMILY
AFTER THE
HOLOCAUST

In the March 1946 volume of the *Hashomer Hatzair* movement newspaper, Zelig Shushan, an emissary from the *Yishuv* in Palestine, described his encounter with the survivors in Europe in an article entitled "The Meeting with the Comrades in the Diaspora."

> We thought that all of the Jews had been killed, that we were the only survivors, that no Jews would come to *Eretz Israel* because each one had been killed in the death wagons, gas chambers, in the crematoria . . . Yet, some of you managed to survive, in the forests, in a bunker, fighting with the partisans . . .
>
> And when I come to you and I see what you have managed to create, how you have already instilled content to your life, when I see the devotion to the kibbutz, to comrades, I see exactly in you the light that I see in the windows around us . . .
>
> You are not alone in your struggle. You are comrades in a large movement "*Hashomer Hatzair*."[1]

These young survivors, he suggested, who had lost mothers, fathers, brothers, and sisters, now carried an obligation to those who had died to continue along the path of *halutziut* (the pioneering way). This was a path in which they would not have to struggle alone, however; they were now part of a larger family, the worldwide movement of *Hashomer Hatzair*.[2] In the aftermath of catastrophe, young survivors such as those addressed by Shushan turned to the kibbutz groups created by Hashomer Hatzair and other Zionist movements after the war. What drew them to the kibbutzim of the Zionist youth movements in such disproportionately large numbers? Why did they choose to join the kibbutzim of the pioneering Zionist youth movements rather than those frameworks created by other political parties? Was it an overwhelming Zionist ideological conclusion reached during the war or a more fundamental need for family, homes, and belonging that drew them to the movements? For the emissaries from the *Yishuv*, and indeed the *Yishuv* leadership as a whole, the success of the kibbutz groups in recruiting young people after the Shoah would play a vital role in decisions leading to the creation of the State of Israel. The perceived Zionist enthusiasm of the Surviving Remnant played no small part in convincing outside observers from the United States, Great Britain, and the United Nations that the Jewish survivors had reached an overwhelming Zionist conclusion after the Holocaust. Administrators and diplomats assigned to finding a solution to the Jewish Displaced Person (DP) situation interpreted the Zionist demonstrations by the youths in the kibbutzim as a sure sign that the DP population as a whole desired final settlement in Palestine. Nonetheless, though the members who joined the kibbutz groups in Poland described by Shushan had made the decision to travel with their group to Germany as part of the *Bricha* (the clandestine movement of Jewish departure from Poland), their membership in the kibbutz did not mean that they were the ardent Zionists they were perceived to be. In fact, their knowledge of Zionist ideology, history, and culture was elementary at best, and their decision to remain within the framework of the kibbutz depended more on the structure and security offered by the kibbutz framework, as well as the emotional and psychological support it provided to them. Using the lens of children and family as a frame of analysis, this chapter will examine the function of Zionism in the kibbutzim of the Zionist youth movements in postwar Poland and Germany, in an attempt to understand the widespread appeal of such frameworks for largely orphaned Jewish youths in the aftermath of the Holocaust. Such an analysis suggests that the kibbutz framework proved appealing for Jewish youths after the Holocaust, many of whom had lost one or both parents, siblings, and extended family during the war, by providing a surrogate family in a structure that sought to recreate the warmth of the prewar home, while offering a sense of camaraderie and purpose in a highly therapeutic and productive social unit. Thus, for many among the survivor youths, what made Zionism most appealing after the war were its functional, pragmatic, and psychological benefits, not its ideological ones. Still, this did not preclude the growth of Zionist enthusiasm once in the kibbutz and the strengthening of ties to the wider Zionist project; indeed the two needs worked hand in hand —it was the desperate need for family and camaraderie that often kept young survivors within the kibbutz group, even when more desirable immigration and living options became available. At the same time, the membership of the young survivors in the kibbutzim and the Zionist youth movements would transform the nature of these movements in the wake of the Holocaust and ultimately aid in the creation of the Jewish state.

JEWISH YOUTHS AFTER THE HOLOCAUST

From the first days following liberation, the age of the surviving Jewish DP population skewed dramatically to those under the age of thirty. A series of reports and surveys presented by various agencies working with survivors in Germany and representing a broad spectrum of interests, from the earliest weeks following liberation and for years thereafter, consistently estimated the proportion of Jewish DPs between the ages of fifteen and thirty at more than half and often above 80 percent of the total Jewish population.[3] Considering that survival required strength, hardiness, selection for labor, quickness of foot and wit, general adaptability, and the ability to cut ties from family and friends, it should be no surprise that young adults were most likely to survive. As youths came together in Germany in the first weeks and months following liberation, a number of them formed kibbutzim, or collective social frameworks affiliated with Zionist youth movements, and *kibbutzei hakhshara* (agricultural training farms), such as Kibbutz Buchenwald or Kibbutz Nili on the estate of Julius Streicher.[4] Such kibbutzim had the appeal of isolating youths from the less-than-ideal existence in the DP camps and providing a replacement family for the one lost during the war. Likewise, many among the youths in postwar Poland gravitated to such frameworks for a variety of pragmatic reasons, including the offers of food, shelter, security, camaraderie, warmth, and the promise of departure from Poland, as well as the offer of something to do on a daily basis. (These kibbutz groups, based on the prewar collectivist models of the Zionist youth movements, differed from the kibbutzim in Israel in that they were not necessarily agricultural in nature, although over time some of the groups did move to one of the forty *hakhsharot*, or agricultural training farms, operated in the American-occupied zone of Germany.) Still, membership in the youth movements came with the expectation of additional "adult" responsibilities often thrust upon adolescents and young adults — namely, conscription to fight in Israel's War of Independence in 1948 and a leading role in the *Ha'apalah* movement in 1947 — in the collective struggle to create the State of Israel.

RECRUITING SUCCESS IN POLAND

The first recourse for many Jewish youths in Poland after the war was to turn to the local Jewish committees that had been formed, seeking answers to their most pressing needs, including food, shelter, health, and security, before they could turn to the larger questions of how and where to continue their lives. Beginning in the summer of 1944 in eastern Poland, Jewish survivors rapidly organized a system of communal and political organizations.[5] From early on, there was a great deal of competition among the Jewish political groups for control of the "Jewish street."[6] In accord with the *Bricha's* effort to organize willing segments of the Jewish public for departure from Poland, the *Hashomer Hatzair* youth movement, in unison with *Dror*, began to organize kibbutzim in a number of cities in Poland in the spring and summer of 1945, including Warsaw, Lodz, Sosnowiec, Bytom, and Kraków.[7] Over the summer of 1945, the movement also opened kibbutzim in Będzin, Częstochowa, Gliwice, and Katowice. The political debate between the various Zionist movements did not eliminate the potential for cooperation among the various movements, with *Left Poalei Zion, Poalei Zion C. S., Dror*, and *Hashomer Hatzair* joining together in June 1945 to form the League for Labor Palestine.[8] In addition to the movements that joined together in the League were the General Zionists and *Mizrachi*, who initially combined with *Gordonia, Akiva*, and *Noar Zioni* to form *Ichud*. *Ichud*, like the United Zionist Organization (UZO) and *Nocham* in Germany, was intended as a political group to represent the unity of the *She'erit Hapletah*, but from early on was involved in a great deal of competition from the pioneering youth movements.[9] The Zionist youth movements enjoyed success in recruiting a growing percentage of surviving Jewish youths into the kibbutz framework for Jewish youths in postwar Poland. According to the calculations of historian David Engel, from the spring of 1945 the total percentage of Jewish youths in Poland who had joined the kibbutzim grew from 7.5 percent to 17 percent by the fall of 1945. Between June and November 1945, the number of Jewish youths living in the kibbutzim of youth movements grew by at least 500 percent.[10] Among the youth movements that emphasized "pioneer" training (*Hashomer Hatzair, Dror*, and *Gordoniah*), the number had increased to 7167 members by the spring and summer of 1946, from as few as eight hundred the winter before.[11] This quest for members would in turn assist in swelling the numbers of Jews departing in the *Bricha*, the semiorganized movement of Jewish departure from Poland. Over the course of 1945–1946, over one hundred thousand Jews left Poland as part of the *Bricha*, over one-third of them youths organized in the kibbutzim of the pioneering youth movements (such as *Hashomer Hatzair, Dror*, and *Gordoniah*) and many of them bound for Palestine via the American zones of Germany, Italy, and Austria. By the beginning of 1947, one American Jewish Joint Distribution Committee (JDC) survey counted sixteen thousand kibbutz members in the DP camps of the American zone of Germany, approximately 10 percent of the total Jewish DP population.[12]

KIBBUTZ LOCHAMEI HAGETAOT 'AL SHEM TOSIA ALTMAN

Among those groups traveling with the *Bricha* from Poland to Germany in November 1945 was a group of 110 young survivors, who had joined kibbutz groups in Bytom and Sosnowiec. The two *Hashomer Hatzair* kibbutzim united after their arrival in the Landsberg DP camp, and like many of the *Hashomer*

Hatzair kibbutzim named after heroes of the wartime resistance, came to take the name *Kibbutz Lochamei HeGettaot 'al shem Tosia Altman* (the Ghetto Fighters Kibbutz named after Tosia Altman; hereafter, Kibbutz Tosia Altman). The kibbutz groups were initially named after the town where they were organized. The decision to name many of the kibbutzim after the movement's resistance fighters who had died during the war was only taken at the first *Hashomer Hatzair* movement conference in postwar Germany at Biberach on December 10, 1945.[13] There several of the kibbutzim were renamed after *Hashomer Hatzair* resistance fighters such as Mordecai Anielewicz (the first groups from Sosnowiec and Bytom), Chaviva Reik, Yosef Kaplan (first from Warsaw and Kraków), Tosia Altman, Aryeh Vilner, and Zvi Brandes.[14] Other kibbutzim carried symbolic names such as "*LeShichrur*" (Toward Liberation), "*BaDerech*" (On the Way), and "*BaMa'avak*" (In the Struggle).[15]

Members of Kibbutz Tosia Altman wrote a collective diary detailing the history of the kibbutz, providing an excellent opportunity to study its experience from within and providing a glimpse of what life was like for young survivors who chose to join the kibbutzim after the war. Forty years after the completion of the diary, it was translated from the original Yiddish into Hebrew by surviving members of the kibbutz.[16] The two *madrichim* of the kibbutz, Miriam and Baruch Wind (Yechieli), who served as the guides, teachers, and spiritual leaders of the kibbutz, had returned to Lublin after spending the war in the Soviet Union. After spending fourteen months in the American zone, eight of which they spent farming the soil of Germany, the majority of the kibbutz left for Palestine in early 1947. They arrived there only in the spring of 1948 following a yearlong internment in Cyprus.

The *madricha* of Kibbutz Tosia Altman, Miriam Wind (née Richter), arrived in Lublin in March 1945. A member of the *Hashomer Hatzair* youth movement before the war, she first escaped from her hometown of Rowno (Rivne) to Vilna in 1939 (at the age of eighteen); after her capture in Romania in 1941, she escaped and spent the years from 1942 to 1945 in Tashkent, where she met her husband, Baruch.[17] Once in Lublin after the war, she met with the postwar leaders of *Dror* (Yitzhak Zuckerman and Zivia Lubetkin) and *Hashomer Hatzair* (Israel Glazer and Shlomo Mann), who instructed Miriam to organize and lead the third postwar kibbutz in Sosnowiec.[18] She separated from her husband, Baruch, who was sent to lead the fourth kibbutz group in Bytom, and began to organize a kibbutz group in Sosnowiec in the beginning of April. The movement focused on organizing kibbutzim in Silesia, where many youths were to be found after repatriation by the Polish government. The close access to Germany would also become advantageous for the *Bricha* movement in the emerging program of departure from Poland. Miriam looked for the first members of the kibbutz at the Jewish Committee in Sosnowiec, where they had gone to look for family. She also wandered the city looking for children to join the kibbutz. Youths arrived on trains, resettled by the new Polish government in Silesia, and were redeemed from monasteries and Polish families where they had hidden during the war.

The *madrichim* like Baruch and Miriam were uncertain of what they would find among these traumatized children and young adults. The youth who composed the postwar kibbutzim and the youth movement leadership in Palestine clearly had rather different understandings of Zionism. The youth movement leadership in Palestine was most concerned over what it referred to as the "quality" of the new membership. Thus, evaluations of these youths by the youth movement and Jewish Agency emissaries tended to evaluate the Zionist potential of these survivors to buttress their numbers in Palestine, to function as the vital added weight that could tip the balance to the creation of the Jewish state. The descriptions of the survivor youths by the youth movement emissaries were far from flattering or optimistic. They emphasized the demoralization, isolation, and indolence of the survivor youths.[19] *Hashomer Hatzair* activists expressed serious concerns over their ability to educate the thousands of refugee youths who filled the kibbutzim. In the words of one: "One needs a great deal of strength of spirit in order to create from this material a new type of man . . . it will take quite a few days and months [of] effort for them to be like us."[20]

Shaike Weinberg (later the director of the Diaspora Museum in Tel Aviv and the United States Holocaust Memorial Museum) wrote an educational program for *Hashomer Hatzair* activists working with kibbutzim, identifying what he understood to be the central characteristics of this "new human material." He characterized the youths by their lack of education, absence of a normal childhood, stunted mental development, and general demoralization and distrust in man, as well as "strong resentment and anger towards the collective lifestyle . . . and a cynical relation to ideals in any form."[21] With this in mind, he urged the *madrichim* to deepen loyalty to the movement, while not arousing in the youths the renewed feeling of being placed in a framework of coercion. The ideal activity was agricultural work in the kibbutzim when possible, or at the minimum a few hours each day of service work. In the cultural sphere, holiday ceremonies (both Jewish and Zionist for social life), general education to make up for lost time, as well as the teaching of Hebrew, Jewish history, the history of Zionism, *Hashomer Hatzair*, and socialism were of central importance. The leadership believed that Zionism, specifically *Hashomer Hatzair* Zionism, had the power to heal this "broken youth" by turning them into ideologically committed Zionists and that such training was an ideal use of time while kibbutz youths waited to leave Europe. Negative assessments of survivor youths notwithstanding, a closer look at the youths who chose to join the kibbutzim, and their reasons for doing so, reveals a relationship that is far more complex. The youths may have been traumatized by their wartime experiences, but they were willing to become active participants in the flourishing kibbutz framework—and in so doing challenged the expectations of the *Yishuv* activists, who questioned the ability of the survivor youths to aid in the building of the Zionist future. In the process, the survivors transformed the very nature of the youth movements, which came to depend on the young survivors for their existence.

JOINING THE KIBBUTZ GROUPS IN BYTOM AND SOSNOWIEC

Most of the young Jewish survivors who joined the kibbutzim in Bytom and Sosnowiec had either lost their entire family or had only one relative remaining. Many had survived in hiding, after the trauma of witnessing the destruction of their families. Some had returned from concentration camps and death marches, while others had managed to conceal their identities or be sheltered by non-Jewish families. This diverse group of youths found themselves together in the communal living format of a kibbutz in western Poland.

The stories of the young members of Kibbutz Tosia Altman and their reasons for joining the kibbutz — first, the relative security of the framework that offered stability, structure, and the warmth of home in the chaos and confusion after liberation, and second, the offers of departure for Palestine and the hope for a better future — provide a glimpse into the experiences of those who joined kibbutz groups after the war.

At the age of seventeen, Haim Shorrer was liberated by Russian troops from his hiding place in a forest in eastern Poland in June 1944. Three months earlier, he had witnessed the murder of his entire family after their discovery in a bunker by Ukrainian collaborators and had only narrowly managed to escape. After four years in hiding and on the run, disconnected from the rest of the world, he now faced liberation, alone and with few prospects for the future. As he recalled years later, "The period following liberation was more difficult than the war itself. Once I was liberated, everyone went on their own path."[22] A Jewish man by the name of Haber adopted Shorrer and brought him to his home in Klosowa, where he sought different forms of work, trying to make a living in Poland for the next year. By the summer of 1945, however, Shorrer left Klosowa and made his way to Bytom, where he joined the kibbutz led by Baruch Wind (Yechieli).

Like Shorrer, Monish Einhorn (Haran) found himself completely alone at the end of the war. Born in 1926 in Zaleszczyki on the Dniester, on the interwar border between Poland and Romania, Einhorn was part of a large family that was completely wiped out during the war. Before a mass deportation of Jews from the area in May 1943, he managed to escape to the forests and survived until being liberated by the Red Army in March 1944. He escaped a German counterattack and traveled to Czernowitz, where he remained until the end of the war, when he was repatriated to Sosnowiec by the newly formed Polish government.[23] Once he arrived in Sosnowiec, completely alone and in foreign surroundings, Einhorn looked for a new home. He found it in the kibbutz led by Miriam. "Everything was new there, life was new . . . It is difficult to describe how important it was. The kibbutz gave a framework to kids who didn't know what to do with themselves, who had no family."[24]

Members of the kibbutzim in Bytom and Sosnowiec often found their new homes in a random manner. Fishl Herszkowitz, a Galician Jew aged seventeen at the time of liberation, had survived in hiding, fighting with a partisan group against the Ukrainians at the end of the war. He first lived with a group of Jews in the area of Husiatyn following liberation, but the constant threats from Ukrainians led him to seek family to the west. He boarded a train of repatriates and arrived in Bytom; when he disembarked, he heard about the *Hashomer Hatzair* kibbutz and, being nicely received by kibbutz members, decided to join it.[25]

Other young Jewish survivors who joined the kibbutz groups in Bytom and Sosnowiec also found the kibbutz by chance, either hearing about it in the streets of the town or running into old acquaintances who told them about the kibbutz. Haim Bronstein was among a group of young survivors from the small town of Skalat (*Skałat*, prewar Polish name) in western Ukraine, who had been resettled by the Polish government in Bytom. Wandering through the streets of the city, he happened to see a blue-and-white flag inside the window of an apartment and overheard voices singing inside. He recognized two old acquaintances from Skalat, who had already joined the kibbutz, and decided that the kibbutz presented a better option than any others available to him at the time.[26]

The recognition of a familiar face among a world of strangers was often enough to convince orphaned survivors to join such kibbutz groups. Aharon Segel was also an unlikely candidate to join the kibbutz in Bytom. He had survived under an assumed identity in the Tarnopol district working as a cattle herder. Nine months after liberation, he returned to his village near Skalat to discover that he was the only one from a family of seven children to survive the war.

I was basically adopted by the head of the community, Moshe Gelbtukh, who gave me a pair of *tefilin* (ritual phylacteries), and I returned from being a devout Catholic to a devout Jew. After six months in Skalat we went to Gliwice, but there was no room for me there, so Mr. Gelbtukh sent me to a *HaPoel HaMizrachi* kibbutz in Kraków. On the way we passed through Bytom, and I met someone who told me that a friend from Skalat, Haim Bronstein, was living in a secular kibbutz in Bytom. I decided that it would at least be better to be with one friend so I stayed in Bytom.[27]

Thus, Aharon Segel went from growing up in a traditional Jewish family to passing as a Catholic during the war and then returning to the Jewish fold, only to finally join a secular Marxist-Zionist kibbutz in Bytom bound for Palestine.

Yolek Weintraub (Yoel Ben-Porat), also from Skalat, was only fourteen at the end of the war. He managed to survive in the forest with an uncle from 1941 to 1944; at the end of the war, he was adopted by a Russian family that wanted him to convert. He instead chose to be repatriated by the Polish government and thus found himself in Bytom. There he ran into Aharon Segel, who told him that he had joined a kibbutz and that Yoel's cousin, Haim Bronstein, was also a member of the group. He had never heard of a kibbutz before, but decided that living with friends would be preferable to being on his own in Bytom.[28] In this way, the group of boys from Skalat all independently found their way into the *HaShomer Haztair-Dror* kibbutz in Silesia.

A number of the kibbutz members joined the kibbutz only after first trying to rejoin Polish society. Salusia Altman (Sarah Ben-Zvi) was born in Częstochowa to a religious family in 1931. When the war broke out in 1939, she was not even nine years old. Her family moved into the Częstochowa ghetto; but when the deportations began, they were hidden in the family factory by the foreman, Jacques. After the ghetto was liquidated, her father disappeared, and she and her mother were placed in the Hasag forced labor camp. Following her liberation from the camp on January 16, 1945, she returned first to Lodz and then to Częstochowa. Although she knew other youths who were joining kibbutz groups, Altman had first sought to return to Polish society, focusing on her education before entertaining any thoughts of departure. However, her encounter with an antisemitic teacher led her to join the kibbutz in Bytom, a little over six months after her liberation from the Hasag camp, with the approval of her mother.[29]

Inka Weisbort also first made an effort to integrate into the newly liberated Polish state by joining the Polish army. Nineteen years old at the end of the war, she had survived a death march from Auschwitz and managed to escape from Ravensbrück in April 1945. After three months recuperating in Germany, she returned to Poland to try to find her family, but found no one. She tried to join a unit of the Polish army in July 1945, but was expelled when her Jewish origins were discovered. She found the sister of her stepfather in Sosnowiec, where she heard about a joint kibbutz of *Hashomer Hatzair* and *Dror*. Having few other options, she decided to join the kids all "crowded into a small apartment" in September 1945.[30] Like Salusia, her first choice was to reenter Polish society. However, her encounter with antisemitism and the slim prospects for a future in Poland led her to look for other social options. This was how she became a part of the kibbutz organized by Miriam.

Many of the young survivors who joined the kibbutzim in Bytom and Sosnowiec (which would later comprise Kibbutz Tosia Altman) came from homes that made them unlikely candidates to join a Zionist kibbutz. Their wartime experiences, while traumatic, were far from uniform, and the process of finding the kibbutz differed for many of them. Yet, many of those who reached the kibbutz decided to remain with it. As Miriam described, the priority was not to find youths with a Zionist background; in fact, this was the least of her concerns: "The only goal then was to rescue the youth . . . to remove them from monasteries, to gather them; they didn't have a home . . . The majority of them came from camps, from hiding with non-Jews (*goyim*) . . . from Ukraine, from towns, from the forest."[31] The youth movement focused on providing shelter for the various youths who would constitute the future of the movement. In so doing, they managed to create a surrogate home and family for youths orphaned by the Holocaust.

THE DIARY OF KIBBUTZ TOSIA ALTMAN

The members of the kibbutzim in Bytom and Sosnowiec provided a snapshot of their everyday life within the kibbutz by keeping a kibbutz diary. Members did not sign entries, but instead wrote them in the first-person plural describing events collectively. This look into kibbutz life reveals the mutually beneficial nature of the relationship between the youths and the youth movement desperate for new members. Miriam instigated the writing of the diary with the second group while the kibbutz was still in Germany and assigned subjects to various members. The journal itself begins with the initial period in Poland; apparently members described these events as they remembered them in the months after their departure from Poland. While it must certainly be treated cautiously as a historical document that underwent editing, with sections whose authorship or genesis is unclear, it provides a rich and exceptional point of view on the Zionist experience in postwar Europe.

The opening pages of the diary from the first three months in Poland testify to the value of the kibbutz to its members in both Bytom and Sosnowiec, while also revealing the beginning of another subtle process in this period, the transition from individual to collective thinking. Some kibbutz members initially had difficulty with the notion of self-maintenance (*meshek atzmi*) and the sharing of clothes and all wages earned at outside work, complaining about the poor allocation of clothing and the need for connections (*protekcja*) to get certain items.[32] Indeed, some members acknowledged that it "was difficult to drop 'I' from one's vocabulary," but the *madrichim* helped to inculcate the value of collectivism in the members. Although ideological development was rather slow in the early period, the two sections of the kibbutz developed socially, learning what was positive versus negative behavior and deciding which members would be allowed to stay and which (like the lazy Yakov Ha-Sandlar) would be expelled for failing to contribute.[33] It was in this early period that members developed pride in contributing to the collective, happy to bring money into their new "home."

Nonetheless, it was quite clear that members of the kibbutz had little knowledge of the ideological debates that had suffused Polish Zionism in the interwar period and soon reemerged despite the unity efforts following liberation. For example, when *Hashomer Hatzair* decided to break off from the other Zionist youth movements in August 1945, the members of Kibbutz Tosia Altman were informed of these developments, but had little understanding of the ideological differences that distinguished them from *Dror* or other movements.[34] Even though Miriam and Baruch used this opportunity to explain the specifics of the *Hashomer Hatzair* ideology and educational program, members were more concerned with division within the kibbutz itself than any division between the movements, perhaps indicating an allegiance that was far more connected to the new "family" than to the movement as a whole.

The kibbutz members settled into a routine in Sosnowiec and Bytom, spending their days at work and their evenings immersed in "cultural" activities such as lectures, discussions, singing, and reading. Activities in the early period in Poland were differentiated between men and women, reinforcing traditional gender roles despite the wartime interlude. Women cooked, cleaned, and did the laundry, while the young men looked for outside work, creating a new home and family for the young survivors that replicated standard gender divisions.[35] Boys and girls slept in separate bedrooms, sharing the available bed space. Tremendous labor was necessary to ensure the day-to-day functioning of the kibbutz, with constant work in the kitchen to keep kibbutz members fed, usually work done by the women. Needless to say, housework was not the most popular assignment among the kibbutz members.

Still, the sense of camaraderie created by living and working together was highly therapeutic for the young survivors. For the women involved in sewing, the group activity provided them with a forum in which to talk about their experiences during the war and in the camps.[36] The young men worked and earned money together, providing for their new family. They looked up to Miriam and Baruch, who were certainly the "mother" and "father" of their respective groups in Sosnowiec and Bytom, despite being only three or four years older than most of their *chanichim* (youth movement members). The "cultural" activities prescribed by Shaike Weinberg constituted an important part of the daily experience for the youths in Sosnowiec and Bytom (and later in Germany as well), as they acquired the "Zionist" tools necessary for their future learning of Jewish and Zionist history, Jewish culture, and Hebrew.

Despite the increasing sense of comfort, after two months in the kibbutz the members began to grow impatient, constantly asking the *madrichim* when they would depart. Miriam in turn looked to the *Bricha* activists in Katowice for guidance on their date of departure from Poland. At the end of October 1945, both groups received the news they had long been waiting for: they would finally be able to leave Poland.

The Sosnowiec group departed on October 29, 1945, taking a train from Katowice to Prague, where the next day they were joined by Baruch's groups arriving from Bytom. Some questioned why they had to continue to conceal their identities after so many years in hiding (and the stationmaster at the Czech border questioned why "Greeks" would choose to go to Prague instead of Bratislava), but they did and thus managed to cross the border and reach Czechoslovakia. (The *Bricha* movement often supplied its groups with false Greek papers to facilitate travel through Europe.) After nearly two weeks in Prague, the group arrived in Munich, where the members began the next stage of their journey, as a united kibbutz in the DP camps of Germany.

The two sections of the kibbutz united in Landsberg (near Munich) with a total of 110 members in mid-November 1945.[37] This timetable meant that the kibbutz in fact preceded much of the *Bricha* from Poland—with the majority of the "infiltrees" into the DP camps arriving in the summer and early fall of 1946, following the Kielce pogrom on July 4 of the same year. Although Kibbutz Tosia Altman eventually spent its last eight months in Germany on a farm, the majority of the 280 kibbutzim (with over 16,000 members) were to be found within the DP camps of Germany, where there were a total of 156,000 Jews by June 1947.[38]

"CRISIS" WITHIN THE KIBBUTZ

Despite entries in the diary that suggest that this renewal of organizational and cultural work within the kibbutz (and contact with the wider movement) fortified members "prepared to face the difficulties of the future," it is clear that the difficult transition to the Landsberg DP camp in Germany took a toll on the kibbutz. According to one entry in the diary written shortly after their arrival in Landsberg, a number of members decided to depart from the kibbutz group; and out of thirty prospective members (aged seventeen to eighteen) who arrived from Prague to join the kibbutz, only five decided to stay, rejecting the idea of *shituf* (sharing) and the poor conditions in the kibbutz.[39] All in all, some fifteen original members (13–14 percent) decided to leave the kibbutz within the first two weeks in Landsberg, not only because of the difficult physical conditions they faced, but also because of political opposition within the camp. Some members discovered acquaintances within the camp and chose to join them instead, leaving the kibbutz for personal and familial, not political, reasons. The difficulty of the transition to Landsberg left the kibbutz in a perceived state of "crisis." Indeed, it seems that while the period in Poland was marked by efforts to attract new membership, the period in Germany for many kibbutzim would be defined by efforts to maintain membership and deepen loyalty to the movement.

While still in the DP camp in Landsberg, the *madrichim* worked to overcome a crisis of low morale through ideological education; and in one of the more fascinating episodes in the diary, the *madricha*, Miriam, decided that a mock trial would be ideal in order to stimulate discussion in the kibbutz and overcome the boredom which had begun to set in.[40] The *mazkir* (secretary general) of the kibbutz, Monish, was put on trial for supposedly deciding to leave the kibbutz to attend a conservatory in Frankfurt. At the trial, his attorneys argued that the kibbutz and Zionism were flawed; the setup of the kibbutz, with its emphasis on *shituf* (cooperative living), prevented a comfortable life in the kibbutz. Many speakers spoke strongly against Monish, arguing that it would be irresponsible of him to abandon the kibbutz.

In the diary, in a personal entry written after the "trial," Monish describes the treatment he faced from members stunned by his "betrayal." He endured shouting, curses, and even spitting. His closest friends seemed to become his greatest enemies. Yehudit stated that she simply "won't allow it," while Paula's reaction was personal: "I no longer respect him as a person, even if he does end up staying."[41] Another female member questioned, "How could he take on the position of *mazkir* when he always knew that he was going to leave?" Friends who previously would loan him a hat or clothes now refused. Others came to him in tears begging him to stay, while Hinda and Tzintza sat in their room "as if they were sitting *shiva* [the week-long mourning period observed by Jews after a death], wiping tears from their eyes."[42]

The dining room of the kibbutz was turned into a courtroom with space provided for the prosecution, defense, a judge, the accused, and the witnesses; the rest of the room was reserved for the audience. Arguing in his own defense while enduring shouts and catcalls from the audience, Monish blamed the faults of the kibbutz and the Zionist movement for his decision to leave. His defense attorneys, Yehudit and Ruth, still unaware that the trial was a farce, also blamed the Zionist movement and the institutions of the kibbutz. Ruth, who was also the administrator for sharing, blamed the idea of *shituf*, asking, "How is it possible that each individual not have his own pajamas and be forced to wear those of another?" Yehudit suggested that the work assignments in the kibbutz were not properly delegated and that a person needed "connections" (*protekcja*) in order to secure favorable positions. Monish indicted the whole concept of collective decision making in his own defense: "If I need to smoke a cigarette, the kibbutz will decide only five per day; if I want to go to the movies, do I have to wait until everyone is ready to go together?!" Finally, the prosecution (Inka, Hinda, and Salusia) spoke, "dismantling the house of cards that I (Monish) built in my charges"[43] and defending the kibbutz and the Zionist movement. After a period of questioning from the audience, the judges left to deliberate and returned with a verdict that was intended to be binding: "Whether by or against his will, Monish must recognize the fact that Zionism is the only way to establish (resurrect) the nation and the kibbutz the only way to actualization (hagshama). He must stay in the kibbutz!" Monish read a statement accepting the verdict of the court, and "all of a sudden, my worst enemies once again became my best friends. . . . I even received two rations of chocolate."[44] Afterward, the members discovered that Monish had in fact been acting.[45] The reactions of the members seem to have tended toward happiness and relief; there is no reference in the diary or in subsequent recollections to any sense of having been manipulated by Monish or Miriam and Baruch.

Accordingly, in the final decision of the "judges," which was meant to be binding, it was decided that Monish must recognize that Zionism was the only way to resurrect the Jewish people and the kibbutz—which, of course, he later said he had known all along. The episode of the "trial" so soon after the arrival and unification of the kibbutzim from Sosnowiec and Bytom points to a number of questions that the kibbutz group would have to face in Germany: how would members be encouraged to remain with the kibbutz now that other, potentially more attractive options were open to them? Why should they choose to stay with Hashomer Hatzair, as opposed to any of the other movements promising aliyah ("ascent," or immigration to the Land of Israel) and perhaps better connections to achieve this goal? Why would certain members choose the kibbutz over the prospect of migration to another country or the option of settling in Germany?

The complaints about the kibbutz and shituf suggest that for many of the members, these ideological goals were only worthy of sacrifice when considered in the light of the greater value of the kibbutz as a new family. Departure from the kibbutz, even if shituf and the lack of individual freedom were to blame, was an inexcusable betrayal. The pressure to conform and follow the dictates of the kibbutz remained strong. The "trial" stood out in the memory of the kibbutz members as a significant event in the development of the kibbutz. Miriam recalled the trial, nearly sixty years later, as a great success; and Monish was surprised by the ease with which he was able to slip into his role, as if he was "descended from a great line of actors."[46] However, the episode of the trial also points to the tensions that could easily boil to the surface when the kibbutz was faced with the crisis of one of its leaders' departure. Those arguing in his defense were quick to blame the narrow constraints of *shituf* and collectivism; his accusers were less concerned with his choice to leave the Zionist path than his decision (especially as *mazkir*) to abandon the kibbutz family, the ultimate act of betrayal.

Was the trial successful? It did reveal the degree to which the members of the kibbutz were susceptible to coercive tactics of ensuring continuing loyalty to the kibbutz group. It also revealed the intense need that many of the members felt to preserve the integrity of their new family following the wartime loss of their own families. In terms of the goals of the *madrichim*, Miriam and Baruch were successful in using the trial as an educational tool to demonstrate to the membership the importance of maintaining the kibbutz. The psychologically manipulative impact of the episode on the kibbutz is striking. Yet, there is no indication that any of the members were sufficiently put off by the manipulation to leave the kibbutz; on the contrary, the episode seems to have reinforced the reasons for remaining with the group for members who may have questioned the kibbutz framework. Nonetheless, it is also of note that the reasons put forth by the members for remaining within the kibbutz had little to do with the ideological basis of the kibbutz or the youth movement. On the contrary, his accusers first vilified Monish for abandoning his comrades in the kibbutz before defending the concepts of collectivism and the goal of *aliyah*.

KIBBUTZ LIFE IN GERMANY

When Miriam and Baruch's kibbutz groups arrived in the Landsberg DP camp near Munich in November 1945, they hoped it would be a brief stop on their ultimate journey to the Land of Israel. They did not realize that they would be forced to remain in the American zone of Germany for nearly fourteen months, moving from Landsberg to Leipheim and then to an agricultural training farm near Eschwege, before being selected by the movement to depart in January 1947 (those who departed in 1947 would be forced to spend one more year in Cyprus before reaching Israel in 1948). The length of the period within the DP camps raised the question of whether the kibbutz could continue as a cohesive group or would remain the most appealing option for the youths who had arrived in Germany. Still, through a focus on materials created by young Jewish DPs themselves living in the kibbutzim, it becomes evident that the time spent by the youths in the kibbutz groups was put to use in deepening Zionist enthusiasm and strengthening attachment to both the Jewish past and the Zionist future. Crucially, as weeks dragged into months and years, it was the sense of attachment to their new family in the kibbutz group that kept members within the group as other housing and immigration options became available over the course of 1946–1947. Those who chose to remain with the kibbutz engaged in a process of transforming themselves from pragmatic Zionists who had joined the kibbutz for the offers of shelter and camaraderie in Poland into individuals eager to acquire the tools necessary for their future lives in *Eretz Israel*.

Although the various Zionist youth movements were divided by ideological differences, the daily experiences of their members shared much in common. Like the kibbutz groups of *Hashomer Hatzair*, the *Dror* and *Gordoniah* groups followed similar patterns in their departure from central east Europe with the *Bricha* and in their experiences once in Germany. Preparation for life in Palestine dominated the activities of most of the movements; what distinguished them was their idea of what the future Jewish state would look like. *Dror* and *Hashomer Hatzair*, for example, emphasized the need to create a socialist society in the new state; *Poalei Agudat Israel* and *Bnei Akiva* worked toward the creation of a state that would be a synthesis of the religious ideals of Torah with a Zionist ethic. Generally, these groups were also formed in Poland, usually as one group in a specific town; later kibbutz groups arrived from Czechoslovakia, Hungary, and Romania. During their time in Germany, they interacted with the central leadership regularly, compiling activity reports, paying dues to the movement, and relying on the movement for educational materials, the movement newspaper, and questions of *aliyah* and internal movement in Germany. After spending the first few months in a DP camp, part of the kibbutz would move to a *kibbutz-hakhsharah* (agricultural training farm) in order to gain experience with agriculture before departure. Such was the experience of Baruch and Miriam's first kibbutz groups from Sosnowiec and Bytom (which later formed Kibbutz Mordecai Anielewicz), living in various DP camps before moving to the movement farm in Eschwege. Over time, certain members would be selected for *aliyah* while others would remain, continuing to learn and train while in Germany. Those who did not depart were often left to hold places and supplies for new groups of kibbutzim arriving from the east.

In Poland, the kibbutz group had focused primarily on planning for departure and creating a cohesive group. Once the kibbutz had arrived in Germany, the educational and cultural work necessary to prepare for "life in Israel" took place in two venues: the DP camp and the training farms that would be opened by the movements in Germany with the assistance of American authorities, the Central Committee, and Zionist movement emissaries from Palestine. The period spent by the kibbutzim in Germany is thus central in the postwar history of the Zionist movement on two levels: first, the arrival of increasing numbers of Jewish DPs in the American zone of Germany over the course of 1946 created a situation in which a diplomatic solution to the Jewish refugee problem would become urgent; and second, the time spent by the youths in the kibbutzim was used to deepen Zionist enthusiasm, prepare them for their future lives, and rebuild the European Zionist youth movements.

Over the next fourteen months, the members of Kibbutz Tosia Altman, like those youths in other kibbutzim of *Hashomer Hatzair, Dror, Nocham,* and other movements, continued to engage in the "cultural" and educational work expected of them, as well as in the agricultural labor instilled in the farm to prepare for their future lives as pioneers in Israel. The sense of collective responsibility bestowed upon the youths as the "future of the Jewish people," a highly developed notion of familial obligation and collective duty after the Holocaust—the cataclysm which had orphaned so many Jews, but at the same time reminded them that they were all bound together—this sense of collective responsibility resulted in a division of labor developed in the DP camps in which the youths, and especially those in the kibbutzim, became responsible for carrying forward the banner of Zionism on behalf of the entire DP population, the *Surviving Remnant.* This would become especially clear when it was the youths, specifically those between the ages of seventeen and thirty-five, who were called upon to "do their duty to the people" and join the fighting in Palestine (something that some eight thousand conscripts from the DP camps in Germany in fact did).[47]

CONCLUSIONS

The experiences of the *Hashomer Hatzair* kibbutzim, as described in the diary of Kibbutz Tosia Altman and the correspondence of other kibbutzim from their time in the DP camps in occupied Germany, suggest a number of explanations for why members chose to remain within the kibbutz framework. From the beginning, on the *psychological* level, the continuing peer pressure and techniques employed by the *madrichim* and leadership persuaded members not to leave the group. The kibbutz granted structure and work, giving members something to do every day and reintroducing them to a daily schedule on the time and calendar of the movement. However, the favorable situation in the DP camps of Germany also gave the kibbutz members time to engage in learning and education, providing members with access to knowledge for which they "hungered." The kibbutz also offered a basis for identity, as membership in the movement provided a sense of belonging to a larger group and a larger family; the identification of the kibbutz with the wartime heroism of the ghetto fighters only served to strengthen this basis of identity. Finally, through the promise of *aliyah,* staying with the kibbutz carried the additional incentive of an expedited route to a future life in Palestine. While the initial psychological and structural factors kept members in the group, the time in Germany offered the movement and the members an opportunity to deepen their attachment to *Hashomer Hatzair* and the ideals for which it stood.

While the kibbutz groups frequently could not succeed at being self-sufficient, they did give the youths a sense of purpose in their lives. In the kibbutzim, youths learned Jewish history, Hebrew, youth movement folk-songs, principles of socialism, and more. The communal setting created a sense of family and tended to emphasize the positive potential of a Jewish future, despite the dark Jewish past. The kibbutz provided pride in being Jewish and offered goals for the future. The kibbutzim represented an alternative to the established Jewish committee or life alone in the DP camps, but a way of life that was not dependent on the official community framework. In this way, the kibbutzim ended up being highly therapeutic for the young survivors, placing them with a similar community of youths who had undergone wartime trauma. The activity within the kibbutz, both in daily work and in education, could help to avert the depression, anxiety, and anger that were certain by-products of the posttraumatic stress many of these survivors were perhaps facing.

Throughout the experiences of the youths in the kibbutzim, a common tension emerged, however, one in which the members had to balance their preparation for a future life in Palestine with the difficulties of everyday existence in the present. Departure for Palestine was certainly not guaranteed; as they waited for a diplomatic solution or their chance to be selected for *aliyah*, members had to work to avoid depression and a growing sense of impatience with their situation. In their "cultural work," kibbutz members acquired the necessary Zionist tools to qualify them for *aliyah*; such exercises simultaneously filled the function of keeping kibbutz members occupied, thereby lessening the potential for boredom, laziness, and demoralization. In classes, reading newspapers, and listening to lectures, kibbutz members learned the politics and geography of Palestine while still facing the reality of continued life in Germany. The appropriation of Jewish tradition and the transformation of a traumatic past into a source of heroic pride perhaps provided members with the psychological balm necessary to continue life in the wake of such tragedy. Still, in some cases, individuals decided to try life outside of the kibbutz, choosing to live independently or join friends and family in other groups.

Just as important, on the diplomatic level the high visibility of the kibbutzim and their manifestations of Zionist enthusiasm demonstrated to outside observers a perceived state of "Palestine passion" on the part of the Jewish DPs. The apparent importance of Zionism for the increasing numbers of arriving DPs confirmed the necessity of the Zionist solution for observers such as Earl Harrison, representatives of the Anglo-American Committee of Inquiry, and the United Nations Special Commission on Palestine, who continued to recommend immigration to Palestine as a solution to the Jewish refugee problem created by the war. The kibbutz could thus also serve as a way for the Jewish DP to leave Europe before he or she really left, to symbolize the rejection of existence in Europe, while simultaneously functioning as a postwar tool of revenge.[48] Above all, it represented a solution to the intense feeling of homelessness and abandonment that accompanied their wartime loss of family — by providing membership in a larger Jewish family.

NOTES

1. *Hashomer Hatzair* 1, (March 1946): 8.

2. Ibid.

3. In June 1945 two Paris-based representatives of the Jewish Agency for Palestine, Ruth Kliger and David Shaltiel, told the heads of the political and immigration departments of the Jewish Agency Executive in Jerusalem that up to 95 percent of the survivors were under thirty-five years old. Kliger and Shaltiel to Shertok and Dobkin, June 11, 1945, Central Zionist Archives, (CZA)-S6/3659, Jerusalem. A survey of Jewish DPs in Bavaria taken in February 1946 found that 83.1 percent of their number was between the ages of fifteen and forty, with over 40 percent between fifteen and twenty-four and 61.3 percent between nineteen and thirty-four. "Jewish Population in Bavaria," February 1946, YIVO Archives, MK 488, Leo Schwarz Papers, roll 9, folder 57, no. 581, YIVO Institute for Jewish Research, New York. A study by the American Jewish Joint Distribution Committee of Jews in the US Occupation Zone in Germany over one year after liberation found that 83.1 percent were between the ages of six and forty-four. "Jewish Population, US Zone Germany," November 30, 1946, YIVO Archives, MK 488, LS 9, 57, no. 682, YIVO Institute for Jewish Research, New York.

4. Judith Baumel, *Kibbutz Buchenwald: Survivors and Pioneers* (New Brunswick, NJ: Rutgers University Press, 1997). See also Baumel, *Finding Home and Homeland: Jewish Youth and Zionism in the Aftermath of the Holocaust* (Detroit: Wayne State University Press, 2009), chap. 1.

5. Natalia Aleksiun, "Where Was There a Future for Polish Jewry? Bundist and Zionist Polemics in Post World War II Poland," in *Jewish Politics in Eastern Europe: The Bund at 100*, ed. Jack Jacobs, 228 (New York: NYU Press, 2001).

6. See also Aharon Weiss, "Jewish Leadership in Occupied Poland: Postures and Attitudes," *Yad Vashem Studies* 12 (1977): 335–65

7. See Yitzhak Zuckerman, *Yetziat Polin* (Lochamei Ha-Getaot, Israel: Beit Lochamei Ha-Getaot, 1988), 82–83, and Zuckerman, *Surplus of Memory: Chronicle of the Warsaw Ghetto Uprising* (Berkeley: University of California Press, 1993), 592–93.

8. See David Engel, *Ben Shikhrur Li-Verihah: Nitsolei ha-Shoah be-Polin veha-ma'avak 'al Hanhagatam, 1944–1946* (Tel Aviv: Am Oved, 1996), 71.

9. Ibid.

10. Engel, *Ben Shikhrur Li-Verihah*, 203n221.

11. Other sources also testify to the expansion in number and membership of the Zionist youth movement kibbutzim in postwar Poland. See Yochanan Cohen, *Ovrim kol Gvul: Ha-Brichah, Polin 1945–1946* (Tel Aviv: Zemorah-Bitan, 1995), App. 5, for a thorough analysis of the development of Zionist kibbutzim in postwar Poland.

12. Report of G. H. Muntz (AJDC Admin. Asst.), Kibbutzim Survey, May 20, 1947, YIVO Archives, MK 488, Leo Schwarz Papers, reel 16, folder 159, pp. 1108–21, YIVO Institute for Jewish Research, New York.

13. Shlomo Shaltiel, ed., *HaYoman: Yomano shel Kibbutz HaShomer HaTzair Lochamei HaGetaot al Shem Tosia Altman* (Giv'at Haviva: Yad Ya'ari, 1997), 69.

14. The above-mentioned kibbutz groups were named after individuals who participated in the Jewish resistance during the war, such as Mordecai Anielewicz (b. 1919, d. May 8, 1943), the commander of the Warsaw ghetto uprising; Tosia Altman (b. 1918, d. ca. May 24, 1943), one of several *Hashomer Hatzair* activists in the Warsaw ghetto uprising; Aryeh Vilner (b. 1917, d. May 8, 1943), one of the founders of the Jewish Fighting Organization, ZOB, in the Warsaw ghetto; Zvi Brandes (b. September 3, 1917, d. August 7, 1943), a leader of the Jewish Fighting Organization in the Zagłębie region; and Chaviva Reik (b. 1914, d. November 20, 1944), born in Slovakia and emigrated to Palestine in 1939 as a member of *Hashomer Hatzair*. She volunteered to join the parachutists' unit and was dropped over Slovakia on September 21, 1944, where she organized Jewish partisan groups to assist in the Slovak national uprising. She was captured and executed on November 20, 1944, at Kremnica.

15. Information on the following kibbutz groups is available at the *Hashomer Hatzair* Archives, Yad Yaari, Givat Haviva, Israel, and in the Ha'apalah Project, 123/Hashomer Hatzair/410, Haganah History Archives, Tel Aviv, Israel:

1. Kibbutz *Mordechai Anielewicz*
2. Kibbutz *Chaviva Reik* in Pocking
3. Kibbutz *Tosia Altman*
4. Kibbutz *Aryeh Vilner*
5. Kibbutz *Yosef Kaplan*
6. Kibbutz *Ma'apilim al shem Zvi Brandes* in Feldafing
7. Kibbutz al shem *Fareinigte Partizaner Organizatye* in Vilna (FPO)
8. Kibbutz *BaDerech*
9. Kibbutz *LaMered*
10. Kibbutz *BaMa'avak*
11. Kibbutz *LeShichrur*
12. Kibbutz *Vatikim* in Herzog (July 1946)
13. Kibbutz *Vatikim* in Schlifing (older kibbutz with families)
14. Kibbutz *Bachazit* (older kibbutz with couples and babies)

(There was apparently another kibbutz named after *Shmuel Breslaw*, but correspondence between it and the central leadership is not available).

16. From the preface to the diary, Shaltiel, ed., *HaYoman: Kibbutz Lochamei HaGetaot al Shem Tosia Altman*.

17. For more on her experiences during the war, see Miriam Wind, "Be-vatei keleh Sovyetim (1939–1940)," *Yalkut Moreshet* 26 (1978): 159–86.

18. Miriam Yechieli, interview with the author, May 30, 2003, Kibbutz Nir David, Israel. For a similar example, see Yaakov Schwartz, "BaDerech LeEretz Yisrael," *Yalkut Moreshet* 55 (1993): 233–55. A prewar member of a *Hashomer Hatzair hakhsharah* in Częstochowa, Schwartz escaped to Vilna in 1939 and spent the latter half of the war in Tashkent. He returned to Lublin with Shlomo Kless, Mordechai Rosman, and Ben Meiri, where he worked preparing forged documents for Jews leaving Poland in the *Bricha*. He led a group

of sixty children (aged seven to eleven) from Poland to Germany in 1946 and eventually reached Palestine.

19. See Aryeh Levi Sarid, *Be-Mivchan he-Anut veha-Pdut: Ha-Tnuot Ha-Halutziot be-PolinBa-Shoah ve-Achareha, 1939–1949* (Tel Aviv: Moreshet, 1997), 197.

20. Zilberfarb to leadership, March 23, 1946, *Hashomer Hatzair* Archives, (1)38.2, cited in Sarid, *Be-Mivchan he-Anut veha-Pdut*, 284. In the words of one emissary: "One needs a great deal of strength of spirit in order to create from this material a new type of man . . . it will take quite a few days and months effort (plowing) for them to be like us . . . we are working and endeavoring to serve as an example and a symbol in our private lives and behavior."

21. An educational program for *Hashomer Hatzair shlichim* and *madrichim* in the kibbutzim of the movement identified the central characteristics of this "new human material," proposal written by S. Weinberg, *Hashomer Hatzair* Archives, (1).2.31, cited in Sarid, *Be-Mivchan he-Anut veha-Pdut*, 284–86 [my translation].

22. Interview with the author, May 29, 2003, Kibbutz Gazit, Israel.

23. Shaltiel, *HaYoman*, 194, and interview with the author, June 7, 2003, Jerusalem, Israel.

24. Interview with the author, June 7, 2003, Jerusalem, Israel.

25. Shaltiel, *HaYoman*, 196–98.

26. Ibid., 190–91.

27. Ibid., 203.

28. Ibid., 184.

29. Ibid., 185.

30. Ibid., 198–201.

31. Miriam Yechieli, interview with the author, May 30, 2003.

32. Shaltiel, *HaYoman*, 48. In one incident in Bytom, Baruch, the *madrich*, staged a theft in order to have a pretext to collect *zlotys* from kibbutz members who refused to share (45).

33. Shaltiel, *HaYoman*, 29. At the kibbutz *asefa* on September 13, 1945, the kibbutz voted to expel the "lazy" Yakov HaSandlar.

34. After the first postwar Zionist conference in August 1945 in London, the brief period of postwar youth movement unity ended as *Hashomer Hatzair* broke off from the other movements. Under pressure from Meir Ya'ari and the leadership of *Hashomer Hatzair* in the *Yishuv*, Chaika Grossman split off from her wartime comrades in *Dror*, despite her reservations to the contrary.

35. Shaltiel, *HaYoman*, 26.

36. Ibid., 27.

37. This timetable meant that Kibbutz *Tosia Altman*, in fact, preceded much of the *Bricha* from Poland, with the majority of the eighty thousand "infiltrees" arriving between April and October 1946 into the DP camps from Poland. See YIVO Archives, MK483, DP Germany, reel 3, folder 29, no. 63, YIVO Institute for Jewish Research, New York.

38. YIVO Archives, MK 488, Leo Schwarz papers, roll 16, 159, no. 1108, Muentz report, May 1947, YIVO Institute for Jewish Research, New York.

39. Shaltiel, *HaYoman*, 66.

40. Ibid., 62.

41. Ibid., 63.

42. Ibid.

43. Ibid., 64.

44. Ibid., 64, from Monish's description of the trial.

45. Monish (Einhorn) Haran, interview with the author, June 7, 2003, Jerusalem, Israel.

46. Noted in interview with Monish Haran, June 7, 2003, in Shaltiel, *HaYoman*, 64.

47. See Patt, *Finding Home and Homeland*, chap. 6.

48. Finally, added to the political symbolism of this choice was the potential for the Zionist settlement on German soil to act as a postwar tool of revenge. The occupation of Julius Streicher's estate by *Kibbutz Nili* in Pleikhershof took on this added level of meaning. As one of its members explained the names of the kibbutz dogs to Leo Schwarz, "Their names are Julius and Streicher. They obey and protect us! It's a pity to humiliate innocent animals with such swinish names. But we couldn't resist the temptation." Leo Schwarz, *The Redeemers: A Saga of the Years 1945-1952* (New York: Farrar, Straus and Young, 1953), 100. For a discussion of marriage and procreation as a form of revenge, see Atina Grossmann, "Trauma, Memory, and Motherhood: Germans and Jewish Displaced Persons in Post-Nazi Germany, 1945-1948," in *Life after Death*, ed. Richard Bessel and Dirk Schumann, 115 (Cambridge: Cambridge University Press, 2003).

JOANNA BEATA
MICHLIC

WHAT DOES A CHILD REMEMBER?

RECOLLECTIONS OF THE WAR AND THE EARLY POSTWAR PERIOD AMONG CHILD SURVIVORS FROM POLAND

In this chapter, I investigate the world of being, thinking, and feeling of Polish Jewish child survivors as they had emerged from the Holocaust. My aim is to present this topic through the children's gaze and thus to illuminate the "world of the inarticulate." Historians of childhood constantly grapple with the question of how to grasp the "world of the inarticulate" and creatively integrate it into the larger historical narrative of the history of a particular group of children or general history of childhood. Early postwar Polish Jewish child survivors' personal testimonies, memoirs, diaries, and letters, as well as artistic works such as drawings,[1] constitute a wealth of evidence illuminating the "world of the inarticulate." This evidence is scattered in various, difficult to comb through, archival collections in Poland, Israel, and the West. Though it cannot be viewed as self-sufficient evidence, it is nevertheless essential for writing the *Alltagsgeschichte* (everyday history) of Polish Jewish childhood both during and after the war, and the social history of the post-Holocaust Polish Jewish family. In my approach to these sources, I draw on the French historian Marc Bloch's position, which advocates that the problems and questions historians pose should determine the kinds of evidence they use.[2] Thus, early postwar children's testimonies should not be expected to deliver the same kind of data as official documents written by adults. Early postwar children's accounts sculpt life from a "raw" child's perspective, giving us a unique access to the modes of thinking, feeling, and expression of a child who has just emerged from the conditions of war and the Holocaust. Of course, we have to take into account the young age and limited cognitive and reflective abilities of their authors, and how adults may have inevitably shaped their thinking and the language in which the children retell the events.[3] The contexts in which these testimonies were created, how, and by whom, matters.[4] Nonetheless, in spite of the conscious and unconscious influence of adults and other age-related and psychological and cognitive limitations,[5] we should view this evidence as the best window we may have into the children's early postwar way of thinking, feeling, and being. They are the only window we may have into the child survivors' fresh and raw memories of the war as captured in the moment of retelling the events, even though some of these unrecorded testimonies may have been edited by the children's interviewers.[6]

The early postwar voices of Jewish child survivors both document the short-term effect of the Holocaust on the youngest survivors and can be useful in reconstructing the map of Polish Jewish relations, especially the complicated chart of rescue and betrayal of Jewish fugitives. The period 1944–1949 was a relatively short, but fundamentally critical time during which the children's future adult lives were taking shape. It was during this period that the children and the adults who cared for them made key decisions about the children's national and cultural identities. For most of the children, this was when they either reunited with their prewar family or confronted the painful lack of reunion because of the murder of their parents and other close relatives. During this period, some of the children found new families through adoption by Jewish relatives and Jewish strangers or non-Jewish individuals, including their former rescuers. In their testimonies of the immediate postwar period, children expressed their yearning for education, and documented the process of leaving Poland and acquiring new personal names and new national identities.[7] Many older children had input and retained agency in shaping their future lives, but the youngest ones, because of their age, hardly had agency in decisions concerning their future lives. Many key themes of this chapter, such as children's attitudes toward their surviving relatives and their former rescuers, and the children's attitudes toward Jewish identity and the loss of families, are similar to the experiences of Jewish child survivors from other Nazi-occupied countries, including France, the Netherlands, and Belgium.[8] Other issues such as the treatment of child fugitives by rescuers are more specifically embedded in the historical experience of the Holocaust in Nazi-occupied Poland and also other East European countries. One could hope that a comparative study aiming at writing a comprehensive history of the rescue of Jewish children in Western and Eastern Europe and the history of European Jewish family reconstitution after the war will emerge in the future. Comparative synchronic historical studies of specific issues, such as attitudes and behavior of rescuers toward Jewish children during the Holocaust and attitudes and behavior of Turkish rescuers toward Armenian children, who had to convert to Islam during the Armenian genocide of 1915–1917,[9] might be useful for a deeper understanding of the treatment of religious and ethnic minorities' child victims of genocide, though such studies may prove difficult to conduct because of sparse sources in the Armenian case.

I focus on Polish Jewish children who lived on the Aryan side in Nazi-occupied Poland, passing as Christian Polish children, and those who were hidden in individual Catholic homes, state orphanages, and Catholic convents and monasteries because of their obviously Jewish appearance. They were all born in 1929 or later. These children constituted a large cohort among the five thousand Jewish children registered by the Central Committee of Polish Jews (Centralny Komitet Żydów w Polsce, CKŻP) in the summer of 1945.[10] The figure of five thousand Jewish child survivors was not final, as it did not include all the young survivors from Nazi-occupied Poland, nor those Polish Jewish children who had survived the war in the Soviet Union with their families.[11] Nonetheless, it clearly indicated the sheer destruction of Polish Jewish children and youths. On the eve of the Second World War, Polish Jewry was considered a youthful community, and most scholars evaluate that in 1939, the number of children aged fifteen years or younger was several hundred thousand.[12] The great majority of these children did not survive the war.

The children who survived the war in the Soviet Union began to be repatriated to Poland from the Soviet Union in early 1946. Of the total figure of 136,000 repatriates who arrived in Poland between February and July 1946, children below the age of fourteen constituted 20 percent.[13] In contrast to the Jewish children who survived the war in German-occupied Poland, child survivors from the Soviet Union had at least one parent or other close relative with them throughout the war. Despite constantly suffering from hunger and various illnesses, the young survivors in the Soviet Union attended schools and enjoyed some basic pleasures of childhood, such as play in nature. Upon encountering those who survived the war under the German yoke, they learned that their wartime experiences, no matter how challenging and painful, were on the whole not as gruesome as of their counterparts. Therefore, in light of what they had heard and observed in daily contacts in early postwar Poland, many of them then and throughout their adulthood decided not to speak about their wartime experiences as part of the same tragedy that had befallen their peer group in Nazi-occupied Poland.[14] Only in the first decade of the twenty-first century, because of new research into modes of survival during the Holocaust and the acceptance of a broader definition of Holocaust survivor, have historians begun to investigate the Soviet wartime experiences of Polish Jewish children and their memories as part of the broader historical examination of Polish Jewish childhood during and after the Holocaust.[15]

What was it like to be a Jewish child in the early post-Holocaust period in Poland? How did children themselves understand and articulate their lives and wartime predicaments, especially their relations with their rescuers?

LOSS OF CHILDHOOD

Jewish children, who were delivered, or who found their way of their own accord, to the various Jewish organizations and Jewish children's homes that began to mushroom in Poland in 1945,[16] were instantly forced to confront the heavy burden of matters concerning their health, identity, family, and the future. Older children and youths were acutely aware that their childhood had been shattered and that they had been consequently transformed into premature adults bearing little resemblance to children. Many accounts articulate this painful reflection, which could be seen as a facet of the crystallization of a future collective Holocaust child survivors' identity. For example, in the testimony of Hinda Dowicz, born on May 15, 1928, in Tarnów, one reads: "We are young old women. Now I am an orphan."[17]

In many child Holocaust survivors' testimonies written after the war, we come across the articulation of the process of the divided "self," between the self of the prewar happy Jewish child, the self of the wartime haunted Jewish child who had often assumed a Polish Catholic identity in order to survive, and the self of the fragile child who just emerged from the genocide. This articulation is a marker of an irreparable destruction of a sense of a unity of self in young survivors. Child survivors continue to articulate this division of self as adults in their late postwar memoirs of the 1990s and the 2000s.[18]

Child survivors also had a profound sense of the loss of years of education and felt starved of knowledge, culture, and learning. Therefore, they immersed themselves in intellectual activities and pursuits trying to make up for the lost years. They not only studied intensely at schools, but also spent much of their free time studiously learning individually and in groups, so they could quickly be transferred to a class level more appropriate for their age. The youngest ones, however, experienced, often for the first time, the pleasures of ordinary childhood, such as playing with toys, playing games in nature with other children, and devouring unknown or forgotten treats such as chocolate, thanks to the assistance of the United Nations Relief and Rehabilitation Administration (UNRRA), the largest international aid organization, and other Western charitable organizations. Children recollected the particularly painful loss of contact with nature, the central space of play and games in ordinary childhood, during the Holocaust. In contrast to non-Jewish children, nature became forbidden space to Jewish children in ghettos and the young fugitives hidden on the Aryan side: "I looked at how all the children played [outside]. I cried and contemplated if I could ever live to a day I could also play as the other children."[19]

Among the youngest there were also children who for the first time had to acquire skills in human bonding, as they had no recollection of being cuddled and kissed by their parents or other adults during the war, and in fact did not know what kissing and cuddling meant.[20]

LOSS OF FAMILY

Next to the loss of childhood, children were acutely aware of their family losses. Therefore, they experienced overpowering loneliness, articulated in this characteristic, common, and brief utterance: "I am now completely on my own in the world."[21]

Intense yearnings for home and family were commonly reflected in the children's testimonies. For children, regardless of having close surviving relatives or not, Jewish children's homes often came to symbolize and represent their "new home." In testimonies they openly articulated their attitudes toward the institutions that took care of them: their closeness and emotional attachment to the staff working in the children's home and to the other children living there. Chana Grynberg, born on January 15, 1932, in Głowaczów in the district of Radom writes: "I have been living here in the orphanage in Otwock since 7 April 1945. I have been fairly treated, equal with other children. I have become a child again and have now 'recovered my home.'"[22]

Though the Jewish children's homes were viewed as "the new, recovered home," the total orphans often felt jealous of those children who had a surviving parent[23] or were visited by parents, other relatives, or former Christian rescuers. For them, even the most caring educators could not substitute for the perished family. They felt pain that there was no one to visit them, that no one was writing to them. Some children's letters to their beloved former rescuers confirm that their authors had longed for a word from their previous guardians, not only because of a strong emotional attachment, but also because they did not want to stand out as different from those children in Jewish children's home who had at least one surviving parent or other close relative:

> Dear Mummy,
>
> I am happy. I am in the Children's Home in Zabrze, near Katowice. How does Papa feel? Did he travel to Zakopane? What is Zbyszek doing? Is Granny still working? Here I have one very good friend named Fredek. He, like myself, lived with a Polish lady. Fredek misses her a lot and I miss you a lot and therefore we are happy to be together. We will soon be leaving for France and I will write to you from there. I ask you to reply to my letters. All other children receive letters. And only I do not receive letters and am very sorry about that. I kiss all of you many times.
>
> Wiktor B.[24]

LEAVING OR REMAINING WITH RESCUERS

Child survivors constituted the most affected and vulnerable social group in the turbulent early postwar period, as developments during this time determined not only the circumstances of their immediate presence, but also their short- and long-term futures. For many, who were well looked after and loved by their Christian Polish rescuers, the appearance of a forgotten or an unknown relative meant a messy and frightening disruption of what they regarded, at that time, as a solid familial life and happy childhood. Therefore, it took them a while to adjust to the idea of leaving the familiar and stable environment in which they had lived for two or three years, or in some cases, even five years. Reluctance to leave their rescuers is exemplified in many children's testimonies. For example, the April 3, 1948, testimony of Jurek Adin, born on June 22, 1933, in Warsaw, speaks of his preference for staying in Poland in close contact with his private tutor from the pre-1939 period, the Polish woman who saved his life on many occasions during the war. Because of their close emotional bond and the woman's total dedication to saving the boy's life, Jurek naturally preferred remaining with her to being reunited with unknown members of his Jewish family who lived in the United States:

> I sometimes went to the Aryan side and many times wanted to remain there but no opportunities arrived. . . . I asked one boy to take me to my private tutor. I could not stay there because she worked as a nurse for the Germans and lived at *Krankenstube*. She placed me with her friend who was already hiding one Jewish boy called Borenstein. . . . My tutor arranged for me to be taken home by Ms. Adela. She told me to go to a particular shop at Belwederska Street from where I would be taken home by Ms. Adela. Ms. Adela arranged a Christian birth certificate for me and registered me as Marian Podbielski. My tutor paid from her pocket to buy my false birth certificate. I spent some time at Ms. Adela's home. She used to go to work in the morning and I was left on my own. In the summer of 1942, I went to a holiday place called Zielonka [a small town in the vicinity of Warsaw] and in August I returned to Warsaw. The priest who baptized me was very good to me and placed me in the children's home of St. Anthony in Świder. . . . I stayed there until 1945, when my tutor came and took me with her to Roszalin. Again I felt so good.[25]

The youngest children, those who were born on the eve of or during the war, were the most shocked by the visits of strangers who came to claim them, since in their eyes, they had never had any other family or a different ethnic, social, and cultural background than that exhibited by their Christian/ethnic Polish rescuers. Like some of the older children, they did not have any memories of their biological parents or of the main facets of Jewish identity. Thus, they not only had to adjust to their new Jewish guardians, but also to the adoption of a new social identity. Jewish identity was a totally new, scary, and foreign terrain—terra incognita.

The testimony of February 22, 1948, by Henryk Weinman gives us an insight into how the youngest were shocked and confused by learning about their unknown painful past and by having to leave those whom they considered their natural and only parents. Henryk was born on March 23, 1941, in Skarżysko-Kamienna in central Poland. He was the youngest son of Tomasz Mieczysław Weinman and Ewa Federow and had three older siblings of whom one already lived abroad. During the liquidation of the ghetto in Skarżysko-Kamienna in late October 1942, his parents perished and he escaped to the "Aryan" side with his two siblings. This was the beginning of their lives in hiding. In January 1943, when he was almost two years old, his older brother Witold took Henryk to Kraków. In a desperate move, Witold decided to leave Henryk at the entrance to the building at Krakowska 45 in the city. The caretaker of that building took Henryk to a nearby Catholic orphanage, where the boy remained until 1945. In 1945, a childless Polish couple, Mr. and Mrs. Janowscy, visited the orphanage and decided to adopt him. As an adopted child under the name of Stanisław Janowski, Henryk lived with his new parents without any awareness of his biological family's background until 1946, when his brother Witold located him. Witold wished to take his brother away from the Janowscy family, but the couple did not agree to it. Therefore, as was typical in such cases, Witold took the matter to a Polish court. After a long legal procedure lasting almost two years, the court granted Witold custody over his younger brother. In the autumn of 1947, Witold placed Henryk in the Jewish orphanage in Częstochowa. In the meantime, Witold also found his sister, Danuta, in Warsaw. She was placed in the same Jewish orphanage in Częstochowa as Henryk.

In his testimony, the seven-year-old Henryk presents the story of the reunion of his biological family from his own perspective. For him, the forced departure from the Janowski couple, the only parents he had known, was the most traumatic and challenging experience to come to terms with:

> I was not aware that I was a Jew. I recall that when I was in the orphanage [the Christian orphanage in Kraków], I heard that being Jewish was something bad—that the Jews were "an ugly nation." . . . I was taken to a different orphanage and mother and father came. They gave me a nice pair of shoes and new clothes. They told me that from now on I would be their child and that they would take me home with them. I went with them without crying. I was very happy. . . . She [mother] later told me that a certain man wanted to take me away and that he was a Jew. "He says that he is your brother but that is not true; you are a Pole." I told mother that I would never leave her. Many times she repeated: "Do not return to the Jews."
>
> [At one point] Witek arrived [at our home] and wanted to take me away. He told me that I would be his brother. I cried out so much and shouted that I would not go with him. Mother and father cried a lot too. All three of us

cried, except for Witold. He took me by force into his car . . . I asked him where he was taking me. I told him that I wanted to go back to my mother, but he did not listen to me. At night, he took me to the train station and we travelled to Częstochowa. In Częstochowa we went to the [Jewish] orphanage. . . . I did not like Witek. After all, to have a mother is more important than to have a brother. Witek told me that it was better for me to be with him and ordered me to forget about my mother. But I shall never forget her because I love her very much. . . . I am happy here [at the orphanage], but I would like to go back to her because I love her.[26]

REGAINING JEWISH IDENTITY AND FREEING
ONESELF FROM ANTI-JEWISH PREJUDICES

Henryk's testimony also reveals that child survivors had to unlearn viewing Jewishness in pejorative or purely negative terms. These children had acquired strong anti-Jewish feelings and attitudes as a result of internalizing various anti-Jewish stereotypes disseminated by the German occupier and also the anti-Jewish stereotypes articulated in the Polish Christian environment in which they had grown up during the war. Typically, they would be afraid of "returning to the Jews," being touched by the "Jewish hand," and encountering Jewish social circles and institutions. For example, nine-year-old Ludwik Jerzycki recalled, in an interview conducted on September 27, 1947, in the Jewish Children's Home in Chorzów, that at first he refused to enter the place: "I cried, I did not want to return to the Jews, because they were saying that the Jews kill children. I was so afraid. But I found out that things are different here. I feel so content. I am not being beaten up. I learn and go to school."[27] This statement, of course, reveals the process of unlearning anti-Jewish stereotypes through building trust among Jewish children in Jewish children's homes, and thus these children's gradual internalization of the positive associations with Jewish identity and Jewish traditions and mores.

Still, some Jewish children were eager to leave their former rescuers, even with an unknown relative or a total stranger—a representative of a Jewish organization. Those were children who were physically or mentally abused by their former rescuers and guardians and were eager to experience a better life and regain a sense of childhood in the care of newly encountered adults. A history of the brutal mistreatment of Jewish child fugitives by those who were supposed to rescue and care for them has not yet been written, though a detailed chart of the abuse and murder of Jewish fugitives by members of Polish society in wartime Poland is in preparation.[28] Because of the short passage of time, the children's early postwar memories of the cruel wartime encounters with adults were still vivid, and they managed to describe them in a simple but powerful manner.

The picture that emerges from the children's early postwar testimonies reveals a disturbing picture of strange intimacy and cruelty in the realm of the home of a rescuer-abuser. What should have been a safe shelter was often for the hidden children a space of daily suffering, isolation, and loneliness. The reasons behind the abuse seemed to be pure cruelty mixed with anti-Jewish prejudice, the knowledge of Nazi persecution of Jews, and the calculated understanding that Jews were simply disposable in the eyes of the German occupier and that one could benefit from the helpless fugitives. Children were capable of expressing what they felt and what they thought as a result of being exposed to different doses of cruelty every day. They articulated their confusion, fear, and helplessness in the face of being dependent on abusive individuals who experienced pleasure from tormenting the young Jewish fugitives. The children also articulated how they coped with the knowledge of being badly mistreated and uncared for by those who were supposed to care.

Some children hidden in Polish villages, who were exposed to mental and physical abuse and long working hours in the fields, typically recalled in the early postwar period that: "They did not care about living any longer." Because of the conditions in which they were confined, paradoxically, these children reached the point of contemplating death instead of yearning for life as most people their age would. A good illustration of the desire to die is represented by the brief, early postwar recollections of how the children reacted to the news of local battles between the encroaching Russian army and the retreating German army in the second half of 1944. Unlike their rescuers, the children did not flee to safe shelters, but stayed in the fields with the cows at risk of being killed by bombs and shooting; they had stopped caring about what happened to them. Recollections of threats of denunciation by cruel and simpleminded rescuer-abusers and of children crying and begging them to spare their lives for one more day provides a brutal and disturbing picture of "rescue" that looks more like a grey zone in which human greed, lack of compassion and respect for young lives, and pure exploitation of the young are central to the relationship dynamic between Jewish children and the rescuer-abusers. From the point of view of hidden children, hard work, making yourself as useful and indispensable as possible, using wit and intelligence in dealing with the rescuer-abusers, and sheer luck were the only means that guaranteed their survival.

On September 3, 1947, in a Jewish children's home in Bytom located at no. 23 B. Prusa Street, Gizela Szulberg recollects matter-of-factly the ways her rescuers mistreated her on a daily basis. Gizela, born on September 23, 1934, into a well-to-do middle-class Jewish family, was fully aware of the fact that her rescuers, the family of Wajdzik in Włoska Wola, could at any time transform themselves into her murderers, since they casually talked about killing her or poisoning her without hiding from Gizela their thoughts and plans concerning the girl. What stopped them from killing her were greed and some remnants of human decency on the part of her main host, the father of the family. At some point, the rescuer demanded that after the war the girl would agree to bequeath them her dead parents' property. This was not an unusual demand among the group of rescuers for profit. Gizela's father had been an engineer and co-owner of a glass factory in Dubeczno, near Włodawa, in Lublin *voivodeship*, so her rescuers knew well that the Jewish orphan girl would be wealthy after the end of the war. Thus, keeping her alive instead of killing her was a more profitable option after they learned that Gizela's parents were dead.

My host had two sons-in-law, terrible anti-Semites, and they constantly said, "We have to kill this Jew or give her back to the ghetto." This is how they talked about me. The wife of the rescuer ordered me to pray to my Jewish God for help. I sat in the room next door and heard everything. The farmer used to say: "I will not kill her; I do not want to have blood on my hands." His wife used to say in response: "You wish to kill me, you do not have mercy over your own children." Our gardener [the brother of Mr. Wajdzik] took lots of money from my parents but did not share the sum with his brother. He would advise him to kill me, and that would be the end of the story. They kept me in a wardrobe and I was often hungry there and had to make my business there too if they had guests. I experienced a lot of unpleasantness. . . . Later, I learnt what happened with my parents. They were in hiding, but at some point, they did not have any funds because a woman [not clear who?] did not want to return their belongings to them. They wanted to visit me but were caught by the Germans and were killed and buried in a ditch. After we received this news, the farmer decided to keep me after all, but demanded that I bequeath my parents' estate to him. All days they would talk only about the estate, nothing else. I wanted to be treated well, so I had promised them that I would bequeath them the estate. In spite of my promise, once they threw me out of the house. I sat near the barn because I had nowhere to go. They found me there later and allowed me to return inside the house.

I was so drained that I did not care any longer what they would do with me. When the spring came, I was looking after the cows in the fields and was happier, because I did not need to be in the wardrobe in a bent position. Until today, my posture is still a little bit bent [as a result of living in the wardrobe]. . . . They caused me so much pain. They hated me because I was a Jewess. They treated me as if I was a Cinderella, and nothing else. I would wake up with the sunrise and would go to fields with the cattle. I had eighteen cattle including the sheep under my care. My legs were so full of cuts and blisters, they looked horrible.[29]

After the war, thanks to her surviving cousin and the Polish police, who had to take her by force from the Wajdzik family, Gizela was finally freed from her rescuer-abusers. However, her testimony of 1946 reveals how mentally and emotionally fragile she still was that year, and how confused she was about her identity because of the loss of her parents and the long and cruel years in hiding with the Wajdzik family. The testimony reveals her lack of confidence and desperate emotional and mental state; it provides clues on how she entered into what one can call a pathological dependency on her rescuer-abusers, as a result of the years of mistreatment at a very young age and the lack of loving care.

After the Soviets came, the people started to tell me: "The Germans will not kill you any longer, you are free." But I could not believe in my luck. In the spring of 1946, I converted to Christianity as a way of thanking them for sheltering me [the Wajdzik family]. I wanted to simply give them my soul. After I went to visit my parents' grave that is the ditch where they were buried. I put violet flowers there and cried a lot. Today I do not cry any longer, my heart has hardened out of fear, because of my experiences. . . . After one of my cousins found me and wanted to take me away from them, but they demanded "A half a million for a child." He did not have the money because he served in the army, and left. I did not even want to say "good-bye" to him; I was so stupid. I wanted to remain with them forever, and to be a Pole, I was so used to that life. But my cousin told the Jews about my existence and they took me from [the] Wajdziks. But at the first attempt of taking me away, I run away and walked seven kilometres back to the farmer. At the end, the police had to come to take me away, they held me by my hands and legs because I did not want to go with them. The Jews placed me in the orphanage, and now I feel good.[30]

Some orphaned children who had survived the war mostly through their wits and determination did not wish to be dependent on any adults after the war. Their wartime experiences made them prone to distrust all adults, non-Jewish and Jewish alike. The daily experiences during the war also taught them to be tough, bold, and impudent in dealings with adults. As during the Holocaust, in the early postwar period they continued to be proactive and determined to making their own decisions about their future. Józef Himelblau, born in 1929 in Warsaw into a middle-class, learned Jewish family in which both parents were teachers, articulates poignantly the feelings of mistrust that continue to color his perspective on human relationships after the war:

My strongest experience from the time of the occupation was when my mother and sister, and my brother, were taken away and I remained alone, without a penny and without anyone to ask for advice. But I held fast and managed.

I was not jealous of Christian children. There was not time to think about this, I was hardened, I had to think about everyday things. How to earn money. We did not proceed with any [Jewish] holidays. I was not once in a church. With my friends one spoke about trading, where to enjoy oneself, about movies, drinking alcohol, smoking cigarettes and other happy things. I did not believe people and I had to help myself alone in all cases. Today I also do not believe people. People say one thing and do something else. The family also does not bring me warmth. I am left entirely to myself and on several people here from the dormitory. I believe them and entrust my life further [to them]. But mostly I believe myself alone. My own strengths.[31]

Józef Himelblau's testimony of January 19, 1948, was taken in a child's dormitory at 25 Narutowicza Street in Lodz, the short-lived center of Jewish life in the early postwar years in Poland.[32] At the time, the young man was catching up on the lost years of education. Józef attended seventh grade in the Jewish public school. His prewar education was finished at fourth grade in a public school. In the notes accompanying the testimony, the interviewer Genia [Genya] Silkes confirms that Józef Himelblau shows "signs of possessing the 'so-called life-spirit,' behaves not like a child, but like a grown-up, and 'does not allow himself to show any sad emotions.'"[33]

In the early postwar period, children feared being associated with Jews not only because of homegrown, antisemitic prejudices encountered during the war in Polish society, but also because of the fresh, intense memory of the German genocidal policies against Jews. This memory led them to associate Jewish identity with living in a state of permanent danger. Therefore, they viewed Jewishness as a "stigmatized identity," an identity with discredited attributes.[34]

Some children continued to play a double-identity performance: in Polish state schools, they continued to act as Christian Polish children, no different from the other pupils, whereas in the Jewish environment, they were "allowed" to return to the Jewish self. These children offer a good illustration of a skillful, long-term split-identity performance in order to physically survive, ready to be utilized under different circumstances. They were encouraged to do so out of fear for their well-being and safety in the Polish environment, as antisemitism permeated the atmosphere in many schools where both Polish teachers and Polish pupils expressed it in a variety of ways. They usually abused and verbally humiliated the Jewish children.[35]

Yehudit Kirżner was born in 1935 in Vilnius, today the capital of Lithuania [prewar Vilna], into a wealthy family in which her father, Grigori, was an owner of a furniture factory. Yehudit's family could count itself among the rare and lucky nuclear Jewish families, because both parents and Yehudit's sister all survived the German occupation on the Aryan side in the Lithuanian countryside near Vilnius. The sisters' prewar nanny played a major role in their survival. After the war, as with many other Jewish survivors, they made their new home in Lodz, where Yehudit's father worked as administrator in a Jewish children's home in Helenówek. At the time Yehudit attended the fourth grade of Polish public school no. 24, and the family lived in a comfortable apartment at no. 44/71 Kiliński Street. In her testimony of December 15, 1945, Yehudit states how on her father's instruction, she performed the Polish Christian identity act on a daily basis at the Polish school, while her "Jewish self" was supposed to lie dormant, ready to be fully expressed only upon the family's departure to the *Yishuv* in Palestine/Israel:

> My father found our residence on Tatarska 20, residence 2, where we lived before the war, and where we had a furniture store. Nothing remained there, the Germans stole everything. We lived for some time in Vilna [Vilnius], later we came to Łódź. We traveled to Łódź for two weeks. In Helenówek we met my aunt. She works here as a doctor. We really liked Helenówek and we settled here. My father received work as an administrator. And I go with my sister to school. It is very happy here. We play, sing and put on performances. I go to a Polish school, with a Polish name. My parents do not want anyone in our school to know that I am Jewish, because I do not look Jewish. My father said that in the meantime, [it should] be that way, because when we will leave for Palestine, I will be able to be Jewish.[36]

Genia Silkes, Yehudit's interviewer, acknowledges that the girl has the perfect physical attributes to continue mimicry acts in the Polish Christian environment. Yehudit is "a tall, blond girl, with light hair, blue eyes, a [?] tiny nose, calm, easy-going." Silkes's observations indicate that for Yehudit the act of being a Christian Polish girl became second nature, as she "does not exhibit any indication of [being] a Jewish child."[37]

Some older children made a conscious decision not to "return to Jews" because of what they had personally witnessed during the war. They were aware of and feared the Nazi image of the Jew as a parasite and subhuman. The Jew, in their minds, was purely the object of German extermination policies, and the Jewish identity came to mean a terrible stigma. For many children, it was not only the German policy and practice toward Jews that made them afraid of regaining their Jewish identity, but also the prejudicial attitudes and behavior of the Polish population toward the Jewish fugitives during the war and Jewish survivors after the war. The children witnessed and experienced a full range of negative attitudes and behavior, ranging from verbal to physical and sexual abuse, constant threats of denunciation, murder of their dearest, and very meager food portions—despite the very heavy workload they were expected to perform on daily basis, especially in the countryside. In her testimony made in the Jewish Children's Home in Kraków, Dora Zoberman, born in 1936 in Kraków, recollects that she and her sister continued to be cautious in their dealings with Polish peasants after the Russian army entered the region. They had a very good reason for their vigilant behavior: less than two weeks earlier on April 25, 1944, their mother and older sister were killed by local Polish peasants after being chased from their shelter in a nearby forest. The next day, the girls' father found his wife's corpse and discovered that her golden teeth and her golden rings were brutally removed by the killers without any respect for her dead body.[38] Soon after, in early May 1944, the widowed father and the half-orphaned girls were suddenly separated near Staszowo during heavy fighting between the German and Russian armies. The grieving girls were left on their own without any familiar adult. In order to survive, they decided to ask a wealthy Polish peasant, Rogala, for work on his farm. To be accepted by the farmer, they announced to him that they were planning to convert to Catholicism. The sisters were reunited with their father only in 1946; but in 1945, the girls' aunt, a survivor of Mauthausen concentration camp, found them at Rogala's farm. This first postwar serendipitous family reunion had happened just before the girls were supposed to convert to Catholicism, which in practice most likely would have meant remaining with Rogala on the farm.[39]

Some young Jewish survivors simply did not want to be associated with a people for whom others had only contempt and hatred. In some cases, these emotions accompanied a deeply split sense of social identity, persisted for a long time after the end of the war, and have played a major part in making choices of friends and loved ones in their adult lives.

> I was attracted to my colleagues from the Jewish dorms and at the same time repelled by them. When I heard them speaking Yiddish, I got goose pimples. I was unable to get used to it. I thought that somebody would come soon and put an end to "it." It seemed impossible that they could be so calm, that they should talk and laugh. I could not find a place for myself among them. I looked at them, and the people I liked the most were those who looked the least Jewish. Those who looked the most Jewish scared me. I ran as far away from them as I could.
>
> This also happened later. I would run away from Jews then I'd come back to them. At times I thought I could be with some Jews, but then I really couldn't. I ran away and pretended I didn't have anything in common with

them. Then I'd be drawn to them again, and I would come back. From the time I was a little child, I had to deny being Jewish, and this has left traces that did not allow me to think, see, or live normally.[40]

Among such children were some who remained in postwar Poland and continued to pass as Christian Poles after the war and to pretend throughout their adult lives that they were someone else. Only in the 1990s and 2000s, as mature individuals, in the new political and social climate in post-1989 Poland, did they feel the need to come out in the open and come to terms with their Jewishness—what they called the return to being oneself.[41] In the last two decades, a number of these children have gradually begun to speak out publicly and write memoirs for the first time about their Jewish identity. They are members of the Association of the Holocaust Children, established in June 1991 in Warsaw, and view it as their "special family," individuals with similar sets of wartime and postwar experiences and with a great deal of understanding for each other's wartime and postwar life trajectories and anxieties, and sharing similar sensitivities and fears.

CONCLUSIONS

War and the Holocaust destroyed the children's families and their childhood. Those children who had found secure and loving shelter among loving and caring rescuers during the war found it difficult, in the early postwar years, to leave that safe world and forge new bonds with forgotten or unknown relatives, as well as with strangers representing Jewish organizations that intended to create a new life for them in unfamiliar locations and in an unfamiliar culture. Some remained in that safe world with the rescuers, who became their adoptive parents, and only as adults did they fully grasp what had happened to them and come to terms with their complex dual identities and painful dual family past. Others were keen to leave rescuers who had physically or emotionally mistreated them, even with family members they had forgotten. Others, as a result of years of mistreatment, had difficulty leaving their rescuer-abusers, as they had lost all confidence in themselves.

Issues of social identity were central in the child survivors' lives. They yearned for their lost years of education and for a loving, solid, and stable family, and dreamed of regaining at least some facets of childhood. They articulated their perceptions, concerns, dreams, and hopes in their early postwar testimonies. They did not have the self-reflective and cognitive abilities of adults and may have been influenced by adult perspectives. Nevertheless, the child survivors were capable of expressing their feelings, thoughts, and attitudes in a profound manner. Their early postwar testimonies may be the best window we have for studying the short-term impact of genocide on children just emerging from genocidal conditions. Some of these testimonies contain unbridled emotion and are fragmented, because the children could not continue to retell the most painful accounts from their wartime existence; but many seem devoid of strong emotion and are narrated in a matter-of-fact manner. One can explain the lack of strong emotions because for many of these children the Holocaust with all its horrific experiences and encounters was the only reality they knew—for them this was the only world of their childhood and growing up, and they did not remember a different reality.[42]

The children's testimonies carry profound observations about the world and about adult attitudes and behavior toward the young. The cases delineated here demonstrate that in spite of a multitude of individual children's wartime biographies, it is possible to detect certain clear patterns and commonalities in the children's microuniverses of wartime experience and interaction with the adult world, whereby one can conjure up a history of a generation or generations of Jewish children and youths from Poland. The children's personal histories constitute a major part of transnational history of post-1945 Polish Jewry—the remnants of the community.

Finally, all the cases attest to the great vulnerability of children in the adult world, not only during the wartime era, but also during the early postwar period. This, of course, is not unique to the experience of Jewish children during the Holocaust, but it highlights some aspects of their tragedy shared by non-Jewish child victims emerging from other genocides. We can place these experiences in a comparative perspective; but at the same time, we have a duty to preserve the historical distinctiveness of the experience of Jewish children in Nazi-occupied Europe, as much as we do to the particularity of children's experiences of victimhood and survival of other genocides.

NOTES

1. In this work I am not focusing on the analysis of children's visual works. This will be carried out in a separate project.

2. Marc Bloch, *The Historian's Craft* (New York: Vintage Books, 1953), 62–69; hereafter, Bloch, *The Historian's Craft*. On Marc Bloch's approaches to social history and evidence, see Daniel Chirot, "The Social and Historical Landscape of Marc Bloch," in *Vision and Method in Historical Sociology*, ed. Theda Skocpol, 22–46 (Cambridge: Cambridge University Press, 1984).

3. On the influence of adults on children, see Colin Heywood, *A History of Childhood: Children and Childhood in the West from Medieval to Modern Times* (London: Polity Press, 2001), 7.

4. On this subject see, for example, Kenneth Waltzer, "History and Memory: Children and Youths at Buchenwald and Belsen," in *Das soziale Gedächtnis und die Gemeinschaften der Überlebenden: Bergen-Belsen in vergleichender Perspektiv* [*Social Memory and Survivor Communities: Belsen in Comparative Perspective*], ed. Janine Doerry, Thomas Kubetzky, and Katja Seybold, 150–67 (Göttingen, DE: Wallenstein, 2013).

5. On the value and limitations of the Jewish children's early postwar testimonies and other methodological issues pertaining to the analysis of these testimonies, see, for example, Joanna Beata Michlic, "The Aftermath and After: Memories of Child Survivors of the Holocaust," in *Lessons and Legacies X: Back to the Sources*, ed. Sarah Horowitz, 141–89 (Evanston, IL: Northwestern University Press, October 2012), and the chapter by Rita Horváth in this book.

6. My position here stands in opposition to the key arguments of Beata Müller in her article "Trauma, Historiography and Polyphony," *History and Memory* 24, no. 2 (2012): 157–95, in which she argues that the early postwar children's unrecorded testimonies "do not offer a direct insight into the child's world, a direct access to a child's voice" because they may have been edited by the children's interviewers, who had their own specific agendas in presenting the children's testimonies. Müller presents an interesting theoretical position about these testimonies as an expression of polyphonic voices, but without providing sufficient analytical evidence for major interruptions into the children's testimonies and the nature of such interruptions, or how the interviewers themselves recorded the testimonies. One can also argue that Müller's absolutist position does not recognize that all texts, even scholarly ones, are to some extent polyphonic because of the stylistic interventions of editors and translators. Though Müller states that the silences matter in the children's testimonies, she does not analyze the functions and the meanings of such silences.

7. On the turbulent history of Jewish child survivors in Poland in the early postwar period as articulated by child survivors themselves, see Joanna Beata Michlic, "Rebuilding Shattered Lives: Some Vignettes of Jewish Children's Lives in Early Postwar Poland," in *Holocaust Survivors: Resettlement, Memories, Identities*, ed. Dalia Ofer, Françoise S. Ouzan, and Judy Baumel Schwartz, 46–87 (New York: Berghahn Books, 2011), and Michlic, "'The War Began for Me after the War': Jewish Children in Poland, 1945–1949," in *The Routledge History of the Holocaust*, ed. Jonathan Friedman, 482–97 (London: Routledge, 2011). On the situation of child survivors through the lenses of Jewish institutions and organizations, see Emunah Nachmany Gafny, *Dividing Hearts: The Removal of Jewish Children from Gentile Families in Poland in the Immediate Postwar Years* (Jerusalem: Yad Vashem, 2009); and Nahum Bogner, *At the Mercy of Strangers: The Rescue of Jewish Children with Assumed Identities in Poland* (Jerusalem: Yad Vashem, 2009).

8. On Jewish child survivors in the Netherlands, see important works by Diane L. Wolf, *Beyond Anne Frank: Hidden Children and Postwar Families in Holland* (Berkeley: University of California Press, 2007), and Wolf, "Child Withholding as Child Transfer: Hidden Jewish Children and the State in Postwar Netherlands," *Journal of Human Rights* 12, no. 3 (2013): 296–308; on child survivors in Belgium and their rescuers, see the pioneering study of Suzanne Vromen, *Hidden Children of the Holocaust: Belgian Nuns and Their Daring Rescue of Young Jews from the Nazis* (Oxford: Oxford University Press, 2008).

9. On rescue and conversion to Islam during the Armenian genocide, see, for example, Ugur Ümir Üngör, "Conversion and Rescue: Survival Strategies in the Armenian Genocide," in *Resisting Genocide: The Multiple Forms of Rescue*, ed. Jacques Semelin, Claire Andrieu, and Sarah Gensburger, 201–18 (New York: Columbia University Press, 2011).

10. On the history of the reemergence of Jewish child survivors and Jewish organizations in the early postwar period, see Lucjan Dobroszycki, "Re-emergence and Decline of a Community: The Numerical Size of the Jewish Population in Poland, 1944–47," *YIVO*

Annual 21 (1993): 3-32. See also Natalia Aleksiun, *Dokąd dalej? Ruch syjonistyczny w Polsce (1944-1950)* (Warsaw: Wydawnictwo TRIO, 2002); and August Grabski, *Działalność komunistów wśród Żydów w Polsce (1944-1949)* (Warsaw: Wydawnictwo TRIO, 2004).

11. For some basic observations about the differences between the situation of child survivors in Nazi-occupied Poland and in the Soviet Union, see Irena Kowalska, "Kartoteka TOŻ z lat 1946-1947. (Żydowskie dzieci uratowane z Holocaustu)," *Biuletyn Żydowskiego Instytutu Historycznego* 6/7 (1995): 97-106. This topic deserves a separate historical analysis.

12. For the study of Jewish youth in pre-1939 Poland, see Moses Kligsberg, "Socio-Psychological Problems Reflected in the YIVO Autobiography Contest," *YIVO Annual of Jewish Social Science* 1 (1946): 241-49; and Kligsberg, "Di yidishe yugnt bavegung in poyln tsvishn beyde velt milkhomes (a sotsiologishe shtudye)" [The Jewish Youth Movement in Poland Between the Two World Wars (A Sociological Study], in *Studies on Polish Jewry, 1919-1939*, ed. Joshua A. Fishman, 137-228 (New York: YIVO, 1974).

13. See *Zarys działalności Centralnego Komitetu Żydow w Polsce za okres od 1 stycznia do 30 czerwca 1946 r.* (Warsaw, 1947), 26. For a discussion of literature on the demographic structure and social life of Jewish community in the postwar period, see H. Datner-Śpiewak, "Instytucje opieki nad dzieckiem i szkoły powszechne Centralnego Komitetu Żydów Polskich w latach 1945-1946," *Biuletyn Żydowskiego Instytutu Historycznego* 3 (1981): 37-51.

14. On the marginalization of the experiences of Polish Jews who survived the war in the deepest recesses of the Soviet Union, see Laura Jockusch and Tamar Lewinsky, "Paradise Lost? Postwar Memory of Polish Jewish Survival in the Soviet Union," *Holocaust and Genocide Studies* 24, no. 3 (2010): 373-99.

15. Currently Prof. Atina Grossmann conducts an important research study on Holocaust survivors who survived the war in the Soviet Union.

16. See Datner-Śpiewak, "Instytucje opieki nad dzieckiem i szkoły powszechne Centralnego Komitetu Żydów Polskich w latach 1945-1946," 37-51; and Joanna Michlic, "The Raw Memory of War: Early Postwar Testimonies of Children in Dom Dziecka in Otwock," *Yad Vashem Studies* 37, no. 1 (2009): 11-52.

17. Testimony of Hinda Dowicz [in Polish], Central Committee of Polish Jews (hereafter, CKŻP), file no. 301/1328, Archives of Żydowski Instytut Historyczny (hereafter, ŻIH), Warsaw.

18. On the split selves in late postwar literary memoirs, see Joanna Beata Michlic, "The Return of the Repressed Self: Michał Głowiński's Autobiographical Wartime Writing," *Jewish Social Studies* 20, no. 3 (2015). For one of the most interesting examples of the expression of split self in the late literary memoirs of child survivors, see Irit Amiel, *Życie: Tytuł tymczasowy* (Warsaw: Czuły Barbarzyńca Press, 2014).

19. Testimony of Sala Sztajnwurcel, CKŻP, file no. 301/2282, ŻIH, 5.

20. Minutes of the conference of the heads of Jewish orphanages under the patronage of the CKŻP, December 12 and 13, 1947, Kraków (second day of the conference), CKŻP, Department of Education, file no. 303/IX/67, ŻIH, 21.

21. Testimony of Jankiel Cieszynski, CKŻP, file no. 301/5514, ŻIH.

22. Testimony of Chana Grynberg, Collection of Franciszka Oliwa, 037/378, vol. 2, 79-82, Yad Vashem Archive, Jerusalem, Israel.

23. In the documentary *My Hundred Children*, the filmmaker Oschra Schwartz follows in the footsteps of a group of former child survivors, including full orphan Jewish boys

who had to fend for themselves during the Holocaust. After the war, in the Jewish children's home in Zakopane run by Lena Küchler-Silberman, the boys were particularly jealous of a Jewish boy who had a surviving father, the dentist in their children's home. Out of jealousy and anger, one day the boys attempted to punish the dentist's boy by hanging him, but fortuitously a member of staff put an end to the boys' dangerous game, which might have ended in a tragedy. These boys as adults remember the episode in the film.

24. Wiktor Baranowicz to the Barański family, October 20, 1946, Zabrze, Poland. A second, undated letter, also written in the Children's Home in Zabrze, contains a similar message; for both, see file no. M31/7081, Archives of Righteous Among the Nations, Yad Vashem, Jerusalem, Israel.

25. Testimony of Jurek Adin, CKŻP, file no. 301/3695, Archives of ŻIH.

26. Testimony of Henryk Weimann, CKŻP, file no. 301/3362, Archives of ŻIH. In the attached statement, the interviewer, Janina Masłowska, stated that Henryk was a nervous boy who was unwilling to talk except about his foster mother, Mrs. Janowska.

27. Statement of Ludwik Jerzycki, to interviewer Janina Sobol-Masłowska, September 27, 1947, file no. 301/2755, 1, Archives of ŻIH.

28. See, for example, Jan Grabowski, *Judenjagd: Polowanie na Żydów 1942–1945: Studium dziejów pewnego powiatu* (Warsaw: Polish Center for Holocaust Research, 2011) (in English translation, *Hunt for the Jews: Betrayal and Murder in German-Occupied Poland* (Bloomington: Indiana University Press, 2013); and Barbara Engelking, *Jest Taki Piękny Słoneczny Dzień . . . Losy Żydów szukających ratunku na wsi polskiej 1942–1945* (Warsaw: Polish Center for Holocaust Research, 2011); and Karolina Panz, "'Dlaczego oni, którzy tyle przecierpieli i przetrzymali, musieli zginąć': Żydowskie ofiary zbrojnej przemocy na Podhalu w latach 1945–1947," *Zagłada Żydów: Studia i materiały* 11 (2015): 33–89. Specifically on the mistreatment of children, see the introduction by Olga Orzeł to the recent publication, in Polish, of fifty-five early postwar Jewish children's testimonies, *Dzieci żydowskie w czasach Zagłady: Wczesne świadectwa 1944–1948: Relacje dziecięce ze zbiorów Centralnej Żydowskiej Komisji Historycznej* (Warsaw: ŻIH, 2014), 7–46. Many of the children's testimonies included in this important publication speak directly about mistreatment and abuse.

29. Testimony of Gizela Szulberg, signed by the interviewer, Ida Gliksztejn, CKŻP, file no. 301/2731, Archives of ŻIH, 1–2.

30. Ibid., 3.

31. Testimony of Józef Himelblau [in Yiddish], signed by the interviewer, Genia (Genya) Silkes, CKŻP, file no. 301/3615, Archives of ŻIH, 9–10.

32. On the revival of Jewish life in post-1945 Lodz, see Shimon Redlich, *Life in Transit: Jews in Postwar Lodz, 1945–50* (Boston: Academic Studies Press, 2010).

33. Genia (Genya) Silkes's observations of Józef Himelblau [in Yiddish], included in the testimony of Józef Himelblau, CKŻP, file no. 301/3615, Archives of ŻIH, 1.

34. On stigma, see the classic study of Erving Goffman, *Stigma: Notes on the Management of Spoiled Identity* (Englewood Cliffs, NJ: Prentice-Hall, 1963).

35. On early postwar antisemitism, see, Jan T. Gross, *Fear: Anti-Semitism in Poland after Auschwitz: An Essay in Historical Interpretation* (New York: Random House, 2006); translation from Polish, *Strach: Antysemityzm w Polsce tuż po wojnie: Historia moralnej zapaści* (Kraków: Wydawnictwo Znak, 2008). For the first comparative study of anti-Jewish violence in postwar Poland and Slovakia, see Anna Cichopek-Gajraj, *Beyond Violence: Jewish Survivors in Poland and Slovakia, 1944–1948* (Cambridge: Cambridge University Press, 2014).

36. Testimony of Yehudit Kirżner [in Yiddish], CKŻP, file no. 301/2077, ŻIH, 8.

37. Observations of Genia Silkes included in the testimony of Yehudit Kirżner [in Yiddish], CKŻP, file no. 301/2077, ŻIH, 1.

38. On robberies of Jewish victims, Jewish fugitives, and survivors, including Jewish corpses during and in the aftermath of the Holocaust, see Jan Tomasz Gross with Irena Grudzińska-Gross, *Golden Harvest: Events at the Periphery of the Holocaust* (Oxford: Oxford University Press, 2012). The latter appeared first in Polish in March 2011. On the taking over of Jewish properties by the German authorities and also by Poles, see the collective volume, Jan Grabowski and Dariusz Libionka, *Klucze i kasa: O mieniu żydowskim w Polsce pod okupacją niemiecką i we wczesnych latach powojennych 1939-1950* (Warsaw: Centrum Badań and Zagładą Żydów, 2014).

39. Testimony of Dora Zoberman, CKŻP, file no. 301/3743, ŻIH, 1-7.

40. Testimony of Irena (Agata) Boldok, née Likierman, born in 1932, "Back to Being Myself," in *The Last Eyewitnesses: Children of the Holocaust Speak*, vol. 2, ed. Jakub Gutenbaum and Agnieszka Latala, 35 (Evanston, IL: Northwestern University Press, 2005). (Originally published in Polish in 2001 by the Association of the Children of the Holocaust.)

41. For an interesting account by a Jewish child survivor who was saved in the convent in Turkowice in northeastern Poland, see the personal story of the distinguished Polish literary critic Michał Głowiński in "Zapisy Zagłady," *Tygodnik Powszechny: Kontrapunkt* 1/2 (March 25, 2001): 14-15. Głowiński is the author of a number of recently published personal accounts of his wartime experiences and his recent "rediscovery" of his Jewishness. See, for example, Michał Głowiński, *Czarne Sezony* (Warsaw: Open, 1999), English translation: *The Black Seasons*, trans. M. Shore (Evanston, IL: Northwestern University Press, 2005); and *Kręgi obcości: Opowieść autobiograficzna* (Kraków: Wydawnictwo Literackie, 2010). See also an interview conducted by T. Torańska, "Polskie gadanie," *Gazeta Wyborcza*, May 23, 2005, accessed on June 10, 2005, http://serwisy.gazeta.pl/df/2029020 ,34471,272112.html.

42. On the death camp in Auschwitz as a space of Jewish childhood, see the memoir by a child survivor and Holocaust historian, Otto Dov Kulka, *Nofim mi-metropolin ha-mavet* (Tel Aviv: Yediot Sfarim, 2003); English translation, *Landscapes of the Metropolis of Death: Reflections on Memory and Imagination*, trans. Ralph Mandel (Cambridge: Harvard University Press, 2013).

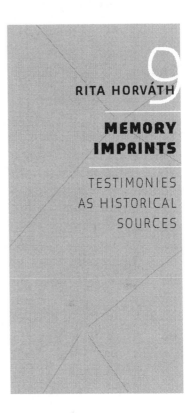

RITA HORVÁTH

MEMORY IMPRINTS

TESTIMONIES
AS HISTORICAL
SOURCES

Literary scholars and psychologists suggest that we need to pay attention — "listen" — differently to testimonies of traumas, especially to testimonies of long-term social and historical traumas such as the Holocaust, than to other kinds of (written and oral) texts.[1] The special methods of listening and understanding developed by Cathy Caruth, Shoshana Felman, Henry Greenspan, Geoffrey H. Hartman, Lawrence L. Langer, Dori Laub, Júlia Vajda, and others consider the testimonies mainly as "human sources." These scholars have not been particularly interested in employing the texts themselves as sources of classical historical research that focuses on chronology and the description of events in intricate casual chains. Nor have they concentrated on clarifying what kind of historical sources Holocaust testimonies may be. This lack of concern with testimonies as classical historical documents has much to do with dominant notions about them in history and historiography.

From the writings of the scholars mentioned above, it is possible to infer that when they talk about history, they draw upon a very broadly defined social-historical definition combined with views from the history of ideas. This all-inclusive, human-centered, philosophical-existential understanding of history that takes account of everything of human concern does not invalidate the arguments of historians who adopt narrower definitions of their discipline. In this chapter, by drawing on and expanding the methods developed by the aforementioned scholars, I attempt to establish survivor testimonies as crucial sources of historical research even according to the narrower definition of the discipline.

The employment of testimonies in this narrower sense is important because the survivor testimonies and the survivors' concept of the role of the witness are informed primarily by classical notions of what constitutes history. In addition to commemorating the dead and their obliterated communities, the most important aim of the overwhelming majority of those who gave testimony was to document the previously unfathomable historical reality that is now called the Holocaust. This goal is evident in both early postwar and late postwar testimonies. The majority of survivors, classical historians such as Philip Friedman among them, intended their testimonies to be used primarily as sources of classical historical research: for the construction of basic chronologies, as well as for description and interpretation of events, event-sequences, and their circumstances.

However, the findings of the psychologists and literary scholars are also essential for the understanding of both the human and scientific significance of the trauma of Holocaust survival, and witnessing. Their work enables us to go a step further in complying with the explicit goal of the testifying survivors to document the Holocaust. Knowing how emotionally invested survivors are in their role as witnesses, how undertaking this role was in many cases already a part of their Holocaust experience contributing to their drive to survive, and what the construction of this role cost them, it is an ethical imperative to employ the testimonies as they were intended: as sources, indeed, as the basis of historical research.

There is a further imperative for drawing on life writings and oral testimonies about the Holocaust in historical research. These sources alone allow the specifically Jewish and individual character of the victims to emerge. They comprise an almost exclusive record of the reactions and characteristics of the victims, something that is not available in the numerous official sources prepared by the perpetrators concerning the destruction of the Jews during this period. In addition, major events and developments of the Holocaust, especially toward its end, are barely documented by any other source. An example is the ill-famed death marches of Jews from Budapest toward the inner parts of the Third Reich. Often we can reconstruct the route of those marches only by relying on survivor testimonies.[2]

However, the use of life accounts as sources of research poses a general methodological problem in respect to historiography. Historians traditionally consider life writings and oral renderings—testimonies, memoirs, diaries, autobiographies, and so forth—to be sources of highly questionable value, merely "anecdotal evidence," mainly because life writings are hopelessly subjective and warped by problems pertaining to the workings of memory and individual psychology.

I would like to take issue with these assumptions and to demonstrate that the traumatic nature of the survivors' memories, contrary to general belief, may actually facilitate historical research. Psychological studies indicate that certain kinds of traumatic memories record exact details obsessively, and that these memories are uniquely impervious to the passage of time and psychological processes that might change them. Unless traumatic memories assert themselves as a special mode of remembering, they are not available to either the conscious or the unconscious workings of the mind. Langer has described this phenomenon.

> Numerous strategies are available to individuals who wish to escape the burden of a vexatious past: forget, repress, ignore, deny, or simply falsify the facts. For reasons difficult to ascertain, what I have called humiliated memory seems immune to these forms of evasion.[3]

Most probably what Langer notes here can be explained by the fact that traumatic memory is a specific type of memory; in many ways, it is not a memory at all. It does not exist most of the time in the mind of the survivor; it is simply not available in any form or way. Therefore, traumatic memories are not subject to the normal functions of remembering and time. According to Laub, a "listener to the narrative of extreme human pain, of massive psychic trauma [. . .] comes to look for something that is in fact nonexistent; a record that has yet to be made. Massive trauma precludes its registration [by the victim's mind]."[4] Caruth, in an attempt to explain why "trauma precludes its registration," suggests that trauma is a "wound of the mind [. . .], a breach in the mind's experience of time, self, and the world," caused by an event that "is experienced too soon, too unexpectedly, to be fully known and is therefore not available to consciousness until it imposes itself again, repeatedly."[5] Hartman, attempting to describe the relationship between a "traumatic kind of knowledge" and art, suggests that "the traumatic event [is] registered rather than experienced. It seems to have bypassed perception and consciousness, and falls directly into the psyche."[6] Since the traumatic event is "registered" but not "experienced," it follows that the record of it, etched into the human mind, is not affected by our everyday mental processes; it remains separate and unassimilated.

Alterations within memories corrupt their documentary value from the point of view of historical research. If we accept, however, that something in the nature of traumatic memories resists change, there is no basis for historians to regard testimonies given closer in time to the events they describe as more reliable than later testimonies. Rather than being suspicious of later testimonies, we need to develop reliable methods for recognizing those kinds of trauma memories that remain unaffected by common mental processes. (The subject matter of the memory is only one indication.) Tellingly, survivor writers such as Primo Levi, Imre Kertész, Ida Fink, Jorge Semprun, and Aharon Appelfeld have consistently protested against the notion of discrediting later testimonies.

Psychology employs numerous trauma definitions: it acknowledges the existence of the intensive individual traumatic event, a series of events, or long-term situations, each one of which completely overwhelms a person and remains unassimilated, with continuing negative effects. In his ground-breaking book, Langer differentiates between "deep memories" and "common memories," adopting the terms used by Auschwitz survivor and artist Charlotte Delbo. By deep memories Langer means "imprints of the Holocaust reality,"[7] whereas common memories refer to recollections of the survivors' long-term historical trauma that do not assert themselves as raw, completely unassimilated, instantaneously traumatizing forces as do the deep memories. Langer also makes the significant claim that deep memories emerge from time to time within narratives relating the survivors' common memories.

The typically multiple traumas of each Holocaust survivor that are re-corded in these two basic ways in the survivors' minds manifest themselves in their life accounts as two main types of texts: the recounting of common memories and that of traumatic deep memories. As a consequence of the trau-matic nature of the entire period, trauma centers emerge in the life accounts rendered by Holocaust survivors, making the process of recollection spas-modic. These trauma centers, which constitute the emotional centers of the testimonies as well, assert themselves as deep memories that time after time violently puncture the process of recounting the survivor's common memo-ries. While those events and situations that are consciously available remain subject to various mental processes and therefore can undergo distortion and modification, the traumatic events and situations that are registered as deep memories remain impervious to change.

Thus not the common memories by themselves, but the relationship be-tween the two kinds of memories — deep and common — with a special atten-tion to the content of the deep memories gives the listener the best possible access to the largely inconceivable realities of the Holocaust. Greenspan for-mulates the interaction between the two kinds of memories as follows: "The seeds of the story's undoing — memories of the worst possible made actual — are thus carried within it. And when they emerge, the story ends. . . . For, in place of narrative unfolding, we now hear a pressured staccato of snapshot images."[8] For Greenspan, "the story" signifies what Langer calls "common memories," which are possible to relate, and can be related to, as narratives. The "pressured staccato of snapshot images" signifies what, in Langer's terms, are "deep memories."

Greenspan's words also call attention to the phenomenon that traumatic deep memories tend to appear as a series of moving images which flash invol-untarily and unstoppably "upon the inward eye" of the witness, completely blotting out his or her surroundings. Sounds, smells, tactile, and taste expe-riences often accompany these "minimovies," and sometimes even constitute the entire memory, but it seems that visual images have a primacy. While testifying, whenever deep memories emerge, survivors have to make a decision about the way they will describe the images moving in front of their eyes, that is, if they choose to describe them at all. In any event, the struggle of the sufferer, who simultaneously, or quasi-simultaneously, views the moving images and tries to commit them to words, is quite visible and/or audible in oral testimonies and leaves discernible traces in written ones.

Interestingly, even when the survivors do manage to relate their deep memories in the form of narratives (illustrative or explanatory, to employ Deborah Schiffrin's terms), the construction of those narratives evinces a struggle for words by which the deep memories forcefully puncture the flow of the overall narrative. The audience, thus, still experiences them as the breakdown of the narrative form.[9]

Constructing the multifaceted narrative structure of testimonies and life accounts of historical traumas involves complex mental, psychological, and textual processes. Deborah Schiffrin has distinguished various types of narratives that are employed in life stories.[10] The two major categories are specific and intertextual narratives. There are three basic types among the specific stories that "recount a specific episode tied to a particular time and place." They "are [all] centered around a single experience, bounded (they have a beginning and end), internally structured (temporally ordered clauses) and evaluated."[11] Based on "function, location, and structure," Schiffrin distinguishes between explanatory narratives,[12] illustrative narratives, and performative narratives.[13] Being "oft-told stories," performative narratives are largely irrelevant to early Holocaust testimonies,[14] but the other two types are particularly characteristic of life accounts containing historical traumas. In addition to simple or specific stories, Schiffrin also identifies intertextual narratives constituting various hermeneutic frameworks for life accounts. Intertextual narratives are "non-contiguous stor[ies] that emerge across a set of narratives [and] other discourse segments that are linked in some way, for example by characters [. . .], type of episode [. . .], interaction [. . .], or goal,"[15] endowing life stories with coherent and otherwise not available meanings. According to Schiffrin, identifying and "analyzing an intertextual narrative is not just a question of adding the specific narratives together; rather, it may require finding a more abstract connection (e.g., theme, evaluation, point, style) that links the different texts together into a coherent framework of meaning."[16] Life writings thus typically offer several different, even contradictory and mutually exclusive, interpretative narratives.

Building on Schiffrin's research, I claim that traumatic deep memories, which are usually related as illustrative or explanatory narratives, often assert themselves as intertextual narratives. Deep memories become intertextual narratives as the same traumatic memories, or closely related ones (routinely connected by repetition compulsion), surface in several contexts within the narrative of common memories. An audiotaped testimony that was collected in the framework of Júlia Vajda's testimony-collection project[17] is a case in point.

Vajda and Szegő produced a detailed analysis of the testimony in question.[18] By employing psychological and literary methods concentrating on gaps, incongruities, repetitions, and emotions in the testimony, the authors identified the major trauma of the survivor, which remained uncommitted to words but emerged several times during the interview. Long silences marked the places where the witness was watching the traumatic minimovie running before his mind's eye that recorded and formed the focus of his Holocaust trauma. I want to add that the witness's main trauma, which he cannot tell but that emerges in several places within his testimony, constitutes an intertextual metanarrative, structuring the entire life account and forming associations with the related common memories. Survivors often describe how traumatic memories emerge suddenly, triggered by factors that are usually unknown to the victim, and blot out the everyday surrounding reality. By contrast, testimonies and other forms of life accounts consciously facilitate the emergence of traumatic deep memories. Rather than responding to triggers that present themselves by chance and work unconsciously, the survivor, by recounting his common memories, himself provides the triggers. Common memories, as contexts for the deep memories, therefore simultaneously incorporate them into an overall narrative and keep them completely apart.

The narrative units surrounding the deep memories may also contain additional triggers that, for some reason, have remained dormant in a particular life account. Greenspan's interview method that entails the repeated recording of the same survivor's testimonies over an extended period of time is especially helpful in identifying the central traumatic memories of a survivor, while also acknowledging that in different circumstances, different trauma centers from the long period of persecution can emerge.[19] There are, however, central traumas that surface every time the survivor testifies. "Leon's" story of the execution of an inmate, which the survivor told several times to the interviewer Greenspan, forgetting each time that he had already described this event, is a case in point. There are other traumatic centers, however, that materialize, or are related, in only a few specific contexts.

What further complicates the relationship of common and deep memories is that some memories can be related as both. The survivor might have a stock way to relate something utterly traumatic, as, for example, the first selection upon arrival in Auschwitz; but other times, when the circumstances are right (for instance, the right audience), the same event can emerge with its entire traumatizing and retraumatizing force as a deep memory.

I must also qualify my claim concerning the usefulness of the "imprint" nature of deep memories in historical research. They can be employed the same way as snapshots can. We have to determine, for example, to what degree the mental recording of the traumatic memory is, like a photograph, already an interpretation, and how its status as an interpretation influences the way in which it is encoded.

Psychological and emotional forces that interpret the traumatic scene already before and for its recording work the most strongly within the center of each traumatic memory. By contrast, details given incidentally while describing scenes that the witness is simultaneously watching with his or her mind's eye are very reliable, because marginal details are recorded without being much interpreted. It is crucial, therefore, to distinguish between the strongly interpreted central elements of traumatic minimovies and the elements that are recorded with only the level of interpretation that is necessary for perception. Details that appeared neutral at the time of the experience and were only later understood and identified as parts of the central trauma, thus becoming elements in the memory's traumatizing force, are usually also recorded without the distortions of a heavy initial interpretation.

A further difficulty concerning the utilization of memories contained as traumatic minimovies is that even though the memories themselves do not change, the way the witness reports them while watching the movie can vary depending on the audience, the immediate situation, his or her stage in life, and most important, depending on the surrounding narratives (determined by common memories, to use Langer's terminology). Langer identifies this particular difficulty by coining the term "tainted memory": "memory sacrifices purity of vision in the process of recounting, resulting in what I call tainted memory, a narrative stained by the disapproval of the witness's own present moral sensibility, as well as by some of the incidents it relates."[20] Audience, situation, and the surrounding narratives also affect which deep memory surfaces. That is why, in order to analyze testimonies by focusing on the identification of traumatic deep memories, we need to rely on a complex literary and linguistic in-depth analysis of the entire testimony, and to pay special attention to the various narratives and narrative frameworks of the texts as well as their thematic and formal interactions with the deep memories.[21]

I claim that traumatic memories, because they largely resist the change-inducing forces of time and psychological processes, facilitate historical research. Therefore, it is a major research task to identify and isolate the traumatic deep memories within testimonies. The technique of literary and linguistic close reading enables us to accomplish precisely this; it aids us in isolating those instances in oral and written texts when the witness is watching one of the traumatic minimovies etched into his or her mind. The most important step in the process of isolating traumatic deep memories is to find the emotional centers of the given testimony. In the testimonies of child survivors, written in Displaced Person (DP) camps soon after the war, I saw that some textual elements prevent or simply do not facilitate the relating of one's loss of family, and some elements help the survivor to address this extremely painful topic. Here I provide two examples that demonstrate various ways in which the enormity of the trauma prevents the deep memories from surfacing within testimonies. In NF's testimony, the magnitude of the trauma together with its continued existential consequences, and in ChB's case, the assumed role of the testifying child, block the emergence of deep memories. The trauma of losing close family members is therefore not related at all in these testimonies or is merely implied. By contrast, in a third testimony (AS's account), we can examine the emergence of deep memories in connection to the complex narrative frameworks of the child's testimony. It is a remarkable testimony, because AS is able to relate the story of losing her mother alongside her last memory of them together at home, but she could not bring herself to verbalize explicitly the fate of her father and younger brother. Therefore, we can study within the same testimony the textual elements that facilitate the telling of these extremely painful stories together with those elements that impede it.

I chose testimonies of children in order to make my point more forcefully, since, from the point of view of traditional historical research, children's testimonies are the most dubious. The reason for this is that children's perspectives are usually extremely narrow, and their understanding of events tends to be even more inadequate than that of adults. Precisely because historians consider children's testimonies as sources of especially limited value, they are the best test cases to determine what kinds of information we can learn by using a literary and linguistic analytic approach.

Upon first reading, early testimonies—both by children and adults—usually seem stark, laconic, and emotionally dry. By conducting a close reading, however, we can demonstrate that the texts are, in fact, bursting with emotion. In early handwritten testimonies, for instance, there are numerous signs to indicate emotional hot spots, such as features of the script—retouches, inkblots, messier handwriting; textual gaps and discrepancies; as well as various grammatical mistakes.

A crucial reason for our initial impression that early testimonies are devoid of emotion is that the loss of the witnesses' loved ones is almost never described in detail and is many times only implied, and at other times, the witness cannot afford emotionally to bring the topic up on the personal level at all. Usually children and adults alike state in general that Jewish families were torn apart and that many family members were murdered. They write general sentences such as, "Without mercy they [the Germans] took the children from the Jewish mothers and killed them,"[22] but do not extend the description to the personal level.

NF, a child survivor, who gave his testimony in the Aschau DP camp (Children's Center) in 1946, for example, does not report the loss of his family in detail.

The translation of NF's testimony:

BOŁSZOWCE

Aschau UNRRA Team 154

NF, born on July 15, 1930 in Bołszowce (Poland)

Education: 6 classes of elementary school. Lived in Bołschowce [different spelling of the town's name], until the war, among the Poles, until the Germans came in. Two months after they came in, in 1941 [The "in 1941" seems to be inserted later as the writing is lighter and it is placed where there was space for it.] the German Gestapo carried out an Aktion—they took out the people in transports to Belzec [Bełżec]. I managed to hide and so I did not fall among those who were taken away. The next day, they gave us an order that within 24 hours we must leave the [town?—word is missing] and go to the ghetto. Life in the ghetto was very bad. Children Aktionen and adult Aktionen did not evade us one day. In a short while, at the beginning of 1942, they liquidated all the ghettos in Galicia, including the ghetto in our town Rohatyn. We sat in the bunker for three days and on the fourth day we went to a forest, not far from our town. We stayed there for one week and then went to another [forest/place?—word is missing]. I and my sister went to look for bread, and when we got back, we did not find anyone there. We are going, but we don't know where. [grammatical mistake: present tense] We went closer to the partisans. We found the partisans and they took us in with great care. We were there until the Russian Army liberated us on April 15, 1944.[23]

[Signature of NF]

NF's written Yiddish is obviously not sufficient, since he writes in Latin characters. The language is so grammatically chaotic that the translator, Yiddish scholar Vera Szabó, had to heavily interpret certain features of the original in order to be able to render it in English. As part of the process, she inserted much of the punctuation as well. In 1946, NF was sixteen years old according to his testimony, or seventeen according to a document kept in the ITS Archives (Bad Arolsen, Germany).[24] Textually the painful emotional intensity of the testimony is evident from the fact that many crucial pieces of information that are directly connected to the witness and his family are formulated in the negative:[25]

I managed to hide and so *I did not fall among those who were taken away.* . . . Life in the ghetto was very bad. *Children Aktionen and adult Aktionen did not evade us one day.* . . . We sat in the bunker for three days and on the fourth day we went to a forest, *not far from our town.* . . . I and my sister went to look for bread, and when we got back, *we did not find anyone there.* We are going, *but we don't know where.* [Italics mine, RH]

We are aware of the most painful gap in the testimony because of the existence of a document in the ITS. According to the document, NF's mother was murdered in the ghetto of Rohatyn in June 1942. The sentence that is formulated in an intensely negative way, *"Children Aktionen and adult Aktionen did not evade us one day,"* is overwhelmed by emotion. It probably implies and hides at the same time the murder of NF's mother, possibly together with some of his siblings, as he also includes *"Children Aktionen."* (The ITS document contains information about only NF's mother.) However, our witness does not tell anything about that matter. Then, in a dryly factual sentence, NF relates how he and his sister remained completely alone: "I and my sister went to look for bread, and when we got back, we did not find anyone there." The testimony's emotional arch peaks in the grammatically faulty next sentence, which also contains a negative formulation that breaks out of the relative safety of the past tense, and from which intense disorientation, fear, and vulnerability radiate: "We are going, but we don't know where." The use of the present tense demonstrates not only the inescapable presence of the traumatic losses, but also how disorientation and aimlessness still rule the world of the testifying youngster now in the DP camp.

The negative formulations are in obvious contradiction to the positive tone of the last part of the testimony relating the survival of the witness and his sister owing to the help of the partisans. While in the previous part of the testimony, the rendering of points of orientation was formulated in the negative: *"not far from,"* in the last section, the point of reference is rendered positively: "We went *closer to* the partisans." In this very short testimony, NF makes sure that he comments on the partisans' unexpected goodness: "They took us in with great care." The testimony ends with liberation, but the focus of the last sentence is still the "there," the place where the partisans saved him and his sister. The grateful and positive tone of the ending cannot become a real celebration of survival and rescue, because the losses are too overwhelming.

When the witness was left alone with a piece of paper to write his testimony/composition, without the continuous and supportive attention of a dedicated, sympathetic adult (teacher or interviewer), he could not emotionally bring himself to record in detail the center of his trauma: the loss of his family.

Another child survivor, ChB, who was born in September 1932, and who takes her role as a witness extremely seriously, relates with amazing accuracy all the Actions (*Aktionen*) carried out against the Jews of her East Galician hometown and the ghetto. By contrast, she does not talk about the fate of her own family, even though she must have lost one family member after another as a consequence of the Actions. Some of the dates and events that she relates are surprisingly accurate, not only for a child, but even for an adult. A number of the dates and events can be corroborated by testimonies of other survivors.[26]

The translation of ChB's testimony follows:[27]

> ChB [her name is written both in Latin and Hebrew letters]
> Neu-Freiman — Munich 45
> Ruschsteiger str. No. 3
> UNRRA team 560
> 17/09/1932
> My Life under the Occupation of the Nazis
> In the year 1941 [on] 8/IX the Germans came to us. After the Germans came[,] the Ukrainians set up a provisional Ukrainian Government and killed us in all the streets. [On] 1/VIII the Germans started to rule in our place. They caught thousands of Jews for hard work. This time there was a great famine because the murderers did not let us leave the town in order to buy bread. And so we suffered privations until the Action [*gzerat hamachteret*][28] happened on the first day of Sukkoth in the year 1942. On Saturday on the 5th hour in the morning[,] a Gestapo unit and Ukrainians surrounded our town. The Action [*gzerat hamachteret*] lasted for two days, they gathered [rounded up] 800 Jews in a train [iron machine] and took them to the town of Belzec [Bełżec]. There they burned them in/by fire. When the Action [*hamachteret*] happened, we[,] by chance[,] escaped/were saved from the hands of the murderers. After the big Action [*machteret,*] not many days had passed and they expelled us to the town of Borszczow [today Borshchiv in present-day Ukraine]. In the year of 1942 [on] X 23[,] they made a ghetto for all the Jews who lived around the town, under the rule of the Nazis. There were 5500 Jews in the ghetto. We lived 15 people in one room. [15 people/room] In the month of Kislev in the year of 1942 they gathered [rounded up] 120 people and took them to the town of Chortkow [today Chortkov in present-day Ukraine] where killing blows were dealt to them. [The text says: "they killed them/dealt them with killing blows." From the next sentence it becomes clear that they were not killed but brutally beaten.] After ten days[,] they returned to the ghetto. Not many days passed and the people who had returned from the prison became ill with typhoid

fever, and the majority of them died. Because of the great crowding[,] the epidemic hit all the people of the ghetto. In 2 months[,] 800 people died. On 17 Adar in the morning[,] a German unit and Ukrainians surrounded the ghetto and killed 200 people. The blood of the Jews ran like water on the streets. In this Action [*machteret*] they caught me and wanted to kill me and by chance I escaped/was saved from the hands of the murderers. On the day of 20 in the month of Nisan in the year of 1943, the Germans again surrounded the ghetto and the Action [*gzerat machteret*] started and in one day they killed 12,000 Jews. After the big Action [*machteret*] on the 1st day of the festival of Shavuot[,] the destruction of the ghetto started[,] which lasted for 15 days. After the destruction of the ghetto, we ran away to our town and there we (hid) were [for] 9 months in. . . . The hunger and the fear were very great. All day they killed Jews in the streets. And thus passed for us the bad years under the rule of the Nazis. On the 12th day of the month Nisan in the year 1944[,] we became free. And out of 5500 people who were in the ghetto there remained 200 sick and weak Jews.

The emotional centers of the testimony are clearly the Actions, and the role ChB assumes is that of the objective witness who aims at recording the experiences of her community. This is an important role that is generally viewed as having intrinsic value, and it does not require the witness to relate her personal traumas and losses. In fact, a more personal tone could be perceived as a factor that lessens the objectivity of the historical account. Informed by this view of what a historical account should be, ChB's testimony is silently dominated by the absence of her personal losses. The absent center of the testimony is probably the fate of her family.

As a witness, the spokesperson for a murdered community, she even corrects her writing as she composes her testimony.[29] ChB undertakes the task of becoming a communal witness partly in order not to have to think about her personal story. The pronouns "we" and "us" in her testimony typically refer to the suffering Jewish community. By this use of first-person plural personal pronouns, she establishes her role as an authentic witness, who was there and who was a member of the community, without getting really personal. We only learn about her suffering as part of the collective.

The use of first-person plural personal pronouns varies in only two places. In the first instance: "When the Action [*hamachteret*] happened, *we*[,] by chance[,] escaped/were saved from the hands of the murderers," the "we" is significant as opposed to what happened to the "I" during a later Action: "in this Action [*machteret*] they caught me and wanted to kill me and by chance I escaped/was saved from the hands of the murderers."[30] The second case —"After the destruction of the ghetto, *we* ran away to *our* town and there we (hid) were [for] 9 months in. . . ." — occurs when ChB continues to use the first-person plural personal pronoun to relate her escape, regardless of the fact that the overwhelming majority of the Jews have been murdered during and as a consequence of the liquidation of the ghetto. This "we" is much more personal than the previous use of "we" denoting the entire community. This "we" seems to denote her own personal community: probably the remainder of her family.

We ache to learn whether she was with her family, but she never gives away that information and quickly returns to her role as an authentic but emotionally distant observer, eventually employing a third-person narration: "And out of 5500 people who were in the ghetto there remained 200 sick and weak Jews." Obviously, ChB was one of those surviving "200 sick and weak Jews" who were liberated "on the 12th day of the month Nisan in the year of 1944," but we do not learn whether any other members of her family survived.

The unique, more personal "we" — hinting at her personal community, probably her family — seems to be merely an unconscious slip. Precisely because she insists on not telling the story of her family, the slip signals her terrible losses. The fact, however, remains: she does not tell anything about her family's fate at all.

As long as the Actions organize the testimony as the reference points as well as the foci of the experience and its representation, the narrative has a very clear structure. After the destruction of the ghetto, however, ChB's narrative becomes much more disoriented. She seems to be aware of that, as she concludes the testimony promptly and abruptly, but with a sort of summary: "And thus passed for us the bad years under the rule of the Nazis." She indicates, therefore, that this is a proper ending. Then, after relating their liberation briefly and objectively, she finishes her testimony on a bleak note emphasizing the losses, especially the loss of the lively Jewish communities of her region: "And out of 5500 people who were in the ghetto there remained 200 sick and weak Jews."

It is a characteristic of children's testimonies that they insist on reporting that their experiences were not unique: they were not singled out; they were not different. Whenever child survivors feel that their experiences were not typical, they report that with special pain. The Polish Jewish girl whose testimony I analyze next adds, for example, the following sentence after describing the abduction of her mother during the first large-scale Action in her hometown: "*I was amongst the first children that remained without her mother and in my house there was a great sadness without my beloved mother*" [Italics mine — RH].[31]

AS's testimony is also highly unusual, because the testifying youngster is able to write in detail about one of her overwhelming traumatic losses, but not about others of similar magnitude. She relates the traumatic loss of her mother, but she is unable to do the same in respect to the loss of her father and young brother. The ordeal of losing her mother emerges within the text of the testimony, and AS describes in detail the moving images of the traumatic minifilm that she is forced to watch over and over.

The translation of the testimonial composition of a Polish Jewish child survivor, AS, who gave her testimony in Hebrew in the Zeilsheim DP camp:[32]

> 1947 01. 30
> Zeilsheim
> How did the seven years of the Hitlerist occupation passed over me
> In the year 1939 the world war broke out[,] and in October in the year 1939[,] the Germans conquered all of the country of Poland. The Germans were very bad to the Jews. They pressured them mercilessly. And one night in the year 1942 this incident happened. At night armed soldiers came to my house. At this time I was sleeping a deep sleep and didn't know what was in store for me.
> They came to me and shouted ["Q]uickly get up[!"] Quickly I got up from my lying(-down) position and entered my parents' [room]. There I saw my mother holding on her knees my 4-y[ear-]old brother and big tears ran down on her face. When I saw this sight, I burst into bitter tears (cry)[,] and at the same time[,] the soldiers came and shouted ["]quickly get out[!] and I with my entire family was driven outside[,] which was lit by big lights [search lights, but she uses Biblical words to denote them] and all the people were standing in one line. When we came[,] one of the leaders of the soldiers ordered [she/us] to move from the place[,] and we all went to the central point. The way was very terrible[,] soldiers were hitting us all the way. And after a while[,] we came close to the central point[.] At the central point there were two sides[:] one side that went to be deported [the same word as she used above for being driven out of her home] and the second side that went to freedom. And I with my entire family went over to freedom. But this joy didn't last long. At the same time there were abductions on the street and the Germans captured my mother too. And I stayed by myself with my father and brother, who was four years old. And I was one of the first children who were without mothers[,] and in my house there was a great sadness without my beloved mother[.] And after a year[,] the Germans again banished [she uses the word "emigrate"] the Jews and me with my father and brother [they] sent to Auschwitz. When we reached Auschwitz at night, soldiers were already waiting for us and when we arrived[,] the separation started. And many people[,] infants and the elderly and also the youth were sent to the crematorium to be set on fire[.] And

joy came to me because by a miracle[,] I remained alive[,] and from that time onwards[,] what happened to my father and brother[,] I didn't know. In Auschwitz[,] it was very bad for me[.] The crematorium was not far from my barrack. And at night[,] when I went outside[,] the sky was full of blood from the crematorium in which people were set on fire. And like that have passed for me two years amidst hunger and great troubles. When the Germans found out that the Russians were drawing closer[,] they evacuated [she uses the same word as above: "emigrated" — *higru*, or banished] the camp[.] It was in winter[,] and on the street there was very cold[,] and we were forced to march many miles on foot and those who didn't have the strength were shot[.] And thus half-dead[,] we arrived at Bergen[-]Belsen. In Bergen[-]Belsen[,] the situation was very terrible. We lived in barracks made of ???? and slept on the ground which was covered by ????. One night, the following catastrophe happened[:] there was a strong wind and it was raining[,] and the wind was so strong that it ripped the barrack apart into tiny little pieces[,] and during that night we remained without a roof on the street[.] The sight was very terrible[,] we were all drenched to the bone, and many people[,] at that night[,] died. And after a while in Bergen-Belsen typhus broke out and many people got sick[,] and I was also very sick and I couldn't stand on my feet[.] And at that time[,] the Germans were scared because the English had been drawing closer and they decided to evacuate [immigrate] all the healthy people and shoot the sick ones. And I was also sick and I heard all these things[,] but I so wanted to win a life of freedom. And in one morning there was a great commotion in the camp and all the armies started to run away[,] because the English were drawing closer. After two days[,] the first English tank arrived at Bergen-Belsen that gave us freedom and I was still sick and couldn't perceive that the hour of freedom had arrived. And that's how the seven years of the German Hitlerist occupation amidst hunger and big troubles passed for me.

[Signature of AS]
Class 5
Henrietta Szold Jewish School

From the testimony we do not learn the age of the survivor, but according to an ITS document, she was sixteen-and-a-half years old when she gave her testimony in the beginning of 1947. She was born on May 18, 1930, in Sosnowiec, Poland.[33] Similar to ChB, AS also wrote her testimony in Hebrew, which was not only not her mother tongue, but a language that she was just then in the process of acquiring.

The choice of language in the DP camps for individual use,[34] publications, or as the teaching language in schools depended on both ideological and practical considerations. Choosing a language in itself amounted to a statement of identity; the chosen language served as both a means of identity construction and a way to establish one's membership in a community. Moreover, choosing a common language actively helped to create that community. Language choice could also signify the rejection of one's past victimization by the countries where that language was spoken.[35]

The fact that the young people wrote their compositions in a language that they had been studying for only a short time greatly influenced the content of the testimonies. They had to express themselves more simply than they probably wanted to, owing to the limitations that their as-yet insufficient knowledge of Hebrew imposed on them. The Hebrew of the testimonies varies in proficiency; ChB's, for example, is more broken than AS's. In numerous instances, one can note phrases clearly translated word for word from the survivors' mother tongues. AS's testimony, for instance, contains a phrase we have translated as, "We were all drenched to the bone." However, she wrote in Hebrew exactly: "We were all drenched till the thread." There is no such expression in Hebrew. However, in Polish, the expression "drenched till the thread" exists: *przemoknięci do nitki*.

AS's composition shows real literary talent. She employs numerous literary devices, her text is deeply informed by them, and she develops archetypical imagery. For instance, she stresses that all the terrible things—the selection in the ghetto and the abduction of her mother, their arrival in Auschwitz and the collapse of the barrack in Bergen-Belsen—happened to her at night. That each of these horrifying events occurred at night is, of course, a question of reality; but the fact that she repeatedly, indeed rhythmically, asserts it, turns reality into a literary device. This is especially noticeable when we realize that AS contrasts the night to the dawn of liberation. Just as Elie Wiesel does in his memoir-novel, *Night*, AS expands the night-dawn (darkness-light) binary into asleep/unaware versus waking up, and seeing clearly versus not being able to perceive reality. The loudness of the murderers and the silence of the victims form another clear binary. She also contrasts suddenness and slowness as well as eagerness and reluctance, both in terms of knowledge. When AS describes her first major trauma, the loss of her mother, she depicts it in terms of a night of initiation, the time when she was cruelly forced to wake up to the unimaginable realities of the historical night of the Holocaust.

She opens her testimony in an impersonal objective voice, as if the occupation of Poland and the oppression exercised by the Germans does not have much to do with her and her loved ones. She portrays the suffering of the Jews in general terms. According to her own metaphor, she was sleeping "a deep sleep." Then suddenly, the testimony becomes tragically personal, and we learn about her initiation into the night of selections and murder. Her waking up brings a clear personal awareness of the Holocaust reality, and is contrasted at the end of the testimony to the joy of liberation, the realities of which could not be immediately appreciated or even observed. In addition to the two-day-long delay, her sickness forced her to remain unaware, unable to perceive the realities of the "morning."

Furthermore, the dynamics of delay and repetition that characterize the major part of the testimony are turned upside down at the end of the testimony. In the beginning, AS is the one who does not want to wake up to an unbearable reality, but the shouting soldiers force her to become completely aware. That part of the testimony is full of verbal and nonverbal delays. Unnecessary repetitions and wordiness effectively postpone relating the story of losing her mother. The directly quoted shouts of the soldiers, which forced her to hurry then, do not hurry the testimony now. In fact, they delay it through repetitions. She slows the narrative down even further by adding superfluous pseudoinformation: "from my lying(-down) position." The most apparent nonverbal means of suspension can be seen on the original handwritten testimony: there are large gaps between certain words. Moreover, these gaps become increasingly larger, whenever AS is about to relate the centers of her trauma. In other words, she asserts some degree of control by not letting herself be rushed.

In relating the liberation scene, the dynamic is the opposite. The suddenness encoded in the phrase "in one morning" and the very specific point of time delineated, "*the hour* of freedom," signify a sharp boundary, though AS relates that, in reality, the process took two long days and could not even be fully observed. She desperately wanted to wake up to a different reality, but the liberators had been delayed. AS's ambivalent feelings regarding liberation are caused mainly by the fact that she alone of her family has remained alive, and now, in order to "perceive that the hour of freedom had arrived," she has to "perceive" her loss in its entirety as well.

In addition, the text also indicates that AS's "waking up" coincides with her forced growing up: she not only loses her mother that night but also takes over the responsibility of caring for her baby brother and father. Her tears, which reflect her mother's grief, imply both identification and a solemn promise. In my opinion, this identification with her mother makes it possible for her to describe in detail the trauma of losing her mother, but prevents her from relating the loss of her brother and father in the first selection in Auschwitz. She could not take care of them anymore; she was forced to abandon her role as a responsible, primary caregiver. She does not say this, but the structure of the testimony suggests it.

AS hides her knowledge about the fate of her brother and father in the text. She states in general that "many people[,] infants and the elderly and also the youth were sent to the crematorium to be set on fire[.]" She then relates that she, a "youth," was saved by a miracle and writes that she does not know what happened to her loved ones, even though her brother was a small child. However, immediately after claiming ignorance about her family's fate, she describes the central trauma of Auschwitz: the function of the crematoria. In other words, she knows very well what transpired, but she could not and cannot bring herself to explicitly put her knowledge into words.

The narrative structure of this testimony is very complex. It contains both illustrative and explanatory narratives as well as intertextual narratives, to use Deborah Schiffrin's terminology. The complexity of AS's testimony's narrative structure is rare among early child testimonies collected by the Central Historical Commission. AS relates the following explanatory narratives, which move the story forward, in order to give added emphasis to certain elements of her chronologically rendered story:

1) Selection on the main square and the abduction of the mother [line numbers on the original handwritten testimony: 15-32]
2) Selection in Auschwitz [34-40]
3) Evacuation and forced march to Bergen-Belsen [44-49]
4) Typhoid fever [59-65]
5) Liberation [65-70]

Two illustrative narratives are also included:

1) The story of seeing her mother for the last time at home [6-14]
2) The story of the collapsed barrack [52-58]

Illustrative narratives do not move the main story forward and therefore can be left out. Their main function is to illustrate or summarize and symbolize a stage in the speaker's life. The illustrative narratives of AS's testimony are made up of emerging traumatic deep memories. Deep memories often constitute illustrative narratives, because their emergence cannot be guaranteed. As I have shown previously, the emergence of deep memories often takes the witness by surprise. Consequently, the narrative units of common memories have to move the life story forward, as the deep memories cannot be counted on to perform that function. The same is true for explanatory narratives; the information can be given without the emergence of a full-fledged narrative of this type. Thus deep memories can also be explanatory narratives.

In AS's testimony, both of the illustrative deep memories are kept apart from the main text by an introductory sentence. The first narrative is introduced by the sentence: "And one night in the year 1942 this incident happened." The second narrative, about the collapse of the barrack in Bergen-Belsen, is marked in a similar way: "One night, the following catastrophe happened." Once again, something that was supposed to provide her with basic protection, that is, shelter her from the raging weather, failed her. The repetitive element of being left unprotected is the basic trauma that asserts itself through the apparent gradation between the terms "incident" and "catastrophe." In this way, the two illustrative narratives together make up an intertextual narrative.

Moreover, the central intertextual theme of being able to protect or failing to protect becomes more complex, guilt-ridden, and painful as the testimony progresses. The two illustrative narratives relate stories in which AS was "abandoned" by exactly those forces that were supposed to protect her. In the traumatic center, which she cannot directly articulate in words, she perceives herself as the one who somehow abandoned those whom she was supposed to protect: her little brother and father. I must emphasize that these feelings of guilt are the survivor's patently and terribly unjust self-incriminatory emotions. The comparison of the absence of explicitly stated loss to the description of losing her mother reveals the existence of these torturous guilt feelings. She says that she was saved by a miracle, since she was young and should have been gassed upon arrival according to the system in Auschwitz; but some benevolent element in the universe did not abandon her even though she was forced to abandon her loved ones. The theme of protection and the lack of it is thus part of several intertextual hermeneutic frameworks that make the interpretation modular, and therefore, flexible. The traumatic centers of the testimony conveyed as illustrative narratives are clearly connected to the ruling archetypal image of the testimony: night. The third event that is stated to have occurred at night is the selection in Auschwitz upon arrival, during which AS loses her brother and father. This deep memory, however, cannot be described in the testimony; it does not become an illustrative narrative. Its emergence merely leaves an illustrative trace: AS's description of Auschwitz at night.

In AS's testimony, the illustrative narrative relating the traumatic deep memory of seeing her mother at home for the last time continues as an explanatory narrative relating the deep memories of the selection in the main square at Sosnowiec[36] and her mother's subsequent abduction. In fact, the illustrative narrative gets its meaning from the later explanatory narrative. The shocking events related by the explanatory narrative are what make the illustrative narrative so significant. Therefore, this illustrative narrative and the following explanatory narrative together relate a sequence of deep memories. To mention one piece of historical information that can be gleaned from this deep memory: we learn that the conventional image of selections as organized pedantically according to some kind of a rationale ignores the fact that they were often accompanied by random, irrational abductions.[37] This arbitrariness caused the victims to lose any remaining feelings of the sort of minimal security that one can make some sense of his or her surroundings and thus be able to attempt to manipulate them to his or her advantage.

Christopher R. Browning differentiates between four basic scholarly approaches that draw upon testimonies: one is "primarily interested in the mode of 'retelling' and narrative construction," another focuses on the survivors' traumas, yet another on the aspects of "collective memory," and his own research, which concentrates on "looking at memory [. . .] in the individual plural" in order to employ testimonies when there are no other available sources. Browning states that in contrast to his own historical approach, the first two approaches "emphasize the effects of the Holocaust upon the survivors and how they have remembered and narrated, struggled and coped with those effects rather than the events of the Holocaust itself."[38] My own aim is to prove that the results of research projects falling into Browning's first two categories could be employed as devices of historical source criticism, enabling us to qualify certain parts of the testimonies as reliable historical sources in the classical sense.

By building on research that focuses on "the mode of 'retelling' and narrative construction" of testimonies and by drawing on trauma theory, we can utilize survivor testimonies and life accounts in historical research in a novel way. A thorough literary and linguistic analysis of both oral and written testimonies allows us to identify the emergence of deep memories within the text of the accounts. Deep traumatic memories are memory imprints, in other words, "snapshots" that have a high documentary value. Therefore, a detailed analysis of survivor testimonies can enable us to draw into the orbit of historical research a new kind of data registered by deep traumatic memories.

NOTES

1. Annette Wieviorka, the historian most dismayed with the recent emergence of what she calls "the era of the witness," noted that "historians have essentially relegated reflection on [testimonies] to literary critics, to the various 'psys' — psychiatrists, psychologists, psychoanalysts — and, to a lesser extent, to sociologists." In Wieviorka, *The Era of the Witness*, trans. Jared Stark (Ithaca, NY: Cornell University Press, 2006), xiv.

2. For example, Kinga Frojimovics reconstructed the main routes of the death marches on the basis of early postwar testimonies given in Hungary in 1945-1946 to the National Relief Committee for Deportees in Hungary (DEGOB). See *Forced Labor Service in Hungary during WWII* [in Hungarian and Hebrew], accessed on May 8, 2010, http://www.tm-it.co .il/avodat-kfiya/show_item.asp?levelId=65137. Christopher R. Browning's research on a Nazi slave labor factory in Starachowice, in the Radom District in Poland, and its evacuation to Birkenau is also based on survivor testimony. Browning also carefully reflects on his methodology in "Survivor Testimonies from Starachowice: Writing the History of a Factory Slave Labor Camp" and "Survivor Testimonies from Starachowice: The Final Days," in *Collected Memories: Holocaust History and Postwar Testimony* (Madison: University of Wisconsin Press, 2003), 37-85.

3. Langer actually calls these kinds of traumatic memories "deep memories"; "humil-

iated memory" is a subcategory of deep memory. Lawrence L. Langer, *Holocaust Testimonies: The Ruins of Memory* (New Haven, CT: Yale University Press, 1991), 96.

4. Shoshana Felman and Dori Laub, *Testimony: Crises of Witnessing in Literature, Psychoanalysis, and History* (New York: Routledge, 1992), 57.

5. Cathy Caruth, *Unclaimed Experience: Trauma, Narrative, and History* (Baltimore: Johns Hopkins University Press, 1996), 4.

6. Geoffrey H. Hartman, "On Traumatic Knowledge and Literary Studies," *New Literary History*, vol. 26 (1995), 537. "Any general description or modeling of trauma, therefore, risks being figurative itself, to the point of mythic phantasmagoria. Something 'falls' into the psyche, or causes it to split" (537).

7. Cognitive psychologist Robert N. Kraft, who—like Langer and Hartman—has studied oral testimonies of Holocaust survivors, also identifies the existence of what he calls "core memories," which correspond with Langer's "deep memories." Robert N. Kraft, "Archival Memory: Representations of the Holocaust in Oral Testimony," *Poetics Today* 27, no. 2 (2006): 311–30.

8. Henry Greenspan, *On Listening to Holocaust Survivors: Recounting and Life History* (Westport, CT: Praeger, 1998), 13. Greenspan comments on the way the survivor struggles to convey the content of the images: "Recounting takes on the language of immediacy and simultaneity rather than remembrance or duration: '*Here* was fire,' said Victor, 'and *here* was always burning rubbish and *here* were always burning people' " (13). [*Italics* are Greenspan's.]

9. Ibid., 11–15. Greenspan quotes survivors, especially Leon, who comments on the breakdown of the story as a genre in the face of such memories.

10. Deborah Schiffrin, "Mother/Daughter Discourse in a Holocaust Oral History: 'Because Then You Admit That You Are Guilty,'" *Narrative Inquiry* 10, no. 1 (2000): 1–44.

11. Ibid., 2–3.

12. Explanatory narratives provide sequences of temporally and causally linked events that explain a transition, and thus occur at temporal/spatial junctures.

13. Schiffrin, "Mother/Daughter Discourse in a Holocaust Oral History," 8–9.

14. Schiffrin defines *performative narratives*, "which also serve either explanatory or illustrative functions," as "marked as oft-told stories in which characters behave in ways emblematic of their general roles, and plots re-create major themes of the life story." See Deborah Schiffrin, "Mother and Friends in a Holocaust Life Story," *Language in Society* 31, no. 3 (July 2002): 309–53, esp. 318.

15. Schiffrin, "Mother/Daughter Discourse in a Holocaust Oral History," 2–3.

16. Ibid., 3.

17. Yad Vashem Archives, O.99—Totalitarianism and Holocaust-Survivors, Testimony Collection, Yad Vashem, Jerusalem. Vajda and her students interviewed survivors by employing a "narrative interview technique" that she had designed by drawing on Fritz Schütze's and Gabriele Rosenthal's work. Concerning the method and its aims, see Júlia Vajda's introduction to the O.99 record group in the Yad Vashem Archives.

18. Dóri Szegő and Júlia Vajda, "'Ne ölj!': Egy el nem mesélhető történet az életbenmaradásról" ["'Thou shalt not kill!': A story about remaining alive that is impossible to relate"], *Múlt és Jövő*, no. 1 (2006): 24–31.

19. Other scholars, including Ronald J. Berger and Sidney Bolkosky, have also been interested in repeated accounts of the same survivors.

20. Lawrence L. Langer, *Holocaust Testimonies: The Ruins of Memory* (New Haven, CT: Yale University Press, 1991), 122.

21. Deborah Schiffrin's differentiation of various kinds of narratives within life accounts is particularly helpful. See Schiffrin, "Mother/Daughter Discourse in a Holocaust Oral History," 1–44.

22. Yad Vashem Archives, M-1/E 881/744, Yad Vashem, Jerusalem. SK's testimony is given in Hebrew in the Zeilsheim DP camp: lines 7–8, in the last sentence of the general story.

23. Yad Vashem Archives, M-1/E 169, Yad Vashem, Jerusalem. Yiddish scholar Vera Szabó translated the text of the testimony from the Yiddish original. The translation is very close to the original Yiddish text.

24. ITS OuS-Archiv, document ID 20883390. Courtesy of Yad Vashem Archives, Jerusalem.

25. William Labov, in his groundbreaking linguistic work on narratives, emphasizes the importance of negative formulations as evaluations within the narratives.

26. Boaz Cohen and Rita Horváth corroborated many of the facts rendered in ChB's testimony while working together with linguist Joel Walters in the framework of the "Voices of Child Survivors: Children's Holocaust Testimonies" project that was supported by the Conference on Jewish Material Claims against Germany from 2007 until 2009, Bar-Ilan University, Israel.

27. Yad Vashem Archives, M-1/E 644/535, Yad Vashem, Jerusalem. The text of the testimony is translated from the Hebrew original by Boaz Cohen and Rita Horváth. The translation stayed very close to the Hebrew text: wherever the English is awkward or faulty, the Hebrew original is also like that. For the language policy in the DP camps, see Boaz Cohen, "And I Was Only a Child': Children's Testimonies, Bergen-Belsen 1945," *Holocaust Studies: A Journal of Culture and History* 12, nos. 1–2 (2006): 153–69.

28. ChB, probably with the help of the teacher, coined this term to denote "Action," which is completely alien for speakers of modern Hebrew. Boaz Cohen suggested possible origins of the coinage: *Gzera*, meaning "decree" or "edict," is an ancient term that signifies draconian anti-Jewish decrees of non-Jewish rulers. *Machteret* means "underground" in modern Hebrew, but here it goes back to the biblical and Talmudic usage of the word, referring to a situation in which a thief who comes clandestinely is legally taken as someone who is prepared to kill. Less likely, the origin of the expression is that it refers to the terrible measures taken against the Jews, who were, in effect, forced to hide. (The perpetrators usually announced that they were taking measures against partisans and all forms of resistance.)

29. See the original, handwritten copy in the Yad Vashem Archives, M-1/E 644/535, Yad Vashem, Jerusalem.

30. The second Action receives an added emphasis in ChB's testimony. It is not the largest Action, yet in connection to this one she adds the Biblical description: "[T]he blood of the Jews ran like water on the streets."

31. Yad Vashem Archives, M-1/E 881/747, Yad Vashem, Jerusalem.

32. Yad Vashem Archives, M-1/E 881/747, Yad Vashem, Jerusalem. Translation from the Hebrew original by Shelly Duvalski and Rita Horváth.

33. ITS OuS-Archiv, document ID 35453066. Courtesy of Yad Vashem Archives, Jerusalem.

34. Children wrote their testimonial compositions in the DP camps in many languages.

35. On the issue of choosing a teaching language and language policy, see Cohen, "And I Was Only a Child," 156–57.

36. From the ITS document, we know that she talks about Sosnowiec. ITS OuS-Archiv, document ID 35453066. Courtesy of Yad Vashem Archives, Jerusalem.

37. On the selections, see "Sosnowiec," trans. Lance Ackerfeld, in *Pinkas Hakehillot Polin: Encyclopaedia of Jewish Communities, Poland*, vol. 7, 327–38 (Jerusalem, Yad Vashem, 2004), accessed on April 10, 2016, http://www.jewishgen.org/yizkor/pinkas_poland/pol7 _00327.html. Since the entries of *Pinkas Hakehillot* were mainly based on survivor testimonies, we can see how the testimonies of adults corroborate AS's depiction of the selection process and the abductions.

38. Christopher R. Browning, *Collected Memories: Holocaust History and Postwar Testimony* (Madison: University of Wisconsin Press, 2003), 37–39.

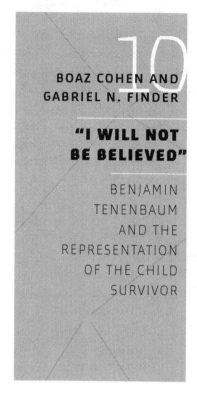

BOAZ COHEN AND
GABRIEL N. FINDER

"I WILL NOT BE BELIEVED"

BENJAMIN TENENBAUM AND THE REPRESENTATION OF THE CHILD SURVIVOR

In 1946 Benjamin Tenenbaum (who later changed his surname to the Hebrew-sounding Tene) returned to his native Poland from Palestine. Born in Warsaw in 1914, Tenenbaum (d. 1999) had received his education in Zionist-oriented schools and belonged to the socialist Zionist youth group *Hashomer Hatzair* (Young Guard). He had immigrated to Palestine in 1937 and, with his friends from the youth movement, helped establish a kibbutz, Eilon, in Western Galilee in 1938. Although he was preoccupied with the development and security of the kibbutz and his own personal responsibilities—he was a newlywed with two young children—the destruction of Polish Jewry in World War II, news of which trickled piecemeal into Palestine, tormented him, and the fate of his father and two sisters preyed on his mind. When the war ended, he resolved to travel to Poland to see the devastation for himself and to search for his family. He had an additional mission in mind: to assume the role of *shaliach* (emissary) to Polish chapters of *Hashomer Hatzair* reemerging from the ruins. But travel to Poland from Palestine immediately after the war was rather complicated. By this time a widely recognized writer of children's books, poet, and translator, Tenenbaum, with the help of Władysław Broniewski (1897–1962), managed to obtain a visa to visit Poland ostensibly to collect new fiction and poetry in Poland for an anthology of Polish literature to be translated into Hebrew. Tenenbaum befriended Broniewski, a leading Polish poet who was considered the poet of the proletariat, while the latter was stationed in Palestine with Polish forces during the war, and he became his Hebrew translator. Tenenbaum's self-appointed mandate, however, was clear: "The movement first, the muses later."[1] After an arduous journey by ship, he arrived in Poland in 1946.

Certain officials of *Hashomer Hatzair*, however, tried to persuade Tenenbaum to place his considerable literary talents in the service of the movement during his trip to Poland. The movement's publishing house, *Sifriyat Ha-Poalim* (The Workers' Library), urged him to write a book on the *Hashomer*

Hatzair's leading role—or so its members believed and argued—in the Warsaw Ghetto Uprising. Moreover, since fighters from the movement who had not died in the insurgency were now leaving Poland, time was of the essence, especially since other movements were threatening to lay claim to the mantle of leadership in the revolt and—from the perspective of its members—distort *Hashomer Hatzair*'s primary role in it. In this vein, David Hanegbi, an editor at *Sifriyat Ha-Poalim*, wrote Tenenbaum to convince him of the urgency of dedicating himself to the task of writing a book on the Warsaw Ghetto Uprising: "You should see this as the major task of your mission—maybe the sole task."[2] In the end, however, the movement's leadership decided to shelve the book temporarily because Tenenbaum was needed for political and educational work during his visit to Poland.

His purpose in traveling to Poland notwithstanding, Tenenbaum continued to pursue his literary projects after his arrival in the country. He translated poems by Jewish poets who survived the Holocaust and worked on the anthology of Polish writers. But he paid an emotional price for this pursuit. "I've hardly started working," he wrote to Hanegbi. "I'm having psychological difficulties working on their world, even the best of them. You have to live here in this country that is our people's graveyard, to breathe this air among people who, as a rule, were glad when 'Jewish meatballs' were frying in the [Warsaw] Ghetto (that's what they called our loved ones during their struggle), in order to understand how hard it is for me."[3]

After an emotional visit to the ruins of the Warsaw Ghetto, Tenenbaum traveled to Lodz, which evolved into the center of Jewish life in Poland in the immediate postwar years.[4] He quite naturally made his way to the headquarters of *Hashomer Hatzair* in Lodz and discovered there a small children's home (or, in the Zionist idiom of the times, a "kibbutz") for Jewish child survivors of the Holocaust run by the movement. The young woman in charge of the orphanage, Nesia Orlovich (later Reznik), who spent the war years in the Soviet Union working with orphaned Lithuanian children, persuaded Tenenbaum to join forces with her and her friends from *Hashomer Hatzair* in Poland and dedicate himself to one overriding task: the physical and emotional recovery of the children. The distinctive contribution of Tenenbaum, the *shaliach* from *Eretz Israel*, to this task, which he and Orlovich conceived of in therapeutic terms, was to teach Hebrew to the children, who ranged in age from six to fifteen, and then teach them the geography of *Eretz Israel* and Jewish history. He also taught them Israeli songs, dances, and games. However, according to Tenenbaum's memoir of his trip to Poland, published in Israel in 1979 under the title *'El 'ir ne'urai* (To the City of My Youth), the children especially liked unstructured lessons, when "with their eyes wide open" they listened enraptured to his tales of heroism and bravery in the *yishuv* (the Jewish settler community in Palestine), especially "the daring and astounding military exploits of the *Palmach* [the Jewish underground in Palestine]" against the British. He did this all with an eye, in line with the mission of *Hashomer Hatzair*, to instilling Zionist ideals in his charges, or as he himself put it, "I sowed the seed that sprouted in the hearts of these children!"[5] The most important of these ideals was to see Israel as their future homeland.

Although Tenenbaum journeyed to Poland with the intention of spending two weeks there, he eventually stayed for almost a year, devoting himself to child survivors in children's homes run by *Hashomer Hatzair*, both in Lodz and in other parts of the country. It was not easy to develop a rapport with the children in the beginning because of their distrust of adults, ingrained in them by necessity in the course of their struggles to survive during the war years. According to Tenenbaum, "I tried to get close to them, to find a path to their hearts, but for the most part I despaired, for all of my efforts were for naught. Whenever I thought I was succeeding in getting close to them, I suddenly noticed that they would get stiff and thrust their thorns, as if to warn, 'Don't touch!'" Over time, however, a strong bond developed between Tenenbaum and the children. He saw how, thanks to the efforts of Orlovich and other educators, "the layer of ice in which the children permitted themselves to be enveloped gradually melted, how they opened like flowers to the sun."[6]

While teaching them, he came to stand in awe of many of them, deeply moved by their accounts of survival during the Holocaust. He was also impressed by the accounts of surviving adults, and he became convinced of the importance of preserving in writing their accounts as well. As Tenenbaum wrote in his memoir, from the moment of his initial encounters with survivors, he was driven to help disseminate knowledge of their ordeal: "Why don't I ask them to put their recollections in writing? Such life stories cannot be allowed to be forgotten. We must take testimonies, write everything down, what happened and how — the whole story of the Holocaust from beginning to end."[7] Yet, in the final analysis, he discerned more enduring value in the accounts of children.

An episode from his memoir is telling. During periodic visits to Warsaw, he had become friendly with Ber Mark, editor of the Yiddish newspaper *Dos naje lebn*, who would later become director of the Jewish Historical Institute. In the immediate postwar period, the Central Jewish Historical Commission, the predecessor of the Jewish Historical Institute, collected testimonies from some seven thousand Polish Jewish survivors, mostly adults, although roughly 430 came from children.[8] On several occasions Mark gave Tenenbaum a large number of testimonies to read, hoping to spark the latter's interest in translating the commission's collection of testimonies into Hebrew. Tenenbaum returned the testimonies to Mark, however, declining to translate them because, in his words, they were "unsuitable for translation," since he was under the erroneous impression that most were written by members of Jewish councils who took pains to deny their collaboration with the Germans, and hence, "[T]hey [did] not convey a reliable picture of what happened." Ber Mark was exasperated.

"You're rejecting all of them in wholesale fashion," cried Professor Mark. "If that's the case, who will write the history of the Shoah? Who is capable of writing only the truth?"

And then—then the words burst from my lips, and I heard them without paying them heed and only afterwards did I grasp their importance.

"Children have written it, we have a truthful record [created by children]."

"Children?" Ber raised his eyebrows in astonishment. "In the first place, what is the number of children who remained alive? Most of them [who are still alive] have already been taken across the border [to Displaced Persons] camps in Germany and Austria. And second, are children actually capable of writing?"

I was silent, for I didn't have an answer. However, while taking leave of my host, descending the stairs, I suddenly stopped in my tracks, and it seemed to me that the thought split my brain in two like a bolt of lightning. What had I said—children? Why shouldn't I try? Why shouldn't I have asked Jewish children to take a seat and each one of them write down his life story?

Thus it began.⁹

Although he hoped to discover unembroidered veracity in the testimony of children of which, he believed, adults were incapable, Tenenbaum was captivated by child survivors no less because after all of the ordeals to which they had been subjected, after the war—Tenenbaum wrote in deep admiration of them—they "came back to life with no less force than a tree whose roots split rocks."¹⁰

Tenenbaum already knew by August 1946, shortly after his arrival in Poland, that he wanted to produce a book of children's testimonies. "The war in the eyes of children with no embellishment" is how he described his vision of the book to Hanegbi. This book would be a "[Hans Christian] Andersen written by children, each of whom went through the seven chambers of hell of the Jewish fate and another one of death, gas, and fire, [and] remained alive in spite of everything, found his way to us, and is writing his life story."¹¹ The book would appeal to a broad readership. "For adults—an enlightening book, for psychologists and educators—research material, for teenagers and children—a kind of twentieth-century Jewish Andersen."¹²

Tenenbaum began collecting children's testimonies in the winter of 1946. It quickly consumed him. In his own words, "a *dybbuk* entered me."[13] He himself traveled the length and breadth of Poland in pursuit of surviving children's testimony. He gathered the first set of testimonies from the children's home of *Hashomer Hatzair* in Lodz. Orlovich brought him essays written by children from the movement's children's home in Ludwikowo. Usually traveling overnight by train, he then visited the movement's other children's homes in other parts of the country. (Train travel in immediate postwar Poland was fraught with danger to Jews, and Tenenbaum himself had a few close calls with Poles on trains.) He further received permission from the Central Committee of Polish Jews, the principal representative body of Polish Jewry in the immediate postwar period, to visit its children's homes for the same purpose.

Two significant obstacles stood in his way, however. First, soliciting the cooperation of child survivors would be no small matter. His method — to be the bearer of gifts. "In each and every place," he writes in his memoir, "upon my arrival, I distributed notebooks to the children — a notebook for each child, and after giving out presents, such as colored crayons, I asked them to write how they spent the war years. The children agreed and wrote."[14] Second, the majority of Jewish children remaining in Poland after 1946 had been repatriated usually with their family members from the Soviet Union, where they had spent the war years, while a large number of children who had survived the Holocaust in Poland now found themselves in Displaced Persons camps in occupied Germany and Austria, en route ultimately — so Zionist leaders hoped — to *Eretz Israel*. To this end Tenenbaum recruited a friend, Marian Kalinovski, a veteran of the Warsaw Ghetto Uprising, who traveled to seventeen Displaced Persons camps in Germany and gathered hundreds of accounts of child survivors attending schools there. All in all, with the help of others, Tenenbaum collected one thousand testimonies — he himself used the term "autobiographies" — from Polish Jewish child survivors. When he returned to Palestine after spending a year in Poland, Tenenbaum translated and published a fraction of the testimonies — seventy in all — which were written primarily in Yiddish and Polish, in a Hebrew-language anthology entitled *'Ehad me-'ir u-shenayim mi-mishpahah* (*One from a City and Two from a Family*), which was published by Sifriat Poalim in Merhavia in 1947.

The seventy testimonies in *'Ehad me-'ir u-shenayim mi-mishpahah* are generally printed intact in their entirety, although a couple of them are printed in full but are divided thematically into two parts, while several appear in the form of fragments. The anthology is organized on both a geographical and thematic basis. Survival in Warsaw and Wilno merit one chapter each, while the remaining chapters are devoted to life in ghettos, in villages and the forest, and in camps and among partisans. The largest chapter, comprising twenty-four testimonies and four fragments, deals with ghettos, the smallest, consisting of three testimonies and three fragments, with life among partisans. The book concludes with a testimonial poem and drawings by a thirteen-year-old girl. Photographs taken of children during the Holocaust are interspersed through the book. Finally, several testimonies are accompanied by photocopies of segments from the originals. In his introduction to the anthology, Tenenbaum calls the testimonies or "autobiographies" in it "typical," since altogether they present a "complete picture" of "the life stories and struggles of a generation of children who grew up and matured and came to know the world in its darkest days."[15]

Tenenbaum took pains to give this collection of testimonies, which was intended to bring the ordeals of child survivors of the Holocaust home to the population of the *yishuv*, a Zionist slant. In his introduction to the volume, Tenenbaum stresses the expressed articulation of Zionist yearnings in the child survivors' testimonies, particularly the wish to immigrate to Palestine and build a Jewish national home there. In this spirit, more than one-third of the testimonies (twenty-eight in all) conclude with the expression of a categorical desire to leave Poland and immigrate to *Eretz Israel*. "I want to leave this land soaked with the blood of our loved ones and come to *Eretz Israel*," writes fifteen-year-old Hadassa Rozen. "Here in the kibbutz we wait impatiently for the day when the word would come: *aliyah* [Hebrew for "ascent," the Zionist term for immigration to *Eretz Israel*]." "And there is no power in this world," she adds, "that can stop us. Our will is stronger than life and death."[16]

The emphasis on *Eretz Israel* is not surprising and can be explained in large part by the centrality of Zionist education in the children's homes. Indeed, a large number of the children whose testimonies appear in the volume resided in children's homes run by *Hashomer Hatzair*.[17] But there was another reason for the strong appeal of Zionism to the children. Their daily encounter with anti-Jewish hostility and even violence made them feel unwelcome in Poland. Following the lead of their Jewish educators and youth leaders, most of whom also had undergone the ordeals of the Holocaust, they envisioned their future in *Eretz Israel*. For this reason, many of the testimonies were actually prepared by children outside Poland, in Displaced Persons camps in Germany, where they had been conveyed by the *Brihah*. The clandestine Zionist organization was responsible for planning and implementing the postwar exodus of Jews from Poland and elsewhere in Eastern Europe to Displaced Persons camps after the massacre in Kielce in 1946, in which Poles, incited by rumors of a ritual murder of a Christian boy, killed forty-two Jews. In the minds of many Jews, including child survivors, the Kielce pogrom provided additional proof, if any was still needed, that Jewish life in Poland was untenable and that the only practical option was *Eretz Israel*.

A Zionist angle makes itself felt in Tenebaum's anthology in yet another way. The testimonies selected by Tenenbaum convey, in harmony with the image promoted in Jewish Palestine of the new Jew, the children's resilience and fortitude. These children, who had endured so much, represented the promise of a better future in a sovereign Jewish state. A portrayal of children's ordeals during the Holocaust, Tenenbaum's anthology constitutes an argument for Zionism on the eve of the *yishuv*'s armed struggle for statehood. This is the context for the emotional appeal that concludes his introduction to the book:

Here sit the children on the ruins of Poland, learning Hebrew and preparing for *aliyah*. Their voices, chanting a Hebrew song, burst forth on the soil of Germany and the beaches of France and Italy. They board and sail on illegal immigrant ships, knock with their small fists on the gates of our houses but they are locked. They are dragged and thrown onto the ships of the great empire [Britain, the mandatory authority in Palestine], and taken to camps in Cyprus. Several of the autobiographies that appear here were written by children who set sail on the ship *Exodus* and were cruelly expelled from the shores of Israel back to Germany. The great empire dealt an additional fatal blow to these little enemies.

But our hearts beat together with the hearts of the tormented. Our sun will rise [and shine] over a long distance [to heal] their wounds. Our home will become a refuge for the orphans and the abandoned. And in the hours that we offer the public and our children the life stories of the little immigrants, we extend our hands once more over barbed-wire fences and the length of the ocean and take the distant wanderers to our sons and brothers.[18]

Like *'Ehad me-'ir u-shenayim mi-mishpahah*, *Dzieci oskarżają* (*The Children Accuse*), the other major early anthology of children's testimonies, which was based on a selection collected by the Central Jewish Historical Commission in Poland and published in Poland in 1946, stresses their competency and strength of character. By contrast, however, of the fifty-five testimonies in *Dzieci oskarżają*, only one includes the wish to settle in Palestine. Instead, many of these testimonies end with expressions of gratitude to the Red Army for liberating the Jews and hope for the rebirth of Jewish life in Poland, which is not surprising given the political climate in which the volume was published, that is to say, the onset of the communist consolidation of power in the country.

From the beginning of his undertaking, Tenenbaum put great stock in one overriding fact: that the testimonies which would appear in his book were authored by the children themselves, unmediated by the intervention of an adult interviewer. Aware of the contemporaneous endeavor of the

Central Jewish Historical Commission in Poland to publish *Dzieci oskarżają*, Tenenbaum underlined this difference between the two volumes in a letter to Hanegbi prior to the publication of his own anthology: "Its book, while interesting, is not written by the children, and testimonies taken by adults are not original testimonies like ours, which were written down directly by the children."[19] Tenenbaum emphasized the significance of this fact, likewise, in the introduction to his book:

> Apart from the historical reality imparted in them, [the autobiographies] are distinguished by the very same truth and directness typical of the perspective and emotions of a child. They lack the self-criticism, to a lesser or greater extent, of an adult author. But their disadvantage is also their advantage. The simplicity evident in their story and the equanimity evident in its unfolding remind one of an old saga or the pages from the Bible, which likewise are factual stories, descriptions of unadorned plots, without superfluous facts and nuances.[20]

"I believe," he wrote in the same vein to Hanegbi, "that an adult, even the best psychologist, when coming to write the children's stories, will never write it down in the same truthful, direct way as the children did in my project."[21]

Ironically, it was Tenenbaum's single-minded objective of preserving the children's tales of survival in their own words that almost led Hanegbi to withdraw the book from publication, because in spite of Tenenbaum's assurance, he was not persuaded that the children themselves were the actual authors of the accounts to appear in the anthology. This concern is understandable because the "autobiographies" evince remarkable acuity for children, the youngest of whom was two when the war started and nine when they wrote their accounts and the oldest of whom were twelve when the war started and nineteen when they wrote their accounts. In other words, all of the child survivors whose testimonies appear in Tenenbaum's book were very young during the Holocaust, the oldest among them barely on the threshold of adolescence.

Yet the children's testimonies taken together reflect an expanded consciousness, a remarkably accelerated rate of maturation. As one child survivor, Masha Kaplan, who was eight years old when the war began, confides in her testimony while recounting the events of a German roundup in her ghetto, "Although I was then a little girl, I understood everything. My eyes darkened and I felt myself sinking under my own weight."[22] Adults who had witnessed and shared their misery during the dark years of the Holocaust were acutely aware of this fact. After speaking to a group of children who were street beggars in June 1942, Adam Czerniaków, the chairman of the Jewish Council in the Warsaw Ghetto, confided to his diary, "They talk with me like grown-ups—those eight-year-old citizens. I am ashamed to admit it, but I wept as I have not wept in a long time."[23] In the words of Sarah Munk, a surviving teacher who had worked with children in the Warsaw Ghetto whose testimony was recorded in *Dzieci oskarżają*, "The dreadful conditions caused the children to age prematurely."[24] In his memoir, Tenebaum, coming from Palestine, describes how he too was struck by how the children whom he had encountered had "aged prematurely."[25] It should not surprise that many adults shared this impression. These were, after all, children who, confronted with the Nazis' genocidal ambitions and the malicious designs of a significant number of local Poles, had by necessity become masters of their own survival in a morally inverted and brutal universe, when there was literally open season on their young lives, in a world in which parental authority and succor had all but vanished when they needed it most. In the process, they had developed razor-edged astuteness and survival skills, set in motion largely by primitive instincts and an almost preternatural will to live while often helping other, frequently even younger, children survive. To take but one of numerous examples from Tenenbaum's book, born in 1930, Mania Bot was nine years old when the war began. From 1942 she hid in a bunker concealed in the forest with her mother and younger sister. After her mother died in June 1943, she roamed the Polish countryside with her younger sister on her back, begging for food from peasants or gathering stalks of wheat growing in the fields. Mania cared for her sister through the winter until the spring of 1944, when after teaching her to recite Polish prayers, she separated from her. Both sisters, claiming to be Christians, eventually found shelter in Polish homes and survived to the end of the war, when Mania found her younger sibling.[26] Mania Bot's account beggars the imagination, yet it is typical of the accounts that appear in Tenenbaum's anthology.

Thus it was that already in the early stages of preparing his book, Tenenbaum anticipated that the authenticity of the children's accounts would be open to challenge. His solution to this potential stumbling block was to include photocopies of examples of the actual testimonies in the children's own handwriting, to which we have referred earlier. As Tenenbaum wrote to Hanegbi in November 1946, "In this book I want to put many photos, not of the children but of photocopies of their handwriting, the childish handwriting, because I think that I will not be believed, that people will suspect me of exaggeration or embellishment. Let the photocopies prove my point."[27] Nevertheless, on the eve of the anticipated date of the book's publication, Hanegbi, anticipating potential challenges to the authenticity of the testimonies, was apparently on the verge of scrapping the whole project unless Tenenbaum made substantial changes to the book. He even suggested that Tenenbaum adapt the style found in the testimonies to sound more childlike.

Tenenbaum stood his ground. In a long letter, Tenenbaum admonished Hanegbi. "Don't jump to conclusions," he wrote, "before you read the entire manuscript. . . . When you read all of it, you'll see the obvious differences in style . . . only then will you see the full picture." His editorial approach, he explained, was dictated by restraint and solicitude for authenticity. "I translated the children's language, and where they waxed eloquent, I took no pains to simplify it." "The photographed pages [of the children's handwritten testimonies] were incorporated for authenticity," he insisted. "Please read them and you'll see that it was not I who gave [the testimonies] this eloquent style." Thus there was no reason to redo their style: "The reader can always see the original style in the [photographed] excerpts we will incorporate, and there he will see the accuracy of the translation." In the final analysis, he argued, the integrity of the testimonies in the book should not be sought in trivial childish "mistakes, unorganized sentences or biographies where every sentence begins with 'because' or 'when.'" The integrity of the book would be reflected rather in its documentary quality: "I believe we gave here the whole story: the attached poems, the photographed excerpts, the demographic details I inserted at the head of each testimony, ([the child's] name, [his] age, the name of [his] parents, and [his] date of birth)—all of these give the book the character of a document."[28]

In the end, Tenenbaum prevailed. He made some slight editorial changes to the testimonies, correcting spelling and grammatical mistakes and adding punctuation marks. But that is about all he did. He explained his editorial approach to his readers in the introduction to the book: "I did not add one embellishment, I did not improve the language. By contrast, the spare style, as it were, in the writings of the children, has a special melody that cannot be replicated [in spite of the fact that] it is largely fraught with errors and impediments."[29]

As Tenenbaum correctly pointed out to Hanegbi, the major distinction between 'Ehad me-'ir u-shenayim mi-mishpahah and Dzieci oskarżają, prepared by the Central Jewish Historical Commission in Poland, was that the accounts in his book were authored by the children themselves, while those in the Polish Jewish volume reflected interviews of surviving children mediated by adult interviewers. Unlike 'Ehad me-'ir u-shenayim mi-mishpahah, Dzieci oskarżają is divided into thematic sections (including sections on life in the ghettos, in camps, on the Aryan side, in hiding, in resistance groups, and even in prison), but otherwise the two anthologies outwardly resemble one another.[30]

It is important to keep in mind that Tenenbaum's book and Dzieci oskarżają are two examples of a wider contemporary phenomenon—the collection of testimonies from child survivors in the immediate postwar years. A great deal of time and effort was invested in listening to child survivors, recording their stories, and then publishing them. Some of these initiatives represented official undertakings, such as the testimonies collected by the Central Jewish Historical Commission in Poland that resulted in the publication of *Dzieci oskarżają*. Correspondingly, the Central Historical Commission of the Liberated Jews in the American Zone in Germany conducted a campaign in Displaced Persons camps and schools to gather testimonies from surviving children. Israel Kaplan, the commission's academic secretary, was the leading force in this project and published the testimony of a child survivor in each of the eleven volumes of *Fun letstn khurbn* (*From the Last Catastrophe*), the commission's scholarly journal devoted to the Holocaust—the first of its kind. But there were also several private initiatives to gather surviving children's testimonies. Tenenbaum's was one, Helena Wrobel-Kagan's was another. Wrobel-Kagan, a survivor of Bergen-Belsen, opened a Hebrew high school in the camp after its liberation in 1945 and asked each of the students to write an essay entitled, "My Way from Home to Bergen-Belsen." It should be noted that the adults who collected the testimonies of child survivors, Tenenbaum included, regarded the exercise as a therapeutic tool to help the children recover from their psychic wounds.[31]

However, for all that Tenenbaum sought to distinguish his book from *Dzieci oskarżają*, he shared the concern with the editors of the Polish Jewish anthology of children's testimonies that the children's accounts would be deemed inauthentic. In her introduction to that volume, one of its editors, Maria Hochberg-Mariańska goes to great lengths to describe the children's awe-inspiring resolve and fortitude, all in an effort to convince the reader of the genuineness of the testimonies that appear in the book. Apparently unsure herself whether her encomium to the children will suffice, she nonetheless feels compelled to make this point explicit: "The children give their testimonies simply and frankly," she writes. "In their recollections, mostly gathered as early as 1945, there is a tone of freshly experienced pain or hope. In preparing these testimonies, we took pains to preserve those impressions —the authenticity of the children's experiences."[32] Moreover, unlike *'Ehad me-'ir u-shenayim mi-mishpahah*, *Dzieci oskarżają* includes, in its final section, testimonies by Jewish adult survivors who labored to rescue Jewish children during the Holocaust in Poland. Several of them stress the resilience, sheer grit, and equanimity of many Jewish children under Nazi occupation.

It seems clear from both of these two earliest anthologies of child survivors' testimonies — *'Ehad me-'ir u-shenayim mi-mishpahah* on the one hand and *Dzieci oskarżają* on the other—that in spite of their different intended readerships, both Jewish but one in the *yishuv*, the other in Poland, their respective editors anticipated and sought ways to deflect potential challenges to their authenticity. It is not difficult to understand why. Normal kids just do not write like that. Of course, that is the point: child survivors of the Holocaust were not like regular children their age, even if, as they often expressed in their testimonies in both anthologies, they wished they could be.

NOTES

1. Benjamin Tenenbaum to David Hanegbi, August 22, 1946, Hashomer Hatzair Archive, Givat Haviva, Israel (hereafter STA), 24.4 (1).

2. Hanegbi to Tenenbaum, June 25, 1946, STA 24.6 (5).

3. Tenenbaum to Hanegbi, August 22, 1946, STA 24.4 (1).

4. On the development of Lodz into the center of Jewish life in immediate postwar Poland, see Shimon Redlich, *Life in Transit: Jews in Postwar Lodz, 1945–1950* (Boston: Academic Studies Press, 2010).

5. Benjamin Tene, '*El 'ir ne'urai'* (Tel Aviv: Am Oved, 1979), 123–24.

6. Ibid., 124–25.

7. Ibid., 148.

8. On this undertaking by the Central Jewish Historical Commission, see Feliks Tych, Alfons Kenkmann, Elisabeth Kohlhaas, and Andreas Eberhardt, eds., *Kinder über den Holocaust: Frühe Zeugnisse 1944–1948* (Berlin: Metropol Verlag, 2008). See also Joanna B. Michlic, "The Children Accuse (Poland, 1946): Between Exclusion and Inclusion into the Holocaust Canon," *Newsletter, Society for the History of Children and Youth*, no. 9 (winter 2007), accessed on April 10, 2016, www.history.vt.edut/Jones/SHCY/Newsletter9/michlic/html.

9. Tene, '*El 'ir ne'urai*, 148.

10. Ibid., 187.

11. Tenenbaum to Hanegbi, August 13, 1946, STA 24.6 (5).

12. Tenenbaum to Hanegbi, August 22, 1946, STA 24.4 (1).

13. Tene, '*El 'ir ne'urai*, 150.

14. Ibid.

15. Benjamin Tenenbaum, '*Ehad me-'ir u-shenayim mi-mishpahah* (Merhavia: Sifriyat Poalim, 1947), 6. It is interesting to note that the collection of children's testimonies Tenenbaum gathered (which are available in the original at the archives of Beit Lohamei Ha-Getaot [Ghetto Fighters House] in Israel and on microfilm at the United States Holocaust Memorial Museum, Ghetto Fighters House Archive [GFH], reels 76–80, call numbers 4193–5212), includes many testimonies by children who spent the war in the far reaches of the Soviet Union. Yet Tenenbaum did not include any of these testimonies in his book. Why did he omit them? One possible answer is that the pro-Soviet leanings of *Ha-Shomer Ha-Tsa'ir*, the movement to which he was so devoted, influenced his editorial choice. Another possible answer is that Tenenbaum, like other Jewish authors of his day, was wary of antagonizing the USSR just when its support was required in the struggle for a Jewish state. On the experiences of Polish Jews who had spent the war in the deepest recesses of the Soviet Union, see Laura Jockusch and Tamar Lewinsky, "Paradise Lost? Postwar Memory of Polish Jewish Survival in the Soviet Union," *Holocaust and Genocide Studies* 24, no. 3 (2010): 373–99.

16. Tenenbaum, '*Ehad me-'ir u-shenayim mi-mishpahah*, 58.

17. On the Zionist education of youthful survivors in postwar Poland, see Avinoam J.

Patt, *Finding Home and Homeland: Jewish Youth and Zionism in the Aftermath of the Holocaust* (Detroit: Wayne State University Press, 2009), chap. 2.

18. Tenenbaum, *'Ehad me-'ir u-shenayim mi-mishpahah*, 11–12.

19. Tenenbaum to Hanegbi, August 22, 1946, STA 24.4 (1).

20. Tenenbaum, *'Ehad me-'ir u-shenayim mi-mishpahah*, 6.

21. Tenenbaum to Hanegbi, November 23, 1946, STA 24.6 (5).

22. Tenenbaum, *'Ehad me-'ir u-shenayim mi-mishpahah*, 150.

23. Raul Hilberg, Stanislaw Staron, and Josef Kermisz, eds., *The Warsaw Diary of Adam Czerniakow*, trans. Stanislaw Staron and the Staff of Yad Vashem (Chicago: Ivan R. Dee, published in association with the United States Holocaust Memorial Museum, 1999), 366.

24. Maria Hochberg-Mariańska and Noe Grüss, eds., *The Children Accuse*, trans. Bill Johnston (London: Vallentine Mitchell, 1996), 235. For the original, see Maria Hochberg-Mariańska and Noe Grüss, eds., *Dzieci oskarżają* (Kraków: Centralna Żydowska Komisja Historyczna w Polsce, 1947), 234 ("Okropne warunki życia przyczyniły się do przedwczesnego rozwoju umysłowego").

25. Tene, *'El 'ir ne'urai*, 187 ("yeladim 'eyleh shehizkinu belo' 'eyt").

26. Tenenbaum, *'Ehad me-'ir u-shenayim mi-mishpahah*, 208–10.

27. Tenenbaum to Hanegbi, November 23, 1946, STA 24.6 (5).

28. Tenenbaum to Hanegbi, September 17, 1947, STA 24.4 (3).

29. Tenenbaum, *'Ehad me-'ir u-shenayim mi-mishpahah*, 10–11.

30. On the structure of *Dzieci oskarżają*, see Michlic, "The Children Accuse (Poland, 1946)."

31. For a thorough description and analysis of the extensive postwar Jewish effort to collect the testimonies of child survivors, see Boaz Cohen, "The Children's Voice: Postwar Collection of Testimonies from Child Survivors of the Holocaust," *Holocaust and Genocide Studies* 21, no. 1 (2007): 73–95. See also Cohen, "Representing the Experience of Children in the Holocaust: Children's Survivor Testimonies in *Fun Letsten Hurbn*, Munich 1946–49," in *We Are Here: New Approaches to Jewish Displaced Persons in Postwar Germany*, ed. Avinoam J. Patt and Michael Berkowitz (Detroit: Wayne State University Press, 2010), 74–97; and Cohen, "And I Was Only a Child: Children's Testimonies, Bergen-Belsen 1945," *Holocaust Studies: A Journal of Culture and History* 12, nos. 1–2 (2006): 153–69.

32. Hochberg-Mariańska and Grüss, eds., *The Children Accuse*, xxix. For the original, see Hochberg-Mariańska and Grüss, eds., *Dzieci oskarżają*, xxv.

UTA LARKEY

TRANSCENDING MEMORY IN HOLOCAUST SURVIVORS' FAMILIES

This chapter analyzes ways in which the memories of Holocaust survivors are communicated and transmitted in their own families. The unique historical situation at the beginning of the twenty-first century, namely, the fact that three generations in Holocaust survivor families now interact with each other, invites new research and discussion.[1] Many Holocaust survivors are still active, sharing their life stories in schools and synagogues. Their children, the so-called second generation, have mostly grown up as first-generation immigrants or refugees in a culture unfamiliar to their parents, and in the shadow of their parents' traumatic experiences during World War II and the Holocaust. They have since embarked on a new experience for which they have not had role models; they have become (or will become) grandparents, often without ever having known their own.[2] By now the grandchildren of the Holocaust survivors, the so-called third generation, have come of age and have begun their own inquiries and research. They have reflected on their family history and discovered their potential to act as "memory facilitators." They are indeed "transcending memory."

This chapter draws on personal interviews that I conducted as a scholar-in-residence at the Hadassah Brandeis Institute,[3] documentary films, testimonies, psychological studies, and other scholarly works from the United States and Israel. While I focus mostly on survivor families in the United States, some of my interviewees in the second and third generations were born and raised in Israel, South Africa, or Lithuania before coming to the United States and developing their own postwar immigration narratives. The literary, artistic, and filmic representations analyzed here are the voices of the second and third generations. They are a small selection from a rich body of work, which deserves a more in-depth analysis than is possible here.[4] For the purpose of this chapter I consider as a second-generation survivor anyone born in or after 1945 to at least one parent who was persecuted for being Jewish in

Nazi Germany or Nazi-occupied Europe. While I recognize the different experiences of someone born in the mid- and late 1940s and someone born in the 1960s to survivor parents, the differences between the younger and older representatives of the second generation are not at the center of this essay.

Drawing on the work of Holocaust Studies scholar Alan Berger, this chapter argues that the second generation and also, I might add, their descendants are ultimately seeking a *tikkun* (mending, repair) of self (*atzmi*) and the world (*olam*).[5] Berger examines works of the second generation in literature and film from the perspective of what he calls "Jewish particularism" (*tikkun atzmi*) and "Jewish universalism" (*tikkun olam*). While *tikkun*, as a moral concept in Judaism certainly has theological roots, this chapter—in accordance with Berger—also considers its nonreligious implications. In addition to Berger's binary concept of *tikkun atzmi* and *tikkun olam*, this essay also includes the notion of *tikkun am* (healing of the Jewish people) as a third option in which the second and third generations demonstrate their search for meaning and identity. Thus, my work shows the intergenerational shift and different ways of searching for *tikkun*.

The search for *tikkun* is closely linked to the post-Holocaust mourning process. All of the survivors' life stories include either forced emigration and expulsion, or survival in hiding and in ghettos, labor, concentration, and extermination camps, as well as the survival of death marches. They were often the only survivors of previously close-knit families from strong, sizable Jewish communities. It was a common experience in Eastern Europe for three generations to live together, and the loss of the extended family was particularly tragic. While there was considerable variation in the ways that Holocaust survivors lived with their difficult experiences, most of their children remember a wall of silence in their families while growing up in the 1950s and 1960s. The survivors' efforts to deal with their trauma, loss, guilt, and shame—all powerful emotions —were often exacerbated by their inability to find the language to share their experiences in a societal climate that was "not receptive to hearing survivors' harrowing tales."[6] In her book *We Remember with Reverence and Love*, Hasia Diner argues that the "myth of silence" had been constructed by a rebellious generation of "historians, literary critics, popular writers and communal notables" in the United States to blame and shame their elders for not having been more concerned with the aftermath of the Holocaust and the lack of support for and understanding of the survivors who arrived as refugees in the United States. The author substantiates her argument by presenting, but often not contextualizing, a vast body of evidence, primarily from U.S. Jewish organizations and communities. She does not, however, conduct oral history interviews or examine individual experiences of survivors and liberators. Most strikingly, Diner eschews an analysis of familial settings, which are at the center of this chapter.

In most postwar survivor families the parents struggled with building new lives, raising children, and trying to shield them from harm and what they considered harmful information. Most second-generation adult children today recall that they did not have any details, but always knew something about "it."[7] Whatever this "it" might have been in any individual family, the second generation often felt an "obsessive need to imagine the Holocaust."[8]

Growing up in families of Holocaust survivors, many children were vaguely aware of their family's painful past. Some were raised in circles of survivor families, while others hardly knew anybody who shared their experiences, worries, and questions. In most cases, however, the adult children recall "always having known about it." One interviewee whose father was born in Austria remembered that she always knew that her father's story was sad, that his parents had died under suspicious circumstances, and that his sister had suddenly disappeared. There was some mystery about her father's past: "But I have to say that I did not really feel that sadness because [of] the way our father presented the story to us when we were small. He would talk a lot about his childhood and family life."[9] This example demonstrates that some survivors were cautious, trying not to further burden their children. The success of their attempts depended on their individual mourning and "working through" process. A male member of a second-generation discussion group featured in the documentary *Breaking the Silence* relayed his father's memories, which always seemed to the son like "fairy tales, or rather adventure stories."[10] One of my interviewees recalled: "It was always talked about, but not in detail, and in steps and at different levels as we aged and our parents thought we could handle more — until I went to Eastern Europe. It was then that my father decided that I really wanted to know about it."[11]

The wall of silence differed from family to family. The memories of one second-generation survivor echo many others, including those of several of my interview partners:

> My mother refused to talk about the Holocaust in a thorough way for a long time. I would only get hints — these people died, that family is extinct . . . The stories were interesting, scary, and meant to be a little removed, except that they smelled of . . . fear, buried and secret not meant to be shared with the kids. That smell came again later when my mother would talk about her nightmares, when she would often get depressed and hopeless . . . My father never mentioned the Holocaust. He refused to talk about it altogether.[12]

Oral history interviews range from stories of survivor parents trying to shield their children from finding out about their Holocaust experiences[13] to stories of parents incessantly talking about their pain and the past.[14] In the first case, the teenage daughter incredulously informed her survivor parents about a terrible event in Europe called the Holocaust that she had learned about in school, and in the second example the teenage daughter begged her mother to stop talking about the horrors she had been through.

The analysis of family dynamics in survivor families is the focus of several studies by the late psychologist Dan Bar-On and his students, who concluded that it is impossible for parents to protect their children from their own oppressive memories: "'Untold stories' often pass more powerfully from generation to generation than stories that can be recounted. In addition, children are sensitive to their parents' need for silencing."[15]

Based on Freud's "working through" process of repressed childhood memories, clinicians have extended this concept and applied it to working with Holocaust survivors and also their children. Bar-On agrees with the clinicians who found that the children of survivors, without having experienced the horrors of the Holocaust directly, "absorbed" them through their parents, "especially if their parents did not talk about these matters in an attempt 'to protect' them [their children]." After interviewing several multigenerational survivor families, Bar-On developed a model of the "working-through process" for the third generation. It includes the five basic stages of knowledge, understanding, emotional response, attitude, and behavior.[16] This paradigm highlights a significant difference between the second and third generation responses. While, according to Bar-On, the third generation reaches an emotional response after having worked through a cognitive process, I argue that this happens in the opposite sequence for the second generation. Whether the survivor parents talked about their Holocaust experiences or did not, they rarely transmitted knowledge about the historical events and their personal experiences. Furthermore, the third generation has gained knowledge about the Holocaust much earlier in life than their parents did. The inversion of the "working-through process" between the second and third generations leads to significantly different communication patterns and subsequently to an easier understanding between grandchildren and grandparents.

When the scholars and writers Helen Epstein, Lucy Steinitz, David Szonyi, psychotherapist Eva Fogelman,[17] and others began their groundbreaking work with descendants of Holocaust survivors in the mid-1970s, some of the most pressing issues at the time were considered the lack of communication, "the phenomenon of intergenerational transmission in the shadow of the Holocaust,"[18] and grief in Holocaust survivors' families (though this was not necessarily the terminology used at that time).[19]

The majority of the second generation has not only grown up without grandparents, but some with the most disturbing images of how they were murdered. At least as haunting was their parents' reluctant revelation that in many cases they once had spouses and children who did not survive the war. The second generation began to live with the ghosts of the past, as this testimony demonstrates:

> I never knew my paternal grandparents, and my father related only occasional anecdotes about them . . . I feel this silence is a direct effect of the painful legacy of the Holocaust. My grandmother Gitla, for whom I am named, remains a mystery for me. There are no family traditions or family rituals passed on from one generation to the next. Only one small and dark photograph of my grandparents remains in my father's possession. It is as though the Holocaust has obliterated the memory of these close relatives.[20]

In the 1970s and 1980s the descendants of Holocaust survivors, many of them in their twenties, realized that despite the diverse circumstances in which they were raised, they also had surprisingly similar experiences growing up. Author Melvin Bukiet highlights the uniqueness of the second-generation childhood experience:

> The Second Generation will never know what the First Generation knows in its bone, but what the Second Generation knows better than anyone else is the First Generation. Other kids' parents didn't have numbers on their arms. Other kids' parents didn't talk about massacres as easily as baseball. Other kids' parents had parents.[21]

Unlike "American parents," their parents spoke with distinct accents, often had number tattoos on their forearms, shrouded themselves in a cloak of secrecy, sometimes alluded to a dark past, and were torn between trying to fit into a new set of social and economic dynamics and maintaining aspects of their "old world" value systems. Several of the parents were the only survivors of their families. In the postwar years the survivors did not know how to deal with the trauma of suffering an unimaginable loss in any other way than to suppress their memories and grief. They also wanted to protect their children from hearing about the horrors they had to endure, and were at a loss for words that could convey their horrific experiences.[22] A scene in the documentary *Breaking the Silence* includes one survivor who was interviewed in the presence of her husband and daughter. She recalls, on-camera, being forced to watch her mother's selection at the gas chamber. The survivor cried out in exasperation: "How do you tell your child that the Nazis killed millions of humans, my mother among them?" Other parents spoke incessantly of the Holocaust, and as a result, some of their children felt so overwhelmed that they could not bear to hear the stories. One daughter describes her feelings:

> I didn't know how to block out these stories. I couldn't cover my ears or turn away my face or even still the turmoil the words created in me. When my

mother talked her words came at me in wave after wave of pain and rage . . .
Not until I was well into high school did I tell my mother that I couldn't listen anymore, and, then, not seeing the pain I had suppressed, she accused
me of not caring about her and left the room.[23]

Whether the survivor parents were silent, talked compulsively about their
pain, or reconstructed anecdotes of courage and adventure, it was difficult for
their children to even begin to fathom what their parents had been through.
In the 1950s and 1960s the research on posttraumatic stress disorder and the
magnitude of repressed trauma after the Holocaust was in its infancy, and
therapy options were limited.

The children of Holocaust survivors grew up in social settings where the
adults "had before and after spouses, before and after professions, incomes,
relations to law, art, politics, success and failure, God."[24] The parents' basic
sense of self had been bifurcated by the war,[25] into a "Before" and an "After."
Their children often expressed their own burden of having "felt the force of
this impenetrable mystery and terrible inheritance, this lack of a 'Before.'"
Susan Jacobowitz, professor of English and a descendant of a Holocaust survivor, states in the introduction to her doctoral dissertation on the second-
generation experience: "As someone [in the] second generation I felt this force
of this 'impenetrable mystery,' this lack of a 'Before' . . . [this] seems to be our
particular burden."[26] Others in the second generation found strength in their
family's past: "[S]omething that I have as a child of survivors which second
and third generation American people don't have is still some connection with
the rich Jewish cultural heritage which is gone now."[27] Writer Eva Hoffman
also feels a significant difference "between coming into this world imbued
with the Holocaust and having experiences of a more normal world before."[28]
Or, as Melvin Bukiet succinctly puts it: "For the Second Generation there is no
Before. In the beginning was Auschwitz."[29] For many in the second generation
that meant to create their own version of a "Before."

Marianne Hirsch, the daughter of Holocaust survivors and a professor of
English and comparative literature, developed a theoretical framework for
the second-generation experience, which she terms "postmemory." The concept of postmemory, in Hirsch's words, "characterizes the experience of those
who grow up dominated by narratives that preceded their birth, whose own
belated stories are evacuated by the stories of the previous generation shaped
by traumatic events that can be neither understood nor recreated."[30] Hirsch
argues that postmemory is not to be taken to literally mean *memories*, but the
complexity of transmission of traumatic experiences through "the language
of the body."[31] Hirsch's notion provides a theoretical framework for the second-generation experience, and invites scholarly discussion on transmission

of traumatic experiences, mourning, and memory. However, it hardly applies to the third generation: Hirsch defines postmemory "as a *structure* of inter- and trans-generational transmission of traumatic knowledge and experience. It is a *consequence* of traumatic recall but (unlike posttraumatic stress disorder) at a generational remove."[32] I would also argue that postmemory requires a complex affective component, which is primarily present in the intimacy and immediacy of a parent-child relationship. The particular psychological aspects of the survivor parent and child relationship, such as mutual over-protectiveness, need for affirmation, guilt, and shame, have been thoroughly researched in the last thirty years and would go beyond the scope of this chapter.[33]

Most of the survivor parents were young adults or came of age during the war. In many cases the war robbed them of their childhood, educational opportunities, youth activities, a regular family life, and often of beloved family members. The survivors often experienced teenage years in hiding or in camps and under the constant threat of death. Adolescence is arguably the most vulnerable time for any young person, but searching for survival under such stark realities is unfathomably difficult. Having been deprived of regular developmental stages such as teenage rebellion, the survivors often could not handle the behavior of their teenage children, whom they many times found to be ungrateful, demanding, and provocative. Their children's adolescence evoked memories of their own horrible experiences at that age. The survivor parents could often not accept their children's rebellion, and reacted in an upset[34] or angry and violent way.[35] One hurt, but ultimately forgiving daughter wrote particularly telling testimony. Her mother was liberated at age sixteen and married another survivor many years later. The marriage did not work out, and her mother was frequently very angry: "She also often belittled us, cursed us in English and in her native tongue and prophesized how we were destined to fail forever because of all our character flaws. These comments caused even more damage than her beatings. She made us feel terrible about ourselves." As much as this daughter must have suffered from her mother's violent outbursts, the daughter has raised her own children in the "opposite way." Her healing process enabled her to parent her own children in a loving, caring way. Her mother must have gone through her own mourning and healing process so that she was able to become a "loving and sweet grandmother," according to her daughter.[36]

One of my interviewees, also a child of an unhappy marriage between two Holocaust survivors that ended in divorce, recalled her difficult home life. Her mother, whom she remembered as "tyrannical, physically abusive, oppressive, lonely, and miserable," turned her life around after a suicide attempt. JF saw her role in the family while growing up as the "housekeeper and peacekeeper" and was conscious of the fact that her mother had elected her to be the "memorial candle," the one child who will carry on her story. However, JF heard the full story only when she was in her forties. Both women have long reconciled their earlier difficult relationship.[37]

Several studies concluded that the survivor parents considered their children born after the war as lifesavers, as symbols, as a triumph, and as substitutes for relatives they had lost.[38] One daughter's testimony painfully illustrates this aspect:

> Sometimes when I didn't want to listen to my mother's diatribes about the war or anything else that may have been troubling her she would say to me, needing to hurt: "But you're my mother to me, and my sister!" And though I wanted to turn away I was held by guilt . . . I did not ask: If I were my mother's mother, who was mine?[39]

Another daughter recalled her mother's obsession with the striking resemblance between her (the daughter) and her own mother: "She always told me I looked like her, and that I remind her of her mother. I do not want any part of this. I want to be me!"[40] Yet another account speaks of the way in which the daughter had internalized her mother's expectations: "My grandmother lives in me as . . . a set of attributes that I somehow tried to emulate, probably to make my mother happy."[41] The Jewish tradition of naming a baby after one of his or her ancestors takes on a new significance after the Holocaust . . . This is the case in particular for Ashkenazi Jews, who traditionally name their offspring after deceased relatives. This tradition of honoring a relative creates a bond not only to the past per se, but to the "Before" that the second generation is so painfully missing.

To symbolize the ancestors who were killed in the camps was a heavy burden for many in the second generation, but to "replace" a child that their parents "lost" during the war was almost unbearable. Of course, a child can never be "replaced," but the parents' unconscious desire to do so was often the source of familial fissures and conflicts. If one or both surviving parents had prewar families that were killed during the war, the overwhelming sense of grief and loss often overshadowed their postwar family life. They might not have been conscious of it, but their offspring often perceived themselves in competition with their prewar siblings, especially when the survivor parent had one child or several children together who were killed.

The literary and filmic treatments of this difficult topic vary from understated sadness and melancholy to self-deprecating humor. Thomas Friedman, in his novel *Damaged Goods*, a "thinly veiled memoir,"[42] captures the heavy silence at home, occasionally punctured by the revelations of family secrets: "I find things out indirectly, discovering the older half-brother when Father told me I need not say the blessing for the first born the morning before Passover. Although my mother's first, counting from Father, the real count, I am second born."[43]

Art Spiegelman also grew up with the paradoxical presence of a brother in absentia and reflects on his relationship to his "ghost brother" Richieu:

I didn't think about him much when I was growing up . . . He was mainly a large, blurry photograph hanging in my parents' bedroom . . . The photo never threw tantrums, or got in any kind of trouble . . . It was the ideal kid, and I was a pain in the ass. I couldn't compete. They did not talk about Richieu, but that photo was a kind of reproach. *He'd have become a doctor and married a wealthy Jewish girl . . . the creep.*[44]

While these examples explore the relationships of fathers and sons, independent U.S. filmmaker Abraham Ravett, similarly to Friedman and Spiegelman searching for *tikkun atzmi*, pays tribute to his mother's first child, her daughter Tońcia, in his visually rich, experimental film *Half Sister* (1985). Both of Ravett's parents had prewar families, but only his mother was willing and able to talk about her little daughter.[45] The filmmaker's brief interview footage of his mother shows her overcome with emotion when relating the event of one terrifying day in May 1944 when the children were separated from their mothers and sent to Auschwitz. As Ravett's mother eventually found out upon her arrival there, the children had been killed. Ravett cuts the footage, and his unfinished sentence, "The last time . . ." lingers with the viewer. Ravett presents visual images that he associates with his half-sister's lost life and cinematographically alludes to the life full of potential that the brutal Nazi annihilation denied her. In the words of Holocaust literary scholar Tomasz Łysak, "The symbolic undoing of her death turns the attention to the void left by the life cut short."[46] Underscoring the filmmaker's intent to inspire "the imagination to conceive a life that would have been,"[47] silences accompany his visual explorations of the only photo of his half-sister Tońcia, about four years old, taken at a studio in Poland.

The existence of their parents' prewar families often contributed to the mystery the children born after the war experienced.[48] In their adult lives, some of these children wonder if their fathers' silence and emotional unavailability might also have been caused by the murder of their prewar families. While in Abraham Ravett's films *Everything's for You* and *Half Sister*, his father's depression and distance are not verbalized, but captured in the father's body language, writer Daniel Vogelmann directly addresses this issue: "Today I think that he [Vogelmann's father] couldn't let himself grow as attached as he had been to Sissel [his father's first child]: how could he have borne another such loss, ever a possibility?"[49] Many survivor parents, often subconsciously, were afraid of emotional closeness to their children. One female survivor admits to her adult daughter, on camera, that she could not allow herself to become too attached to her out of fear that she could lose her, as she had lost everyone she loved in the camps.[50] A daughter of a survivor put it even more strongly: "My mother did not want to have a child because she saw what happened to her other one [in the camps]."[51] One of my interviewees, born in postwar Poland, always suspected her mother's overprotectiveness to be because of her having had a prewar family. The interviewee felt too ashamed to ever ask her mother, and her mother, who had survived Auschwitz, never talked about her past in detail.[52]

Many adult children of Holocaust survivors felt burdened by the lack of a "Before," a time in which their ancestors lived their normal lives. In order to see, feel, and experience their ancestors' former places of residence in villages and towns all over Europe, the survivors' descendants often embarked on the multigenerational, so-called "trips to Europe," which became watershed events in the family dynamics and in the children's and grandchildren's biographies.

Marianne Hirsch contemplates her relationship to the "world of yesterday," her parents' *Heimat* of Czernowitz, which of course is not her parents' world anymore.[53]

After embarking on a multigenerational trip to Czernowitz (Chernivtsi) with her family, Hirsch relays a common experience: "In a profound sense, nostalgic yearning in combination with negative and traumatic memory—pleasure and affection layered with bitterness, anger and aversion—are internalized by the children of the exiles and refugees, members of the 'second generation.'"[54]

Depending on their ages, the unfathomable magnitude of the Holocaust that their parents had experienced on the most personal level had a different impact on the adult children when traveling through Europe. One of my interviewees became more religious, others questioned religion, and the Orthodox Jew and son of Holocaust survivors Menachem Daum challenged what he perceived to be his two sons' insular dedication to studying the Torah. With his 2005 documentary *Hiding and Seeking*, the filmmaker sought to contribute to his sons' religious tolerance by having them meet the Polish Catholic farmer family, the Muchas, who had sheltered their maternal grandfather and his two brothers for twenty-eight months in war-torn Poland, risking their own lives.[55] Daum intentionally used the emotional family trip to Poland not only as a lesson toward a deeper understanding of the family's history, but also to contribute to reconciliation between Jews and gentile Poles.[56] This documentary is one of the few films that focus on multigenerational interaction and portray the family dynamics between three generations. Daum's sons, who follow their paternal grandfather's strict orthodox teachings more closely than their father's humanistic and conciliatory views, reluctantly decide to join their father on the trip to Poland, for their own reasons. Early in the film Daum's father-in-law, Chaim Federman, resents the family trip to Poland and warns against the gentile Poles as being dangerous and treacherous, despite the fact that Polish farmers saved him and his brothers. Maybe after more than sixty years Chaim still felt ashamed that he and his brothers neglected to adequately thank their rescuers and let them know that they made it safely to the United States after the war? While Daum was inspired by his search for *tikkun olam*, his sons were motivated to learn more about their family history and visit the sites of their ancestors' survival. In his speech toward the end of the film, Daum's son Tzvi Dovid acknowledges to the Muchas that "there is such an overwhelming sense of insurmountable debt that my grandfather has literally become paralyzed to act upon it." In the end, Daum's story of redemption comes full circle when we learn that Chaim and his brother have set up an education fund for the Muchas' grandchildren and that the Muchas were officially honored as "Righteous among the Nations" by Yad Vashem.

Canadian actor and filmmaker Saul Rubinek already as a young boy wanted to see the cellar in which his parents survived for thirty-six months during the war. Two years after the publication of his book about his parents' lives, *So Many Miracles*, Rubinek produced a documentary with the same title in 1987.[57] Rubinek's parents initiated the trip back to Poland, wishing to see their Polish rescuers again. The parents showed their son Saul, whom they raised in Canada, the places of their youthful happiness in Poland, where they fell in love, and where they endured the most painful moments of their lives. While in hiding, Rubinek's mother gave birth to a baby daughter, who immediately died. The film captures, on camera, the emotional reunions between Rubinek's parents and the Polish family who had hid them, and between his mother and her former girlfriend, who urged her to visit their former teacher, which she did. Rubinek and his parents narrate the film, and Rubinek intercuts the mid-1980s footage of reunions and interviews with archival photographs and dramatic reenactments. This stylistic choice is meant to give the film more texture and to visually recount and illustrate his parents' experiences before and during the war. Overall, the movie has an upbeat mood; and as Rubinek stated in a 2007 interview, he would not have been able to make the documentary if his parents had not had their optimistic outlook and positive attitude.[58] While Daum's agenda in producing his film *Hiding and Seeking* was from the onset explicitly the search for *tikkun olam*, Rubinek's parents helped him see this as a goal in the process of filming in Poland.

The return to their parents' places of childhood and youth and the search for the sites where their families once lived has been the motive for many descendants of Holocaust survivors. Comedian Deb Filler invokes humor when telling about the 1990 trip with her father to his former hometown Brzozów, stopping in Prague on the way. Her father admonishes his daughter, whom he calls "Bebbski," for not following the rules in a Czech restaurant:

> You have to do as you're told here. If you didn't behave in the camps, they'd shoot you!
> I was incredulous. I looked at him and said: "Dad, we're not in the camps!"
> He seemed surprised.

The trip to her ancestors' former hometown in Poland, to their former store, and finally to the memorial that marked the site of their murder was a profoundly emotional and cathartic experience for Filler. At the actual places where her ancestors once lived and were murdered, Filler "could feel years of grief being tapped."[59]

One of my interviewees related her experiences when visiting her paternal and maternal ancestors' former hometowns in Germany with her father and her eight-year-old son. Her parents' families were able to escape Nazi Germany after having endured the "Aryanization" of their property, persecution, and abuse. DF's mother was very conflicted about her daughter and grandson's trip to Germany in 1998. In a letter she recalled her memories of a beautiful countryside and a carefree life, but also of beatings of the Jews, antisemitism, and the loss of her family in the Holocaust. DF's mother has not returned to Germany because of her vivid and painful memories. DF and her son actually went in the house that her great-grandfather had built and were shocked to see items that clearly once belonged to her family. DF felt an eerie sense of both having come home to her ancestors' culture and unease. Her inner conflicts regarding her background connect with her wishes that her son would carry on the family's legacy.[60]

An Israeli–born American filmmaker, Ornit Barkai also traveled with her daughter to Europe in search of her mother's past and filmed there in 2001. Her mother, too, could not bear to return to her former home in Dorohoi in Romania from where, in November 1941, she was deported with her two older sisters and an uncle to the concentration camps in the then Romanian-controlled region of Transnistria. The film *Past Forward* is primarily narrated by the voiceover of Barkai's daughter; on-camera interviews with several Ukrainian officials and old villagers in Kopystirin (the wartime Romanian name was Capusterna), where her then six-year-old mother spent two years of internment; and interviews with Barkai's mother during family visits to the United States, painfully recalling her life in hiding in a pigsty in Kopystirin before she and her sisters moved into a villager's house. The film is not linear and favors an associative approach over chronological accuracy. It focuses on the interplay of footage from the road trip through the Ukraine with Barkai's mother's on-camera and her daughter's off-camera narration. The juxtaposition of Barkai's mother's recollection of hunger and misery in the village and that of one eyewitness who claims that his family saved ten Jews provides one indirect answer as to why Barkai's mother chose not to travel with her daughter and granddaughter to the places of her past, where she was victimized and traumatized. Although or because Barkai largely remained behind the camera and focused on the interactions between her mother and her daughter, her film's composition is strongly influenced by seeking *tikkun atzmi*. By focusing on the grandmother-granddaughter interaction and narrative, Barkai both finds healing for herself and ensures that the family legacy keeps living on through her daughter.

While both men and women in the second generation have consciously decided to carry on their families' legacies, it is perhaps not surprising that women have written the majority of second-generation autobiographical accounts about their families' painful past. They often were designated or designated themselves to be the "memorial candles" for their families, as psychotherapist Dina Wardi puts it. She argues that perhaps because of the matrimonial line of Halachic law, the survivors tended to choose girls more often than boys as "memorial candles." She concludes, "Another reason is that in Jewish families the role of taking care of emotional problems within the family is generally a feminine role."[61] This, however, is rarely unique to survivor families. Eva Fogelman attributes the identification of survivors' daughters with their mothers to the "identity and development of the female offspring."[62] The 2001 Israeli documentary film *Last Journey into Silence* portrays problematic mother-daughter relationships in the setting of a mental institution. Filmmaker Shosh Shlam explained the reasons for and approach to her haunting film in an interview:

> I am the daughter of a Holocaust survivor who alone survived his entire family. As a child I lived with the nightly screams and inherited the pain, the wound that is bleeding still. The inner bleeding led me to search for survivors, those whose lives are flooded by night. I began my quest for survivors in hospitals throughout the country. Then I heard a hostel was about to be opened for Holocaust survivors, the first of its kind in the world, at Shaar Menashe Hospital. Survivors who were hospitalized for thirty or forty years in mental institutions were going to live there . . . I chose women to get away from my father. . . . Silence was the story. They [the survivors] were imprisoned inside the hell of their memory, which they carry inside. They do not remember the Holocaust; they live it. They survived the death marches but in fact died in them.[63]

Shlam films the daily routines at the facility and the routine visits of three daughters to see their mothers, who have for decades suffered severely from posttraumatic stress disorder. Her film explores the inner trauma of the older women, who have lost any concept of time, as well as the selfless kindness of their daughters, who have long surrendered to the role reversal that their mothers' emotional and mental conditions have required of them.

The children of survivors frequently were able to engage in dialogues with their mothers much longer, not only because often their mothers were more open about their harrowing pasts, but also because a disproportionate number of male Holocaust survivors predeceased their wives.[64] One of the few exceptions was the tragic story of Art Spiegelman's mother, who committed suicide in 1968. There are many reasons why the majority of wives outlived their husbands in survivor families, such as general life expectancy and gendered roles in household and society, but postwar strategies for coping with trauma and gendered responses to societal expectations regarding emotions and decision making also played a role. As the first group of second-generation survivors began grappling with their families' tragic past, some of their fathers died prematurely and left their children with many unanswered questions. Ravett includes some of those questions in his film *Everything's for You*, which he edited and completed ten years after his father's death. Subsequently, the temporal and spatial distance between the father's image and son's sound can be overcome only in the last stages of the film production process, as a posthumous tribute to Ravett's father. Ravett deals in several of his films with what he considers the dilemma of his upbringing, which he is still "unpacking."[65]

Certainly the second generation has been examined, reexamined, and examined itself in literature, art, film, psychological studies, and other scholarly works. After the societal and familial silence about the Holocaust was shattered, the (self-) designation as the family's legacy carrier in the second and now in the third generation usually falls to the female family members. The message "you are the continuing generation" became louder and clearer as the survivor parents aged:

> Behind us are death and infinite emotional emptiness. It is your obligation and your privilege to maintain the nation, to reestablish the vanished family and to fill the enormous physical and emotional voids left by the Holocaust in our surroundings and our hearts.[66]

While some of the second-generation offspring have been very outspoken and have become prolific writers, filmmakers, and artists, and along with many of their peers have dedicated their life and work to this legacy, others still feel too close to the trauma, as this testimony of a second-generation survivor on the effect of her family's Holocaust memory on her daughters shows:

It's affecting them again the same way the horror was passed on to my brother and me—by the intimation of things too horrible to express, by atrocities too incomprehensible to render meaningful, by the notion of vast and threatening evil . . . Helping her [the older daughter] to deal with it was excruciating. You can learn to bear, to love, to survive, but ultimately you cannot render positive meaning to the horror.[67]

Many in the second generation might have enjoyed what they perceived to be a close connection to a lost world or been haunted by the question of how their lives as part of European Jewry would have turned out without the Holocaust. However, the third generation has a very different perspective. They want to find out who their great-grandparents were, where and how they lived, and what happened to them during the war. Having been socialized in the United States or Israel with a robust sense of Jewish identity, they relate to the lost communities of their grandparents and their persecution during World War II often on an intellectual level. An exception was my interviewee Rebecca, at the time of the interview a graduate student at Brandeis University. She commented on her very emotional trip to Poland in 2005, when she traced her ancestors' forgotten communities, pensively walked through old Jewish graveyards, trying in vain to find her great-grandfather's grave. She enjoyed imagining "how it once was," and found a closer connection to her grandmother by seeing where she once lived before she settled in Israel.[68] Rebecca's mother had been instrumental in researching the family history and instilling a passion in her daughter for uncovering secrets from the past.

In some families, the second generation was not able to unlock the family history. Like many others, RS's mother felt "tortured" by her father's nightmares when growing up, and she "did not want to have anything to do with the Holocaust."[69] The second generation has in many cases laid the groundwork for their descendants to carry on the family history and the legacy of the Holocaust. But even if they had not opened the way, the third generation has many times taken it upon themselves to research and tell their grandparents' stories, even to their parents, who often do not know any details about their own parents' lives before and during the war.[70] The grandparents often found it easier to relate their experiences during the Holocaust to their grandchildren rather than to their own children, and to help them with school assignments trying to understand the historic events on a personal level.[71] The grandparent-grandchild relationship is less fraught with psychological and interpersonal conflicts than the parent-child relationship. Grandparents are often emotionally more available and more open to telling their grandchildren about their experiences during the Holocaust. In addition to the interpersonal aspects, a societal acceptance and validation makes it easier for the grandparents to share their stories—and for the grandchildren to want to hear them. The survivor generation has created a special bond with their grandchildren's generation. Psychologist Eva Fogelman found that "it is easier for survivors to share their lives with their grandchildren."[72] Unlike their parents, who in many cases grew up without grandparents, the third generation developed close relationships with their grandparents through multigenerational family interactions.

The third generation is transcending parts of their grandparents' memory that they either received in direct conversation with them, narrated by their parents, or both. Their quest, much less burdened with interpersonal and emotional issues compared to that of their parents, tries to situate their family's past in a geohistorical context. Drawing on Hirsch's concept of "postmemory," my notion of "transmemory" might provide a useful model for the third generation. Similar to "postmemory," the term "transmemory" does not address literally personal memories, but rather the reverberations of memories from past generations. This chapter argues that the third generation transcends these memories in the new millennium. I use the term "transcending" with its religious connotation in the sense that many in the third generation have either maintained or, even more, intensified their religious observance in comparison to their ancestors. But the third generation is also "transcending" memory in a nonreligious, philosophical, existential way. By contextualizing their family history in a geohistorical and political framework, the third generation seeks to make the memory of the Holocaust relevant for today and the future. They also seek to "transcend" the lessons of the Holocaust in order to stop current genocides and prevent future ones.

The relationship between the survivors and their children was often determined by a "double wall" between them. One of my former students in the Oral History course, descendant of a survivor herself, recognized this "double wall" when interviewing Holocaust survivor SB from Austria. He was initially very reluctant in answering personal questions and much preferred to talk about his political views and to lecture about the Holocaust. Both Hillary and SB felt the existence of a wall between them. In Hillary's first interview with SB, she felt that he "put up a wall," answering some of her questions in a guarded way and avoiding others. But when SB shared his observation with her in the third interview that he sometimes felt like he was "talking to a wall," Hillary realized the existence of a "double wall." Her "working-through process" culminated in the dance piece *A Moving History*, which she choreographed as part of her senior thesis at Goucher College. Hillary transcends SB's and her own relatives' memories and the interaction between her and the survivors into movement. The symbolic dismantling of a "wall" became not only the primary set device, but also one of the central themes of her choreography. She concludes: "The wall also depicts the process of breaking down the boundaries everybody has, especially when disclosing painful and personal details of the past. However, through breaking down these walls, truth, knowledge, understanding and healing can surface."[73]

As a final reflection, after a guided tour through Poland, another one of my former students wrote a letter to his deceased survivor-grandparents. In the letter he tried to explain and justify his participation in an international student program in which he traveled to Germany and Poland, which included several concentration camps. He concluded his letter:

> I recognized that my ultimate purpose in grappling with the Holocaust is twofold. One is to honor your humanness . . . Both of you survived the Holocaust and, while this had a profound effect on your lives and will [continue to] have on the fate of our family, this tragedy didn't define either one of you . . . The second purpose is to continue this dialogue with Jews and non-Jews alike for the sake of my grandchildren (should they someday materialize).[74]

Being two steps removed from the horrors of the Holocaust, many in the third generation are also searching for *tikkun*, but they have shifted or are in the process of shifting from *tikkun atzmi* to *tikkun am* or *tikkun olam*. In his novel entitled *Everything Is Illuminated*, Jonathan Safran Foer, himself the grandson of a Holocaust survivor, fictionalizes his own trip to the Ukraine in search of the woman who might have saved his maternal grandfather's life during the war. He is concerned not only with his own geographical and spiritual journey, but also with gaining an understanding of a different time and a different culture. The fact that Foer managed to do all that with a subtle sense of self-deprecating humor and an accomplished play with language made his novel widely popular. Not all grandchildren of survivors feel the need to explore present-day Eastern Europe as author Jonathan Safran Foer did. One of my interviewees, Ilan,[75] at the time of the interview a senior at Brandeis University, firmly states that he would not travel to Eastern Europe or Germany, "out of respect for my ancestors. It is just inappropriate." However, he feels deeply committed to carrying on the family legacy and searching for *tikkun am*. For him, one of the most important lessons of the Holocaust is that the Jewish people need to be united, including in their support for Israel. Another interviewee, RG, is in total agreement regarding unwavering support for Israel since it gave her grandparents a new life, and it has become a very important part of her own life. She takes the opposite approach, however, regarding visiting her ancestors' former homes. In her opinion the only way to show respect for her ancestors is to literally trace their steps and walk on their cobblestone streets.[76] Yet another former Brandeis student, RS, also stresses the importance of supporting Israel as a safe haven for Jews, but unlike RG, she did not want to visit her grandmother's towns on her trip to Europe because she did not want to endure the hostility of the current occupants of her family's former, now dilapidated home. Some of her family members actually went back for a visit, but it was a terrible experience for them. RS echoes what they must have reported upon their return to the United States: "Back to what? It is not their home anymore." RS feels very strongly that she has the responsibility of preserving her family history. Since RS cannot connect to her grandmother's lost Jewish community in Uzhgorod in western Ukraine, she focuses instead on the few tangible objects that her grandmother was able to save. In telling her family history on the basis of few everyday objects, RS transcends time and space. The candlesticks that held the candles her great-great grandmother lit in her home in the 1800s still serve this purpose in RS's life. Their odyssey from a *shtetl* in eastern Europe to a new home in the United States tells of the horrible twentieth-century tragedy, the Shoah. RS's senior thesis argues for the symbolic character of these objects, which to her also signify Jewish identity.[77] They symbolize lives lived and lives lost, love and tragedy. RS's inquiry into the past engaged her grandmother in such a way that "by focusing on the objects . . . she was able to comfortably tell their stories." After sixty years, RS's grandmother felt the need to share her and her family's story with her granddaughter, who vowed to carry on the family legacy. Both are grateful to each other for the mutual trust and the opportunity "to pass on her story to the next generations." RS's desire to preserve her family story and her grandmother's donations to the Museum of Jewish Heritage in New York suggest their interest in the continuity of Jewish traditions and *tikkun am*, the healing of the Jewish people.

"Transmemory" is a multilayered process influenced by familial and societal dimensions first and foremost, which addresses the notion that the third generation directly interacts with their grandparents-survivors, listening to their memories of the Holocaust, examining artifacts and family heirlooms that their grandparents brought to the United States, and inviting their grandparents to speak at their schools. The grandparents are now, much more so than when they raised their own children, in a position to reflect on their experiences in and memory of the Holocaust, to research their lost Jewish communities in Europe, and to engage in dialogues with historians, teachers, writers, and younger generations. Even though some of my interviewees in the third generation experience the burden of their grandparents' feelings of guilt placed on them, the generational remove allows for an emotionally more balanced response. RG recognizes that her grandmother's projections of "guilt" onto her are the result of a life of deprivation and discrimination. The geohistorical knowledge of the Holocaust allows RG and many others in her generation to contextualize their grandparents' experiences and responses. The third generation is also affected by what they sometimes perceive to be snide comments by their grandparents regarding today's comfortable lives and educational opportunities. The grandparents do not mean to be critical, but the comforts of a carefree childhood and youth that they first noticed in their own children and now in their grandchildren sometimes trigger the memories of their own losses, for which the mourning process will never be fully completed. According to Eva Fogelman and other psychologists, the second and also the third generation, to differing degrees, are engaged in a mourning process along with the survivors.[78] While the third generation is the "memory facilitator," the second generation, in their double role of children and parents, facilitates the mourning process in many survivor families.

The survivors also want to come to terms with their past and leave their personal legacy and that of the Holocaust with their grandchildren. In several families the grandchildren have consciously chosen to become more observant than their grandparents and transcend memory on a religious level.[79] These grandchildren consider the religious tradition in their families tragically interrupted by the Holocaust and see their role in mending this rift. On yet another level, some grandchildren are transforming their grandparents' memories into books of remembrance, research projects, storytelling events, art, and even dance.

Several psychologists have argued that the members of the third generation tend to be "higher achievers than their peers" (Fogelman),[80] that they feel a sense of pride and awe toward the survivors (Hogman),[81] and that their survivor-grandparents' love and attention toward them have resulted in a greater resilience compared to their peers (Sigal).[82] One descendant describes her unique form of transcending her grandmother's experiences: "Since my grandma is reminded of her experience every time when she looks at her arm [with the tattooed number from Auschwitz] I got a Star of David tattoo to remind me never to forget what happened, and to show my pride. The Holocaust also influences my everyday life because it had made me realize that similar torture and systematic murder still occur today."[83]

We do not yet have enough gender-related data analyzing differences in the third generation in carrying on the family legacy. Empirical impressions confirm, though, that the role of the "remembearer" (Nava Semel)[84] continues to be primarily female. In self-selected groups such as Internet forum discussion groups and among my interview partners, the young women clearly outnumber the young men. Future research would need to delve deeper into the causes and the extent to which this is the case. One of my third-generation male interviewees grew up with a general knowledge about the Holocaust, but his family did not acknowledge that the Holocaust was not only a collective, but also an individual and personal experience. His grandmother, who survived the Lodz ghetto and the Auschwitz concentration camp, "never ever talked about it with anyone else but my sister."[85]

Further research would also need to address the question of how the third generation has affected the position of the second generation. With the coming of age of the third generation, the shift from trauma to legacy, from *tikkun atzmi* to *tikkun am* and *tikkun olam* is beginning. A comparative study between the United States and Israel would be a necessary step in understanding similarities and differences in the ways the third generation acts as "memory facilitator" not only between the generations, but also in their respective cultures.

NOTES

1. See the seminal studies of multigenerational families in Israel and Germany by Dan Bar-On, *Fear and Hope: Three Generations of the Holocaust* (Cambridge: Harvard University Press, 1998) and Gabriele Rosenthal, ed., *The Holocaust in Three Generations: Families of Victims and Perpetrators of the Nazi Regime* (London: Bloomsbury Academic, 1998). Multigenerational studies in the United States include, among others, PhD dissertations by Jaye Houston, "*L'Dor v'Dor*: Legacies, the Holocaust Female Survivors, and the Third Generation" (Claremont Graduate University, 2005), and Michelle A. Friedman, "Reckoning with Ghosts: Second Generation Holocaust Literature and the Labor of Remembrance" (Bryn Mawr College, 2001); and books by Laura Levitt, *American Jewish Loss after the Holocaust* (New York: New York University Press, 2007), and Lea Ausch, *Three Generations of Jewish Women: Holocaust Survivors, Their Daughters and Granddaughters* (Lanham, MD: University Press of America, 2002).

2. While most children in the second generation grew up without grandparents, this was not necessarily a universal experience. Geohistorical differences and individual circumstances allowed for exceptions. Most notably, multigenerational survivor families came from the Budapest ghetto in Hungary, parts of Transnistria under the Romanian control during the war, and Western Europe. The most important variables include age, location, and rescue possibilities.

3. I am indebted to Joanna Beata Michlic, director of the "Project on Families, Children, and the Holocaust" at the Hadassah Brandeis Institute (HBI). I was privileged to be part of this project at HBI in the spring 2010 semester.

4. This especially concerns Israeli feature films and literary works in both the United States and Israel.

5. Alan Berger, *Children of Job: American Second-Generation Witnesses to the Holocaust* (Albany: State University Press of New York, 1997).

6. Aviva Kempner, *Keeping the Family Name Alive*, in *Daughters of Absence: Transforming a Legacy of Loss*, ed. Mindy Weisel, 121 (Herndon, VA: Capital Books, 2000).

7. Author interviews with LG, March 12, 2010, Weston, Massachusetts; StS, January 15, 2010, Baltimore, Maryland; and DK, April 25, 2010, Newton, Massachusetts.

8. Efraim Sicher, *Breaking Crystal: Writing and Memory after Auschwitz* (Champaign, IL: University of Illinois Press, 1997), 71. The equivalent in the Israeli context is the reference to "coming from there."

9. LG, interview with the author, March 12, 2010, Weston, Massachusetts.

10. *Breaking the Silence: The Generation after the Holocaust*, produced by Eva Fogelman and Edward Mason, directed by Edward Mason (PBS, 1984), documentary film.

11. StS, interview with the author, January 15, 2010, Baltimore, Maryland.

12. Dolly Goodman, "How Has the Holocaust Affected My Life?" in *We Shall Never Forget!: Memories of the Holocaust*, ed. Carole Garbuny Vogel, with the assistance of the sons and daughters of the Holocaust Survivors Discussion Group, 2nd ed. (Lexington, MA: Temple Isaiah, 1995), 419f.

13. StS, interview with the author, January 15, 2010, Baltimore, Maryland.

14. Toby Mostysser, *The Weight of the Past: Reminiscences of a Child of Survivors*, in *Living after the Holocaust: Reflections by the Post-War Generation in America*, ed. Lucy Y. Steinitz with David Szonyi (New York: Bloch, 1975), 5.

15. Dan Bar-On, *Fear and Hope: Three Generations and the Holocaust* (Cambridge: Harvard University Press, 1995), 20.

16. Ibid., 17f.

17. Helen Epstein, *Children of the Holocaust: Conversations with Son and Daughters of Survivors* (New York: Penguin Books, 1979); Lucy Y. Steinitz with David Szonyi, eds., *Living after the Holocaust: Reflections by the Post-War Generation in America* (New York: Bloch Publishing, 1975); *Breaking the Silence: The Generation after the Holocaust*, produced by Eva Fogelman and Edward Mason, directed by Edward Mason (PBS, 1984), documentary film.

18. Bar-On, *Fear and Hope*, 26.

19. Eva Fogelman (and other psychologists), based on Freud's definition of trauma, maintain that trauma itself cannot be transmitted. The second generation was raised by traumatized parents, but by and large did not experience trauma themselves.

20. Geraldine Bronstein Ertel, "How the Holocaust Has Affected My Life," in Vogel, *We Shall Never Forget!*, 221.

21. Melvin Jules Bukiet, ed., *Nothing Makes You Free: Writings by Descendants of Jewish Holocaust Survivors* (New York: W.W. Norton, 2002), 14.

22. Robert Jay Lifton, in Fogelman and Mason, *Breaking the Silence*.

23. Toby Mostysser, "The Weight of the Past: Reminiscences of a Child of Survivors," in Steinitz, *Living after the Holocaust*, 5.

24. Helen Epstein, "Normal," in Weisel, *Daughters of Absence*, 6.

25. Ibid.

26. Susan Jacobowitz, "The Holocaust at Home: Representations and Implications of Second Generation Experience (Art Spiegelman, Thane Rosenbaum, Lily Brett)" (PhD diss., Brandeis University, 2005), 3f.

27. Fortunoff Video Archive for Holocaust Testimonies, Yale University, tape 94, as cited in Lawrence Langer, *Holocaust Testimonies: The Ruins of Memory* (New Haven, CT: Yale University Press, 1991), x.

28. Eva Hoffman, *After Such Knowledge: Memory, History, and the Legacy of the Holocaust* (New York: PublicAffairs, 2004), 182f.

29. Bukiet, *Nothing Makes You Free*, 13.

30. Marianne Hirsch, *Family Frames: Photography, Narrative and Postmemory* (Cambridge: Harvard University Press, 1997), 22.

31. Marianne Hirsch, "The Generation of Postmemory," *Poetics Today* 29, no. 1 (spring 2008): 109.

32. Ibid., 106.

33. Cf. Berger, *Children of Job*, 14f.

34. StS, interview with the author, January 15, 2010, Baltimore, Maryland.

35. JF, interview with the author, January 31, 2010, Waltham, Massachusetts.

36. Anonymous, "Cognitive Dissonance," *Passing the Legacy of Shoah Remembrance, l'Dor v'Dor, Yom Ha Shoah Commemoration*, April 12, 2010, Temple Emanuel, Newton, Massachusetts.

37. JF, interview with the author, January 31, 2010, Waltham, Massachusetts.

38. Dina Wardi, *Memorial Candles: Children of the Holocaust* (London: Routledge, 1992), 27.

39. Toby Mostysser, "The Weight of the Past: Reminiscences of a Child of Survivors," in Steinitz, *Living after the Holocaust*, 10.

40. Fogelman and Mason, *Breaking the Silence*.

41. Gabriele Rosenthal, ed., *The Holocaust in Three Generations: Families of Victims and Perpetrators of the Nazi Regime* (London: Cassell, 1998), 43.

42. Berger, *Children of Job*, 38.

43. Thomas Friedman, *Damaged Goods* (Sag Harbor, NY: Permanent Press, 1984), 72f.

44. Art Spiegelman, *Maus II* (New York: Pantheon Books, 1991), 15.

45. In Ravett's film *Everything's for You*, his father briefly mentioned his prewar children, a son and a daughter, killed at ages eight and eleven. A photo of Ravett's father and his first wife, pushing a baby carriage, is floating across the screen. In an attempt to elicit his father's memories more easily, Ravett asks his questions in Yiddish, whereas his father continues to answer them in heavily accented English.

46. Tomasz Łysak, "Experimenting/Experiencing Loss—Abraham Ravett's (Auto)biographical Experimental Films," in *Cultural Representations and Commemorative Practices*, ed. Tomasz Majewski and Anna Zeidler Janiszewska, 347 (Lodz: Officyna, 2010).

47. Abraham Ravett, *Half Sister*, accessed on November 3, 2012, http://www.faculty.hampshire.edu/aravett/half_sister.html.

48. I use the term *prewar families* in a broad sense here, referring to a time before the Nazi occupation and subsequent atrocities. The time frame varies depending on country and location.

49. Daniel Vogelmann, "My Share of the Pain," in *Second Generation Voices: Reflections by Children of Holocaust Survivors and Perpetrators*, ed. Alan Berger and Naomi Berger, 73 (Syracuse, NY: Syracuse University Press, 2001).

50. Mrs. Gelfman, in *A Generation Apart*, directed by Jack Fisher (New York: City Lights Pictures, 1983), documentary film.

51. Fogelman and Mason, *Breaking the Silence*.

52. EE, interview with the author, January 13, 2010, Baltimore, Maryland.

53. Marianne Hirsch and Leo Spitzer, "'We Would Not Have Come without You': Generations of Nostalgia," *American Imago* 59, no. 3 (2002): 257.

54. Ibid., 261.

55. *Hiding and Seeking: Faith and Tolerance after the Holocaust*, produced and directed by Menachem Daum and Oren Rudavsky (PBS, August 30, 2005), video.

56. Menachem Daum, "Film Update: Hiding and Seeking: Faith and Tolerance after the Holocaust," August 30, 2005, accessed on November 25, 2012, http://www.pbs.org/pov/hidingandseeking/film_update.php#.ULvGoRz3Lno.

57. *So Many Miracles*, directed by Vic Sarin and Katherine Smalley (Canada: Alternative Pictures and CBC, 1987), DVD, 58 min. Available from the National Center for Jewish Film, Waltham, Massachusetts.

58. Ibid. Saul Rubinek, interview with Max Roper, 2007, DVD.

59. Deb Filler, "Kicking and Weeping," in Weisel, *Daughters of Absence*, 83.

60. DF, interview with the author, February 10, 2010, Waltham, Massachusetts.

61. Wardi, *Memorial Candles*, 32.

62. Eva Fogelman, "Transforming a Legacy of Loss," in Weisel, *Daughters of Absence*, xxxiv.

63. Aimee Pozorski and Petra Schweitzer, "Time and Trauma in *Last Journey into Silence*: A Conversation with Shosh Shlam," *Reading On* 1, no. 1 (2006).

64. In my samples, which include interviews and testimonials of the writers and filmmakers whose works are analyzed here, fifteen husbands predeceased their wives as opposed to four wives who predeceased their husbands.

65. Abraham Ravett, interview with the author, March 13, 2010, Northampton, Massachusetts. Cf. Berger, *Children of Job*, 147.

66. Wardi, *Memorial Candles*, 30.

67. Dolly Goodman, "How Has the Holocaust Affected My Life?" in Vogel, *We Shall Never Forget!*, 421.

68. Rebecca Gil, interview with the author, April 19, 2010, Boston, Massachusetts.

69. Rebecca Shapiro, interview with the author, March 8, 2010, Waltham, Massachusetts.

70. LK, interview with the author, March 9, 2010, Waltham, Massachusetts, and MB, interview with the author, March 30, 2010, Baltimore, Maryland.

71. See Barkai's documentary *Past Forward*, in which her daughter's narration is based on an essay she wrote as a school assignment. In Israel and South Africa, the "roots projects" also aim for the students to get a sense of history by interviewing their grandparents. Cf. Bar-On, *Fear and Hope*, 32, and Robin Porter (name changed), interview with the author, March 11, 2010, Waltham, Massachusetts.

72. Eva Fogelman, "Psychological Dynamics in the Lives of Third Generation Holocaust Survivors," *Hidden Child* 16 (2008): 10–12, accessed on November 30, 2012, http://www.drevafogelman.com/_psychological_dynamics_in_the_lives_of_third_generation_holocaust_survivors__94110.htm.

73. Hillary Hoffman, "A Moving History" (senior thesis in choreography, Goucher College, Baltimore, Maryland, 2010), 31f.

74. David H. to his grandparents, submitted to the author, 2005.

75. Ilan (name changed), interview with the author, February 8, 2010, Waltham, Massachusetts.

76. Rebecca Gil, interview with the author, April 19, 2010, Waltham, Massachusetts.

77. Rebecca Shapiro, *Memories Never Die: The Significance of Objects in a Survivor's Tale* (senior thesis, Brandeis University, 2010).

78. Eva Fogelman, "Impact on the Second and Third Generations," in *Children Surviving Persecution: An International Study of Trauma and Healing*, ed. Judith Kestenberg and Charlotte Kahn (Westport, CT: Greenwood, 1998), 85.

79. Author interviews with TP, March 11, 2010, Waltham, Massachusetts; Ilan (name changed), February 8, 2010, Waltham, Massachusetts; MB, March 30, 2010, Baltimore,

Maryland; LK, March 9, 2010, Waltham, Massachusetts; AP, March 12, 2010, Waltham, Massachusetts; and RS, May, 13, 2010, Boston, Massachusetts.

80. Eva Fogelman, "Psychological Dynamics in the Lives of Third Generation Holocaust Survivors," accessed on November 30, 2012, http://www.drevafogelman.com/_psychological_dynamics_in_the_lives_of_third_generation_holocaust_survivors__94110.htm.

81. Flora Hogman, "Memory of the Holocaust," *Echoes of the Holocaust*, no. 4 (June 1995), accessed on April 22, 2016, http://www.holocaustechoes.com/4hogman3.html.

82. John Sigal, "Resilience in Survivors, Their Children and Their Grandchildren," *Echoes of the Holocaust*, no. 4 (June 1995), accessed on April 22, 2016, http://www.holocaustechoes.com/4hogman3.html.

83. 3GNY: Descendants of Holocaust Survivors, "Family Histories: Roni Bronstein," accessed on March 19, 2010, http://3gnewyork.org/wordpress/family-histories. In Israel, several descendants in the second and third generation have recently decided to have their survivor relatives' Auschwitz numbers tattooed on their bodies. The Israeli documentary film *Numbered (Sfurim)*, directed by Dana Doron and Uriel Sinai (New York: kNow Productions, 2012), examines this phenomenon. See also "Proudly Bearing Elders' Scars: Their Skin Says 'Never Forget,'" *New York Times* (online), September 30, 2012, accessed on November 10, 2012, http://www.nytimes.com/2012/10/01/world/middleeast/with-tattoos-young-israelis-bear-holocaust-scars-of-relatives.html?pagewanted=2&_r=0&hp. Mexican filmmaker Ariel Zylbersztejn addresses one little girl's obsession with her grandparents' tattooed numbers in his 2009 narrative short film *JAI — Los Numeros de la Vida* (available on YouTube) in an endearing, lighthearted way.

84. Nava Semel, *And the Rat Laughed* (Melbourne: Hybrid Publishers, 2008).

85. RS, interview with the author, May 13, 2010, Boston, Massachusetts.

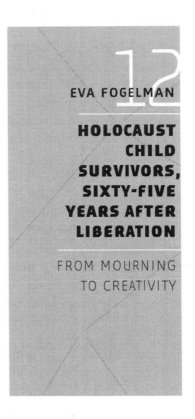

HOLOCAUST CHILD SURVIVORS, SIXTY-FIVE YEARS AFTER LIBERATION

FROM MOURNING TO CREATIVITY

Most of the world does not contemplate children as survivors of the Holocaust; surely it is understandable why this is the case. After all, the image that most have is that of Jews spilling out of the cattle cars, selected to go either "left or right," and the children—all of the children—selected for death. An entire generation of European Jewish children was subject to the nightmare of *Sophie's Choice*,[1] except, of course, that the Sophie in the William Styron novel was a Polish Catholic, and so she was given a choice, though an impossible one. No Jewish mother was given the choice to save one of her children. The world expected that Jewish children would not be among the wretched, skeletal, survivors.

The child survivors were the true lost children of the Holocaust. While they managed to survive by dint of a confluence of miracles, instincts, and *mazel* (plain old luck), they were largely ignored in their life after Auschwitz. This, of course, was true of the adult survivors as well. The Jewish community in Palestine—the *Yishuv*—thence constituted the core population of the new State of Israel, which celebrated an image, indeed an ethos, of the fighting, fully emancipated, and finally repatriated Jew. The new spirit of the Zionist age informed a societal agenda, to look forward and not back. Survivors were given the responsibility to rebuild their lives, and were told in effect not to speak of the past. And many of them did not wish to speak of the past, nor were they capable of revisiting the past.

Moreover, historians determined that, in learning about the Holocaust, nothing useful could be gained by talking to the survivors. An eyewitness to such an atrocity was deemed to be too damaged, too traumatized, and was therefore unreliable to offer an accurate account of what had happened. For historical purposes, the survivor was considered a biased witness, whereas the perpetrators were considered to be the ultimate truth tellers. Former Nazis were believed; Holocaust survivors were thought of as natural liars. Given this atmosphere of neglect and cynicism, the survivor had every reason to remain silent and be marginalized. This was even truer of the child survivors, who were considered too young to recall, or to understand, the significance of what they had seen. And, of course, there were so few child survivors that it was easy not to notice them.

It is estimated that only 6 to 7 percent of the Jewish children of Europe lived through the Holocaust and experienced liberation. It is impossible to calculate how many survived. Some are still hidden. What can be said with some measure of certainty is that the youngest were the most vulnerable; hence, most of the babies, toddlers, and preadolescents during that time did not live long enough to become adults. Their potential was destroyed before it could be realized.

Many children given to neighbors and convents in different parts of German-occupied Europe for safekeeping were never returned. Yet, parenthetically and ironically, there were children who survived the Holocaust and died three years later on the battlefields of the new Jewish State, in the 1948 War of Independence. As soon as some of them got off the boats — after all they had been through — they were sent out with rifles to fight those who would kill them in their hoped-for homeland.

Although Jewish children had witnessed everything and lost so much before they matured, this cohort of Holocaust survivors — the children who survived — were largely ignored by their surrounding societies. Despite the huge focus on Anne Frank — the quintessential hidden child of the Holocaust — and her diary, the world did not seem to realize that there were children and teenagers who, improbably, survived genocide. These young survivors were neglected by virtually everyone and by every organizational entity that purported to care for those the Nazis had failed to kill. They remained anonymous in the culture, and fell under the radar of the Jewish community as well.

Scholars, social workers, and reparation authorities did not pay much attention to child survivors either. Orphaned child survivors were placed in institutions. For example, Kfar Batya, a kibbutz in the Mizrachi movement, took in Yaffa Eliach and Judith Kallman, who was also a "kindertransportee" in London. Roman Kent, now chairman of the American Gathering of Jewish Holocaust Survivors, and his brother were placed in an orphanage and eventually with families in Atlanta, Georgia. In some extraordinary cases, the children's own survivor parents neglected child survivors. The parents had forgotten how to parent, or they did not see the point of parenting since the Holocaust proved that parents, no matter how fiercely loving and protective they wanted to be, could not protect their children from the Nazis and their collaborators.

The neglect that most of these children experienced when they were liberated resulted in complicated consequences to their identity formation and their ability to heal. Their survival was beyond human comprehension; it is not surprising, therefore, to learn that each child survived in his or her own unique way. After the war they soldiered on, refining their survival instincts in a new world where such extreme and otherworldly abilities no longer applied. The one skill they possessed—how to survive—was not easily adaptable. They were overqualified for the next step forward. No roads would lead them back to the past, and many did not wish to reclaim their past. There was no home to return to. An example of such a child is Samuel Pisar, the noted international attorney, who was on his way to becoming a "murderer" until his aunt took control of him and shipped him off to school in Australia, where he was cared for by his adoptive family and able to reshape his life.

The Holocaust child survivors did not constitute a monolithic group. Young people who were thirteen or under when the Third Reich was established include those who were born in Germany in the 1920s and those born during the war in ghettos; there were children in hiding, or with a disguised parent who fled from place to place. The majority of them were born in the late 1920s and 1930s; and in Hungary and even Poland, many still were born in the early 1940s. Formal education—or the lack of it—played an important role in these children's lives as well. Many were upset that their schooling was interrupted and that their life circumstances made it almost impossible to continue their education after liberation. Edith Cord, born in Vienna, realized very quickly, by age eight, that education would be her ticket out of poverty. Her family fled first to Italy and then to France, where she was hidden in a convent school, and she already understood that she would never be able to matriculate unless she applied herself. Edith resented having to move from place to place, and each time she attended school she could not finish her courses because she had to flee. After the war, Edith completed six years of university work in two years and earned her degree in Nice. When Edith emigrated to the United States, she earned her doctorate, and her first career was that of professor of modern languages. There were also other child survivors who managed to receive their education, and they did very well. The late Andrew Grove founded Intel; Jack Tramiel founded Commodore and Atari, the first personal computers; and Fred Taucher invented Domain Name Servers (DNS). Indeed, without their contributions, our world would be a very different place. Elie Wiesel and Yaffa Eliach were the first to teach Holocaust studies in the City University of New York. Jerzy Kosinski wrote novels and transformed himself into a man both of letters and of mystery.

At times these child survivors chose professions that were preordained, inspired by their wartime experiences. Nathan Sobel was a founder of NACHOS, a child survivor organization in New York. As a ten-year-old living on his own, he navigated his way through the streets and slept in back alleys of a major

Polish city. His "street smarts" and "hands-on" understanding of the way a city works served him well when he became city planner in New York. Roman Kent always says he earned his PhD in Auschwitz. Of course, they all knew that actual universities did not offer this kind of a curriculum. A real and more useful academic degree would eventually be practical. Many child survivors became miserable knowing that a formal education might ultimately be denied to them as they desperately reentered the world. Ernest Michel, another Auschwitz survivor, became one of the United Jewish Appeal's most prominent executives. In Auschwitz he dreamt of organizing a World Gathering of Holocaust Survivors; in 1981 he did exactly that, yet he always felt he was educationally inferior to his peers because he did not finish sixth grade. That changed after he received two honorary doctorates—one from the City University of New York and another from Yeshiva University.

For child survivors who decided to struggle with new languages and who were determined to make their own way in their new lives, the possibilities were endless. Many of them came naturally to the helping and healing professions because they could empathize with pain and suffering. Others, especially those in Israel, took different paths. After receiving their educations on kibbutzim, they became career officers in the Israeli army, scientists who helped build Israel's defense industry, doctors who built medical systems, and teachers—all for the purpose of protecting and saving the Jewish people.

Some became government leaders. The former Dutch minister of the interior, member of the senate, and mayor of Amsterdam, Ed van Thijn, was incarcerated in Westerbork; in Israel, the late Josef Lapid became the head of the Shinui Party in the Knesset and served as justice minister. The late Tom Lantos, a survivor and a member of the United States House of Representatives, played a major role in American foreign policy.

Just as professional identity could be influenced by experiencing persecution and losses, so could one's Jewish identity. Despite the initial diversity of Jewish identification among the child survivors, for many returning to their Jewish identity is a lifelong process that is changing to this very day. There are child survivors who are just discovering that they are Jews, while others intensified their Jewish religious observance after liberation. For example, the head of the Boston University Hillel, Rabbi Joseph Polak, survived the Bergen-Belsen concentration camp with his mother. Before the Holocaust, it was not so obvious that he would become a rabbi. His Jewish future was sealed by a bargain his mother made with God. While she was a prisoner, Rabbi Polak's mother, much as Samuel the Prophet's mother had done, swore that if she survived with her son she would raise him in the Orthodox tradition. She kept her vow, and now her son carries on her legacy by teaching his students how to be Jewish. In 2015 Rabbi Polak published a personal memoir, *After the Ho-*

locaust the Bells Still Ring, that he views as a way of unearthing his past as an infant child survivor.[2]

Some child survivors, used to hiding and concealing their true identities, were ambivalent about identifying themselves as Jews. This was certainly true of novelist and lawyer Louis Begley, a past president of the writer's organization PEN American Center. His autobiographical novel, *Wartime Lies,*[3] describes how he and his mother survived the Holocaust, although in the book, the adult is his aunt. For whatever reason, he refuses to participate in Holocaust commemorations and organizations and refuses to address the subject publicly. Child survivors such as Begley, who carry rage and ambivalence, need to "heal."

In order to heal, individuals undergo the process of mourning, which ultimately results in the channeling of feelings into creativity. When a group is victimized, the healing of individuals is dependent on a convergence of personal characteristics, past socialization and experiences, and the social situation. The validation from others of pain and suffering enhances the potential for restoring the self. For child survivors of the Holocaust, this necessary step came very late; nonetheless, even at this late date, sixty-five years after the war, such recognition of suffering is making a difference in their waning years. Since most child survivors received little or no validation of their traumatic childhoods, their capacity to mourn and heal was hampered. Older survivors wrongly believed that those who were young during the German occupation did not remember what happened to them. But the children, even if they had not yet learned to speak, remember very well being forced out of their houses into ghettos, or escaping in the middle of the night to hide with neighbors or total strangers. They remember changing their names and their family narratives to take on new identities, or living with other children in orphanages, convents, or Christian boarding schools; and there are those who remember deportations. Older survivors assumed that these children did not see, smell, touch, hear, or feel what was going on around them. When adult survivors got together with other adult survivors, the child survivors sitting at the same table or eavesdropping on the conversation about the war were excluded. An adult survivor mother rarely asked her child, "Do you remember your father?" If Jewish children had non-Jewish rescuers, in many cases, their survivor parents prevented them from contacting the rescuer out of fear over the child's competing loyalties. But the genie could not stay in the bottle forever. The children's emotions would eventually come out.

In 1979, when the Holocaust survivor movement came alive and spread to every corner of the world, child survivors took advantage of the opportunity to bear witness. Instead of remaining in a state of psychic numbness and social withdrawal, they began to search for others with similar backgrounds with whom they could mourn and share, and their collective voice began to be heard. For the first time, empathetic listeners provided opportunities to help child survivors do the inner work of integration. This integration starts the process of incorporating the past into one's identity and provides ways to mourn. But mourning is not so simple. While they do remember, it is challenging for child survivors to tell the story of what happened to them because they do not remember events as a sequential narrative. They remember fractured images, especially if the memories occurred in their preverbal stage. Child survivors remember incidents kinesthetically, as physical memories.

After years of being told they were too young to remember, child survivors admit there is, what the psychologists would call, some narcissistic gratification in telling their stories their own way, and this has happened more often in recent years. As the older survivors become incapacitated and curtail public appearances, child survivors are sought out and asked to share their stories with the world. This validation of their pain, suffering, loss, and adaptation makes child survivors feel understood, often for the first time. That others want to know what happened to them enables them to feel that they, too, along with the older survivors, can contribute to the recording of history.

In the mid-1970s, as a daughter of survivors involved in the Holocaust education and commemoration movement, I became involved in raising consciousness about the plight of child survivors almost by accident. I was leading groups for sons and daughters of Holocaust survivors in Boston, when I stumbled across child survivors for the first time. It happened when a potential group member approached me and said: "I saw an ad that says you're leading an awareness group for children of Holocaust survivors. I don't know if I belong." I asked to meet with her to discuss it, and it turned out that she was not alone. There were a number of prospective group members who were children during the war and who had at least one parent who had survived. These former children described feeling like members of both the survivor community and the second generation—having struggled with their own unique psychological dynamics.

As a result, I organized what became known as intergenerational groups. The child survivors later called themselves the 1.5 generation, caught between the first and second generations. There were soon more avenues available to them for sharing their stories. The Center for Holocaust Studies in Brooklyn, founded by Dr. Yaffa Eliach and Stella Wieseltier in the late 1970s, was one of the first oral history projects in the United States that made a point to include child survivors. In 1981 psychoanalyst Judith Kestenberg initiated the International Study of Organized Persecution of Children, a project of Child Development Research, which to date has interviewed fifteen hundred child survivors. She, her husband Milton, and I organized monthly meetings with child survivors who had already been interviewed and child survivors who would be interviewed, and a few who never shared their testimony. As time passed, such groups and interviews were held in other major cities around the world, and child survivor organizations were established and flourished.

In the late 1970s, Myriam Abramowicz and Esther Hoffenberg directed and produced *As If It Were Yesterday*, a film about hidden children in Belgium. After showing her film worldwide and meeting many hidden children, Abramowicz had a vision, that of bringing child survivors together, such as Ernest Michel and the older Holocaust survivors had done at the World Gathering in Jerusalem in 1981. She approached Jean Bloch-Rosensaft and me to turn her vision into a reality. With the help of Judith and Milton Kestenberg of Child Development Research and the Anti-Defamation League, the First International Gathering of Hidden Children was held in 1991 on Memorial Day weekend in New York City, where sixteen hundred child survivors validated their own unique suffering and survival. Particularly affected were the hidden children. As the upcoming event was written about in *Newsweek* and *New York* magazine and in local newspapers, hundreds of child survivors started to come out of hiding. As had been the case with the World Gathering, this event also provided a major opportunity for communal mourning, something that is vital for survivors recuperating from historical trauma. The First International Gathering of Hidden Children gave the "children" an opportunity to mourn together in a collective voice. But first they had to accept that those they mourned were gone forever.

In each survivor's recovery, there comes a moment of realization that loved ones are indeed dead. Every psychological process of mourning begins with shock and follows set stages that are dynamic, not static. At times they overlap, and can reverse or replay themselves during the course of a lifetime. For child survivors of the Holocaust, mourning is even more complex because of multiple deaths and the chaotic, life-altering circumstances surrounding the experience. Every child survivor has to mourn a multitude of relatives he or she knew and did not know, or knew and did not remember.

There are child survivors who witnessed the actual murder of a parent, a sibling, a grandparent, or other relative. That indelible image continues to be their living nightmare, etched in their minds forever. Some witnessed the slow death of the person they loved as they withered away from starvation or disease. For others the shock came after the war, from seeing a name on a list or being told that someone was dead. That permanent loss destroyed the fantasy that sustained the child, who had hoped that a loved one was still alive. That sense of hope went a long way toward providing a will to live under unbearable conditions. Now that hope was gone, and shock was left in its place.

After liberation, most survivors experienced an unconscious resistance to giving up the defense mechanisms that served them well under extreme conditions of terror. That attitude leads to the second stage, denial. Often, when one is jolted into accepting the death of a loved one, denial takes over and serves as a coping mechanism. But according to popular wisdom, "Denial is not a river in Egypt." It is a painful state of being. That is why, in many cases, denial stretched into months and years before the person could enter the confrontation stage. When denial is a defense, there is resistance to giving up the hope that protected the victim from anxiety and from reliving a nightmare.

There were those who discovered only after the war that a loved one had died. But when a child witnessed the death of a parent or loved one under extreme conditions of terror, there was no opportunity to mourn at all; the situation provided no physical or psychological space in which to grieve. The enormity of the process of adapting to life after liberation sapped all of one's energy. Many children were being handed off to strangers in places completely different from what they knew. Adults were making up for lost years, establishing new identities, moving from being a "victim" to being a "survivor," and had no time to lavish care on the children. Most often that also meant physically moving from place to place until a permanent home could be found, and establishing new relationships, communities, and occupations far removed from their previous lives in Europe. Child survivors leaving Europe had to adjust to completely new cultures and languages, an adjustment that interfered with the stages of mourning. Under those circumstances, it often took an external trigger or a personal encounter with death to jolt an individual into delayed mourning many years after the deaths of his or her loved ones. The external triggers could be as simple as watching a movie and having flashbacks, or losing a spouse or other loved one, which released a flood of emotions that transcended the immediate loss and incorporated losses from the past that were never mourned.

Additionally, there are those who are forever trapped in denial, because moving from denial to confrontation requires established facts to prove that the person is indeed dead. In many cases, such information is impossible to find. And sometimes information comes in unexpected ways.

One of my own case studies is about Paulette, who was born in France in 1935 to parents who fled Germany shortly after Hitler came to power.[4] For many years, although she hardly remembered him, she struggled to grieve for her father, who was deported to the Drancy internment camp near Paris when she was just seven. Her mother hardly spoke to Paulette about him. I encouraged Paulette to check the Nazi hunter Serge Klarsfelds's book on French deportees, where she found the date of her father's deportation to Auschwitz. But without an official date of death, it was difficult to engage in mourning. By the time she was ready to ask questions, Paulette's mother had been diagnosed with dementia and could not offer any answers. Then, sixty years after liberation, Paulette received a telephone call from a woman in Paris, who had found her father's suitcase in an attic in a town in the French Pyrénées where they had hidden; there were yet a few people still alive who remembered them. With great trepidation Paulette made plans to retrieve the suitcase and meet the people whom she, too, had known in childhood. She learned what a kind, intelligent man her father was, and how well he was liked by the townspeople. When Paulette was handed the suitcase, she became very emotional. She could not believe she had her father's papers. On one of the last pages of his diary, he wrote "*Merde, merde, merde.*"

"It must have been a terrible day," she said.

What Paulette discovered was that her father had made every attempt possible to save his family by pleading for refuge from people around the world. He never received responses to his pleas. His devotion to his family was clear from his papers; but while she was growing up, her mother had given her a different impression, and Paulette assumed her father had abandoned them.

To cope with the uncertain facts of her father's death, Paulette began the next stage: confronting his death. She worked on a scrapbook that combined photos, artifacts, and a narrative of her life to share with her own family. This became an all-consuming, painful venture that forced her to put her experiences into words. It was overwhelming. Although she continued to write, she handed the suitcase and its contents to the person assisting her, and asked him to review the information for her. She could no longer handle the emotional flooding the papers provoked.

A few weeks ago, Paulette called to say that her daughter-in-law had received a phone call from the Looted Art Registry, who found two rare books in France with bookplates indicating they had belonged to her grandfather. The person who provided the information also let her know that her father was on convoy 62, which arrived in Auschwitz on November 20, 1943, and that he was killed on November 30, 1943. Her first response was, "I never knew his *yahrzeit* [death anniversary]." She went on to say that she thought he had died in April or May 1944.

A different kind of "knowing" sets in when one has an actual date of death. Suddenly Paulette's memory was sharpened. She now remembers the bombing of Paris, waking up in a bomb shelter, and going out with her father to empty her potty near a tree. She remembers different locales she fled to with her mother, with or without her father, and where she celebrated her birthdays. She remembers how, during the winter, her father fetched water from a frozen well by breaking the ice and how they grew vegetables in the spring. She has many more memories, but the important ones for understanding the psychological impact of her years as a hidden child, who later in life confronts her father's death and his love for her, are various unconnected vignettes or images: when she cut herself while helping a neighbor peel potatoes and was afraid to go home because she had been spanked twice by her father when she was rude to her mother. The first time she was spanked by him, she had asked her mother to teach her to crochet, and her mother had no time. The second time, she had tangled up some wool, and her mother said she had no time to fix it.

Paulette also remembers going to town with her father and holding his hand, but he was distracted, in deep thought. She remembers he chain-smoked and that he had a pink onyx ring. She also remembers the lullabies he sang to her. The last time Paulette saw her father, he brought her a pastry that she shared with an older playmate, who was hurt when he fell out of a tree. Her father encouraged her to share the pastry with the boy. After her father was deported, Paulette's mother took her across the Swiss border. In a foster home there, Paulette learned to pray, and began to ask God to protect her father. Many months later, her mother told her that her father had been killed. When Paulette realized that God had not answered her prayers, she stopped believing in anything. She also did not respond appropriately, because she had not seen her father for a very long time. For years, Paulette had a "thing in her head" and believed he could not be dead. "For years I used to think, who knows? Intellectually I knew my father was dead. Yet when I saw the movie *Tomorrow Is Forever* I thought he might be alive."

Her mother did not tell Paulette that her father had tried to help them escape. Paulette told me, "I always thought that if he would have loved me enough, he would have escaped from the camp. I didn't know that if he escaped others would get punished. He had a strong sense of right and wrong and wouldn't want to jeopardize other lives. He worked in the underground and he went to Paris because his mother was dying and he got caught." Paulette was probably also angry that he spanked her and sided with her mother. This anger is less conscious than the anger she felt for being abandoned. Paulette now understands that she is mourning her father while also mourning the fact that he did not love her unconditionally.

This summer Paulette plans to go to Europe, and she hopes to retrieve the books that have brought her to this point. She wants to continue working on her creative project and may even write a book when it is finished. Paulette's story exemplifies the complexity of accepting the fact that a loved one has been killed, and she now faces the fourth stage of mourning: the expression of feeling. How can she be angry with someone who suffered so much and was killed in Auschwitz? The feelings that emerge in this phase are survivor guilt, anger, rage, depression, a sense of helplessness, and a need to undo the suffering of the deceased. At times survivors get stuck in this stage and feel too guilty to enjoy their own lives because they feel they should have died instead. There is often an overidentification with the suffering of the deceased, and this can cause psychological challenges if one is stuck in this stage.

Politics can also be a trigger. Amazingly, *glasnost* in the former Soviet Union opened the floodgates of mourning for many survivors and child survivors. Child survivors wanted to search for their rescuers, and rescuers were searching for the children they saved and had given back to their parents, to relatives, or to Jewish agencies.

When I was director of the Jewish Foundation for Christian Rescuers (then housed at the Anti-Defamation League), a man called and told me his wife had been rescued in Lithuania and wanted to know if we could offer the rescuer financial aid.[5] Our representative in Lithuania told us that that the rescuer, whom I'll refer to as Drinka, wanted to visit the United States. The rescuer also sent a letter to the child she saved, Geula, who was then a fifty-one-year-old social worker, married with two children and residing in Pennsylvania. After liberation, Geula was retrieved and raised by an aunt because her parents did not survive.

After living with her parents in the Vilna ghetto for a year, Geula was hidden by a Lithuanian Christian family, whom her father had befriended while they were strolling with a baby carriage outside the ghetto. Geula had no memory of her parents of origin. Despite the fact that Geula was not eager to correspond with her rescuer, Drinka would write to her regularly. Eventually, Drinka lost touch as Geula's family moved around. Once contact was renewed, Geula was ambivalent about seeing her former rescuer, but was being pressured to do so by the local rabbi. He told Geula that the least she could do to repay her rescuer was to bring her to the United States. Geula felt terribly guilty and asked me what she should do. I replied, "Well, if you don't want to bring her, you don't have to." She was relieved when a professional told her she could stop feeling guilty.

At that point, I asked Geula to tell me her story. The story she told came from her aunt; Geula was too young to remember events in a coherent sequence. Geula's father worked outside the Vilna ghetto and returned every night. One day he saw a Christian woman with a stroller and asked her if she would hide his little girl. When Drinka shared this request with her husband, he said, "It must be a sign from God that you were walking there at just that moment. We must take the child." The following night they went to the appointed place and picked up a sack containing Geula, then just a toddler. Her biological father also gave them a piece of paper that had Geula's name written on it. The couple had two children of their own and realized that their neighbors would be suspicious if they had a third child without a pregnancy, so they moved to a neighborhood where no one knew them. As we talked, Geula suddenly remembered that when she was about four years old, she was crying from a nightmare. She went into Drinka's bed and wanted to be held. Instead, Drinka put a finger over her mouth to stop her from making noise and sent her back to her bed. This frightened Geula, and she was very scared of Drinka after that incident. Verbalizing her fears made Geula aware that her childhood feelings about Drinka were not appropriate in the current situation. Geula changed her mind about the visit, and made plans to bring Drinka to the United States and to have her honored by Yad Vashem as one of the Righteous Among the Nations of the World.

Confronting the past, expressing the emotions that come with it, and then doing something meaningful, such as recognizing goodness and paying tribute to a former rescuer, is the essence of channeling feeling into the final stage of mourning. What is of interest is that now, more than sixty-five years after the war, some child survivors are just now shedding the state of denial and are moving into confrontation.

The Hidden Child Foundation in New York receives numerous telephone calls that ask for help in the search for lost family members. But what do you do if you have no information to go on? How could one move from denial to confrontation under such circumstances? Wladyslaw Sidorowicz,[6] a doctor from Ukraine, thought he was Catholic until recently, when he discovered that he and his father did not have matching DNA. His parents were Ukrainians who married before World War II. They had a daughter as well. In retrospect, he recalls that he felt he did not belong to his family. He was different. He had ash blond hair and green eyes, while the rest of his family had black hair and brown eyes. He was academically oriented in a family where intellectual pursuits were forbidden and punished, and although his sister was eight years older than he was, he helped her with her homework.

Wladyslaw's father spent some time in the Gulag and then joined the Polish army formed by the Russians. After the war, the family was reunited in southwestern Poland, but his father had become a different man, a raging alcoholic who was physically abusive. His mother protected the boy from his father's rage, and she paid a heavy price. Later, Wladyslaw finished medical school —third in his class of 250—and when his father fell ill and was hospitalized, Wladyslaw read the medical chart and saw that their blood types did not match. That incident triggered a decades-long quest to find his real father, because his mother refused to give him any information about his past. In 2007, his own daughter suggested that he get his DNA tested, and he was shocked to learn that his DNA is Semitic and that he was not biologically related to the woman he always knew as his mother. She had previously alluded to this, albeit vaguely, by saying to him, "The Sisters saved your life." He estimates that in 1945, when he was between seven and sixteen months old, he was cared for by nuns, who gave him to a family in Ukraine.

"Can you imagine not knowing who you are, what your real name is, or when you were born? Who was left in your family?" he asked. The good doctor moved to South of Fallsburg in upstate New York, where he now lives, and is continuously searching for his lost identity as he studies Judaism. In this case and in others like it, the movement from denial to confrontation is almost an impossible task. We are all defined by our roles in our family, our sexual identity, religious identity, professional identity, and national identity. Living without closure and without an identity impedes adaptation to the real world, and as a result, to this day some child survivors are affected.

At the end of the war, the Jewish children who were hidden were not brought to the town square to be given back to their families or Jewish agencies. Jewish organizations had to hunt them down; lawsuits were rampant in Poland and Holland as families fought to keep children who were not their own. In addition to mourning their own biological parents, many child survivors also had to mourn their foster parents. This became very complicated for those who had a surviving biological parent, or both parents, who wanted loyalty and love expressed to them and not to a stranger. They had no understanding that as a result of their pressure, their child had experienced a loss.

The final stage in the mourning process — the search for meaning — is often misunderstood. Survivors are not searching to find meaning in the murder of their loved ones, or meaning in why God did not protect them from starvation and degradation. They leave that to the philosophers and theologians. Each survivor searches for a way to lead a meaningful, productive, enriching life in the here and now. Some want to assuage their feeling of survivor's guilt by showing others that they are worthy of having survived, so they search for ways to do meaningful work, or choose to become involved in a mission that will make the world a better place. Child survivors grapple with transcending a civilization that went awry. This is a creative process, a form of searching for meaning that is not always conscious. There is a driving force that a survivor may feel but cannot necessarily put it into words. Literary critic Lawrence Langer is correct when he claims he is "dubious" about "wresting meaning" from the literary texts of annihilation.[7] The creative works of survivors or their other endeavors — whether they are work-related or avocational — force the survivor to work through the emotional flood that engulfs them. That effort is of utmost importance because the goal of this phase of mourning is to channel those overwhelming emotions into other avenues so that the survivor can function properly on a daily basis.

The late George Pollock, a psychoanalyst, taught us that creativity is derived from mourning.[8] In psychoanalytic parlance, it is a form of sublimation, and hence a defense against overwhelming feelings. Yet, the creative process does not always alleviate intense emotions and is not a panacea.

Dr. Yehuda Nir, a psychiatrist, wrote the wartime memoir *Lost Childhood*.[9] In it he recounts how his mother survived by working as a maid for a Nazi and how his father was killed. As a boy in hiding, he had many close calls and continues to be consumed with rage toward the Germans. He uses any public forum he can find to express that rage, first in his book and now in the production of an opera based on his book. Nir's rage borders on irrationality when he says that all the rescuers honored by Yad Vashem are bogus, and insists there were no good Germans, Poles, or Hungarians. Nir's case proves that trying to channel deeply rooted emotions through a creative outlet cannot always be successful.

Writing—the literary response—has become a significant way for child survivors to channel their emotions and engage in a creative search for meaning. There are many writers in this category, and the Israeli author, Aharon Appelfeld, who survived the Holocaust as a child in Bukovina, is an excellent example. Thane Rosenbaum, novelist, essayist, literary critic, and law professor, has said that Appelfeld's novels follow a literary motif common to many books written by children who survived the Holocaust. The child is often depicted as born into a world of hiding—a perpetual game of hide-and-seek where the idea is to never be found. Often they are represented as hiding as a Christian, whether in a convent or a farmhouse or racing through forests and towns with an older relative or non-Jewish rescuer. But the reader understands that these children are essentially alone. Surely this is how people understand the circumstances of the child in Jerzy Kosinski's *The Painted Bird*.[10] In Appelfeld's new autobiographical novel, *Blooms of Darkness*,[11] a Jewish boy is saved by a prostitute, who keeps him in her room and hides him in her closet as she services her clients, many of whom are German officers. In the morning, she retrieves him and cares for him; and as the war comes to an end they must flee, and it is the boy who rescues the prostitute who had rescued him.

Unlike Appelfeld, most child survivors are not writers by profession and often just have one book in them. When they write, it is a way to remember those who were murdered in the Holocaust. Their books provide an opportunity to speak in public, to get validation from readers and audiences, and to remember the dead collectively. This was surely true in the case of playwright Arte Shaw, a child survivor from Tashkent, who wrote the Broadway play *The Gathering*, in which a Holocaust survivor, who became an artist, takes his thirteen-year-old grandson on a *bar mitzvah* trip to Bitburg, Germany, to protest President Ronald Reagan's plan to lay a wreath on the graves of the Waffen ss.

The creative approach can take many forms—the visual arts, film, theater, writing, performance, even architecture. It can be done by raising consciousness about man's inhumanity to man through education and human rights work, or by working as lawyers or activists to help others in distress. Another way to search for meaning is by living a life that expresses the continuity of the Jewish people, and connecting to and recapturing the culture that had been damaged or destroyed. There are child survivors at the forefront of keeping the Yiddish and Ladino languages alive, who are immersed in studying Jewish texts, who are raising future generations who will grapple with the quality of Jewish life in the modern world. Some of them are even leaders of Hasidic sects in Brooklyn—for example, the Munkaczer and Dinever dynasties are headed by brothers who are both child survivors.

In every victimized group, myths are created to describe the members of that group. Anecdotal evidence instead of research is often used to support and justify those myths. But myths and legends can be laid to rest. Historical and psychological data now provide evidence of the coping and adaptation mechanism of the population of Holocaust child survivors. We now understand more clearly the enormity of the experience and history of child survivors. We face a twofold challenge: to avoid stigmatizing child survivors and at the same time to validate child survivors' experiences, in order to enable each person to lead a productive life that has a positive impact on society.

The child survivors have taught us all that it is not possible to rush the mourning process, that grieving cannot be measured with an egg timer or a stopwatch. It is not a race. In the aftermaths of more recent genocides— Bosnia, Rwanda, Cambodia, Congo, Sri Lanka—survivors are often forced to speak too soon, when the wounds are too fresh. Many of those genocide survivors, many of them children, are simply not psychologically ready to speak. Truth and Reconciliation commissions, especially in South Africa, force the belief that in order to heal, survivors must immediately testify to what happened, to recount in their own words what they witnessed and how they feel about having survived with the knowledge that others died. We now know that while the intentions were sincere, the process of forcing victims to speak to their losses too soon is unreasonable and psychologically harmful.

What is most important is that genocide survivors be permitted to reenter the world of the living, to experience the simple pleasures of a warm bed or a gentle, reassuring hug, and a secure environment. There will always be time to speak and remember, but testimony, as moral and as important as it may be, is not a substitute for security. Survivors, and especially child survivors, who were forced to become experts in hiding, need to know that it is safe to come out. They are not easily convinced.

The silence will be broken, but not immediately. There is a fine balance between wanting survivors to speak too soon, or too late. It is the responsibility of those in the field of healing others to be patient for the sake of the survivors, and allow them to speak when they are ready. Healing is often a solitary process. Healers are enablers, but not magicians. Healers cannot make pain go away or disappear. They can only create environments where trust is restored and where healing can begin.

NOTES

The author would like to thank Jeanette Friedman, Thane Rosenbaum, and Jerome Chanes for their assistance in preparing this chapter.

1. William Styron, *Sophie's Choice* (New York: Random House, 1979).

2. Joseph Polak, *After the Holocaust the Bells Still Ring* (Jerusalem: Urim, 2015). The memoir won the 2016 National Jewish Book Award in the category of autobiography and memoir.

3. Louis Begley, *Wartime Lies* (New York: Knopf, 1991).

4. This study case is further elaborated on in E. Fogelman, "Mourning a Ghost: A Challenge for Holocaust Child Survivors," in *Healing after Parent Loss in Childhood and Adolescence*, ed. Phyllis Cohen, K. Mark Sossin, and Richard Ruth, 201–17 (New York: Rowman and Littlefield, 2014).

5. This story is further elaborated on in E. Fogelman, "Effects of Interviews with Rescued Child Survivors," in *Children during the Nazi Reign: Psychological Perspective on the Interview Process*, ed. J. S. Kestenberg and E. Fogelman, 81–86 (Westport, CT: Praeger, Greenwood Publishing Group, 1994).

6. Wladyslaw Sidorowicz, "Do You Know Me?" *Hidden Child* 17 (2009): 17.

7. Lawrence L. Langer, "Introduction: On Writing and Reading Holocaust Literature," in *Art from the Ashes: A Holocaust Anthology*, ed. L. L. Langer (New York: Oxford University Press, 1995), 7.

8. G. H. Pollock, "The Mourning-Liberation Process and Creativity: The Case of Käthe Kollowitz," in *The Mourning-Liberation Process*, vol. 2 (Madison, CT: International University Press, 1989), 549–73.

9. Yehuda Nir, *The Lost Childhood: A Memoir* (New York: Harcourt Brace Jovanovich, 1989).

10. Jerzy Kosinski, *The Painted Bird* (New York: Houghton Mifflin, 1965).

11. Aharon Appelfeld, *Blooms of Darkness: A Novel* (New York: Schocken, 2010).

IN DEFENSE OF EYEWITNESS TESTIMONIES

REFLECTIONS OF A WRITER AND CHILD SURVIVOR OF THE HOLOCAUST

In my practice as a writer, I have found children's accounts *more* reliable than accounts of the adults, because children rarely have ideological, political, or other reasons to manipulate information. I like Joanna B. Michlic's characterization that "child survivors' testimonies are hooked on truth." Her view that child survivors' experiences are "worthy of a closer examination and are indispensable in writing the history of wartime childhood" is confirmed by Aharon Appelfeld, a child survivor himself. In his essay "Horror and Art,"[1] he says that adults had a past, a point of reference, while we young children had no such thing. For adults the Holocaust was a period of madness, while for us it was normality. Adults tried to repress their memories, while children accepted them as reality. Attending the meetings of a child-survivors' group for many years, I often heard complaints from group members that they did not receive what the psychologist Eva Fogelman calls "validation of their pain and suffering" and were dismissed as children who "did not know anything." As in many study cases of individual child survivors, I often surprised my mother by recalling details from our Jewish war on the Aryan side. "How did you know that?" she wondered. We children in our formative years had our eyes and ears wide open. At the meetings of child survivors, I also heard complaints from those who had been reunited with relatives in America — in some cases earlier in Western Europe — that their relatives did not want to know and often forbade them to talk about their Holocaust experiences. In some cases one may call it insensitivity, in others a defense mechanism. "Try to forget, I'll reward you for those years, I'll do everything so you'll forget," her father would persuade the heroine of one of my actual stories.[2] Another child survivor is driven mad when she hears a rabbi explaining that the Holocaust was a punishment for the Jews not being pious enough, or a universalistic theory that "the Holocaust was a gift for the world."[3] Adjustment had ambiguous forms: "I feel fine in New York. I like to vanish into crowds on Lexington Avenue and in the subway. I married twice

and didn't try after that. I didn't want to have children. I'd rather be by myself"
—says still another female child survivor.[4] And even in America, where Jews
after the Holocaust were not only tolerated but accepted, a child survivor saved
by Catholic nuns tries to keep her assumed identity: "I felt no guilt or shame
about lying. Had it not been for lies, I would have long been dead. . . . Besides,
I really did not know who I was."[5] I met several people still afraid of their true
identity in the Washington-Baltimore child survivors' group.

My book *Children of Zion*[6] is a selection of children's voices from interviews
compiled in Palestine in 1943 by the Eastern Center for Information of the
Polish Government in Exile. Called *Palestinian Protocols*, they included testimonies of Jewish children who in the fall of 1939 got out or were forced out of
German-occupied Poland and found themselves under the Soviet occupation.
Less than a year later, they were deported with their families to Soviet slave
labor camps, mainly in Siberia. Another year later, under the Moscow-London
agreement and pressure from the Western Allies, they were released from
the camps, where they had lost many members of their families, and moved
south, where they subsequently suffered even heavier family losses because
of starvation and epidemics in the overcrowded cities of Soviet Central Asia.
As orphans or semiorphans, they were evacuated in 1942 with the newly
formed Polish army to Tehran, from where the Jewish Agency brought them
to Palestine. Mostly from small Polish towns and *shtetlech*, the children spoke
about the destruction of those little-known or unknown Jewish communities,
including the mass murder that—according to their accounts—had started as
early as September–October 1939. Named *Yaldei Teheran*, or "Tehran children,"
they were in fact the first survivors of the Holocaust.

In order to extract the child's voice, I cleansed the testimonies of the wooden
style of bureaucratic reporting and the interviewers' interference (which Rita
Horváth calls "overwriting" in her essay on early postwar Hungarian interviews with child survivors). It sometimes required recasting the sentences,
but I never changed the content and tried to retain the basic character of the
child's account. Here are samples from that underreported part of history to
demonstrate the weight and reliability of children's testimonies:

> We lived on the street for three weeks. My father and mother got sick with
> typhus and my little sister and I took care of them.

> We lived with other refugees, most of whom had typhus, dysentery, and
> other diseases. They refused to take them to hospital and most of them
> died as they lay next to us.

> We slept in the open and my parents caught a cold. I tried in vain to get
> the hospital director to admit them. I managed to place them with an

Uzbek but I had nothing for them to eat [. . .]. Finally, I dragged them into a horse-drawn cab — no one helped me — I dropped them in front of the hospital and went back on foot. I was feeling sick and I knew I had typhus.

Many died on the street and there was no one to bury them.

My five-year-old brother, Zissel, got sick. I went every day [to the hospital] to find out how he was. One day I found his little bed empty. They told us he had died and had been buried, but they refused to show us his grave.

I went to find out how my brother was feeling. They told me he had died in the night. I sat in front of the hospital all day waiting to take my brother's body to the cemetery. In the evening, they told me that the funeral had already taken place, but they refused to show me where the grave was.

[My father] was taken to the hospital and I never saw him again. I don't even know where he's buried.

I saw [my mother] fall asleep in such a strange way and then become as hard as stone. For four days, I sat by her and guarded her. Then some strangers came and took her somewhere.

[Papa] slid off his straw mattress onto the floor. I tried to drag him back but he was very heavy . . . His eyes had always been blue but now they were of a completely different color and tears were running from them. I saw my mother die, then my father. They both died of hunger.

My father and mother got sick with typhus. They refused to give us a cart to take them to the hospital. They died on the same day. We cried all night and the next day buried them ourselves.

My father was forty-two, my mother forty-one. I sold their clothes to bury them in the Jewish cemetery in Bukhara, and I had a gravestone erected for them.

My brother Shloime died on the way to the hospital, and Aron in the hospital. We knew we were dying.

[In the orphanage] we would get four hundred grams of bread a day, but we were afraid our father would die of hunger, so my little brother and I would eat only half and give the rest to him so he wouldn't die.

[In the orphanage] we would get three hundred grams of bread a day and a plate of soup. Part of the bread we would take to our older brothers and sisters, even though there was a severe penalty for that.

I would creep out of the orphanage and go to my mother with the bread I didn't eat. One day I found her in such a state that I didn't want to go back to the orphanage, but she would not let me stay.

We had a bad time in the children's home where the Polish children called us dirty Jews, but from time to time, we would sneak out and take whatever we could to our parents.

Since leaving for Tehran, I've had no news of my family, and I'm probably the only one who survived.

I didn't say good-bye to my mother, because I was afraid they would find out I wasn't a complete orphan. What became of her later I don't know.

To this day, I don't know whether my father is alive, or where he is.

Where my parents and brothers are I don't know.

We were seven brothers and sisters. Only I survived.

I had six brothers and three sisters. Now I'm all alone.

When I was left alone in the world, I was brought to Palestine.

We were four children in our home, but only I came to Palestine.[7]

The "Tehran Children's" accounts indicate the Nazis' murderous intentions even before the so-called "Final Solution" that began after the German invasion of the Soviet Union. They also confirm that inhuman mass deportations by freight trains to slave labor camps were a Soviet, not Nazi, invention. Which leads to a question: why a great power that carries on a lucrative trade in oil, natural gas, weapons, and nuclear technology does not pay — and is not even asked to pay — compensation for the slave labor and the deaths of hundreds of thousands of innocent foreign civilians, mostly Poles and Polish Jews?

I have my own evidence supporting Fogelman's statement that "the youngest were the most vulnerable [and] the least likely to survive" — but with some nuances. Two little girls were smuggled out of the Warsaw ghetto at about the same time, late February–early March 1943. Each was entrusted to a gentile woman. Each of the women had received a certain amount of money and kept the girl for a time before passing her on to a Catholic establishment for abandoned children. From there — according to both women — each girl was passed on to an orphanage run by nuns, yet only one survived. As I wrote in *The Victory*[8] (a sequel to *The Jewish War*[9]), my stepfather had brought home a girl from an orphanage hoping she was his daughter. Then another Jewish man appeared claiming she was his child. A Solomon lawsuit followed. Each woman insisted that the child in the courtroom was the one she had helped to save. Eventually, the other party produced a nun who had saved the girl's original birth certificate proving she was the other man's daughter, and my stepfather lost his child—for the second time. Afraid of causing pain, I did not dare to ask about more details; but more than fifty years later, I had a chance to see copies of the protocols from the court proceedings. According to witness testimonies, one girl was about one year older than the other. The younger, born in October 1939, did not even know she was Jewish. I remember that she insisted on not being Jewish, no matter how hard we tried to convince her that it is not so bad to be a Jew . . . The older girl, on the other hand, knew *too* much and—as the woman in court said—"She talked too much," in particular about her time in the ghetto. The court came to no conclusion on what had happened to the five-year-old who "knew too much," but it transpired from the testimonies that she had been abandoned in the street and picked up by police, who of course asked her a few questions. I was in Warsaw with my mother at the same time (from March through June 1943), and as I wrote in *The Jewish War*, one day I got lost in the street. I knew too much, too; but I was six and a half, and I knew I should *not* "talk too much."[10] Thus, in the first case, the younger child had a better chance of survival than the older, while in my own case the opposite was true.

A younger child could be more easily adopted; but an older child had a chance to be hired by a farmer, and I knew such survivors among my peers. There was also a special category of children: street-smart youths who crossed the Warsaw ghetto walls back and forth, and who after the liquidation of the Ghetto became homeless on the Aryan side. I remember boys who sold cigarettes in the street, screaming: *"Papierosy swojaki, papieros!"* "*Swojaki*" meant "homemade" (not in the sense that they were healthier, but cheaper). About ten years ago, I read a memoir by Joseph Ziemian, *The Cigarette Sellers of Three Crosses Square*.[11] It turns out that most of the cigarette sellers were Jewish. I also remember boys and girls singing in the courtyards and on streetcars and trains. They sang forbidden but very popular anti-German songs, and they too appear in Ziemian's book as homeless Jewish orphans on their own, whom he regularly contacted and helped on behalf of *Żydowski Komitet Narodowy* (Jewish National Committee).

My mostly autobiographical short novel *The Jewish War* is divided into two parts: "The Father" and "The Mother," as if especially for Dalia Ofer's research on the roles of men and women. In the first part, Father is the leader. He decides when to run and where to hide, provides food and shelter, and does everything that is expected from a caring husband and father. He is resourceful, tenacious, courageous, yet he is losing the war one step after another. In the second part, Mother takes over. She decides to obtain forged Aryan identity cards and to move to Warsaw. Father is against it, but he cannot stop her. The question was: who could save the child? He wanted to keep me, because she had a better chance of survival without a little boy who was circumcised; yet she insisted that only she could save me, and she was proven right. This was one of those "role-reversals between husbands and wives," about which Lenore Weitzman wrote in her essay included in this volume. *The Jewish War*, which is more than an autobiography, emphasizes the universal difference between the masculine and the feminine elements, pointing out that under certain existential circumstances the more flexible feminine element with its unconventional ways and means is the winner.

The famous pedagogue and educator Janusz Korczak (1878–1942), in his diary written in the Warsaw ghetto, quotes a boy from his orphanage who wrote in an essay: "My father was a fighter for a piece of bread."[12] It was always my view as a witness that in the Nazis' war against unarmed Jewish civilians — which I had called "the Jewish war" as early as 1965 — fleeing, hiding, and obtaining food for the family was a form of resistance and defiance. Everybody was a fighter in that war — no matter what gender or age.

In the Warsaw ghetto — as in the Kraków ghetto from which Joanna Sliwa, in her chapter, has cited so many painful details — children often became the sole providers for their family, and risked and lost their lives in the process. In Lodz, which had been annexed by the Reich, the ghetto was so isolated from the Polish Aryan side that no interaction was possible. There the children fought for their lives by slaving as hard as adult laborers and — as in the Kraków ghetto situation presented by Sliwa — pretending they were older than their actual age. Her remark that ironically the ghetto was often "the only safe place to be" is reminiscent of the bitter diary of Calel Perechodnik (1916–1944), who wrote that because the Jews were robbed, blackmailed, informed on, tricked, deceived, and exposed even by people who ostensibly offered them shelter, they came out of their hiding places and returned to the ghetto to be together with other Jews, which meant to die among the Jews rather than in a hostile territory where it was hard to tell a friend from a foe. Mentioning an acquaintance who had managed to jump out of a train to Treblinka, Perechodnik bitterly comments that "had Kejzman known what lies ahead for him, he would have remained in the train."[13]

In the memoirs of Jan Kostański, which I coauthored with him,[14] Jan, a gentile teenager at the time, recalls not only the street cigarette sellers, but also boys who helped the Polish national underground as smugglers of arms and supplies, and as messengers during the Warsaw Uprising of August–September 1944. Popular and generally admired like the Parisian *gavroches*, many of those children fell in the fighting and were buried under crosses, as nobody knew their Jewish identity. In most cases, they were the same street-smart youths who before the annihilation of the ghetto had smuggled food in.

They are also remembered by Bogdan (Dawid) Wojdowski (1930–1994) in his *Bread for the Departed*,[15] which in my opinion is not only one of the best Holocaust novels, but also a reliable—though "subjective"—eyewitness testimony.

Most Holocaust accounts published in America follow a pattern: first an idyll, then a disaster, then fight or flight for survival, and finally the victory of good over evil. But in reality there was no idyll. There was a disaster and fight or flight for survival, but no true victory, and no happy ending. The Holocaust was a tragedy without a catharsis. Anne Frank's "cathartic" statement: "In spite of everything, I still believe people are really good at heart"[16] was written before her arrest and arrival at Auschwitz and Bergen-Belsen. Alvin Rosenfeld doubts she could have retained that view in the barracks, where she was dying an inhuman slow death with thousands of others.[17] A girl exactly her age, who was dying there at the same time yet miraculously survived, says at the end of her narrative in my *Drohobycz, Drohobycz and Other Stories*: "The world had ended and I was supposed to go on living, I didn't know how."[18] All the other narrators in that collection of documentary stories also coped with this existential question.

An Oscar-winning documentary film tells the story of a young Jewish woman who survived deportation and slave labor; married her liberator, a U.S. Army officer who happened to be Jewish; and had children and grandchildren—a happy ending. But a Holocaust story does not end there. The "wall of silence in the families" that Uta Larkey discusses in her essay is confirmed by Ruth Wajnryb, who interviewed twenty-seven men and women of the second generation born and brought up in Australia. She writes that parents kept silent, because they did not want to pass their suffering on to their children; and the children did not ask, so as not to reawake their parents' pain—thus both sides mutually protected each other. Moreover, children were afraid of what they might learn. The silence did not help: the children felt their parents' pain and in addition feared what was unknown to them, and in this way the trauma was being passed on.[19] The documentary about a Holocaust survivor who happily lives ever after had simply ended too early. Had it lasted a little longer, it would have ended on a different note. After my own experience with return to the place of tragedy—recorded by a documentary film entitled *Birthplace*[20]—I seriously doubt whether Deb Filler, the comedienne cited by Larkey, really understood her father's trip to his hometown if she found that experience "cathartic."

A digression: Larkey has mentioned Daniel Vogelmann of the second generation. Daniel's half-sister Sissel was born in 1935 in Florence and arrested on December 20, 1943, with her father, Schulim Vogelmann, originally of Przemyślany, Poland, and her mother Anna Disegni, the daughter of the chief rabbi of Turin. Deported on January 30, 1944, from Milan with transport no. 07, they arrived on February 6 at Auschwitz, where Sissel and her mother were immediately put to death. Her father survived as prisoner no. 173484, and after the war married Albana Mondolfi of Bologna. Daniel, their son, was born in 1948 in Florence. In 1980 he founded the publishing house La Giuntina, specializing in Jewish subjects. (La Giuntina published, among other pieces, some of my short stories in Italian translation).[21] Daniel Vogelmann has written several collections of poetry, including a cycle about his half-sister Sissel, which I have translated into Polish. His father, before his death at seventy-one, said that after Auschwitz he is 2071 years old, and I know that his son Daniel is not a happy man.

The Victory, which I wrote more than forty years ago, is still a rare literary attempt at dealing with the aftermath of the Holocaust and the absence of actual victory or even catharsis. I am one of those child survivors for whom — as Michlic put it — "the war did not end in 1945." In my preteen group in the Jewish children's home at Helenówek near Lodz, we did not speak about the past, but about the present and future. A reflection on this came later when we were growing up and saw the void around us. The other reason why we kept silent about our past was that nobody asked us about it: "You were too young to know." But we did know, or at least felt and internalized our fear. In a collection of accounts entitled The Last Witnesses: Children of the Holocaust Speak, a woman who survived, passing as a gentile child, recalls that after the liberation, "The people I liked the most were those who looked the least Jewish. Those who looked the most Jewish scared me. I ran as far away from them as I could."[22]

I felt something similar. After intensive Catholic instruction, culminating in confession and communion (though without baptism), I did not want to become a Jew again. The priest did not intend to instill hatred, but if one believed the story of Jesus, one could not help resenting the Jews; and so for some time after the liberation, I insisted on saying my nightly prayers and going to church on Sunday. Children felt much safer within a religion that "saved" them from being Jewish. I suppose that retrieving Jewish children from convents and Catholic families was complicated by this crucial factor. Such must have been the situation in Poland, Belgium, and France, with Cardinal Aaron Jean-Marie Lustiger (1926–2007) as perhaps the best-known case in point.

The Jewish children's home in Helenówek helped me become a Jewish child again. There we were taught work ethics, collectivism, and shituf,[23] not unlike in a kibbutz. As I depicted it in The Victory, the few survivors from my mother's shtetl Dobre moved to a common apartment in Lodz and shared their income from a common stand in the marketplace, as well as food from a common kitchen as in a kibbutz. About a dozen demobilized Jewish soldiers shared an apartment, where we Jewish boys liked to visit them, and they liked to see us.

Orphaned adolescents flocked to a Jewish *bursa* and lived there as one family. After I left Helenówek and returned to my mother and stepfather in Lodz, I spent my after-school time at Zionist youth clubs. In addition to ping-pong and chess (the traditional Jewish sports), we practiced boxing. Gabriel Finder writes that boxing in the Jewish Displaced Person camps had psychological appeal as a way to develop courage, agility, and self-defense skills.[24] It had the same appeal for us Jewish boys in postwar Lodz. Many of us were signed up with kibbutzim, so that we could be taken out of Poland before our parents would be able to leave. Most boys and girls in the Lodz Jewish day school, which I started attending in 1947, were wearing the various colors of Zionist organizations; and every break between classes resounded with singing and dancing the *hora*. Zionism seemed to be — as Avi Patt put it in his chapter in this book — "an obvious conclusion to wartime experiences and the postwar anti-Semitism," and the Zionist youth movement seemed "the best response to the psychological needs" of survivors, especially the young. Zionist emissaries may have facilitated the mass exodus from Poland, but they did not need to exert much influence.

In my collection *Drohobycz, Drohobycz*, the most optimistic story is one that ends in Israel: "When I landed here, the young man who received refugees held out his arms to me. I stayed in his arms. God wanted to repair the wrong, and I was born a second time — when I placed my feet on this ground and when I gave birth to my children here."[25] But it was not always the case. Amos Oz remembers that Holocaust survivors were resented as those who "went to death like sheep," and their stories evoked not empathy but shame.[26] Aharon Appelfeld, who came to then-Palestine in 1946, was one of those who had to cope with such an unfriendly climate: "What could we, boys of twelve, do with so many memories of death? Relate to them, live them? We learned to keep quiet."[27] "One had to suppress the trauma and keep silent, because nobody was able to listen to it, and if they did, they did not understand," confirms Irit Amiel, another child survivor from Poland.[28] Most of the protagonists of her true stories never regained mental balance,[29] and some assumed false identities as native "*sabras*," changing even the biographies of their parents. My mother, who lived in Israel from 1957 to 1960, was on several occasions shamed for "not fighting back." Let me once again testify: 1) My father was one of the fighters for a piece of bread, and thanks to him my mother and I survived the first phase of our Jewish war; and 2) my father and mother did more fighting than the members of the armed young men and women in the Warsaw ghetto, and my mother won. Of my childhood friends, the most successful in Israel were those who had survived the war in Soviet Russia and as such did not have to face any "shame." The situation has changed after the "revelations" of the Adolf Eichmann trial, which for us survivors were not revealing at all.

On May 9, 1995—fifty years after the greatest disaster in Jewish history—I was in Tel Aviv, the most beautiful of Jewish cities. I stood in a hotel window overlooking the sea, where ships of the Jewish navy were parading, and from behind the horizon emerged fighter planes marked with the blue six-pointed star by which our enemies degraded us in our past. With supersonic speed, the jets came straight at the skyscraper buildings and in the last split second vertically rose up into the pure blue of the Mediterranean sky. This *was* cathartic, and I lived to see and feel it. The Zionist dream had saved over half a million Jews and millions of their descendants; nobody had saved more Jewish lives. I truly respect the sincere dedication of the Bundists and idealistic Jewish communists, but it is the Zionists who have liberated us, and I do not believe there ever was a more miraculous miracle. Or that there ever will be. What worries me is the short memory of the people who do not appreciate it.

NOTES

1. Aharon Appelfeld, lecture at the Second International Conference of Hidden Children, Jerusalem, July 12–15, 1993.

2. Henryk Grynberg, *Drohobycz, Drohobycz and Other Stories*, trans. Alicia Nitecki (New York: Penguin Books, 2002), 84.

3. Ibid., 140–41.

4. Ibid., 203.

5. Ibid., 216.

6. Henryk Grynberg, *Children of Zion*, trans. Jacqueline Mitchell (Evanston, IL: Northwestern University Press, 1997). Originally published as *Dzieci Syjonu* (Warsaw: Karta, 1994).

7. Ibid., 133–66.

8. Henryk Grynberg, *The Victory*, (Evanston, IL: Northwestern University Press, 1993). Originally published as *Zwycięstwo* (Paris: Institute Litteraire, 1969), 77–83.

9. Henryk Grynberg, *The Jewish War* (Evanston, IL: Northwestern University Press, 2001). Previously published in English as *Child of the Shadows* (London: Vallentine, Mitchell, 1969). Originally published as *Żydowska wojna* (Warsaw: Czytelnik, 1965).

10. Ibid., 33–35.

11. Joseph Ziemian, *The Cigarette Sellers of Three Crosses Square* (New York: Avon Books, 1977). Originally published as *Papierosiarze z Placu Trzech Krzyży* (Warsaw: Niezależna Oficyna Wydawnicza, 1989).

12. Janusz Korczak, *Pamiętnik* in *Wybór pism Korczaka*, t. 4 (Warsaw, 1958), 573.

13. Calel Perechodnik, *Czy ja jestem mordercą* (Warsaw: Karta, 1995), 92.

14. Henryk Grynberg and Jan Kostański, *Szmuglerzy* (Warsaw: Twój Styl, 2001). Republished in Henryk Grynberg, *Janek i Maria* (Warsaw: Świat Książki, 2006).

15. Northwestern University Press, 1997. Originally published as *Chleb rzucony umarłym* (Warsaw: P.I.W., 1971).

16. Quote after Alvin Rosenfeld, "Anne Frank and the Future of Holocaust Memory," Joseph and Rebecca Meyerhoff Annual Lecture, United States Holocaust Memorial Museum, October 14, 2004.

17. Ibid.

18. Henryk Grynberg, *Drohobycz, Drohobycz and Other Stories*, trans. Alicia Nitecki (New York: Penguin Books, 2002), 12. Originally published as *Drohobycz, Drohobycz* (Warsaw: W.A.B., 1997).

19. Ruth Wajnryb, *The Silence: How Tragedy Shapes Talk* (Sydney: Allen and Unwin, 2001).

20. *Miejsce urodzenia*, directed by Paweł Łoziński, "Kronika" Film and Television Productions, Warsaw, 1992.

21. Henryk Grynberg, *Ritratti di famiglia*, trans. Claudio and Maria Madonia (Florence: La Giuntina, 1994).

22. Wiktoria Sliwowska, *The Last Eyewitnesses: Children of the Holocaust Speak*, vol. 2 (Evanston, IL: Northwestern University Press, 2005), 35.

23. Hebrew for "common property."

24. Gabriel Finder, "Boxing for Everyone: Jewish DPs, Sports, and Boxing," in *Studies in Contemporary Jewry*, vol. 23: *Jews and the Sporting Life*, ed. Ezra Mendelsohn, 36-53 (New York: Oxford University Press, 2009).

25. Grynberg, *Drohobycz, Drohobycz and Other Stories*, 57.

26. Amos Oz, *Opowieść o miłości i mroku* (Warsaw: MUZA, 2005), 17-18. First published in English as *A Tale of Love and Darkness* (Boston: Houghton Mifflin Harcourt, 2004); originally published in Hebrew as *Sipur al ahava ve-khoshekh* (Jerusalem: Keter, 2002).

27. Aharon Appelfeld, "A Testimony," lecture at the conference on *The Survival and Transformation of Jewish Cultural and Religious Values in Literature after World War Two*, Bellagio, Italy, November 20-25, 1982.

28. Irit Amiel, *Wdychać głęboko* (Izabelin, PL: Świat Literacli, 2002), 6.

29. Irit Amiel, *Scorched* (London: Vallentine, Mitchell, 2006). Originally published as *Osmaleni* (Izabelin, PL: Świat Literacki, 1999).

BOAZ COHEN, a historian, is the chair of the Holocaust Studies Program at Western Galilee College in Akko, Israel, and senior lecturer at Shaanan College in Haifa, Israel. He is the author of *Israeli Holocaust Research: Birth and Evolution* (2013), editor of *Was Their Voice Heard? The Early Holocaust Testimonies of Child Survivors* (in Hebrew, 2016), and coeditor of *Holocaust and Film* (2013) and *Survivor Historians* (2015). His current research is on early Holocaust historiography, Holocaust testimonies, and early testimonies of child survivors and adult interest in them.

GABRIEL N. FINDER is Ida and Nathan Kolodiz Director of Jewish Studies and associate professor in the Department of Germanic Literatures and Languages at the University of Virginia. He coedited with Eli Lederhendler, *A Club of Their Own: Jewish Humorists and the Contemporary World*, volume 29 of *Studies in Contemporary Jewry* (forthcoming 2016), and with Laura Jockusch, *Jewish Honor Courts: Revenge, Retribution, and Reconciliation in Europe and Israel after the Holocaust* (a 2015 National Jewish Book Award finalist in the Holocaust category). He is coauthoring a book with Alexander Prusin on the Polish trials of Nazi war criminals from the end of World War II to 1960, and is writing a book on the Polish Jewish honor court from 1946 to 1950.

EVA FOGELMAN is a psychologist in private practice in New York City. She is codirector of International Study of Organized Persecution of Children, a project of Child Development Research and the Kestenberg Holocaust Child Survivor Archive at the Hebrew University of Jerusalem. Dr. Fogelman is the author of the Pulitzer Prize-nominated book *Conscience and Courage: Rescuers of Jews during the Holocaust*. She is currently working on a sequel to her award-winning documentary *Breaking the Silence: The Generation after the Holocaust*.

KINGA FROJIMOVICS, a historian and archivist, is director of the Hungarian section in Yad Vashem Archives and a project researcher at the Vienna Wiesenthal Institute for Holocaust Studies. She is author of the book *I Have Been a Stranger in a Strange Land: The Hungarian State and Jewish Refugees in Hungary, 1933-1945* (2007). Her current research project focuses on Hungarian Jewish forced laborers in Vienna in 1944-1945.

HENRYK GRYNBERG, child survivor of the Holocaust, is a Polish poet, essayist, and novelist living in the United States since 1967. Available in English are his *Children of Zion* (1997); *The Jewish War and the Victory* (2001); and *Drohobycz, Drohobycz and Other Stories* (2002, which was awarded the 2002 Koret Jewish Book Award).

RITA HORVÁTH, a literary scholar and historian, is a research fellow at the International Institute for Holocaust Research in Yad Vashem and a research associate at the Hadassah-Brandeis Institute at Brandeis University. She is author of *The History of the National Relief Committee for Deportees, 1944-1952* (1997) and coauthor, with Anna Szalai and Gabor Balazs, of *Previously Unexplored Sources on the Holocaust in Hungary* (2007). Her current research project focuses on testimonies of child Holocaust survivors.

UTA LARKEY is an associate professor at Goucher College. She coauthored the book *Life and Loss in the Shadow of the Holocaust: A Jewish Family's Untold Story* (2011). Her current research project focuses on Jewish displaced persons (DP) camps in postwar Germany.

JENNIFER MARLOW is an assistant professor of European history at Bethel University in McKenzie, Tennessee. She is currently finishing her book manuscript entitled, "Jewish Families and Catholic Domestic Servants in Poland, 1919-1950." Dr. Marlow's research interests include Polish-Jewish relations, Holocaust rescue, and childhood.

JOANNA BEATA MICHLIC is a social and cultural historian, and founder and director of the HBI (Hadassah-Brandeis Institute) Project on Families, Children, and the Holocaust at Brandeis University. She teaches at Leo Baeck College, London, and is a senior honorary research associate at the UCL Centre for Collective Violence, Holocaust and Genocide Studies, London. Her major publications include *Neighbors Respond: The Controversy about Jedwabne* (2004; coedited with Antony Polonsky); *Poland's Threatening Other: The Image of the Jew from 1880 to the Present* (2006); and *Bringing the Dark Past to Light: The Reception of the Holocaust in Postcommunist Europe*, coedited with John-Paul Himka (2012). She is currently working on two monographs on the history of Jewish child survivors, 1944-1950, and rescuers of Jews in Poland: history and memory.

DALIA OFER is Max and Rita Haber Professor of Holocaust and East European Studies at the Hebrew University of Jerusalem (emerita). Her book *Escaping the Holocaust: Illegal Immigration to the Land of Israel* (in Hebrew, 1990; English translation, 1998) received the 1992 Ben Zvi Award and a National Jewish Book Award. She coedited with Lenore J. Weitzman, *Women in the Holocaust* (1999), and with Françoise S. Ouzan and Judy Tydor Baumel-Schwartz, *Holocaust Survivors: Resettlement, Memories, Identities* (2012). She is also editor of *Israel in the Eyes of the Survivors* (in Hebrew, 2015), and *The History of the Jewish Police in the Viliampole (Kovno) Ghetto* (in Hebrew, 2016). She is currently researching the topic of family in East European ghettos during the Holocaust.

AVINOAM PATT is the Philip D. Feltman Professor of Modern Jewish History at the Maurice Greenberg Center for Judaic Studies at the University of Hartford, Connecticut. He is the author of *Finding Home and Homeland: Jewish Youth and Zionism in the Aftermath of the Holocaust* (2009); coeditor, with Michael Berkowitz, of a collected volume on Jewish displaced persons, titled *We Are Here: New Approaches to the Study of Jewish Displaced Persons in Postwar Germany* (2010); and coeditor, with Mark Shechner and Victoria Aarons, of *The New Diaspora: The Changing Face of American Jewish Fiction* (2015). He is currently coediting a new volume on "The JDC at 100" and conducting research for a new book on the early postwar memory of the Warsaw Ghetto Uprising.

JOANNA SLIWA is a PhD candidate at the Strassler Center for Holocaust and Genocide Studies at Clark University in Worcester, Massachusetts, and a Saul Kagan Fellow in Advanced Shoah Studies (Claims Conference). Her current research examines daily life during the Holocaust in Kraków, Poland, through Jewish children's experiences.

KENNETH WALTZER is professor emeritus of history at Michigan State University and former director of MSU's Jewish Studies Program. He is completing a book on the rescue of children and youths at Buchenwald and was the historical consultant in the making of the film *Kinderblock 66: Return to Buchenwald*.

LENORE J. WEITZMAN has been a professor at the University of California, Stanford University, and Harvard University, and is currently the Robinson Professor of Sociology and Law (emeritus) at George Mason University in Virginia. She is the author of five books, including the award-winning *The Divorce Revolution*, which won several academic awards and led to the passage of fourteen new laws in the state of California. She coedited *Women in the Holocaust*, with Dalia Ofer, a finalist for two Jewish Book Awards, and is now completing a book on the "*Kashariyot*," the young women who were secret "couriers" for the Jewish resistance during the Holocaust.

Note: page numbers followed by n refer to notes, with note number.

Historical Commission), 201-2, 204, 205, 206

children's testimony: avoidance of loved ones' deaths in, 180-86, 189-90, 191; children reluctant to give, xxiii; collection of, xviii, 200, 201, 205-6; intertexual narrative in, 191; language used for, 187-88; locating traumatic memory in, 179-92; narrative types employed in, 177, 190-92; postwar accounts, value of, 28; status as evidence, x, xvi, xvii-xix, 27-28, 153-54, 167-68, 169nn5-6, 199, 203-7, 234, 249; as therapeutic, 206; wealth of, 153. See also *The Children Accuse* (Central Jewish Historical Commission); *'Ehad me-'ir u-shenayim mi-mishpahah* (Tenenbaum, ed.)

child survivors: avenues for sharing stories, 238-39; in Britain, xxi; critical events of postwar period, 154; disrupted development in, ix, 156, 234-35; distrust of adults in, 163-64, 198; double-identity performances in, 164-65; education deficits in, 154, 156, 167, 235, 236; guilt/shame felt by, 56, 59, 90, 191, 210, 242-43; healing ability of, as compromised, 234-35; heterogeneity of, 235; and loss of family, effects of, 157; loss of identity in, xv-xvi, 111, 112, 117-18, 120, 122, 156, 158, 159-60, 163, 237, 244-45, 256; means of survival in, 155; as neglected group, 233-34; neglect of by parents, 234; 1.5 generation, 238; and ongoing antisemitism, 138, 139-40, 164-66; parents' efforts to recover, xx, 120, 121, 123, 159, 245, 252-53; and recovery of identity, xv-xvi, 141-42, 146, 147, 148, 197-98, 256-57; rejection of stigmatized Jewish identity by, 166-67, 250, 256; repressed memories, return of, x, xv-xvi, 241-42; and rescuer-caregivers, difficulty in leaving, 157-60, 167; sense of divided self in, 156; successful careers of, 235-36; uncanny maturity of, 203-4, 206-7; yearning for home in,

157, 167. *See also* mourning process in child survivors; orphans

child survivors, young: increasing opportunities to be heard, 238; lack of agency in, 154; lack of basic socialization in, 156; lack of memories in, as misconception, 237, 249, 256; loss of childhood in, 156; memories in, as disjointed, 238

clothing, marked, requirements for, 36, 73

confiscation of Jewish property, 71, 110-11, 220

creativity, as product of mourning, 237, 245-47

Czerniaków, Adam, 48, 203-4

Daum, Menachem, 218-19

Davidson, Shamai, 103-5

Deutsch, Izráel, 67, 69-71, 74, 76, 81n2

documentation on ghetto life, limitations of, 3, 7, 10, 11, 21, 22, 28

documents, survivors' lack of, xxii, 244-45, 252-53

Dror, 134, 135, 146

Dwork, Debórah, xix, 27-28

Dzieci oskarżają (Central Jewish Historical Commission), 201-2, 204, 205, 206

Eastern European Jews, as focus of this work, xi, xx, 51

education: anti-Jewish laws and, 71; child survivors' need for, 154, 156, 167, 235, 236; gender-based distinctions in, 5; public, Jews and, 4

Educational Institute for the Blind (Budapest), 69

'Ehad me-'ir u-shenayim mi-mishpahah (Tenenbaum, ed.): collection of testimonies for, 200, 201, 207n15; concerns about believability of, 203-5, 206-7; contents, described, 200-201; evidentiary photocopies of testimonies in, 201, 203-4; maturity of children and, 203-4, 206-7; origins of, 198-99; testimonies in as unmediated, 202-3, 204-5; Zionist slant of, 201-2

Eichmann, Adolf, 75, 87, 257

Hanegbi, David, 197, 199, 203, 204–5

Hashomer Hatzair (Young Guard): break-off from other Zionists, 141, 151n34; *Bricha* and, 146; and child-parent relations, 19; children's homes in Poland, 197, 200, 201; education programs, 136; leaders of, 135; organization of kibbutzim, 134; political goals of, 146; as surrogate family, 131; Tenenbaum and, 196–97, 207n15; and Warsaw Ghetto Uprising, 196–97; Zionist mission of, 198, 201. *See also* kibbutz groups, postwar

healing: as compromised process in child survivors, 234–35; mourning and, 210; second- and third-generation survivors' search for, 210, 217, 219, 221, 225–26, 228. *See also* mourning process in child survivors

heroic traditions, *vs.* realities, xxiii–xxiv

Hidden Child Foundation, 243–44

hidden children: bonds with rescuers, xxiv, 111, 112, 114, 122; neglect of testimony by, xxii–xxiii; parents' yearning for, 23; recovery of as Jewish priority, 123; renewed public presence of, xxiii; social networks established by, xxii–xxiii, 239; unreturned, 234, 244–45

Hiding and Seeking (Daum film), 218–19

hiding of adults: inside ghettos, 32–33, 34, 59–60, 71; outside ghetto, 120–21

hiding of belongings, 12, 14, 15, 17–18

hiding of children: deaths resulting from, 34; penalties for, 26–27

hiding of children inside ghettos during raids, 26, 31–34, 41, 59–60

hiding of children outside ghettos: and abuse by caretakers, xxiv, 160–64; and blackmail by caretakers, 120, 162; and caregiver demands for permanent custody, 120, 121, 123, 159, 245; and danger of informants, 32; false ID and, 158; in Soviet Union, 155, 200, 207n15. *See also* gentiles passing off Jewish child as relative; smuggling of children from ghetto

Hirsch, Marianne, 214–215, 218

history, broad *vs.* narrow definition of, 173

Hitler, Adolf, 68, 76

Holocaust: child deaths in, xvii, 123, 155, 234; deaths of Polish Jews, 123; impossibility of happy ending in stories about, 255–56; Jews in, as fighters, 254, 257; as ongoing trauma, xxiii

Holocaust survivor movement, 237–38

Hungary: anti-Jewish laws in, 71, 73, 74, 83n23; "exempted" Jews in, 74, 76; German invasion of, 71, 72, 87; ghettoization and deportations in, 72, 75–76, 82–83n23, 87; yellow-star houses in, 74, 75, 76, 83n23, 83n29

Ichud, 134

International Red Cross, 76, 77–78, 79; Tracing Services records, 86, 96

Israel: as Jewish safe haven, 258; shaming of survivors in, 257; survivor careers in, 236; War of Independence, 234. *See also* Zionism

Israelite Deaf (and Mute) Institute (Berlin), 68–69

Jewish Displaced Persons (DPs): adoption of Hebrew by, 187–88; collection of children's testimony from, 200, 201; as demoralized, 136; difficulties of life for, 137; evacuation from Poland, 200; as issue, and decision to create Israel, 132; predominance of young adults among, 133, 149n3; sense of collective responsibility in, 147

Jewish Historical Commissions, xviii, 198, 201, 206

Kalina, Antonin, 95, 96, 101, 102

Kanizsai, Dezső, 67, 69, 70, 71, 72, 74, 79

Kasztner train, 74–75, 80, 83n27

kibbutz groups, postwar: and decision to create Israel, 132, 146–47, 148–49; education programs in, 136; growth of, 133–34, 146; names of, 134–35, 150n14; new members' limited ideological interest, 132, 136; path to Israel, 146; percentage of Jewish youth joining, 134; reasons for youths' interest in, 133, 136, 139–40, 147, 149, 152n48, 257; rescue of young Jews as priority of, 140; sense of collective responsibility in, 147; sense of identity provided by, 147, 148; as surrogate family, 131, 132, 133, 137, 141, 147; vital impact of, 136–37. See also Kibbutz Tosia Altman

Kibbutz Tosia Altman: agricultural training by, 145, 146; in American zone of Germany, 135, 142–47; and collective thinking, transition to, 140–41; cultural and ideological education in, 141–42, 146, 147, 148; daily life in, 141; diary of, 135, 140; formation of, 134–35; and gender roles, 141; journey to Israel, 135, 145; low ideological interest of new members, 141; mock trial of departing member in, 143–45; morale-boosting measures, 143–45, 147–48; naming of, 135; reasons for joining, 137–40; as surrogate family for survivors, 141, 145, 147

Kibbutz Mishmar Ha-emek, xxii
Kielce pogrom, 124, 128n67, 201
Kraków, expulsion of Jews from, 29
Kraków ghetto: children's active resistance in, 27, 31, 32, 33, 36, 40–41; creation of, 27, 29; deportations to/from, 30, 35; forced labor in, 30–31; hiding of children in, 31–34; liquidation of, 27, 30, 38, 39, 40, 115–16; major German actions in, 30; number of residents, 29–30; smuggling of children from, 26, 37–40, 115; smuggling of children into, 35; smuggling of goods by children in, 26, 36–37

Langenstein-Zwieberge camp, 98, 99, 100
Langer, Lawrence, xix, 173, 175, 176, 179, 245
Law for the Prevention of Offspring with Hereditary Diseases (1934), 68
Levi, Primo, 86, 175
Ligocka, Roma, 33, 34, 38, 40

Lodz, as postwar center of Jewish life, 197
Lodz (Litzmannstadt) ghetto: deportations from, 9; deportations to, 9, 53–54; food shortages in, 7; isolation of, 23, 254; life in, 10, 20–21, 22; liquidation of, 60; portraits of, 64–65n21. See also Through the Window of My Home (Selver-Urbach)
Lodz Ghetto Chronicle, 7–10, 21

mourning process in child survivors, 237–48; and creativity, 237, 245–47; "denial" stage of, 239–42, 245; difficulty in articulating memories and, 238; "expression of feeling" stage, 242–45; facilitation of, 246–47; factors affecting, 237; guilt and, 242–43; "search for meaning stage" in, 245–47; shock of witnessing loved-one's death and, 239; time required for, 246–47; unknown fate of loved ones and, 240–42; validation from others and, 237–39, 249; writing as tool for, 246

nannies, hiding of children by, 110–24
National Institute for the Israelite Deaf-Mute (Budapest), 69–79; closing of by Communists, 79; closing of by Nazis, 72; deportation of students to Pest ghetto, 78–79; early history of, 69; efforts to protect children, 73, 80–81; internment camp at, 74–75; internment camp raids by Arrow-Cross, 76, 77–78; life before invasion, 71–72; non-Jewish students in, 69, 82n9; postwar operation of, 79; relocation of students to orphanage, 72; student experience at, 70–71; students backgrounds in, 69–70; students' postwar return to, 67, 79
Neolog Jewish Community of Pest, 69, 71, 79
Night (Wiesel), 85, 86, 88, 90–91, 93, 102, 188

Ofer, Dalia, xix, 48, 51, 253
One from a City and Two from a Family (Tenenbaum). See 'Ehad me-'ir

u-shenayim mi-mishpahah (Tenenbaum, ed.)

Operation T-4, 68

Orlovich, Nesia, 197, 198, 200

Orphanage for Boys of the (Neolog) Jewish Community of Pest, 72-74

orphans: appeal of Zionism to, xxi-xxii, 134; jealousy of children with parents, 157, 170-71n23; lingering sense of loss in, xxii, xxiv, 157

Otwock ghetto, 12-18, 23

parents: children's estrangement from in 1930s, 5-6, 19; culturally defined roles of, 4, 5, 16, 21-22, 46; of deported children, loss of will to live in, 22; focus on economic responsibilities, 5, 6; hardships of early 20th century and, 4; of hidden children, yearning of, 23; middle-class, access to gentile supporters, 23; and returned child, restoring relations with, xxiv, 234; single mothers, risk of deportation for, 9-10; stress-induced conflict between, 13-14, 16. *See also* family life; social roles of family members

passing as gentile: characteristics required for, 44-45n46; circumcision and, 37, 117. *See also* gentiles passing off Jewish child as relative

passing as gentile, by adults, 13, 14, 16, 18, 121

passing as gentile, by children: to avoid capture, 23, 41, 243-44, 252; to get food, 53; and loss of identity, xv-xvi, 111, 112, 117-18, 120, 122, 156, 158, 159-60, 163, 237, 244-45, 256; for smuggling of goods, 36-37

passing as gentile in postwar Poland: ongoing antisemitism and, 164-66; rejection of stigmatized Jewish identity and, 166-67

Perechodnik, Calel and Anna, 11-18, 254; backgrounds of, 11, 14-15; daughter's birth and childhood, 12, 15, 22; death of Anna's brothers, 12, 14-15; deportation to camps, 11, 14, 16, 17, 18; deportation to Otwock ghetto, 12; early optimism of, 12, 13, 15, 22; efforts to hide daughter, 13, 14, 15; happy marriage of, 6, 11-12, 15; hopes for escape, 13, 14, 16; stress-induced conflict between, 13-14, 16

Perechodnik parents, 5, 6, 16-18

Pest ghetto, 67, 75-76, 78-79, 83n29

Płaszów camp, 30, 39, 40

Poland: Jews killed in, 123, 155; postwar antisemitism in, 124, 128n67, 139-40, 164-66, 197, 200, 201; postwar evacuation of Jewish children from, 200; postwar struggle among Jewish groups in, 133-34; resistance, Jewish children in, 254. *See also Bricha*; kibbutz groups, postwar

Ravett, Abraham, 217, 222, 230n45

religious faith, Holocaust and, 224, 227, 236-37, 242, 249

Rescue Committee of Budapest (*Vaadah*), 74-75, 80

Rohatyn ghetto, 181, 182

Rosenfarb, Chava, xv, xxixn1

Rwandan genocide, xii

second-generation survivors, 210-23; definition of, 209-10; desire to know more, 210; and family legacy, 215-16, 221-22, 232n83; as Heirs of the Holocaust, xxvii; impact of parents' emotional struggles on, 212, 215, 218, 222-23, 255; as mourning facilitators, 227; and murdered previous family as haunting memory, 212-13, 216-18; and parent's emotional distance, 217-18, 224-25; postmemory experience of, 214-15; search for healing in, 210, 217, 219, 221; and split identity of parents, 214; and survivors anxious to talk, 211-12, 213-14; and survivors reluctant to talk, 210, 211-12, 213, 255; trips to sites of parents' past, 218-21, 255; working-through process for, 212, 224-25, 227; young survivors as, 238